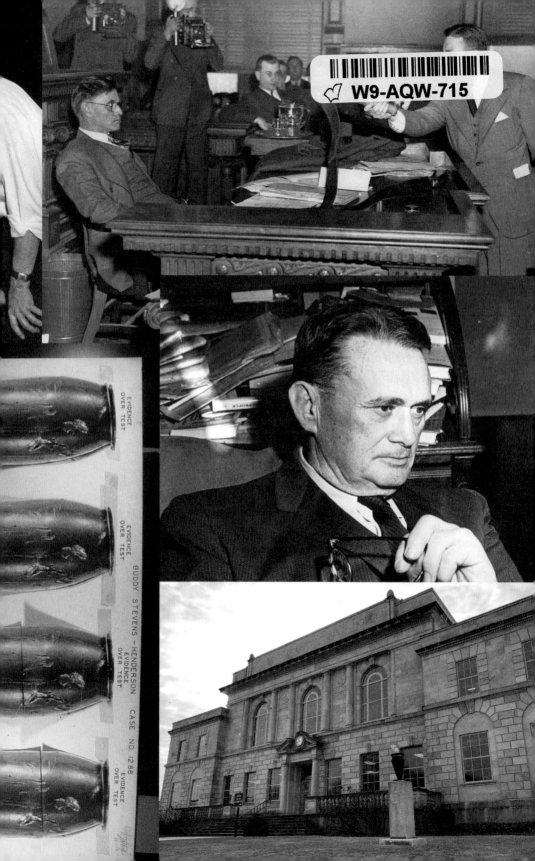

EVIDENCE OVER TEST

EVIDENCE OVER TEST

BUDDY STEVENS - HENDERSON

EVIDENCE OVER TEST

CASE NO. 1288

EVIDENCE OVER TEST

THE THREE
DEATH SENTENCES
OF CLARENCE
HENDERSON

THE THREE
DEATH SENTENCES
OF CLARENCE
HENDERSON

A BATTLE FOR RACIAL JUSTICE AT THE
DAWN OF THE CIVIL RIGHTS ERA

CHRIS JOYNER

ABRAMS PRESS, NEW YORK

Photographs on endpapers, clockwise from top left:

The .38 Special police revolver the state claimed fired the shots that killed Buddy Stevens. (Photograph by the author)

Fulton County Crime Lab director Dr. Herman Jones (right) oversees the collection of tire track evidence at a crime scene prior to the Stevens murder. (*Atlanta Journal-Constitution*)

Dan Duke, at the time a prosecutor for the Fulton County Solicitor's Office, angrily shakes a barbed Ku Klux Klan whip in the face of Governor Eugene Talmadge during a 1941 clemency hearing the governor held for Klan members convicted in the beating death of a man the prior year. (*Atlanta Journal-Constitution*)

Atlanta *Constitution* editor Ralph McGill was known as the "conscience of the South" for his moderate views on race, but he also was an ardent anti-Communist and used his daily column to harass Communists and their fellow travelers. (*Atlanta Journal-Constitution*)

The historic Carroll County Courthouse in Carrollton, Georgia. The trials of Clarence Henderson were conducted in its massive courtroom. (Photograph by the author)

A prosecution exhibit used to compare the bullet extracted from Stevens's leg with test bullets fired from the .38 revolver. (Photograph by the author)

Communist Party organizer Homer B. Chase (left) with a deputy sheriff in Cartersville, Georgia. Chase was jailed in June 1949 when he refused to post a $5,000 "peace bond" for allegedly threatening a would-be Communist recruit. (*Atlanta Journal-Constitution*)

Carl "Buddy" Stevens's grave marker in the city cemetery in Carrollton, Georgia. (Photograph by the author)

Sheriff B. B. "Bunt" Kilgore (right) in a photo taken soon after the murder of Buddy Stevens. The handling of investigation by state and local police became a sore issue in the case. (*Times-Georgian*)

Carrollton Presbyterian Church, where Buddy Stevens picked up Nan Turner for a date on October 31, 1948. (Photograph by the author)

Library of Congress Control Number: 2021934987

ISBN: 978-1-4197-5636-8
eISBN: 978-1-64700-387-6

Printed and bound in the United States
10 9 8 7 6 5 4 3 2 1

Abrams books are available at special discounts when purchased in quantity for premiums and promotions as well as fundraising or educational use. Special editions can also be created to specification. For details, contact specialsales@abramsbooks.com or the address below.

Abrams Press® is a registered trademark of Harry N. Abrams, Inc.

ABRAMS The Art of Books
195 Broadway, New York, NY 10007
abramsbooks.com

For my father

CONTENTS

PREFACE

The story of the death of Buddy Stevens and the trials of Clarence Henderson has been part of my life for almost my entire career as a journalist. In fact, this story got its hooks in me before I even knew I *had* a career.

In the fall of 1998, I had been working in newspapers for two years, starting as a general assignment reporter for the *Times-Georgian*, a small daily in Carrollton, a college town about sixty miles west of Atlanta, and working my way up to features editor. That I had risen so quickly should give an impression about the size of the paper rather than the size of my ambition. I had walked through the doors of the *Times-Georgian* in 1996 never having written a single newspaper article. My high school had no paper, and I never considered writing for either my undergraduate or graduate school papers. Interviewing for a vacant position in the cozy newsroom, I brought my master's thesis in history as my writing sample, a clueless move that elicited raised eyebrows and grins from the paper's editors.

Likely I would not have gotten the job were it not for the recommendation of a friend from my days at the University of West Georgia, a four-year state college that defines much of life in Carrollton. Fortunately, the editors thought enough of the recommendation (and my willingness to work for the near-poverty wage they offered) to offer me the job and later the promotion.

That happy circumstance was why I was in the position—acting on a tip from my father—to pull down the very first bound volume of the *Carroll County Georgian*, from 1948. Carefully turning the yellowed pages, I found the edition for Thursday, November 4, and the headline: "One Suspect Held, No New Clues as Stevens Murderer Is Sought." My father, Van Joyner Jr., had attended what was then called West Georgia College in 1944 and knew Carl "Buddy" Stevens Jr. in passing. Buddy was a Carrollton boy, a "townie" about the same age as my father, and when he was gunned down on a dark, rainy night in 1948, word spread among my father's classmates. Dad remembered the murder, but not a lot else. By the time of the murder and the mad search for Buddy's killer, Dad had already served in the Navy, graduated from the University of Georgia, and was back in Atlanta, newly married to my mother. But the death was big news at the time, he recalled.

"You should look into that," Dad advised. "I don't think they ever figured out who killed him."

From the start, I was engrossed—first by the murder mystery, then by the dramatic legal battles that followed. I progressed from photocopying a few broadsheet pages to spending many memorable hours tracking the twists and turns of the Stevens case in the university library with microfilmed rolls of the *Georgian* and its competition, the *Times–Free Press*. I've always been the talker in the newsroom—the reporter who would hang up the phone and turn to his colleague to say, "Hey, you won't believe this!" Fortunately, my friends at the *Times-Georgian* were patient and encouraging as I prattled on about my latest find. So was Stanley Parkman, the statesmanlike former publisher, who spent a few hours every week tucked away in a back office, working on his weekly column. Parkman sold the *Times-Georgian* and the other newspapers in his West Georgia chain years earlier to a Kentucky-based chain, but he stayed on as a columnist and "publisher emeritus."

The more I dug into back issues of the *Georgian* and the *Times–Free Press*, the more I became convinced the story of Buddy Stevens's murder said something about post–World War II America. From race relations to fear of Communism to the ambition and paranoia of the postwar generation, it all played out in miniature in Carrollton. And Carrollton's version of the fractured postwar American psyche was just as high stakes as anywhere else—life and death in the case of Buddy and the man accused of killing him. And the deeper I got, the more I realized how strong the themes of the episode still echoed in the news of the day.

When I finally decided to seek out the court records associated with the case, I walked into the Carroll County Superior Court Clerk's office anticipating a struggle. Finding half-century-old county records is a scattershot proposition. Fires, burst pipes, and plain negligence can quickly turn a good story into a dead end.

"I'm looking for some court records," I recall telling the clerk behind the counter. "Pretty old court records."

"Which case?" she asked.

"It was a boy, shot to death in 1948," I said. "Carl Stevens Jr. He went by 'Buddy.'"

Without moving from her station, the clerk reached below the counter and lifted a heavy wooden box. It was the old box that used to hold slips with potential jurors' names on them. Before computers, a bailiff would draw names to decide who would be summoned for jury duty. The clerk reached inside the box, pulled out a sheaf of about seventy legal-sized pages, and slid them over.

Over the years, enough people asked for the records that they never got filed away. Some of those people, like me, claimed to be researching a book on the case, she told me. I was elated and immediately agreed to pay for copies of everything—an extravagance on my salary at the time.

It turned out that what I got was not a court transcript, but a legal brief prepared for the appeal of the verdict of the first trial. It read like a transcript might if you omitted the lawyers' questions and instead rewrote them into the answers of witnesses. Even so, it gave a vivid picture of the trial and the personalities involved. I faithfully took the pages and assembled them and my newspaper research into binders, organized by date and subject matter. I had binders for the murder and manhunt, the trials, communism, race relations, and the various lawyers, officials, politicians, and scoundrels who I believed were central to the story. Once I had the information meticulously organized, I put them on a shelf. And later into a box, moving them from apartment to apartment to rental house to purchased home. The binders traveled hundreds of miles, across the Southeast, as I pursued a newspaper career.

Yet no matter where I was, the story followed me. Over drinks with reporters in a favorite bar, invariably I would bring up "the book." One day I would write it, I said. But it wasn't until my career brought me back to home to work at the *Atlanta Journal-Constitution* that the day finally arrived. I think it was probably when I listened to the first season of the podcast *Serial* that I was inspired enough to begin. *Serial* was a national sensation mostly because of its storytelling. The host, Sarah Koenig, took a largely unknown criminal case and walked listeners deep into its mysterious world. It was a wormhole of characters and details that had us question the meaning of justice in America. I believe the murder of Buddy Stevens and the trials of Clarence Henderson tell the same kind of story. That evening, I sat down on my couch with the first binder in my lap and reacquainted myself with the cold and rainy night of Halloween 1948.

Of course, the man holding the binder was different from the one who organized it. More seasoned, so to speak. I realized pretty soon that my research of two decades prior was, at best, a good start. I began writing, but I also started digging deeper. I filed records requests and made cold calls to living relatives of some of the people involved. I read histories of the period and made trips to the Georgia state archives and the Library of Congress in search of the documents needed to flesh out this story. My white whale became the actual court transcripts of the three trials of Clarence Henderson. While I had a detailed brief of the first trial, I had little else, and to my terror, they were missing from the stacks of bound cases kept by the clerk of court.

In the intervening years, Carroll County had built a new county courthouse next to the "historic" courthouse where the trials had taken place. The clerk told me that all the records had been picked up and placed in the new courthouse, but if the Stevens case had never been properly filed, then they might have been discarded or inadvertently left in the drawer of an old desk somewhere. I had to face the possibility they could have been forever lost.

During my research I stumbled upon a fascinating book about Herman Jones, the founder of the Georgia Crime Lab and an important figure in criminal forensics. The epilogue of the book, *Georgia's Crime Doctor*, centered on the firearms identification in the Stevens case and included photos of prosecution exhibits and passages from what appeared to be a transcript. I contacted the author, Jay Jarvis (to whom I remain indebted), and asked how he had found the transcripts. Jarvis told me he worked with an investigator with the district attorney's office to get them. That investigator had retired, but I managed to locate her. She said she had found them in the evidence room, but that was before the new courthouse was built. Who knew where they were now?

I emailed the clerk the new lead. Last seen in the old evidence room, I wrote. Within the hour, I got a phone call. "I have them," the clerk said. More than just the transcripts for the trials, he had the prosecution exhibits, a .38 revolver, and the bullet extracted from Stevens's body the night of the murder. Like everything else in the old courthouse, movers had taken everything from the old evidence room and put it in the new one. The items from the Stevens case sat untouched on a shelf in the new evidence locker for years.

It is thanks to such good fortune I was able to tell the story of Clarence Henderson as well as the curious and colorful figures who came to his aid, including communist organizer Homer Chase and fiery defense attorney Dan Duke. But I hope this book is more than that.

As a history student, I was fascinated by the post–World War II period. Most Americans think of the period as one of boundless optimism as a country, weary of war and the Great Depression, cast its eyes to a brighter horizon. But I also knew it was a period of tremendous fear and a time of great social upheaval. America's unanswered questions about race, sublimated during the war, came raging back. African Americans who fought a "Double V" campaign for victory abroad and at home during the war had begun a generational struggle for civil rights but also faced the prospect of massive resistance from white-led governments in the South. Industrious leaders, white and Black, were optimistic about America's future, but also deeply concerned about radical political movements and the threat of international communism. Cities expanded and industry thrived, but such progress also threatened an older social order of class and gender. In short, there was much to gain and everything to lose, so when a young, promising lad like Buddy Stevens was gunned down, seemingly at random, the shock waves were intense.

And it's there that we start.

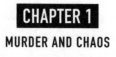

CHAPTER 1

MURDER AND CHAOS

October 31, 1948. Carrollton, Georgia

Nan wasn't sure how far she had walked. It was dark and it had begun to rain. She was barefoot, and the burrs and stalks from a recently plowed cotton field dug into her feet. She was terrified.

At first it seemed the masked gunman only wanted money. He had taken a few bills from Buddy when they were still at Buddy's car, but now it was clear the man wanted more. His voice was rough; his country drawl was pronounced. "Someone is waiting out here to see you," he said. But no one was there. It was just Nan, Buddy, and this man—a silhouette shining his flashlight through the dark and the rain.

Nan and Buddy had been walking for half an hour, but it seemed longer since the man ordered them out of their car. Directing them with the barrel of his gun, he marched them up and over two wire fences, across pastures, and into thickets. Buddy carried her at times. Along the way, the gunman had become more agitated and aggressive. He barked orders, some of which Buddy refused, making the man only more angry. To force Buddy to comply, the man had beaten him badly with the butt of his gun and whipped him with branches ripped from a scrub tree. Buddy walked beside Nan, nearly senseless but still upright. Blood was streaming down from a cut above his eye.

When they reached the edge of a clearing, the man had them lie on the ground a few feet apart—Buddy on his stomach, Nan on her back. When the man ordered Nan to remove her underwear, Buddy summoned the last of his strength to make a final, desperate lunge.

"Run, Nan!" he yelled, his wide eyes and blond hair briefly illuminated by the man's flashlight. Nan ran into the dark field toward distant lights off to the northeast. She wasn't far when she heard the first shot. She turned to see the second flash of gunfire explode the darkness. In that brief moment, she saw Buddy fall to his knees.

She turned and ran toward the distant lights.

* * *

The shots that killed Carl "Buddy" Stevens Jr. went right to the belly of Carrollton. Stevens's family had become fixtures in the local community since moving to Carrollton in 1929, when Buddy was a young boy. They bought a house on Ward Street, two blocks north of the downtown square. Carl Sr. worked as Carrollton's city clerk and became active in the local Kiwanis Club. His mother, Charlcie, kept the house in order and entertained as the family moved among the white social and political elites.[1] Buddy went to the public schools and was an Eagle Scout.

On the night of his murder, he was a twenty-two-year-old Army veteran, just returned from thirteen months in Korea as part of the U.S. occupying force there after World War II. He was a fit, rangy sophomore at Georgia Tech in Atlanta, about sixty miles east. In the wake of his death, the Carrollton Kiwanis Club issued a statement declaring Buddy as a Georgian "exemplifying noble traits of American manhood." He was the embodiment of the aspirations the white professional class had for their children. He had come to Carrollton that weekend just to visit Nan, an eighteen-year-old former Miss Carrollton, whose troubled home life and closeness with a local minister made her the frequent topic of rumors.

Buddy's background was important, but so was where he died. The Stevens murder didn't happen on some dead-end street in a backwater cow town. The young man's body fell right in the middle of an aspiring white-collar community. When they encountered the gunman, they were parked at the end of Sunset Boulevard in the new Sunset Hills Country Club development. Their desperate march at gunpoint had taken them across what would soon become the club's golf course.

The whole scene was a short walk from West Georgia College, a two-year junior college with a progressive mission to grow the school into a four-year institution in less than a decade. They left their car a half block behind the home of superior court judge Samuel J. Boykin, a community leader and the youngest of three Boykin brothers, all lawyers.[2]

At the end of World War II, Carrollton dared hope its future would connect this onetime frontier village to a wider world. Stevens's bullet-ridden corpse embodied their fears of what the world had in store.

Buddy's murder—and the revelations that followed—shocked Carrollton to its marrow. Its ripples spread to Atlanta, where they stoked fears of racial violence mixed with the developing activism of the civil rights movement and an obsession with the threat of communism. They would even be felt in New York City, in the office of the National Association for the Advancement of Colored People's top lawyer, Thurgood Marshall, who one day would break the color barrier on the nation's highest court.

* * *

Nan ran a half mile, barefoot across muddy broken ground, to the house of George Syme.[3] She was hysterical, disheveled, and incoherent. Syme reached for his telephone and called the police. When the first officers arrived, Nan had recovered enough to tell them what had happened, but she was not sure where. She also said she never saw her attacker. Either on her own or with prompting, she did say he "sounded like a Negro."

It was late when Carroll County sheriff Bernard "Bunt" Kilgore and a hastily rounded-up posse discovered Stevens's body. The sheriff brought with him Buddy's father, Carl Stevens Sr.; local doctor Elwyn V. Patrick; and Jim Hillin, an investigator with the Georgia Bureau of Investigation.[4] Murders weren't uncommon in Carroll County, but they usually weren't mysteries, either. Judge Boykin would have one or two every court session. Men killed their wives, their neighbors, or their coworkers. Rarely was someone killed by a stranger, particularly when that someone was a well-educated white boy from a good family. Yet Hillin had been dreading something like this for months.

Buddy was found on his knees, slumped over and propped up by some low shrubs and stumps. Patrick reached down to take his pulse. Nothing. Along with the wound to the chest, Buddy had been shot in the arm and leg, but he put up a hell of a fight. He was beaten and the gash over his right eye had bled a lot. Police found a beanie cap at the scene—possibly Stevens's from Georgia Tech—and a child's blue sweater they believed had been used as a mask by the murderer.[5]

The rain had stopped as the search for Stevens's murderer got under-way, but it was wet and cold. The morning would bring the first frost of the season—hog butchering time for local farmers. The conditions hampered the efforts of bloodhounds brought in from neighboring counties to search for Stevens's killer. The fact that the dogs' handler was a little drunk didn't help.

Stevens's body was taken to Kytle-Aycock Funeral Home, where a crowd had gathered outside. Dr. Patrick was joined at the funeral home by Eldred C. Bass, a young physician only a few years older than Buddy. Bass was known as "Sonny" because he was the son of Eldred Bass Sr., the local grocer.[6] The two doctors made a cursory examination of Stevens's body, agreeing the gunshot wound to the chest was the fatal wound. Rather than probe there for evidence, they moved on to examine the wound to Buddy's right leg, where, just under the skin below the knee, Patrick found a bullet, which he retrieved using a scalpel and forceps.[7] Based on the location of the entry wound, it appeared the bullet entered from below, moving upward toward the knee. Patrick couldn't be sure about the angle. Perhaps the bullet struck bone and ricocheted, he thought.[8] He dropped it into a paper billing envelope provided by the funeral home.

The dogs and men who had worked late into the night searching for the killer were back at it the next morning, Monday, November 1. The murder already was big news. The *Atlanta Constitution* carried the story on its front page with a banner headline: "Tech Student Slain by Gunman." The newspaper reported that police said there had been "several previous crimes of a minor nature" in which the suspect was a "masked Negro."[9]

Along with local police, the state sent the highway patrol and the Georgia Bureau of Investigation (GBI) to lead groups of locals in search parties. Within hours they had a suspect. A pretty good one, too, except that he was white.

A motorist told police he picked up a white boy limping along on Tyus Road on Sunday night, less than a mile southwest of the murder scene. Junior Teal, a tall, twenty-three-year-old sawmill worker and bootlegger, was "scratched and bruised." He was barefoot. His torn shirt was stained with blood and lipstick. More telling, perhaps, was that the shirt also had a blue stain the same shade as the blue from the child's sweater found at the scene.[10]

Police found Teal and arrested him, but he claimed innocence. He said he had gotten drunk earlier in the day and gotten into a fight in Roopville, a rough crossroads town south of Carrollton. He claimed he had spent the day with bootleggers, who would eventually provide his alibi.[11]

It's not unusual that Teal would be out walking. He didn't own a car and usually hitched rides from anyone heading the way he wanted to go. Although he was young, Teal was a rough character and known to local police.[12]

Word of the arrest spread quickly. That afternoon an angry mob gathered outside the Carrollton jail. Teal was inside and state troopers assigned to guard him were having some trouble with the townsfolk. Georgia had a history of rough justice at the hands of mobs. Lynchings were common across the South, and although Black men were the typical victims at the hands of an angry white mob, a rope could be found for Teal.

Carrollton police chief Rada Threadgill was nervous and asked state officials to take Teal to Atlanta, in part for safekeeping, but also so police could use some relatively new crime-fighting tools: the lie detector and the paraffin test.[13]

The polygraph machine, in its modern form, had only been in use for about a decade, and the paraffin test used to detect gunshot residue was newer. Teal was the guinea pig in Georgia—the first criminal suspect to submit to a polygraph, and he got two of them. He would tell the story for the rest of his life.

The polygraph was new to the state police, and Major Wayne Henson, head of the Georgia Department of Public Safety and the state's top cop, was eager to show its value. He was cautious about it, too, so he was coy with reporters over whether he would announce the results of the tests on Teal.

"The only benefit we can derive from its use is to have the courts accept it," he said. "Therefore, we want to study this first case at length and be sure of our facts before we say anything."[14]

But in short order the police lost interest in Teal as a suspect in Stevens's murder. Just a day after his arrest, Teal was speaking to reporters from jail. Photographed next to a thick-necked jailer, Teal told reporters, "I don't know nothing about that business in Carrollton."[15]

Discarding Teal as a suspect, police turned to other emerging scientific techniques to solve the Stevens murder. Dr. Herman Jones, a biochemist, had founded the South's first modern crime lab just a little more than a year earlier. Nicknamed the "Crime Doctor," Jones had transformed police investigations in Georgia, bringing the heft of science to bear on gumshoe police work. The local press was enthralled at the 4,400-square-foot lab, where "scientific crime detection works by split-hair precision and fact." With rows of test tubes and beakers, powerful microscopes, a spectrograph to analyze metals—the lab "leaves nothing to chance," the *Atlanta Constitution*'s crime reporter wrote in 1947.[16]

The day after the murder, Hillin of the GBI took the bullet extracted from Stevens's leg to the crime lab for examination, leaving it with Jones's chief lieutenant, George Cornett.[17] Cornett's first conclusion was that Stevens had been shot with a round fired from a pistol with a "right-hand twist," meaning the rifling of the barrel of the gun caused the bullet to rotate to the right, or clockwise, as it left the barrel. That twisting made marks on the bullet that, when stood on its end, leaned right. It also was a 9mm bullet. Jones told the press police were looking for an automatic, probably a foreign gun.[18]

As state and local police continued to search for a suspect, the Stevens family put their only child to rest. Buddy's funeral at the First Methodist Church was Tuesday, just two days after his death. He was buried in the city cemetery, a sad end to a life imbued with promise.

Buddy's death enraged as much as it shocked. Carrollton's leadership demanded action, and police were urged forward by the local newspapers, which provided breathless coverage of every development. The *Carroll County Georgian*, in particular, alternated between sensationalized reporting of every rumor and hopeful dispatches indicating police were hot on the trail of the killer.

Stanley Parkman, the young publisher of the *Georgian*, was at a Rotary Club meeting when he heard the news of Buddy's death. The murder would be the biggest story of his career, but the first part of it wouldn't publish for days. Stevens was killed on a Sunday night, but the *Georgian* wouldn't have another edition until Thursday. The first accounts came from the *Atlanta Constitution*. Consistently, the *Georgian* would be the last to report on developments in the Stevens murder, but no paper covered it in such detail.

Parkman was tall—well over six feet. He wore spectacles, which, combined with a weak chin and stooped shoulders, gave the father of three the bookish look of a scrivener. He was a gentle, pious man, the product of a strict and stark upbringing by his father, a struggling plantation manager. But he also was ambitious.

Parkman came to Carrollton in 1944 to work for the *Times–Free Press*, a weekly paper run at the time by a dyspeptic man named Clyde Tuttle. Tuttle was not a Carrollton native, either. A publisher from North Carolina, he had bought the paper during the war and proceeded to irritate the locals with editorials criticizing the lack of advertising support he was receiving.

A year into his tenure, the thirty-year-old Parkman was approached at church by a group of businessmen with an offer of support to leave Tuttle's paper and start his own. Parkman's patrons raised the money and bought stock they agreed they would eventually sell back to their young protégé. In return, they got what they wanted: the *Georgian*, a newspaper with a disposition more favorable to their interests.[19]

Under Parkman, the *Georgian*'s agenda was anything but hidden. In fact, the "*Georgian* Program" ran in every edition on the editorial page, right under the masthead. The program embodied Carrollton's striving, progressive ideals: better roads and schools, more markets for agricultural products, a professionalized city government. Other parts of the plan—"Greater Civic Pride," "Spirit of Cooperation"—showed through in the *Georgian*'s coverage of events.[20]

The newspaper was there to build up the community as much as cover its daily happenings. Construction updates at the city hospital were front-page news. Minor farm victories—"Two Carroll County Boys Win Awards for Potatoes" anchored one front page—got the same treatment.

Given his investment in Carrollton and his dependence on the good graces of the city fathers, what he did in his first edition after Stevens's murder was all the more impressive. In a column headlined "Error Made in Judgment," Parkman revealed what few knew: A masked man had been stalking couples and raping women in lovers' lane attacks for months. Moreover, Parkman said he knew about the attacks and covered them up at the request of Carrollton police chief Rada Threadgill, who had waved the young Parkman off the story lest he scare the culprit away before an arrest could be made.

But Buddy's death had shaken him, and he spilled it all.

"On at least four previous occasions within the past two months, couples have been robbed, and in at least two cases it is said that the girls have been criminally assaulted by a criminal operating in exactly the same manner as the one who committed this awful murder Sunday night," he wrote. In the editorial, Parkman didn't accept all the weight for his decision. He made it clear the police shared guilt.[21]

"At the urgency of the officers the newspapers did not report these prior cases," Parkman wrote. The editorial was oddly written and marred with typos. Parkman was nervous.

"At that time and since then I had been hounded by the fear that before the assailant was caught he would attempt an attack upon some fine young couple and the boy in the case would not stand idly by," he wrote. "I felt that sooner or later there would be a boy involved who would risk his life at the point of a murderer's gun rather than see his sweetheart, wife, or companion mistreated."[22]

For Parkman, it was confirmation of his fears. His was a booster publication, but the tradeoff was too great.

"Now the worst has happened," Parkman wrote.

Then he wrote a strange sentence that leaves one wondering what, exactly, was going on.

"Of course, in all the previous cases, evidence has been lacking, there has been little apparent concern among those directly affected, and actually the officers were uncertain as to what crime had been committed and what to do about it."[23]

White couples in a Deep South community had been unconcerned that a Black man had attacked them? That he had raped a white girl? And white police were unsure this was a crime? This suggestion throws into doubt a central aspect of the Stevens case: that the attacker was Black.

The editorial was brave for Carrollton and a break from the contract Parkman made with the city's power brokers. The day it ran, an enraged Threadgill, who was both older and much smaller than Parkman, burst into the young publisher's office. The police chief theatrically took off his badge and gun, slamming them onto Parkman's desk, and challenged him to step outside and settle it.

"Well, Rada, there's a murderer loose in this town," Parkman began. "You can beat me up, but I'm not going outside of this building whether you've got your gun on or not."

Parkman had size and youth on Threadgill, but the young publisher knew that wasn't enough.

"I knew that was a fight I was destined to lose," he said later.

Instead, Parkman suggested that the police chief beating the hell out of the newspaper publisher would make quite a story. Threadgill left.[24]

While Parkman knew about the earlier attacks, the *Times–Free Press* was in the dark. On the same day as Parkman's revelation, the competing paper seemed shocked by the news and wondered "if such matters should not be given publicity."[25]

Carrollton was on edge in a way difficult to fathom with modern sensibilities. "It was chaos," one of Nan Turner's classmates recalled decades later.[26] Murders happened all the time in rural West Georgia. It was a violent place filled with hard-living bootleggers, gamblers, sawmill hands, and tenant farmers. The newspapers were filled with the brutal outcomes of domestic strife and friendships coming to an abrupt end at the point of a gun.

But the death of Buddy Stevens was different. He wasn't a bootlegger or sawmill hand. He was a veteran, a Georgia Tech student, and the scion of a fine family. Also, the murderer was a stranger—to him and everyone else. He was a dark, shadowy threat to order.

Or was he? Perhaps something even more sinister was at work. Rumors swirled, particularly around Nan Turner, Buddy's date. Townsfolk gossiped about a turbulent family life and other adult men on her periphery, including a local minister. Maybe the crime wasn't random. Maybe it was one of passion and Buddy got in the way?

Two weeks had yet to pass following Buddy's murder, and Parkman was imploring his readers to remain calm.

"Tensions are running high and more and more people are suffering from nervous conditions," Parkman reported in a front-page plea for calm on November 11, 1948. "It is an important matter for the welfare of the community that all of us control our emotions as best we can. The continual flow of rumors, most of them unfounded, makes for excitement that causes loss of sleep and anxiety."[27]

While rumors surrounding Nan Turner complicated life for Parkman, most Carrollton residents were anxious for more existential reasons. Turner said she had been assaulted by a Black man, stoking the worst racial fears of a small Southern town.

Nan's speculation, whether genuine or planted, that the attacker she never saw was Black spread quickly, and anger in Carrollton grew. The toxic mix of sex, murder, and race was too much for a rural Georgia town to absorb.

"A great many people have purchased guns," Parkman reported. "These things are being kept in readiness until the vicious murderer is captured, and as long as they are kept in readiness there is a constant danger that any slight disturbance would cause the death of some innocent person."[28]

There was no lack of police attention to the crime. Captain Clarence McLemore, director of the Georgia Bureau of Investigation, personally took the lead in the investigation. The GBI—a bureau within the Department of Public Safety that patterned as the state's answer to the FBI—was about a decade old and McLemore had come up through the state patrol.[29]

The GBI hadn't completely ruled out a white attacker. In at least one prior attack, the man behind the mask told his victim he had blackened his face with greasepaint. But with no other witnesses and a trail gone cold, police began rounding up and interrogating Black men and holding them for days or longer without charges.[30]

Swept up in the initial wave of arrests was Lawyer Hicks, a sixty-year-old Black farmer from Roopville. Hicks, married with two teenage children, seemed an unlikely person to have been stalking white couples ten miles away from home. Yet the *Georgian* reported "a number of telling clues pointed to Hicks" and that couples involved in the earlier attacks identified Hicks as their attacker. But others, including Nan Turner, didn't pick him out of a police lineup arranged in Atlanta.[31]

By November 6, the *Constitution* had more details on Hicks, including that he had been accused by a thirteen-year-old white girl who said the man had "criminally attacked" her. The girl's story was backed up by six of her friends. The GBI's McLemore said the girl's story was similar to other accounts of the serial attacker. The girl, identified in the papers as a "farm girl," was reportedly attacked six weeks before Stevens's death. She claimed she was walking with a boy and five other "farm youths" down a country road at night when a masked attacker with a gun approached them and made them all lie down on the road. The masked man separated the thirteen-year-old from the group and raped her, the paper said. The victim and witnesses allegedly identified Hicks by a speech impediment.[32]

The Black-owned *Atlanta Daily World* was less convinced of the story, calling Hicks an "aged farmer" and noting that witnesses described their attacker as "tremendous in size and strength." Bolstering its case, the *Constitution* described Hicks as a "husky Negro."[33]

In the investigation's initial days, the *Constitution* announced "2 Arrested in Tech Student's Slaying." Without stopping to wonder how two men could be arrested for a slaying done by one suspect, the *Constitution* urgently reported that two Black men were in custody: Charles McCann of Carrollton and Charles Rufus Thomas of Lowell, a community ten driving miles south of Carrollton. The *Constitution* didn't give much ink to McCann, because it appeared the evidence pointed to Thomas.

"Carrollton residents, who said they identified Thomas for law enforcement officers, reported he had teeth marks on his wrist, scratches over most of the upper part of the body and a scar on his lip," the newspaper reported. "The description fits almost exactly the description given by the young West Georgia College coed who witnessed the slaying, police said." This is a remarkable claim, considering that earlier Nan Turner had been unable to identify her attacker by anything other than the sound of his voice. The *Constitution* reported that Thomas and McCann were taken to Atlanta for "safe keeping," but the newspaper had been unable to verify they had made it to the jail. Threadgill refused to say where they were.

"There are too many irons in the fire now; I don't care to talk about it any further," he said.[34]

Threadgill likely was leaning on his connections with Sheriff Lamar Potts of neighboring Coweta County to secretly hold his prisoners, an arrangement that kept them away from potential lynching parties while also isolating them for long interrogations.

Along with Hicks, Thomas, McCann, and original suspect Junior Teal, investigators also scooped up Emanuel Thomas and J. B. Plant. All but Teal were Black. Threadgill said an additional three Black men had been picked up for questioning but had been released after being held for a week.

It was clear that any Black man was a suspect. A couple of weeks after the murder, a drunken Willie Lee Satterfield got into an argument with a taxi driver on downtown Carrollton square and was arrested on a disorderly conduct charge. "He was questioned extensively to determine if he had any connection with the Stevens case," reported the *Times–Free Press.*[35]

The dragnet ranged far and wide. More than one hundred miles away in Chattanooga, Tennessee, police arrested Joseph Abdoe, described as a Cuban from New Castle, Pennsylvania, and held him in connection with the murder. Abdoe was unlucky enough to be found with a foreign-make 9mm pistol, the kind of weapon believed to have been used to kill Stevens.[36]

With no new leads, the governor's office offered a $500 reward for information, and with local donations, the reward climbed to $1,000 in a week—about four months' earnings for most. The *Times–Free Press* referred to the unknown suspect as "the human fiend" and noted that a number of suspects had been grilled by state police. Still, there were no leads.[37]

As the weeks passed, locals began expressing a growing unease. "The hunt for the fiend slayer of Carl (Buddy) Stevens continued Tuesday," the *Times–Free Press* reported. The newspaper noted that the county commissioners had taken the unusual step of swearing in Denver Gaston as a county policeman. Gaston, a state patrolman, had beaten Sheriff Kilgore in August in the Democratic primary. He was unopposed in the general election, held November 9, and was sheriff-elect. Although he was not due to take office until after the new year, the commissioners decided to get him on the Stevens case right away, regardless of how awkward it might be for Kilgore to supervise the man who just beat him at the polls. The commissioners also hired a former Troup County investigator to help with the Stevens case, in what the newspaper called "an all-out attempt to solve the Stevens murder and the recent wave of attacks in the county."[38]

Police departments for twenty miles in any direction had made the case their top priority. Yet, nearly a month out from the murder, there was still no suspect.

CHAPTER 2

CARROLLTON

Present-day Carrollton, Georgia, is a city of about 27,000 people located forty miles west of Atlanta and just fourteen miles east of the Georgia-Alabama line, where rolling hills and dense pine forests form the southern tip of the Appalachian Mountains. The city is the county seat of Carroll County and is primarily known in the state as the home of the University of West Georgia, a four-year state college where former House Speaker Newt Gingrich taught history in the 1970s before leaving academia for politics.

When Buddy Stevens's family moved to Carrollton during the Great Depression, the city had less than 5,000 people. The area had a reputation for being wild and remote, a holdover from its history as the edge of the Georgia frontier. The region was the last area of the state to be settled and was still wild country nearly a century after General James Oglethorpe founded Georgia as a royal colony in 1733. At least, that is how white Georgians saw it. In reality, native peoples had lived there for centuries, with that part of western Georgia forming the boundary between the Creek to the south and the Cherokee to the north.[1]

In the 1820s, the Cherokee Nation was centered in New Echota, a village in the northwest Georgia mountains some eighty miles north of modern-day Carroll County with a market, houses, and a bicameral legislature.

The nation stretched from Alabama through Tennessee and the Carolinas, but about half of the 14,000 souls, by an 1826 count, lived in western Georgia, where they were pressured intensely by thousands of white Georgians pushing westward. Return J. Meigs, a federal Indian agent assigned to the Cherokee, described the white pioneers as having a "shrewd & desperate character" with nothing to lose and holding "barbarous sentiment toward Indians."[2]

The Cherokee may have occupied western Georgia, but white leaders in Georgia and Washington ignored their claim to it. The Compact of 1802, an agreement between Georgia and the federal government, gave the state legal right to the land—as soon as the natives could be removed. In exchange, Georgia agreed to abandon its expansive claims on the lands that make up present-day Alabama and Mississippi.[3]

In 1822, President James Monroe named two members of Georgia's congressional delegation as Indian commissioners and assigned them the task of negotiating the removal of the Cherokee from western Georgia. The Cherokee—under the leadership of Chief John Ross, the mixed-blood son of a Scottish trader—refused to budge, holding the white negotiators to the terms of the earlier treaties ceding the land to the Cherokee.[4]

Stonewalled, the white men attempted to bribe Ross and the other Cherokee leaders. The bag man was a Creek chieftain named William McIntosh. The episode ended badly, with Ross loudly calling out McIntosh's betrayal in public. McIntosh left New Echota, forever banned from the Cherokee Nation.

The Creek chief met his end in 1825 when his fellow tribesmen discovered his plan to sell *their* lands to the Georgians and killed him at his plantation on the Chattahoochee River, ten miles southeast of Carrollton.[5] McIntosh's plantation is preserved to this day as a public park. It's a serene place if you can divorce yourself from its history of betrayal and violence.

The Creeks would attempt to take the land back, but ultimately were forced to abandon their lands east of the Alabama border, including Carroll County.[6]

With the natives removed, the state held a land lottery in 1827 to divide the county among its new white settlers. Winners paid $18 for a 202-acre lot.[7] In dividing the frontier, the state gave special weight to families caring for orphans, the mentally ill, or the children of convicts, along with Revolutionary War veterans and their widows. All of the former Creek and Cherokee lands were disbursed with the exception of the McIntosh Preserve, from which the state hoped to operate a commercial ferry, as the assassinated chief had done.[8]

But the county was not parsed out by lottery because it was so desirable. Far from it. Much of it was remote, hilly, and forested—poor land for cotton or tobacco. Add to this a 180-mile-long border with the Creeks to the west and the Cherokee to the north, both of whom were aggrieved by the turn of events, and the west Georgia frontier was a desolate and dangerous place. In 1830 a group of early Carroll settlers appealed to the governor for assistance as they were "daily exposed to the wild depredations and ravages of an enraged people."[9] That year President Andrew Jackson, a famed Indian fighter, gave the settlers and those like them exactly what they craved by signing the Indian Removal Act, a legislative weapon that set the stage for the genocidal forced migration known as the Trail of Tears.

Wrested from native hands by contract or force, most of the Carroll County lots were traded rather than developed, often for pennies an acre. Some were bartered. A lot purchased by a fortunate lottery winner could be traded for a cow or a rifle. One early Carroll County innkeeper rejected a complete lot as payment for a single night's stay. Keep in mind, the innkeeper already was in Carroll County and turned down more of it.[10]

Early settlers named the county after Charles Carroll, the last surviving signer of the Declaration of Independence. Naming counties after Declaration signers was something of craze in the Early Republic and into the Jacksonian Period. Carroll was eighty-nine when the county was chartered in 1826. Thirteen other states have Carroll Counties in his honor. He never visited the one in Georgia.[11]

It's just as well. Carroll County was no place for octogenarian Founding Fathers. In its early years, the county was terrorized by a group of outlaws called the Pony Club who raided white and neighboring Creek encampments alike, stealing horses and earning their name. The Pony Club operated with impunity, thanks to friendly elected officials, but on Election Day in 1832 a group of residents organized by the sheriff fought the gang in the Carrollton town square, beating the outlaws with rocks and sticks. The vigilante group, called the "Slicks," were accused of assault, but the grand jury instead gave the group a commendation for their heroics.[12]

With a reputation as a wild and lawless outpost, it is little surprise the county's first public building was a jail, a timber structure with doors equipped with "first-rate patent padlocks."[13] The jail was an important feature of early Carrollton. Historian James C. Bonner, whose chronicle of Carroll County stands as the most comprehensive to date, wryly noted that the local government had few responsibilities "except for the Indian problems and the apprehension and punishment of cattle rustlers and horse thieves."[14]

The county's reputation as a poor spot for anything besides land speculation changed shortly after its founding with the discovery of gold in its northern half. Carroll quickly became part of a wider Georgia gold rush, the nation's first. Mines in Carroll County centered around the new town appropriately named Villa Rica, where miners dug out 1,250 ounces of gold a year. The enterprise was made more profitable because slaves were used in the mining operations. One mine, known as the Big Cut, produced $500,000 in gold in the three decades leading to the Civil War.[15]

Gold fever brought even rougher characters to Carroll County, and Bonner noted Villa Rica "was known more for its vices than for the prominence of its citizens."

"Many street fights and violent deaths occurred on its noisy, old streets," he wrote.[16]

Aside from its forced mining operations, Carroll County had a lower percentage of African American slaves than other areas of the state, because it was poorly suited to Georgia's most lucrative agricultural products. In the 1830s, the county was 90 percent white. It would be same three decades later, on the eve of the Civil War, when 40 percent of the state population was of African descent.[17]

Because its population had relatively little reliance on slave labor, Carroll County was a hotbed of unionist sentiment in the run-up to the Civil War. A three-man delegation to the state Democratic Party convention in 1860 voted with the minority to preserve the union, earning the county the nickname the "Free State of Carroll."[18] But the county's political resistance to secession faded a year later as young men volunteered to fight for the Confederacy. It also did not translate into anything approaching an egalitarian view of Blacks—enslaved or free. After the war, Carroll County remained as it always had been: solidly grounded in notions of white male supremacy. Racial attitudes were neatly summed up in the later remembrances of Joe Cobb, a local newspaper reporter, in his book *Carroll County and Her People*, a 1906 volume regarded as the first local history.

"Notwithstanding the false charges and prejudice of many Northern abolitionists and fanatics," Cobb said, Blacks in Carrollton were "happiest and best contented" under slavery. After all, he said, they never had to worry about food or clothing or what they would be doing the next day. The white man took care of it for them. "Now the jails and other prisons are filled with the new generation," he lamented. These lazy, uppity Blacks had resorted to crime to support themselves and their families, he wrote. "And so the Negro question will be unsettled for years to come."[19]

Prevailing racial sentiments were expressed regularly in the local press, which began in earnest in 1872 when a printer named Edwin Sharpe began publishing the *Carroll County Times*. Carrollton had had other newspapers over the years, but the *Times* was a more substantial organ that leaned hard toward the county's future growth. In its pages, Sharpe praised Carroll County as a "white man's country" that "had never been cut down and butchered up, as had Middle Georgia, by the curse of slave labor."[20]

That's not entirely true. There were sizable slaveholding operations in the southeastern area of the county, where the Appalachian foothills gave way to flatter lands along the Chattahoochee River more suitable to large-scale agriculture. After the Civil War, the county's African Americans exercised their freedoms by shifting away from those areas to the northern edges of Carrollton, where they founded segregated neighborhoods with names like Dogtown and Sticktown. In these new settlements, Bonner notes, a Black man was free "to own a dog or a gun."[21]

In this way, Carrollton was fairly typical of Southern cities. As freed Blacks—and the freeborn generation that followed—migrated to urban areas to find jobs, establish businesses, and build their own communities, the racial attitudes of whites hardened. Historian Gail Williams O'Brien suggests that the establishment of segregated Black districts were the product of "an intensification of white racism and a hardening of racial boundaries."[22] Simply put, Blacks were segregated into ghettos because whites did not want them to live in their neighborhoods. Tragically, having a Dogtown or Sticktown on the edge of a white city like Carrollton only fueled white mistrust. In Carroll County, whites and Blacks had never lived so close, in such numbers, while knowing so little about each other.

The urban segregation of whites and Blacks had a dramatic effect on policing. White police officers served white citizens at the pleasure of white politicians. They offered Blacks no protection from whites and little from other Blacks. In fact, the bar for evenhandedness was set so low for African Americans that, in 1901, Carroll County sheriff Joe Merrill briefly became a national folk hero for refusing to turn a convicted Black murderer over to a lynch mob when the Georgia Supreme Court agreed to a temporary stay of his execution.[23]

More often police were often unwilling to patrol Black neighborhoods and viewed Blacks with whom they did have contact as "bad niggers." The police themselves were often unskilled, poorly trained men expected to work long hours for low pay. While it was a job lower-class white men might envy, policing was not a middle-class profession until well into the twentieth century.[24]

Apart from its shifting racial dynamic, the post–Civil War period dramatically transformed Carrollton. In the decades prior to the war, the city had been a relatively small encampment, with most of the population living on subsistence farms outside the city, in the county. And even by 1872, while Carrollton was the largest city in the old Creek lands, it still had just five hundred residents, no brick buildings, and miserable, muddy tracks for streets. Yet, town leaders had hopes for a brighter future. Despite its small population, Carrollton had fifteen lawyers practicing in the early 1870s, enough to found the Carrollton Law Club, members of which spent evenings debating fine points of jurisprudence, such as whether a man had a legal right to murder someone caught "debauching" his wife.[25]

By 1900, Carroll County had just sixty-five total nonagricultural businesses. Two dozen of these were general stores, and most of the rest were serving agricultural needs. Tanners, blacksmiths, and tack shops were common. Yet, Carrollton became known as one of the more industrialized parts of the state, particularly with the founding of a number of textile mills. Mandeville Mills, founded in 1902, was the largest of these and was one of the city's largest employers through the 1940s.[26] At one point Mandeville Mills employed four hundred workers with a weekly payroll of $350,000 and $2.5 million in annual sales.[27]

As the city modernized, it sent one of its own to Washington, DC, to become a national leader in industrial reform. Carroll County's representative in the U.S. Congress, William C. Adamson, chaired the Committee on Interstate and Foreign Commerce, where he lent his name to the first piece of legislation establishing an eight-hour workday and organizing the first

U.S. Department of Labor.[28] Later, Carrollton would rename its town square in honor of the great man.

As it attempted to cast itself as a job-generating, modern city, Carrollton was striving to reconcile its hoped-for future with the ghosts of its bloody frontier past. In 1906, in a commemoration of the county's founding, the local judge, W. C. Hodnett, gave a stem-winding speech about the Creek and Cherokee and "the need to conquer them and to remove them."

"We are not here today either to defend or to criticize the action of the government in acquiring this land as it did and at the price paid for it," the judge said. "Opinions may differ on that subject. We are here for a more notable purpose. The citizens of Carroll do not forget. . . . The actions of the men commemorated here today made it possible for the conditions to be as we find them now. Instead of a thinly settled country with immense forests full of prowling Indians and wild beasts as it was seventy years ago, as you travel along the roads it is almost impossible to get out of sight of a house, the homes of a happy, industrious and prosperous people. Besides, we have numerous broad highways, and one of the best little cities in Georgia, with reliable merchants, accommodating banks, factories, mills, shops, etc. This is an age of progress, and Carroll is no laggard."[29]

Part of being no laggard was Carroll County's early embrace of formal education. In the midst of its hardscrabble, frontier beginnings, the county founded its first private academy in 1829. Within a few years the school had 145 students, including two dozen girls. Bowdon College, a coed college west of Carrollton, was founded in 1856—the first institute of higher learning in the former Creek and Cherokee territory.[30]

But the act that would embody Carroll County's vision as a progress-oriented community was the founding of a somewhat inauspicious A&M school—essentially, a training school for agricultural youth—in Carrollton in 1908. The Fourth District A&M School, so named because the Georgia legislature had decreed one such school for each of its congressional districts, opened in an unusually cold winter. Students living in the dorms had no heat or running water. In the following year, illnesses ran through the school, killing four boys. Yet the school cemented itself as a sturdy institution in what remained largely a rural farming village.[31]

The school's trajectory changed in 1920 with the arrival of Irving S. Ingram, a visionary young principal. At twenty-seven, Ingram had little academic training, but he would guide and transform the A&M school into West Georgia College, a two-year college, by 1933. Ingram led the young college for decades.

Just before Buddy Stevens's murder, Ingram reported that the fall of 1948 "was most satisfying in every respect." The college was experiencing its highest enrollment ever, thanks to returning veterans from World War II, which had the result of stabilizing the college's income after the loss of some financial aid from the state. In 1948 the state appropriation for the college was just $75,700, or $127.23 per student. Although Ingram pointed out that the per capita expenditure at West Georgia was dramatically lower than at similar schools around the nation, he was optimistic.

"While the funds were not ample, the year was the first year in the history of the school which approximated a sufficient annual income," Ingram wrote to the chancellor of the university system. "For the first time the college was not embarrassed."

Ingram said he hoped for more funds from the state to offset "a decrease in the veteran enrollment" expected in coming years.

While Carrollton's elite were constructing a country club across from campus, Ingram complained about inadequate facilities. For instance, there were no permanent dorms for male students. Young men were housed in a shop building that the president described as "poorly lighted, improperly heated, crowded and noisy. No parent has been satisfied with it."

The unpaved main road through campus "is impassable in winter," he reported.

In the fall of 1948, West Georgia had an enrollment of 743 students. For the first time since the end of the war, more than half were men. Of the 506 male students, 293 were veterans.[32]

In a state where the average white male citizen had an eighth-grade education, Ingram saw his mission as instilling a progressive attitude toward higher education in Carroll County. In his annual report to the state, he captured perfectly the dichotomy of a postwar America brimming with optimism yet fearful of the threats—internal and external—that could bring the whole thing crashing down. West Georgia College was a bulwark against those threats, he believed.

"The clientele of the Junior College does not normally come from the traditional college families," Ingram wrote. "The majority come from families of the average income group who must depend on practices of strictest economy to educate their children." More than half of West Georgia's students came from farm families.

The students from these modest families would become Georgia's community leaders, "average people who are destined to be in key positions," he wrote. "Their education will be the most stable influence against the overwhelming 'isms' that seem to be engulfing the world."[33]

He expanded the imprint of the college on rural Carroll County by offering free "College in the Country" lectures for rural whites who had not been able to complete a formal education. He also—controversially—extended education into the Black population through "Negro schools" and listed the African American director of the program alongside white West Georgia faculty in the college catalog.[34]

His attitudes on race were forward-thinking for a man of his time and place. In a letter to the *New York Times* published just weeks ahead of the Stevens murder, Ingram described himself as a "Southern liberal," especially in terms of issues of race. But he begged for patience. A gradualist, Ingram complained that integration "extremists" were undermining more progressive Southerners like himself by providing political fodder for the reactionary politics of the South's racist politicians.

"Southerners will work out the situation if let alone," he wrote. "God knows we have many things wrong with us, but we are making amazing progress."

Just prior to the Stevens murder, Carrollton was focused on another major achievement. To complement a growing college, Carrollton's white leadership had rallied around the idea of a building a new, modern hospital.

On October 21, 1948, the *Georgian* reported a joint city-county venture to begin construction of a full-service hospital. The effort had begun before World War II when local wholesale grocer C. M. Tanner put up $75,000 in seed money and challenged the community to raise the additional $25,000 needed.[35] Construction was delayed by the war, but organizers continued pushing and raising money. The needed federal approvals came just ten days before Buddy Stevens was gunned down, and it was the lead story in Parkman's *Georgian* as donors were encouraged to make good on their pledges.[36]

Buddy Stevens died as Carroll County was on the cusp of a new era. As police searched for Buddy's killer, much was at stake for his hometown.

A DESPERATE MANHUNT

From the bloody and impoverished frontier to an industrious, educated, and modern city, Carrollton was blossoming. That is why the death of Buddy Stevens struck so deep and why the mystery of his murder was so troublesome.

Two weeks had passed since the Halloween homicide and police had yet to make an arrest, so it was news when Buddy's parents showed up at the monthly city council meeting. The Stevenses were grieving parents who had lost their only child, but they were also influential figures in Carrollton's white professional class. When Buddy was gunned down, they were in the midst of building their dream house in Sunset Hills, the very spot where Buddy and Nan had been abducted. By Christmas they would move in, becoming only the second residents of the development, after Judge Sam Boykin.[1]

The council meeting was a pageant of small-town decorum. Charlcie Stevens, Buddy's mother, spoke for the family. She began by praising the police, an act designed to soften the field for the coming criticism.

"We want to personally express our appreciation for the efforts that have been put forth to apprehend the criminal who murdered our son," she said.

However, she suggested, those efforts might have been enhanced had the city police only known what they were doing. The city might benefit from FBI investigative training to learn the most modern methods, she said. It was clear she had done her research, because she knew that such classes were offered to local police several times a year. In fact, Carrollton police had held such a training in 1947, but a number of new officers had been hired in the expanding city police force since that time, she said.

Under the circumstances, Mrs. Stevens said, mothers and their daughters were afraid to leave their homes knowing that her son's murderer was at large.

"Many mothers in Carrollton are extremely distressed now as a result of this tragedy and for the benefit of the public we should seek to provide the very best police protection possible," she said. Members of the council solemnly nodded their heads. It was uncomfortable. Some people were crying, but not Mrs. Stevens, who said she hoped her son's death would spark "keen interest" in providing the force with proper training.

It was a tough spot for Stanley Parkman, whose newspaper was founded on boosting the city, not criticizing it. Swallowing hard on civic pride, he couched his words carefully, calling Mrs. Stevens "the valiant mother" and reporting that she offered improvements "that have become obvious as a result of this crime."

The paper didn't print those "obvious" suggestions, but reasonably one might expect that Mrs. Stevens was referring to the management of the crime scene. News photos from that night showed investigators casually handling pieces of evidence at the scene, hats perched on the backs of their heads.

Then Mrs. Stevens dropped a bomb. The city patrolman who took the initial call from Nan Turner didn't respond by dispatching city police to the scene. As the result of a rollback of a recent annexation, the attack had occurred just outside the city limits. Call the sheriff, the patrolman advised. That confusion gave the suspect additional time to make his escape. This was news to the city council. They knew by now, of course, that the murder happened outside of the city, but they were unaware that the initial call was ignored.

Sensing the rising tide of blame, Police Chief Threadgill jumped to his feet, telling the council that the patrolman followed the correct procedure and called him at home for orders. The chief said he rounded up a posse and was on the scene that evening.

In the next edition of the *Georgian*, Parkman described that extraordinary session as "one of the highest compliments ever paid to the mayor and City Council of Carrollton."

That's one way to look at it.

Weeks passed following Stevens's death, and white Carrollton was nervous. Rumors began spreading around town that "prominent people" were involved in the murder.

The loose talk angered Chief Threadgill, who released a mildly threatening statement.

"These wild rumors that are going around are completely unfounded and we are willing to talk to anyone about them and straighten them out," he said.

Parkman took the front page with an editorial masquerading as a bylined news article upbraiding city folk for spreading gossip.

"These rumors, such have broken out over the weekend, not only do serious damage to the person involved but they are damaging to the entire community," he wrote in the peculiar way the *Georgian* had of making every story boosterish.

Folks could hardly be blamed for filling the information void with guesswork. A serial rapist—a Negro?—was loose and attacking young white women. And Chief Threadgill wasn't reassuring anybody that police were close to capturing him.

"There have been no new arrests in the case for more than a week," the chief said. "We have started at the very beginning of the case and are checking all the evidence at hand. We are checking all similar cases that took place before the Stevens case."

At the very beginning? No wonder there were rumors of well-to-do and powerful people involved. It smelled like a cover-up.[2]

In another story, the *Times–Free Press* announced that the GBI had assigned the case to a two-man team. Tom Price, "a veteran investigator," was joined by James T. Hillin, and they were devoting their efforts full-time to the case.

Price and Hillin started from scratch: witnesses were brought in for questioning, they went to the crime scene, rumors were run to ground.[3]

But two weeks into the job, Price and Hillin were no further along. On December 9, Parkman placed a reminder on the front page that the case was still unsolved. The reward had grown to $1,200 and any tip could break the case, he wrote.

"It is a deadly serious matter," Parkman wrote. "The next victim could be your son or daughter or even you."

Parkman wrote that Price and Hillin were open for business, but if someone wanted to pass that case-breaking tip on to the *Georgian* instead, that would be just fine.

"For the safety of the community, to clear away our doubts and suspicions," he wrote, "in the name of decency, this case needs to be solved."[4]

On the same day, the *Times–Free Press* took a different approach, appealing to a different audience.

"An appeal to local Negroes," the featured editorial began. "Much of the evidence—and it is not too convincing—in the Stevens murder case and the series of attacks preceding it indicate the man was member of your race." The tone was reasonable, with Clyde Tuttle noting that "all races have their good and their bad as well as the deranged or manic type." Then came the hard sell for Blacks striving to make good with white Carrollton.

"Negroes will be doing their race and the improvement of racial relations a good deed by assisting in every way in the searching investigation that is being made of the murder and attacks," he wrote. "Talk to the police."[5]

The way whites looked at it, race relations in Carrollton were fine. The December 16, 1948, edition of the *Georgian* carried a front-page article recounting a recruiting visit by the Ku Klux Klan. In a tone a bit smug, the brief used anonymous sources to report the Klan recruiters didn't have much luck. But the superior tone wasn't some paean to racial reconciliation. Instead, it was an olive branch to the job local police were doing in holding down unrest.

"General opinion is that the officers of the law are doing a fine job maintaining order and need no outside assistance of the KKK type," the newspaper reported.[6]

At the dawn of the 1950s, Georgia was an intensely segregated state, the result of decades of the native white ruling class clawing back what Reconstruction had sought, however briefly, to install. Georgia author and social critic Lillian Smith argued segregation emerged from an unholy bargain between rich and poor whites that elevated poor whites minimally, but enough to justify the system itself. But Smith said the system could only survive for as long as individuals would accept the corruption of it.[7]

As for whites, they did accept it. Moreover, they defended it, not only with terrorist organizations like the Ku Klux Klan but also through the mechanism of government. In 1953, Georgia attorney general Eugene Cook, a politician who mixed his strong segregationist stands with rabid anti-communism, penned a long letter to his opposite number in Virginia to bolster that state's defense against integrating public schools. In building his case that the state's ratification of the Fourteenth Amendment was disconnected from the idea of integration of schools, Cook listed the variety of ways Georgia had sought to keep the races apart. For example, interracial marriage was a felony punishable by up to two years in prison. While in prison, the law required whites and Blacks to be kept in separate institutions. Also in Georgia, churches, cemeteries, private schools, and colleges were exempt from property tax as long as the separation of the races was observed.[8]

Historian Numan V. Bartley wrote that as Georgia swayed under the increasing weight of an untenable and "decaying social institution that had lost intellectual respectability, segregation was mounting a moral quandary within the American conscience."[9]

But white resistance to reform was strong. Talmadge and other white Georgia leaders urged massive resistance to challenges to "the Southern way of life." In response, Blacks voted with their feet, leaving the state and the South by the millions, heading north to cities with better jobs and less restrictive covenants. Segregationists in Georgia waved the Confederate battle flag at them as they left. By 1956, in response to *Brown v. Board of Education*, the Supreme Court case declaring segregated schools unconstitutional, Georgia's General Assembly voted to incorporate the battle flag into the state flag itself as the dominant motif, an unmistakable message.[10]

The bargain between rich and poor whites to maintain segregation, while driven by deep-seated beliefs in white superiority, was not simple race hatred. Bartley wrote that more practical considerations were at work as well. The fall of segregation would decimate the school systems of poor counties, which catered only to the children of whites, and barely that. A flood of Black children, "impoverished, deprived, and undereducated" by generations of social, political, and economic disfranchisement, would drive down educational attainment to levels even below their current meager status.[11]

In the late 1940s, the schools in Carroll County struggled to pay salaries and ran monthly budget deficits. Were it not for the largesse of some of the county's leading men, the schools would have folded entirely—and that's with a segregated system that seriously tried to educate only the white majority. Aside from their lack of resources, the prospect of integration and federal control were anathema to white leaders. In 1948, Lieutenant Governor Marvin Griffin came to Carrollton to deliver a stemwinder of a speech to the local Rotarians that aimed at heart of the issue. The *Georgian* carried a summary of the speech on the front page: "In concluding his address, Mr. Griffin warned against begging for too much federal aid and especially for school purposes. He said he is afraid too much federal money for schools will bring in federal control of our school system which is one additional long step away from liberty." A decade after this speech, during Griffin's scandal-plagued term as governor, he would threaten to close the state's public schools rather than integrate.[12]

Within a decade, white reformers in Atlanta would adopt a new approach for "the City Too Busy to Hate." While the die-hard white supremacists urged state leaders to close the public schools before integration, moderates like Atlanta mayors William B. Hartsfield and Ivan Allen weighed the dying carcass of segregation against their city's future prospects as a truly global city of commerce and chose the latter. Hartsfield, and later Allen, who came to the city's top office via the Chamber of Commerce, urged the city's business class to keep the public schools open as a symbol of the city's commitment to economic progress. Black voters flocked to the white moderate candidates, pushing them ever more toward integration.[13]

But that day was far off in Carrollton, where Judge Boykin said in the local press that the city was not ready for the races to collide, even to serve the most desperate hopes of the commercial class. Still, Boykin and other civic leaders took pride that, while segregated, Carroll County was no haven for the uglier aspects of white supremacy, like the Ku Klux Klan.

Shortly after the new year, Carrollton's white leaders got the news they had longed to hear. Police had arrested a twenty-seven-year-old farmhand named Tyler North for the murder of Buddy Stevens. The *Atlanta Constitution* broke the story on January 13, 1949, under the banner headline "Carroll Slaying Suspect Bound Over." In Carrollton, the *Georgian* and *Times–Free Press* headlines were more pointed, each identifying North as a "Carrollton Negro." The relief was palpable. The *Times–Free Press* reported that the arrest was a surprise, since "the general public had assumed that the case had been dropped."

In fact, North had been arrested several weeks earlier and held in secret, along with a half dozen other Black men police were interrogating. The *Constitution* crowed that it had known about the arrest for some time but had not identified North at the request of law enforcement. Why, exactly, was North a suspect? The police weren't saying. Prosecutor Wright Lipford, whose formal title was solicitor general for the Coweta Judicial Circuit, released a statement to the press saying the evidence against North would be provided to the grand jury—in three months.

Newspapers described North as a "light-colored Negro six feet tall and weighing about 175 pounds." Lipford told reporters North had left his home south of Carrollton shortly after the Stevens murder and was arrested in Atlanta. The farmhand was married with three children and had lived in Carrollton his entire life, with the exception of the time he spent while in the Army in the South Pacific during World War II. The papers reported that he was taking classes offered under the GI Bill, which might have been why he was in Atlanta.[14]

Perhaps fearing violence or just to give him a more convenient location to question the suspect, Lipford stashed North in the Newnan jail, twenty miles away, where he was under the watchful eye of Lamar Potts. Potts was sheriff of Coweta County and something of a folk hero. He made national news with the 1948 conviction of John Wallace, a powerful land baron from a neighboring county who had murdered a white tenant farmer and burned the body. The story, which combined a willingness to confront the powerful with impressive forensic advances, had captured the imaginations of Georgians, who had grown used to government corruption. Much later, Margaret Anne Barnes's retelling of the incident as *Murder in Coweta County* would become a bestseller and be made into a TV movie starring Johnny Cash as Potts and Andy Griffith as the villainous Wallace.

There were apparent similarities between the Coweta and Carroll cases. North had been arrested, in part, based on the forensic work of Dr. Herman Jones and the Fulton County Crime Laboratory. The *Constitution* reported the lab found traces of human blood on North's corduroy britches. Police had raided North's home and seized the pants prior to his arrest, likely on a tip, although every Black man was a suspect in the murder.[15]

The *Georgian*'s Parkman took to the editorial page to praise investigators and express confidence using an odd bit of logic. Because North had been in custody for weeks before it was announced that he had been charged, Parkman reasoned, it was safe to assume the case had to be strong against him.

"Since the arrest of this suspect, and the early belief on the part of the investigators that he was guilty, they have been able to more or less take their time, being more careful than usual to see that everything tied together,"

Parkman wrote. "There was no rush about making the formal charge and announcement of the charge to the public."

One might reasonably argue the opposite: North was held in secret for weeks because the police *weren't* sure he was a good candidate for the murder and were saving themselves from embarrassment.

Carrollton had been searching for this kind of relief. Someone had been caught and the city could rest easy. But Parkman said the Stevens murder had caused some introspection among residents about the future.

"We realize that some of the horrible things we read about can happen to us in peaceful, quiet Carroll County," he wrote. "I hope the officers have the right man."[16]

The grand jury selection was announced in late March with an all-male, all-star cast. The group included the mayor, a city councilman, the dean of the college, several downtown businessmen, and a former deputy sheriff. Jeff Aldridge, vice president of Mandeville Mills, one of the city's largest businesses, was selected as foreman. Of course, all of the men were white. The Stevens case was one of three murders before them.[17]

Once seated, the grand jurors were greeted by Judge Samuel Boykin in the cavernous courtroom in the Carroll County Courthouse. The courtroom's ornate patterned ceiling and white plaster walls had recently been refurbished by a work crew of county inmates, at least some of whom must have rued the irony.[18]

As if the deck wasn't already stacked against North, Boykin—who would preside if North came to trial—instructed the grand jury to investigate the taxicab industry in Carrollton, which he claimed played a central role in the serial rape of white women in the city. The effect of Boykin's instruction was that the grand jury who would hear evidence against North was, on its own, investigating the crime he was said to have committed. But no one was going to question the judge's wisdom.

It would be hard to overestimate how important Judge Samuel J. Boykin Jr. was to Carrollton. He bore his father's name but was the youngest of three Boykin boys, all born in Carrollton and all attorneys. Heavyset, with dark features, Boykin wore thin, wire-frame glasses, his dark hair combed back from a receding hairline framing a round, pleasant face. The effect was professorial. Sam went to Georgia Military College between the world wars and got his law degree from the University of Georgia. After school, he spent two decades in and out of state service as an attorney, secretary, and treasurer for the politically influential State Highway Department.

In 1942, the Boykin brothers threw their support behind Attorney General Ellis Arnall in the Democratic primary race to unseat Governor Eugene Talmadge. Talmadge had held the seat for a decade but angered the party's educated elite when he fired the University System's Board of Regents after the board countermanded his removal of two UGA professors believed to support integration. The stunt caused all of Georgia's colleges to lose their national academic accreditation. Carrollton was an aspiring college town and the Boykin brothers would have none of it. Arnall, a progressive Democrat and lawyer from neighboring Coweta County, defeated Talmadge in the primary. As Georgia was effectively a one-party state, Arnall's victory in the fall was assured, and the Boykins celebrated by hosting a banquet in the new governor's honor in Carrollton with Sam as a master of ceremonies.[19]

The following year, when Arnall nominated the senior judge of the Coweta Circuit to an open slot on the state supreme court, he tapped Sam Boykin to take his place. Carrollton had known few judges in its history. It had been less than thirty years since the death of Judge Sampson W. Harris, a Confederate colonel who presided over the court for decades after the war.

"His heart was full of sympathy for the sons of Confederate soldiers and towards the old slavery-time Negro," his former court reporter recalled.[20]

By the fall of 1948, voters had twice reelected Boykin to the position. Much of Boykin's ability to influence the direction of Carroll County came from his use of the grand jury system to conduct wide-ranging investigations. The *Georgian* obsequiously described Boykin's grand jury instructions as "masterpieces of straight-spoken conviction." In just a few years he had deputized juries to investigate the county's unequal property tax formula, which had hampered funding the public schools, and the blacktopping of the county's many dirt roads, which kept the county isolated. Now he was instructing a grand jury to investigate a criminal ring run by cabdrivers.[21]

"From information presented to me by the solicitor general and other investigating officials, it is clear that the person or persons murdering our people and raping our young girls has, in almost every incident, had transportation to and from the scene of the crime," he said, his voice echoing through the large courtroom. "And that transportation has invariably been furnished by taxi cabs operating in Carrollton."[22]

Boykin said the city had favored veterans as taxi drivers and needed to crack down.

"Some of them seem to think this gives them a right to rape and murder," he said.

"We have something in Carrollton and Carroll County worse than the Ku Klux Klan," the judge soberly told jurors early Monday morning of April 4. "We have people going around murdering and raping young people.[23]

"The courts and law enforcement cannot clean up the city and county by themselves. They must have help from the people, the people who sit on our grand juries and in other influential situations," he said.[24]

In part, the blame lay with the people of Carrollton, he suggested. They allowed these attacks to occur "at regular intervals" without a public community response. Now people around Georgia were considering whether it was safe to send their children to West Georgia College, he said.[25]

Within hours of Boykin's grand jury charge, the mayor and city council had invited Lipford to a meeting to discuss ideas on how to regulate the taxi drivers. Lipford told the council that taxis were involved in at least four lovers' lane assaults prior to the Stevens murder.[26]

Boykin also told the grand jury that federal authorities had been brought in to investigate a "dope ring" that was peddling morphine and other drugs. "Other counties have made it so hot for dope peddlers recently that they have migrated to Carroll County," he said. "Now it is up to us to keep them on the move and to drive them from our borders as soon as possible."

Along with drugs, Boykin said the trafficking of illegal beer, wine, and liquor was "alarming." Carroll was a dry county.[27]

The grand jury was shaken. Rape, murder, and dope rings? It was horrifying, and it had all been laid at their feet. When North came before them, they saw they could do something about it, and Boykin had already pointed the finger of guilt right at his Black face.

The men heard the charges leveled at North on April 5, a little more than five months after the murder. Jurors met behind closed doors, but the room held few secrets close. Witnesses came and went throughout that Tuesday and the following day, and many spoke to reporters. The *Georgian* reported that the jury was investigating links between the Stevens murder and other cases of women being assaulted.[28]

On April 7, the *Georgian* headline blared: "Grand Jury Indicts Negro for Stevens Murder."

Despite the serial nature of the attacks, North was indicted only for the Stevens murder and not for the prior rapes. But press accounts indicated police were working to link North to those attacks.

The *Georgian* listed the remainder of the indictments, always indicating whether the person indicted was Black. In cases where a Black suspect was indicted for murdering a white person, the white person was named. In cases where the victim was Black, the *Georgian* just listed the race with no name. Among the cases was Earnest Elliot, a Black man from Temple, who was accused of killing a white man, B. C. "Smutt" Karr, during an argument. That case had not caught the public's attention the way Stevens's killing had. Likewise, Foster "Pappy" Ellis, a Black man accused of killing a Black woman, earned a brief mention in the local papers. Ellis's alleged victim didn't even merit that kind of exposure.[29]

The following day, the same grand jury issued indictments for rape to Leonard Pendergrass, a fifty-six-year-old taxi driver and former city police officer, and sawmill operator John Cumby, fifty-seven. Both of the attacks preceded the Stevens murder and the charges—particularly against Pendergrass—raised eyebrows. Wasn't this what Boykin had warned about when he charged the grand jury? The curiosity wasn't lost on the *Times–Free Press*, which noted police were still working on the rapes prior to Stevens's death, but that confounded the theory that North was the fiend behind them all. So far, there was no evidence produced to connect North with them. For that matter, no evidence had been made public to connect North with Stevens.

And then there is Pendergrass, whom the *Times–Free Press* noted was the only link between taxi drivers and the series of rapes.

"It is expected that the investigations will by no means stop," the paper reported.

Pendergrass would become an important link for police in indicting yet another man in the Stevens case, but that would come later.[30]

Despite having held North for more than three months, Lipford was not ready to move forward with a criminal trial, to the great disappointment of local townspeople who packed the downtown courthouse in hopes the Stevens case would be called. Lipford's delay was something of a surprise. Commonly, trials—especially those involving Blacks—moved quickly after an indictment. But the solicitor and Sheriff Denver Gaston were both relatively new to their posts, and everything was not running smoothly in Boykin's courtroom. Defendants and witnesses in some cases were not available and cases were not ready, souring Boykin's mood. But the Stevens case was another matter. Lipford wasn't ready to put North on trial, and the rape trials of both Pendergrass and Cumby were also continued until the June term.

Cheated of the main event, the standing-room crowd witnessed the murder trial of Foster "Pappy" Ellis, the Black man whose Black victim wasn't named in the brief mention his indictment merited. Ellis had been indicted along with North on April 5, 1949. Seven days later he was standing trial.

It turned out that his victim had been his wife, Mary Parks Ellis, whom Pappy had killed with a shotgun. Ellis claimed the shotgun went off accidentally and he did not mean to shoot his wife. After the blast he called an ambulance, but Mary was beyond help. After hearing testimony from a dozen witnesses in the one-day trial, the jury found Ellis guilty but recommended mercy. Boykin sentenced him to life in prison.[31]

"A VERY DARK NEGRO"

When the June term arrived, Lipford still was not ready. He asked the case be continued until the fall. This worried white people. When North was finally indicted, Carrollton heaved a sigh of relief and rumors spread that local police, aided by Price and Hillin of the GBI, were about to break the case wide open. The delay until June was greeted with more disappointment than concern. But why this *second* delay?

Buddy's parents publicly expressed their confidence in Chief Thread-gill's continuing investigation while also announcing they had nothing to do with the delay. Behind the scenes, leaders in the town began pressing for more resources. Following the indictment, Price and Hillin were split up and transferred to work GBI cases elsewhere in the state. The Kiwanis Club of Carrollton, where Buddy's father was an important member, met in early June and drafted a resolution for Governor Herman Talmadge, the son of the late governor Eugene Talmadge, asking they be reassigned back to the case full-time.

"We are fully aware that it is a difficult case, a killing without rhyme or reason, and that to bring it to a satisfactory solution will require still more effort and still more manpower," the Kiwanis resolution read. Price and Hillin were "sorely needed to help substantiate the evidence now available which can bring the perpetrator of this crime before the bar of justice." Across town, the Lions Club took up a similar resolution asking for more help from the GBI.

The pressure worked, to an extent. Within a week, Hillin (although not Price) was back in town and working with Sheriff Gaston, questioning a group of boys who said they heard the shots the night of Buddy's death.[1]

For the first time in months, there was real public concern that the man responsible for killing Buddy and attacking a half dozen young women might still be at large. In a June 14 editorial, the *Times–Free Press* noted that North was "one of many suspects" and had been indicted solely on circumstantial evidence. That the newspaper knew the evidence against North, presented in secret before a grand jury, shows how deep the concern ran among the town fathers. There was a real fear that Threadgill, Gaston, and Lipford had the wrong man and that was why they had yet to bring him to trial.

"Meanwhile, young people have started parking in the same old 'lovers lanes,'" the *Times–Free Press* worried, "and the city might wake up some morning with another Stevens case on its hands."[2]

A new jury pool was selected three months later and North was on the docket. Criminal session would begin October 10, 1949, nearly a year after Buddy's death. Not on the docket was Leonard Pendergrass or John Cumby.[3]

If North was to stand trial for Stevens's murder, at least he would have adequate counsel. Myer Goldberg, a Newnan lawyer and state legislator, had been assigned to represent him. Goldberg brought with him his partner, Henry Payton. On the prosecution side, Lipford had enlisted the aid of Shirley Boykin, a Carrollton attorney in private practice and, unbelievably, the older brother of the judge.

The Stevens case was the single most important story in the county.

As the October criminal session of Carroll County Superior Court convened, Solicitor Lipford announced North would at last be brought before the bar of justice, but not for the Stevens murder. Instead, North was called to stand trial for assault "with intent to rape" a local white girl in an incident the summer before Stevens's death.[4]

The allegation had been drummed up late in the investigation into North, and a grand jury indicted him just a week before the October criminal session began. In fact, North had been in jail for months on the Stevens murder charge when Lieutenant Price of the GBI located the Carrollton teen, who was staying with family in Savannah, and asked her to testify. While not the charge Carrollton was expecting, attempted rape of a white girl by a Black man was shocking and played into every fear and fantasy white Southerners held about their Black neighbors. In fact, one reason why North had such competent counsel was because of a history of Black suspects being represented by inept or uninterested white lawyers. In 1932 the U.S. Supreme Court overturned the convictions of nine Black youths accused of raping two white girls in the landmark case *Powell v. Alabama*, which formed the basis for the "Fairness Doctrine" that governs criminal procedure to this day.

Yet, fear of Black-on-white rape is one of the most powerful tropes in America's long and ugly history of racism. Crusading journalist Ida B. Wells took the idea to task in *Southern Horrors: Lynch Law in All Its Phases*, her 1892 pamphlet on lynching, in which she said whites used rape as "a deed dastardly enough to arouse Southern blood, which gives its horror of rape as excuse for lawlessness."

A half century later, North was arrested under the charge of killing Stevens, but also because he was thought to be the Black "fiend" who tried to rape Nan Turner. The same man who raped a half dozen white women before the fatal Halloween attack. If—even in a supercharged, racial environment—such a charge couldn't be supported by the evidence, Lipford, Threadgill, Gaston, and the GBI would have to turn North loose.

Into this gap came a young woman, eighteen by the time of the trial, willing to testify that North came into her room and tried for force himself on her.

"He said, 'I don't want no nigger for a wife. I want a white girl,'" the girl told prosecutors. North tried to kiss her and said he wanted to take her north and marry her. Did he rape her? "He didn't get that far," she said. He did, she claimed, tell her to meet him the next day and they would leave together.[5]

The girl came from a poor white family and North did know them through his boss, a white man named Lloyd Phillips, who took them food. On the stand, the girl turned on Phillips, saying she told him of the "attack" and that he had said he would kill North. Moreover, prosecutors alleged that Phillips had hosted a chicken dinner for the girl, her sister, and her mother at North's home, a serious breach of racial etiquette, adding to fuel to the fire of racial intermingling.[6]

Under cross-examination, the girl denied she had been married or that she had a child, but then she backtracked. She did, in fact, have a child, but she said the baby lived with relatives in a town an hour south of Carrollton. The defense produced thirty character witnesses, many of whom said the girl was "of bad character."

In the end, North took the stand. "I'm not guilty of the things with which I am charged," he said.

The jury deliberated ninety-five minutes before finding him guilty. Judge Boykin sentenced the father of three to twelve to fifteen years in prison.

After the trial, Gaston arrested Phillips, who had testified on behalf of his employee, and charged him with "accessory before the fact to assault and attempt to rape." Of note, Lipford dropped the rape charges against Pendergrass and Cumby.

Once again, Lipford had failed to bring the Stevens charges up before a jury. Newspapers reported North could still be brought back to stand trial in the Stevens case, but serious doubts began to emerge. The *Times–Free Press* reminded readers that North had been indicted in April, but only "after a series of suspects had been picked up, grilled and released."[7]

Less than a month after North's surprise conviction on assault, Lipford announced North would be tried in a special court term just after Thanksgiving. The announcement couldn't have filled the Stevens family with confidence.

"I believe we should present the evidence we have in hand to a jury in Carroll County at the present time," the prosecutor said. The statement sounded like a man who believed his case against North was not good but also was not getting better.[8]

Lipford was spared potential embarrassment when, a week before the trial, North's lawyer, Myer Goldberg, took a leave of absence to deal with an eye ailment. To prepare for surgery and save his sight, Goldberg's doctors had prescribed an indefinite leave of absence from practicing law. Boykin approved yet another postponement.[9]

It was becoming increasingly clear that Lipford wouldn't pin the Stevens murder on North. In fact, in a few months, North would be released on a $2,000 appeal bond, an incredibly rare accomplishment for a Black man convicted of the attempted rape of a white teenager.[10]

Of more concern to white Carrollton, prosecutors and the police were again without a suspect in the Stevens case.

But just as the trail had gone cold, an amazing, almost magical coincidence occurred, taking the Stevens investigation in an entirely new direction. The problem with the case against North was that it was entirely circumstantial. What investigators needed was a murder weapon and they needed to put it in the hands of a new suspect. And he needed to be Black.

Almost at the very hour Boykin signed the order granting yet another postponement in North's prosecution, fifty miles away, in a downtown Atlanta pawnshop, Leon Beeber, a forty-two-year-old Jewish immigrant from Poland, paid $25 to a Black man from Carroll County named Elijah "Eli" Luther Cosper for a silver Smith & Wesson .38 revolver with a black grip.[11] Why Cosper, who was blind, had a handgun was a mystery. He and his wife, Floy, had a small produce business and hauled their goods to market in Atlanta.

Two weeks later, on December 8, 1949, an Atlanta police detective called on Beeber looking for a Smith & Wesson, serial number 527398, reported stolen in Carrollton sixteen months earlier. The detective snatched up the gun and delivered it immediately to Hillin at the GBI.[12]

The original owner of the gun was a white taxi driver and former Carrollton police officer named Leonard Pendergrass, the very same man who had been indicted on charges of rape in April. Lipford held Pendergrass for months before deciding in October not to prosecute. When the gun was turned up in Beeber's pawnshop, Sheriff Denver Gaston revealed that Pendergrass had been present for an earlier lovers' lane attack in August 1948, two months before the Stevens murder, when the masked man claimed his second victim. According to Gaston, Pendergrass drove a young man named Lee Hardman and his date out to a quiet area a few miles south of town near a Methodist church.

Much of this story seems strange, including Pendergrass's claim that he loaned Hardman the .38 Special revolver he kept from his time on the city police force the day of the attack. Pendergrass said he left the couple at that dark crossroads. Gaston said the couple was later approached by a masked man with a flashlight who robbed them and raped the woman. Among the items stolen was the revolver.[13]

When the Atlanta police realized the gun was reported stolen in Carrollton, it was sent to the Fulton County Crime Lab for ballistics tests to see if it had been used in the Stevens murder. Dr. Herman Jones, the lab director, initially had said the bullet that killed Buddy was a 9mm round commonly fired by foreign-make semiautomatic pistols. The recovered gun was a .38 revolver. A 9mm bullet will not chamber correctly in a .38 revolver because the brass casing is too large. However, George Cornett, a firearms expert at the crime lab and Jones's second-in-command, managed to discharge some 9mm bullets from the .38 revolver and matched the test slugs to the one recovered from Buddy's body.[14]

After that, things moved quickly. Cosper and his wife were swept up by police and sweated. Under questioning, Cosper said he had bought the gun a year earlier from another local Black man, Laymon Almon. Almon, who also had been arrested, told police he bought the gun from a twenty-seven-year-old sharecropper named Clarence Henderson in December 1948, two months after the murder.[15]

That night, Henderson heard a loud rapping on the door of the one-room sharecropper's shack he shared with his wife, Lizzie, and two children. "Open up, nigger!" a loud voice commanded. "It's the sheriff." Henderson lifted the crossbar and a half dozen uniformed white men, led by Sheriff Gaston, rushed in, pushing Henderson so hard he stumbled back.

"Get your clothes, nigger. You're going to jail," one of the men said.

"Jail? What have I—" he started, but his question was cut off with a blow to the jaw.

"For killing a white man!"[16]

Henderson was arrested for the Stevens murder by a posse of the first order. When the handcuffs went on, Gaston, Carrollton police chief Rada Threadgill, investigators Hillin and Price, and their boss, the new chief of the Georgia Bureau of Investigation, Captain Delmar Jones, were there. Governor Talmadge must have had another appointment.[17]

The sharecropper was a convenient suspect because Carrollton police already knew him. Two months earlier, around the same time Lipford dropped the rape charges he had used to hold Pendergrass, the grand jury indicted Henderson on an unrelated assault charge.[18]

For more than a year, white police investigators had been arresting and questioning men from Carroll County's small, largely agricultural Black community.[19] A dozen men had been detained; many more had been questioned. White newspaper editors had appealed to their Black readers to turn over the monster in their midst. And police and prosecutors had indicted and jailed Tyler North for a crime they, at last, determined he had not committed.

At no time had Henderson emerged as a suspect. Until now. Now people were talking, and fingers were pointing at the father of two with a third on the way. In the white press he was described as "a very dark Negro," while the Black-owned *Atlanta Daily World* described Henderson as a "farm youth" arrested on "a hunch."[20]

Sheriff Gaston said Henderson told several different but equally false stories about his relationship with the gun. Chief Threadgill added the damning evidence that "several Negroes have been questioned who stated they saw Henderson with the gun prior to the Stevens murder." The details of that story would change over time. In the meantime, investigators continued untwisting the tortured trail of the murder weapon.[21]

After the North debacle, Lipford had no desire for a repeat performance with Henderson. While he had waited months to bring what evidence he had against North before a grand jury, now armed with a murder weapon, Lipford announced he would seek a special grand jury session on Henderson soon after the new year.

Lipford also announced a new arrest. Harvey "Bo" Dunson, another Black man, was being held as a material witness. Gaston filled in the blanks, saying that Henderson had claimed he got the murder weapon from Dunson. Dunson denied the claim, the sheriff said.[22]

True to his word, Lipford arranged a special session of the grand jury on January 12, 1950, less than a month after Henderson's arrest. In fact, two grand juries were empaneled: one to indict Henderson on murder, the second to indict him on armed robbery for the $15 taken out of Buddy Stevens's wallet. One of the members of the robbery grand jury was Ralph Threadgill, the brother of the Carrollton police chief.[23]

The Stevens case had been the most difficult ever undertaken in Carroll County, Lipford said, perhaps the most difficult investigation ever in Georgia. But they had their man. Once Henderson was indicted, Lipford said he would ask the grand jury to set a trial date within the month.[24]

In the meantime, investigators leaked out information about Henderson aimed at reducing any suspicion or sympathy potential jurors could muster. Apart from being "very dark," police said Henderson had a criminal record and was considered "somewhat of a bully among the Negroes in the vicinity."[25]

It is true that Henderson had a long history with police. The 1940 U.S. Census records the then seventeen-year-old Henderson as a resident of the Georgia State Highway Work Camp—a prison chain gang.[26]

For Lipford, this was a better fit than North, a father and veteran of the South Pacific, bettering himself under the GI Bill. North was so upright, even his white employer had risked jail to testify on his behalf. But Henderson, while also a father of two, was a rank criminal, a jet-black Negro not even liked among his kind, according to the white narrative.

Lipford called more than two dozen witnesses into the secretive grand jury session. Among them were Dr. Herman Jones, head of the Fulton County Crime Lab, and Eli Cosper, the blind truck farmer who pawned the pistol Jones's lab identified as the murder weapon. Beeber, the immigrant pawnbroker, also was called. Their testimony came at a rocket pace, with the session lasting a little more than two hours before the grand jury released its indictment of Henderson. Judge Boykin announced that the trial would start less than two weeks later. Jury selection would begin the very next day.[27]

Two local lawyers were assigned to represent Henderson. Claude Driver of Buchanan, in neighboring Haralson County, was one. In 1950, Driver was preparing a run for the state house of representatives against another lawyer, Harold Murphy.[28]

Henderson's other attorney was William Wiggins, a Carrollton lawyer who had just opened his firm in 1948. Some years later Wiggins, too, would serve in the state legislature, but at the time of the Henderson trial he was just starting out, a young lawyer without much experience assigned as indigent defense counsel for what the prosecutor had already described as one of the most complex cases in Georgia history.

Over the course of a long career, Wiggins would serve as a part-time prosecutor in city and state court, work as counsel for the Georgia Department of Transportation on right-of-way cases, and spend decades as Carrollton city attorney. But right now he was charged with defending the man accused of killing one of Carrollton's shining lights.[29]

Despite Lipford's itch to get started, the team of Driver and Wiggins scored a small victory when Boykin agreed to postpone the start of the trial for week so they could prepare their case. Lipford would keep his pledge to bring Henderson to trial in January. Opening arguments would be January 30, 1950.[30]

The murder of Buddy Stevens had roiled white Carrollton for fifteen months and had shaken Black Carrollton as much or more. Police had pulled in a dozen or more Black men and one white man in their search for the culprit. Later there would be accusations of police abuse, not uncommon for the Deep South.

Investigators had made mistakes. It took an hour to locate the body, and while Stevens fell where he was shot, just one of the three bullets that struck him was retrieved. Men and dogs trampled the crime scene. The prime suspect, Tyler North, was held for most of the year on charges of the murder, only to be later discarded as a suspect, then charged with a suspicious "assault" in an unrelated case.

With a weak case against North, the chances seemed remote that the Stevens murder would be solved. Then, in a stroke of good fortune, the murder weapon turned up in a pawnshop miles away and was traced back into the hands of Clarence Henderson. It was as if the missing piece of a machine had fallen magically into place.

CHAPTER 5

THE FIRST TRIAL

There was much at stake as dawn broke on Monday, January 30, 1950. "Long Investigation Nears End," the *Carroll County Georgian* proclaimed in a banner headline before the trial.

"One of Carrollton's most baffling crime investigations, which had its start the night of October 31, 1948, will come to a climax here next Monday when Clarence Henderson, 27-year-old tenant farmer, goes on trial for his life," the newspaper reported. "Judge Samuel J. Boykin, of Carrollton, will preside over the trial, which is expected to be the most sensational hearing in many years."[1]

Trials in Carrollton were held in the Carroll County Courthouse, a sturdy, Italian Renaissance Revival building, since its construction in 1928 at the intersection of Newnan and Dixie Streets. The building's single courtroom had a high ceiling and was large enough to seat several hundred spectators. Boykin sat at the front behind a low oak desk situated on a riser. The witness stand was on the right, followed by the jury box.

Carrolltonians packed the cavernous courtroom the morning of the trial. Whites filled up the front of the courtroom, with managers from textile mills seated alongside rough farmers with time on their hands before the spring planting. Blacks were given a segregated section in the back. Racial tensions were high. For more than a year, local whites had fumed over the pace of the investigation. Despite rumors of white suspects, police had never identified anyone other than a Black man in connection with the murder. In a show of force, more than thirty armed state troopers rimmed the courtroom to keep the peace. And as they entered, men and women both were searched for concealed weapons.[2]

Henderson waited in a hallway to be called. He wore a light shirt underneath dark denim overalls and a jacket. He carried a wide-brimmed hat in his manacled hands. Before he entered the courtroom, the bailiff stopped him in a narrow stairway. After a short pause, Sheriff Denver

Gaston arrived with two state troopers, Police Chief Rada Threadgill, Tom Price of the GBI, and a photographer. Henderson stared impassively, looking deep into the lens while the white men took their places around him to capture the moment. The flashbulb popped and the squinting defendant was led into the courtroom.

The trial started with testimony from Eldred Bass and Elwyn Patrick, the two doctors who examined Stevens's body the night of the murder and retrieved the evidence bullet from his leg. Patrick testified that he had been at the scene of the murder and examined Stevens's body before it was moved. Stevens was in a kneeling position with his chest "humped over," he said. Both doctors agreed that Stevens likely died as a result of a bullet to the heart. Former sheriff Bunt Kilgore was next and briefly questioned about the chain of custody of the bullet, which he said he immediately handed over to Lipford's next witness, GBI agent Jim Hillin.

Hillin had been investigating the series of lovers' lane attacks in Carrollton throughout the summer and fall of 1948 and had been called to the scene the night of Stevens's murder.[3] Lipford asked Hillin if he had received the bullet from Kilgore the night of the murder. Hillin said he had gotten the bullet from the sheriff and delivered it to the Fulton County Crime Lab. Then Lipford asked if Leonard Pendergrass had reported to him the serial number of his gun stolen in another attack in August. Driver objected to the question—one of the few objections Henderson's defense team would make.

"I don't see how it is material what Mr. Pendergrass or somebody else did," Driver complained. Boykin said he would allow the question "for the time being" and give the prosecutor room to the connect it with the issue at hand.

Hillin said he received the serial number from Pendergrass and turned it over to his superior at GBI headquarters.

"Do you recall the date you gave your office the serial number of this gun? Was it in 1948 or 1949?"

"It was in 1948. It was several days or a week after Mr. Stevens was killed," Hillin said.

When the Atlanta police discovered the gun in Leon Beeber's pawnshop and delivered it to him, he in turn took it to the Fulton County Crime Lab for testing, he said.

In cross-examination, Wiggins pressed Hillin for details explaining why Pendergrass had reported the serial number.

"How long was that after the death of Stevens?" Wiggins asked.

"Several days," Hillin said.

"Had you talked with Mr. Pendergrass before he gave you this?"

"Yes, sir. I talked to Mr. Pendergrass after Mr. Hardman got held up."

Curious now, Wiggins asked, "He didn't give you the serial number until after the murder?"

"Hardman had the same number from Mr. Pendergrass prior to that time and gave it to me," Hillin said.

So Hardman had reported the pistol and serial number to Hillin as stolen prior to Stevens's death? "How long before?" Wiggins asked.

"I would say about a week or less than a week. Mr. Hardman had the gun taken off of him in a holdup," Hillin said, again referring to the August attack.

Wiggins wrapped up his cross-examination without settling why Hillin, who was assisting local police in investigating a series of rapes, waited two months to get details on a stolen gun from an eyewitness to one of the attacks or why he waited even longer to talk to the gun's owner.[4]

Leon Beeber, the pawnshop owner, was called to say he took the gun in pawn from Eli Cosper. He identified Cosper from the witness stand.

"You know him merely by sight?" Wiggins asked in cross-examination.

"Yes, because he is blind," Beeber said. It was one of a number of questions Wiggins asked that day where he did not seem to anticipate that the response would favor the prosecution.[5]

Beeber was dismissed from the stand and Boykin called for a lunchtime recess. Court would resume at 1:00 P.M. with the testimony of Nan Turner, Buddy Stevens's date and the only eyewitness to the crime. The crowd of spectators, white and Black, filed out of the courthouse. The day was sunny and unusually warm. Temperatures would reach the mid-70s.

When the hundreds of spectators arrived back from lunch, they found the courtroom doors locked. Boykin had decided, with agreement from the Lipford and Henderson's defense lawyers, to clear the courtroom for the next witness. Only the lawyers, the press, and close family members of the parties involved were allowed in.[6]

Nan Turner took the stand and swore an oath to tell the truth. Then she was asked her name.

"Mrs. Nan Hansard," she said.

It had been eighteen months since Stevens's death and Nan had moved on. The prior July, Nan started a new life with a friend of Buddy's, Walter Hansard, who was studying dentistry at Emory University in Atlanta.[7]

That Nan was allowed to testify in relative privacy was a nod to the protected status in which white women were placed in 1950s Georgia. This was particularly true in the arena of sex. Although all of the white attorneys had agreed that the general public would be barred from hearing her testimony, Boykin had the authority to clear the courtroom without their approval. State law gave judges the discretion to clear the courtroom of some or all spectators in "any case of seduction or divorce, or other case where the evidence is vulgar and obscene, or relates to the improper acts of the sexes, and tends to debauch the morals of the young."[8] So it was that Nan began her testimony before a largely empty courtroom.

With a few short questions, Lipford set the scene for the jury. Buddy picked Nan up for their date in front of Carrollton Presbyterian Church at 7:45 P.M. From there, the couple drove a few blocks south to the Green Front Café, a sandwich shop near the railroad tracks popular with the younger set, where Buddy bought a pack of cigarettes.

Then they drove to Sunset Hills and parked at the end of Sunset Boulevard, a dead-end street. From there, Lipford let Nan tell the story.

"We had been there about an hour," she said. "We had been listening to the radio."

By her reckoning, it was approaching 10:00 P.M. The night was cold and rain threatened when the couple was startled by a flashlight shining through the driver's-side window. A man's voice ordered them out of the car.

"At first I couldn't see him," Nan said. "He talked like a Negro. I couldn't see his face."

"What are you two doing here?" the voice demanded. It was dark, and a light was shining in their faces, but they could see he had a gun in his right hand. The man held the gun in front of the flashlight and Nan saw the long barrel. It looked dark.

"Put your hands up," he ordered, motioning at Buddy. The man ordered Buddy and then Nan to get out of the car and for both of them to start walking to the end of the street. Nan was barefoot, having left her shoes in the car.

"We got to a small embankment," Nan said. The man told them both to lie facedown on the ground.

"You got any money?" he said.

"Fifteen dollars," Buddy replied, handing back the cash from his pocket.

The man turned to Nan.

"You have any money?"

"No. I don't have any," she said.

"Yes you have. Where's your pocketbook?"

"I don't have any money," she said.

The man ordered them up and told them to keep walking. It was a dark, moonless night. It had started to rain. The man motioned with his flashlight off the road toward a cotton patch. The cotton had been harvested and the field was plowed up, leaving stalks and bolls behind.

"Somebody is waiting out there to see you," the man said.

The lie was chilling. Buddy told the man he didn't think there was anyone out there.

"I have a little Christmas party down there," he said. "Maybe there is somebody who wants to see you."

The man was nervous, telling Buddy to keep his hands away from his body, unsure if he was armed.

When they got to the plowed-up cotton patch, Nan complained that the bolls hurt her feet.

"Why aren't you carrying her?" the man said to Buddy.

Buddy picked her up and struggled to carry Nan over the uneven ground as they moved from cotton patch to pasture. The group went up and over a wire fence and farther from the car and nearby houses. Nan turned to look back.

"Turn your head back," the man warned.

He whistled, as if to signal someone. *Was* someone waiting?

The plowed field was soon to become a fairway for the Sunset Hills Country Club golf course. The jewel of the new development, the course was designed by rising star Robert Trent Jones, who had just teamed with golf legend Bobby Jones to build a course in Atlanta and redesign a couple of holes at Augusta National Golf Club, home course of the Masters Golf Tournament.

Another fence. Nan and Buddy went up and over. The man didn't follow.

"What do you have in your pocket?" he asked, perhaps still nervous about whether Buddy was armed. Buddy handed over the package of cigarettes. They were far from the car when the voice made his next demand. From behind his gun, he told Buddy to rape Nan.

"I won't do it," Buddy said. "I'd rather die."

Angered, the man swung hard across the fence, hitting Buddy with the butt of his gun and opening a gash several inches long above his left eye.

Agitated, the man crossed the fence and stalked the pasture. He ordered Buddy, who was bleeding from his head wound, to take off his shirt and then marched the couple up a small hill about 150 yards away, where he forced Nan to lie on her back with Buddy on top of her.

The man walked to the edge of woods and brought back some branches. "I'll make you," he said to Buddy, and began whipping him while ordering him to rape Nan.

"I won't do it," Buddy said again and again.

The man picked up a thick branch and hit Buddy in the back of the head. He asked Stevens for his parents' names and where they lived, kicking Buddy all the while. In the swinging light of the flashlight, Nan saw the man was wearing a woven leather shoe. Not only was the shoe not practical for force-marching people across a chilly, darkened field, but it was not a workingman's shoe. An unlikely choice for a sharecropper like Henderson.

The man ordered Nan and Buddy to stand and walk to the edge of the nearby woods. As he was walking, the man hit Buddy in the back with a stick, knocking him down. Again the man ordered the couple to lie on the ground. This time he had Buddy lie facedown on the ground and had Nan lie separately on her back and remove her underwear.

To stop Nan's protest, he gagged her with her own scarf and covered her face. The man positioned himself above Nan. Nearby, Buddy lay on the ground, badly beaten and bleeding from the gash above his eye. Buddy started to move, but Nan pleaded with him to stay still. Buddy said nothing. A long minute passed as the man loomed over Nan. He moved down on top of the girl and ordered her to put her knees up. Buddy saw his opening. He lunged, knocking the man off-balance. Nan scrambled to her feet. The men grappled, with Nan's attacker holding her by one knee and using his other hand to defend against Buddy's attack.

Summoning his strength, Buddy pushed against the man, knocking Nan down in the process. "Run!" Buddy yelled. She managed to free herself and, in a flash, she was up and running. Then she heard a shot. In the hush of the courtroom, Nan said, "I saw Buddy falling back."

As she ran, she heard two more shots. Perhaps unsure of the direction back to Buddy's car, Nan ran northeast across open country toward the lights of homes in the distance.[9]

Under cross-examination, some of the details of Nan's testimony changed. She said the man had them lie on the ground while he was on the other side of the second fence, rather than after he had struck Buddy with the gun. At one point she testified she was still trying to escape when the first shot was fired, while in another part of her testimony she was running from the scene when she heard all three shots.

Even her direct testimony was inconsistent. Nan said she saw the man's hands. He was Black, she said, but she immediately followed it up with "he talked like a Negro."

In its April 7, 1949, edition, reporting on the North indictment, the *Georgian* said Nan Turner "first said she believed her assailant was a Negro. Later she said she couldn't be sure." By the time Henderson was charged, that confusion had been forgotten.[10]

Wiggins questioned some of the details of Nan's testimony, honing in on where the man had been in relation to her and Buddy throughout the ordeal. For instance, Wiggins wanted to know how the man could have so effectively controlled them when they were on one side of a barbwire fence and the man was on the other. He also questioned Nan's account of Buddy's heroics, considering she was gagged and blindfolded when the most dramatic events occurred.

"Buddy moved. I imagine the Negro started to get up. He held my knees and told Buddy not to move," Nan said.

"You say he held you with your knees and you were trying to get up?" Wiggins asked. "How do you know he had you by your knees?"

"He had one hand on me," Nan said, beginning to cry.

"Where did he hold you?" Wiggins asked. Nan, tears running down her face, didn't answer.

"How could you tell he had his hand on your knee?"

Finally, she broke down and sobbed. Boykin hit his limit. "Don't ask that question again," the judge warned.[11] Nan was excused from the witness chair and Boykin ordered the doors to the courtroom be opened. Hundreds of people streamed in—whites first, then Blacks.

If Nan provided the most dramatic testimony of the day, the most damning came from George Cornett. Cornett was a former *Atlanta Constitution* photographer and policeman with the Fulton County Police Department. When Dr. Herman Jones founded the Fulton County Crime Laboratory, he chose Cornett as Watson to his Sherlock. Cornett was the lab's chief photographer and fingerprint examiner. Ballistics is, in part, photography, but Cornett had worked a dozen years honing his skills in firearms identification as a forensic investigator and was in demand at trials across the state. Authoritative, bespectacled, fiftyish, square-faced, with a high-and-tight haircut, Cornett was an expert witness out of central casting.

Cornett testified that he received the bullet retrieved from Stevens's leg on November 1, 1948, the day after the murder. The gun, a Smith & Wesson .38 Special, came to him thirteen months later, on December 8, 1949—the very day it was retrieved by Atlanta police detective Harkins from Beeber's pawnshop and delivered to Hillin of the GBI.

The first order of business was to explain why he believed the 9mm bullet that pierced Buddy Stevens's leg came from a .38 caliber pistol. The answer, Cornett explained, lay in the ridges and valleys created when gun manufacturers drilled the barrels of their firearms. Ballistics experts call the ridges "lands" and the valleys "grooves." The measured distance between the top of one land to the top of the land on the opposite side determines the caliber of the weapon. In this case, the distance was 0.38 inches. All of this rifling leaves marks on the softer lead of a bullet as it twists its way out of the barrel.

The Stevens bullet had five lands and five grooves, meaning it wasn't fired from a foreign-make 9mm weapon, as had initially been suspected.

"Most 9 millimeter ammunition of foreign make have six lands and grooves," Cornett said. "Some of them have four, but I don't know any that have five."

No, he said, that bullet had been fired by a Smith & Wesson .38 with a right-hand twist—just like the weapon pawned at Beeber's.

Of course, lands and grooves weren't the only sticking points that needed explaining. A 9mm bullet won't load correctly in a .38 revolver. First, .38 Special ammunition is "rimmed," meaning there is a flange at the back of the bullet casing meant to hold the bullet in the proper position within the chamber of the revolver, while the 9mm bullet's flange is much smaller and nearly equal to the width of the jacket.

Apart from the lack of a proper flange, a 9mm bullet won't fit in a .38 revolver. The 9mm lead slug itself is slightly smaller, but the brass jacket around it is slightly bigger.

"It lacks .007 of an inch," Cornett told the jury. "This bullet will not chamber up in a Smith & Wesson."

To make it fit, Cornett did something he had never done in his twelve years as a ballistics expert. He filed down a test bullet to make it fit in the evidence pistol. It was precise work. Cornett said he filed the brass jacket around the ring where the lead slug fit into it. If he filed it too much, it would slip in the revolver's chamber. The bullet had to be filed to fit, but not so much that it wouldn't slip forward and away from the pistol's hammer.

For one to believe Cornett's testimony, one must accept an astounding chain of events that led to this exercise:

An Atlanta police detective discovered a weapon in a downtown pawn-shop reported as stolen from Carrollton. He rushed the gun that day to GBI agent Hillin, who in turn rushed it to the Fulton County Crime Lab for ballistics testing. Then, without knowing whether the bullet would fit, or fire properly if it did, the assistant director of the lab devised a method to make ammunition designed for a 9mm automatic chamber up in a .38 Special.

It was remarkably cooperative, efficient, and ingenious police work.

Cornett said he wasn't sure what he was doing would even work. "I cut one 9 mm and examined the projectile to see whether it would explode in the chamber or not," he said. That would be something if, after a year of searching, the ballistics expert exploded a round in the suspected murder weapon. Cornett, in fact, filed down three bullets.[12]

After firing the 9mm slugs into a "recovery box," a four-foot-long box stuffed with cotton, Cornett retrieved the test bullets, marked them, and placed them under a comparison microscope with the bullet taken from Stevens's leg. The comparison microscope—which allows the user to simultaneously view two bullets side by side—was relatively new as a crime-fighting tool, as was the entire field of forensic ballistics. It was invented in the 1920s by the forensic scientist Calvin Goddard, a pioneer in the field. Goddard used the microscope during the appellate stages of the trials of Nicola Sacco and Bartolomeo Vanzetti, Italian American anarchists accused of murdering a security guard in the course of robbing a factory in Massachusetts. The Sacco and Vanzetti trials were national news in the 1920s, the product of the twin bugaboos of immigrants and anti-capitalist ideology, and Goddard's invention got considerable publicity as a result.[13] Still, Cornett was obliged to describe the mechanism in some detail to jurors who might not have heard of it.

"You look through the eye at the test bullet and you see the test," he said, "and with the other, you see a portion of the evidence bullet. The microscope brings them out plainly and you see a portion of both at the same time."[14]

When Cornett compared the Stevens bullet with the 9mm slug he filed down and fired from the .38 Special, the resulting markings were identical, he said. Lipford had enlarged photos of the bullets to show the jury the markings. Cornett walked jurors through each of the photos, comparing the width of grooves and lands between bullets.[15]

In his cross-examination, Driver concentrated on the differences between the test bullet and the one taken from Stevens. It wasn't a smart move. Yes, Cornett said, the Stevens bullet does look different than the test bullet.

"The evidence bullet has gone through tissue and bone," he said. This wasn't a science lecture. A man was dead and Cornett dug in.

"My opinion is the evidence bullet was fired from this evidence pistol," he said.

"You could have been mistaken," Driver offered.

"I don't know I've ever been mistaken," Cornett said. "I know I am right, the same gun fired the test and the evidence bullet."

"You could not be mistaken?" Driver said, losing ground fast.

"No, sir," he said, "not on this."[16]

On redirect, Solicitor Lipford produced a rusty, broken file, reportedly found in Henderson's home. "Who delivered to you that file?" he asked Cornett.

"Mr. Jim Hillin of the GBI."

"State whether or not you made a microscopic examination of the file."

"I did."

"What did you find?"

"Found brass," Cornett said.

"Cartridge case is made out of what material?" Lipford asked.

"The same," he said. "The brass on the file was a little bit more discolored than the one I used, because it was fresh brass I used."[17]

Cornett was many things. He was a photographer, a policeman, and second-in-command in the state's only modern crime lab. However, his expertise in the microscopic examination, comparison, and identification of metal filings was not established. Neither Driver nor Wiggins objected.

Wiggins did object to the introduction of the file as immaterial. "It is not connected in the case," he said.

True, police found a file. Cornett identified dust he determined to be tarnished brass. But there were no shell casings found with the tool or any testimony showing Henderson had used the tool on bullets.

"I couldn't say it was off a cartridge case unless I had the cartridge case it was from," Cornett said.[18]

Lipford promised the judge the state's witnesses would provide more context about the file, and Boykin overruled Wiggins and allowed it in provisionally.

Cornett's testimony was already known to many in the courtroom thanks to a dramatic preview published two days earlier by the *Atlanta Constitution*'s crime reporter, Keeler McCartney. McCartney was in the first decade of his thirty-eight-year run on the crime beat for the *Constitution* and had a knack for gaining the confidence of police and criminals alike.[19] His long and detailed scoop on the ballistics evidence ran on the front page and read like a pulp novel. The story included a blow-by-blow account of how Cornett solved the ballistics mystery and reconstructed dialogue between investigators.

"This is an impossible situation," Cornett told GBI Agent Jim Hillin. "The death bullet is a 9mm pellet made for a foreign-make automatic. Yet

I'm positive it was fired from an American Smith & Wesson revolver . . . a .38 Special."

In the article, McCartney wrote that Cornett filed the tests bullets and fired them from his own service revolver *before* the murder weapon was discovered to test his theory. Cornett never testified to that in Henderson's trial. If true, investigators had a theory—even before they had a gun or a suspect—that required them to find a metal file.[20]

At the trial, Lipford next called Lieutenant Tom Price, the lead GBI investigator, to testify about how the file was found.

"We were looking for a pair of shoes," Price said, "leather shoes with laces criss-crossed."

Under Wiggins's cross-examination, Price seemed uncertain about when and where the search was conducted. At first, Price said the search was conducted either the day after Henderson was arrested or perhaps the next day at a home northeast of Carrollton in Sand Hill. His explanation didn't paint the clearest picture.

"The house where we failed to find the file we searched first after Clarence was arrested and found it in the home at Sand Hill, where we found the file," he started.

No, he said, not Henderson's father-in-law's house, where the sharecropper was arrested en masse by the sheriff, police chief, and head of the GBI. It was Lizzie's home: Clarence's wife's.

"I don't know where his wife is living now," Price said. "I found it over there where she was living at the time he was arrested."

Price described vaguely the location of the first house searched as on the road heading south of Carrollton.

"Was anyone living there when you searched the house?" Wiggins asked.

Yes, Price responded. Lizzie Henderson.

"I thought you said she was living in the house at Sand Hill," said Wiggins, now thoroughly confused. Sand Hill was northeast of Carrollton, not south.

"She was at the time the file was recovered," Price replied.

And when was this search conducted?

"I couldn't be positive," Price said, stumbling along. "It could have been anywhere from three to five days."

Unraveling Price's testimony, it would appear investigators searched Henderson's home south of Carrollton with no results. Instead, they found a metal file in a drawer some days after Henderson's arrest in another house a dozen miles away where his wife, apparently, was staying. Again, this was a piece of evidence needed to buttress Cornett's theory that Henderson filed the copper jackets of 9mm bullets to fit a .38 Special, so finding such a thing was crucial.

Confusing as it was, Price's testimony was enough, in Boykin's judgment, to allow the state to introduce the file into evidence. The jury could sort it out.

Following Price's muddled testimony on the file, Wiggins pressed him about the other lovers' lane attacks. It was the first and only time the defense attempted to poke holes in the state's theory of the case by bringing up the other attacks.

"You investigated several cases in this county of rape and armed robbery?" Wiggins asked.

"Yes."

"Has there been any arrest or conviction?"

"We convicted Tyler North of assault with intent to rape," Price said.

What Price did not tell the twelve white men on the jury was that North was indicted in the Stevens murder, held for months, and never prosecuted. He also did not tell them that North had been convicted based on accusations completely unrelated to the lovers' lane attacks. For whatever reason, Wiggins didn't pursue.

"What other cases did you investigate?"

"Six of robbery, one assault with intent to rape and one murder," he said.

One assumes the murder would be this case. Price didn't explain the cases in detail or why he referred to the six prior cases of attacks as robberies when the newspapers and Judge Boykin had indicated they were rapes. In fact, in his long recitation of the case in the pages of the *Georgian*, reporter Hal David clarified Price's testimony: "Five rapes, one attempted rape and one murder."[21]

Wiggins might have missed his chance to pry into the North case because he had his eye elsewhere.

"Will you give me the names of the rape cases other than Tyler North, who you say has been convicted?" Wiggins asked.

"Lee Hardman and Mrs. Parker was involved in one case," Price said.

Hardman was the man who was robbed of his pistol, the very gun now suspected to be the murder weapon. This was the first time the rape victim in that attack had been mentioned. And then only as "Mrs. Parker."

Wiggins pressed but Price was fuzzy on the details of this attack. "I would have to refer to my notes," he said.

Wiggins asked Price if he had tried to connect the Parker rape and the other attacks to Buddy's murder. "I don't remember," Price said.

"Do you know the circumstances of the Hardman case?" Wiggins asked.

Suddenly the judge's older brother rose from the prosecution table. "I object to it," Shirley Boykin said. "Are we going to try six cases in one?"

"The same facts are involved in all six," Wiggins replied. "They were all committed in the same way."

Judge Boykin shook his head. "You don't have that right," he said. "If you go into that, you will have to go into each one of these cases."

"Can I go further?" Wiggins asked.

"I don't think you should go further on that line," the judge advised.[22]

Lipford knew Hardman was the shakiest part of the story of the gun. Hardman initially told police he believed he had been robbed of the gun by Leonard Pendergrass, the cabdriver and former cop who actually owned the pistol in question. The prosecutor called Hardman, who quickly testified that he lost the weapon in a robbery the summer before Stevens was murdered. It was under cross-examination that Hardman's story took a chilling and decidedly familiar turn.

Hardman worked as a mechanic for the same cab company that employed Pendergrass.[23] The two men were close enough friends that Hardman would borrow Pendergrass's gun from time to time. One such time was August 25, 1948, about two months before Buddy Stevens was shot to death. Hardman had a date with Mrs. Parker, and Pendergrass drove the two of them to Stripling Chapel United Methodist Church. Before picking up his date, Hardman asked to borrow Pendergrass's police issue .38 revolver for the occasion. It was a Wednesday evening, so it is possible the Hardman and Parker attended the church's midweek service, which would have let out around dusk. Wednesday church services were such a part of daily life in Southern communities like Carrollton that most businesses, banks, and government offices closed at noon to give families time to get home and prepare for them. For decades after the practice of closing early ended, Carrolltonians still marked high noon Wednesday with a prolonged blast from a tornado alert siren.

Stripling Chapel United Methodist Church was a small brick church just a few miles south of Carrollton. Today it's near a Walmart and a home improvement store, but in 1948 it was out in the country. Whatever Hardman and Mrs. Parker were doing there as darkness fell, it didn't go to plan. As had happened to couples all summer, a man with a flashlight and a gun accosted them inside their car.

"His voice sounded like a colored person," Hardman said. The man shined a flashlight in his face, so he didn't get a good look at him, he said.

"He told me not to move."

"You didn't get the gun?" Wiggins asked in cross-examination.

"I reached back for the gun and he shot at me," Hardman said. The man missed.

"How close was he to you?" Wiggins asked.

"I don't know, probably as close as from me to you," Hardman said, pointing to Wiggins across the front of the courtroom about fifteen feet away.

"What did you do after he fired at you?"

"What could I do?" Hardman shrugged. The pistol was in the pocket of his raincoat and both he and Mrs. Parker were sitting on it, he said.

Whoever was behind the flashlight was certain enough that Hardman was armed that he was willing to fire a warning shot at the slightest movement. It was there, at gunpoint with his hands in the air, that Hardman thought he recognized something in the man's voice. It was Pendergrass. Hardman had told this to the grand jury in secret, but now he wasn't so sure.

"It could have possibly been a white man or a Negro," he said. "I thought it was Pendergrass. I didn't make the statement positively it was Pendergrass."

"You thought it strong enough to go before the grand jury and swear it was Pendergrass," Wiggins said. "You say now, conclusively, it was a Negro?"

"I say from his voice I thought it was," Hardman said.

How could Hardman have told the grand jury the voice belonged to Pendergrass, the white ex-cop he knew personally, only now to hedge? Hardman had plenty of time to hear it that evening when the voice came from behind a flashlight and a smoking gun.

"Was it a long conversation or just a few words?" Wiggins asked.

"Quite a discussion," Hardman said.

"Did you argue with him?"

"Yes, I argued."

"Was he drinking?"

"Yes," Hardman said. "He was very rough. He forced me up from where I was sitting and got off 15, 20 or 30 feet."

"You got up and left the raincoat with the gun in the pocket on the ground?" Wiggins asked. "How far from the raincoat did you go?"

"Possibly 100 feet."

Wiggins sought more details, but very few emerged. Hardman couldn't say which hand held the flashlight and which held the gun. He never saw his face and his attacker's vocal characteristics kept changing. The man continued to march Hardman away from the car. "I don't know how far I walked, something around 200 feet," he said. "He held the flashlight in front. He was walking along slowly behind me."

Once he was well away, the man with the flashlight let Hardman go. Hardman ended his testimony by saying he walked through the woods to a nearby road and flagged down a car.

"Did you leave your raincoat?" Wiggins asked.

"Yes, sir."[24]

The jury never heard the rest of the story. Newspaper accounts say that Mrs. Parker, who was never called to testify, was raped that evening by the man with the flashlight. But they now had an alternate theory: the rapist terrorizing Carrollton was ex-cop Leonard Pendergrass, whose service revolver was used to gun down Buddy Stevens.

Lipford called Pendergrass to the stand solely to testify that he loaned the pistol to Hardman and that Hardman told him it was stolen. Pendergrass confirmed the gun was his and that he had owned it five or six years before it was stolen. He said he reported the loss to the Carroll County sheriff "and, later on, to Mr. Hillin."

In cross-examination, Pendergrass said Mrs. Parker wasn't in the cab when he lent the gun to Hardman. Likely she never knew it was stuffed in the pocket of the raincoat she was sitting on when the man with the flashlight marched her date into the woods.

"We were here in Carrollton," Pendergrass said. "He was going down to see a woman." Hardman had borrowed the gun on several occasions, keeping it a few days before returning it, he said.

"One time he went down to Mrs. Parker's house and he said he had seen some Negroes walking around the house and he wanted to protect [her] and he kept it down there for a few days."[25]

So Hardman borrowed a pistol from Pendergrass on August 25, 1948, then lost it the same night to a man he first swore to be Pendergrass, but later testified it was a Black man who attacked him and Mrs. Parker. If the jury believed that, Lipford now had to walk the gun back from the downtown Atlanta pawnshop where it was discovered in December 1949 and put it in Clarence Henderson's hands. To accomplish this, he called on a series of witnesses from Carroll County's small and undoubtedly frightened Black community. He began with Eli Luther Cosper, the blind produce farmer who took the pistol to an Atlanta pawnshop.

"LET ME GO HOME"

The afternoon was wearing on as a bailiff led Eli Cosper to the witness stand. From the back, African American spectators craned their necks for a better view as one of their own stepped into the cold light of the white man's court. Once settled, Prosecutor Lipford asked Cosper a series of leading questions, each of which the farmer answered with as few words as possible.

"Your name Eli Luther Cosper?"

"Yes, sir."

"Do you know Laymon Almon?"

"Yes, sir."

"State whether you bought a gun from Laymon Almon."

"Yes, sir."

And so on.

When Lipford asked Cosper when he bought the gun, Cosper couldn't recall, so the prosecutor helped.

"December last year?" Lipford asked.

"Yes, sir," Cosper replied.

Leon Beeber, owner of the pawnshop, had testified earlier in the day that Cosper had pawned the gun on November 21, 1949.[1]

Cosper testified he bought the gun for $20 and pawned it later that day in Atlanta for $25.

On cross-examination, Cosper was a little more talkative.

"What business did you have with a pistol?" Wiggins asked the blind man.

"I wanted to make a little money" he explained, "and I made five dollars."

Cosper said he intended to get it back and sell it later for more money. The pawnshop had other .38 Specials priced at $50, he said.

"Why didn't you go back and get it?" Wiggins asked.

"It had the law about it, and I was afraid," he said. "I heard it was a stolen gun."

Cosper said he had bought the gun from Laymon Almon in September.

"September?" Wiggins replied, startled.

Cosper caught himself. "December, I guess it was December," he said. Regrouping, he said, "I know it was a Monday morning."

Wiggins wanted to know more about Cosper's decision to buy a gun and trade it in pawn to make a quick buck.

"How did you know the gun was any good or not? You couldn't see."

Cosper shrugged. "No, sir, but I thought I could get more for it."

"How long had Laymon Almon had the gun?"

"I saw him with the gun, I think, in 1948—about a week before Christmas," he said.

Cosper "saw" Almon with the gun almost fourteen months earlier? Wiggins was dubious.

"Who told you it was a week before Christmas?" Wiggins asked.

This confused the farmer. "I knew it," he said.

That wasn't what the attorney meant. "Didn't someone just *tell* you it was a week before Christmas?" he said.

Cosper paused, then shook his head. He wasn't taking this white man's bait.

"I know it was a little before Christmas," he said. "Yes, it was a week or two before Christmas."[2]

Eli Cosper's testimony was muddled and gave every appearance of a poorly coached lie. But the state's next witness, Eli's wife, Floy, was harder for the defense to shake. Under questioning from Lipford, Floy Cosper said she had seen Henderson with the pistol at a dance she threw at her house right before the cotton harvest in August 1948.

"The boys was arguing out in the yard and Clarence come out there," Floy said. "This boy and girl from LaGrange was fussing and Clarence come out there and told the boy not to hit the girl anymore."

Floy said the boy took offense and "started up on Clarence."

"Clarence pulled out the gun and shot straight up," she said, "and the boy got in the car and they left."

The date of the party was August 28, three days after Mrs. Parker was raped at Stripling Chapel United Methodist Church and the gun stolen.

"That is the gun he had," Floy said when asked to look at Pendergrass's .38 Special. "It had these marks on the handle."

It's not clear what marks she was talking about. The gun, which decades later remained locked in an evidence room in the Carroll County Courthouse, does not have any marks on its black handle that would be memorable seventeen months after seeing it at a dance party. Nonetheless, Floy Cosper's testimony was damaging and important. She said she saw Henderson with the gun immediately following its supposed theft and before Stevens was shot to death with it. Wiggins tried to shake her testimony or, at the very least, add to it.

"Do you know Junior Clark?" Wiggins asked.

Mrs. Cosper repeated the name with a curt nod.

"Did you see Junior Clark that day?" Wiggins said.

"Yes, sir." Another nod.

"Didn't you see Junior Clark with that gun down there?"

Floy answered flatly, "No, sir."

"Didn't you see some shooting a little before that?"

Again no. Floy Cosper was a strong woman. She took care of her blind husband. No doubt she kept his small produce business afloat. Moreover, she and all of the Black witnesses knew the jeopardy they were in. For months, white police had grabbed and shaken Carroll County's Black community in an attempt to rattle out a suspect. Now that they had one, they would have justice. A white prosecutor with all the power of the Jim Crow courts behind him was asking them questions before a white judge and white jury over the death of a white man. Floy Cosper knew what was at stake.

"You didn't tell Clarence to take that gun away from him?" Wiggins asked.

Mrs. Cosper paused. "Not *that* gun," she said.

So Clark *did* have a gun that night. The attorney peppered the woman with questions, trying to put Pendergrass's gun in Clark's hands.

"Do you know where Junior Clark got his gun? . . . Have you seen Junior Clark and Clarence Henderson have any trouble? . . . Didn't you see Henderson take a gun from Junior Clark?"

No, no, no, she said.

"You were there that night?" Wiggins asked.

"Yes, sir."[3]

It wasn't much; probably not enough. Reasonable doubt was a tremendously high hurdle for a white jury when it came to Black defendants charged with crimes against whites. In a circuit court in the Deep South under such circumstances, even Thurgood Marshall, then head of the NAACP's legal defense team, considered it a win if he got a guilty verdict that didn't include the electric chair.[4]

Lipford continued to piece together the gun's extended travelogue. He called Laymon Almon to the stand and asked him to identify Henderson.

"There he sits," Almon said, pointing.

Almon then said he bought the pistol from Henderson for the price of $18 plus a wristwatch in trade. This was about three weeks before Christmas 1948, or a little more than a month after the Stevens murder. He sold it to Eli Cosper about a year later, he said.

Lipford had put the gun in Henderson's possession from August to December 1948, exactly the period needed to pin the murder on him, and he needed to keep it there. In a written statement before the trial, Henderson said he lent the pistol out during the time of the murder to Junior Clark. Lipford called Clark next.

Clark wasn't the state's strongest witness, but he was motivated. Clark was in jeopardy and his record wasn't clean. If Henderson was attempting to construct a story that Clark had the gun at the time of the murder, he had to fight back or face the gaze of white justice himself. Clark began by saying he had seen Henderson with a pistol. "I don't know exactly what month, but I've seen him with one," he said.

Lipford asked him to describe the gun. "It was a black one," Clark said. Not particularly helpful. The police-issued .38 in question was nickel plated.

Was it a revolver or an automatic? "It was a revolver." And what more do you remember about it? It was a blue steel .38, he said. That's a description of a different gun. Not helpful.

Lipford asked if he had ever seen Henderson with another pistol—a silver one.

"Yes, sir," Clark responded. "It was nickel plated."

Was it this pistol? Lipford asked, holding up the gun.

"Yes, sir, that is the one. I seen him with this, I don't know exactly how long it was after I seen him with the first one," Clark said. "I seen him with the black one first. The next time I saw him with this pistol," he said, pointing at the alleged murder weapon.

Clark said he had seen Henderson the day after Stevens was killed. "He asked me if I had heard about the killing," Clark said. "He said it was up here in Carrollton."

"State whether or not he said he had been to Carrollton," Lipford said.

Claude Driver rose. "I object to him leading the witness," he said to Boykin.

"Yes," the judge said. "Don't lead the witness."

Lipford nodded, then turned to Clark and asked perhaps the most leading question: "Did you ever see Clarence filing any bullets?"

"Yes, sir," Clark said, without hesitation.

"You know what kind of bullet this is?" Lipford asked, holding up one of Cornett's filed 9mm shells.

"I don't believe I do," Clark said.

Lipford paused, then extended his hand with the bullet in the palm. "You have seen him file that type of bullet?"

Driver jumped up again. "I object to that examination as leading," he said.

"Yes," Boykin said. Then, nodding to Lipford, he instructed: "Don't lead him."

Lipford turned back to Clark and asked another leading question. Actually, an order. "State whether you ever saw him do anything to these bullets," he said.

"That is a conclusion!" Driver complained.

"I overrule your objection," Boykin said.

Clark said he had seen Henderson file bullets just like the test bullets prior to the murder of Buddy Stevens.

Believable or not, Lipford now had sworn testimony from witnesses who saw Henderson with the gun prior to the Stevens murder, one who saw him with it after the Stevens murder, and now one who saw him filing bullets in his home.

Wiggins did his best to undo the damage, questioning Clark on his recollection of Henderson's bullet-filing operation. Clark said Henderson had bullets all around and was filing some down. He said he saw some already in the .38.

"It was a long bullet," Clark said. "It was long. He said he bought them up in town and they was the wrong bullet."[5]

65

The "long bullet" is a curious and specific memory that doesn't fit neatly with the state's theory of the case. First, Clark seems to be suggesting that the bullets were too long and were filed down in an effort to shorten them. Cornett had already testified that the 9mm murder bullet was too *wide* to fit the .38 Special and had to be filed to fit the more narrow chamber.

Also, a 9mm bullet is not a "long" round. It's about an inch in length. However, a .38 Special round is half an inch longer than that—a significantly longer round for a handgun.

The young defense attorney did ask Clark whether he had ever borrowed a gun from Henderson. Yes, he said, but not the murder weapon. He had borrowed the other gun, the black one, the night of Eli and Floy Cosper's party—the same party where Floy Cosper said she saw Henderson fire his gun into the air to stop a man from beating his date. Clark said he accidentally discharged the gun into the floorboards of the Cosper home. "I liked to shot my own foot over there," he said.

"Who was in the house when the shot was fired?" Wiggins asked. "Was Cosper's wife in there?"

Floy Cosper had testified she hadn't seen Clarence take a gun from Clark the night of the party. Clark shifted uncomfortably. As a state witness, he hadn't heard Floy's testimony and wasn't sure why Wiggins wanted to know. He told him as little as he could.

"I don't remember whether she was in the room or not," he said.

"Was she in the house?

"Yes, sir," Clark said.

How about Eli Cosper? Was he in the room when Clark fired a round through his floorboards?

Yes, he was, Clark said.

"They ask you what you were doing?" Wiggins said.

"No, sir. They asked me who that was shot and I told them it was me."[6]

Floy Cosper may not have lied on the stand, but she didn't tell the entire truth, either. Nor had Clark been entirely forthcoming. After Clark's testimony, Lipford called Sheriff Gaston to the stand to testify that Clark was arrested the night of the party for shooting and injuring a man named James Sampson, with whom he had fought at Henderson's home some days or weeks earlier. Despite shooting another man, Clark was released a few days later.[7]

Lipford followed Clark with a series of additional witnesses from Carroll County's African American community, all of whom testified, to one degree or another, to having seen Henderson with a nickel-plated revolver. Despite the intense interest in the trial, the white press largely ignored the testimony provided by Henderson's Black neighbors. Lipford and Wiggins were barely listening themselves. The prosecutor only wanted these witnesses to show Henderson was seen with a nickel-plated pistol; Wiggins wanted to show Clark had a pistol too. But these witnesses offered conflicting details about Clark's trouble with Sampson. If anyone had been paying attention, the testimony introduced new confusion into the state's timeline. But Henderson's defense team didn't seem to hear what, exactly, these Black witnesses were saying.

C. H. Cook, a man who claimed to have known Henderson all of his life, said he bought the blue-steel .38 from Henderson sometime in 1948 but recalled he also had a nickel-plated gun. "I couldn't swear that was the gun," he said, pointing at the murder weapon.

On cross-examination, Wiggins asked Cook if he had ever seen Clark with a similar gun.

"I just don't know," Cook said. "I've seen him with a nickel-plated, but I don't think it was near as large as that."[8]

A neighbor, J. T. Brown, recalled Clark and Sampson had their trouble over at Henderson's house. "That was a Sunday evening," he said. The next morning Brown said he stopped by Henderson's house and saw him with a shiny revolver.

"I don't know whether that is the gun or not, but one just like it," he said. "He wanted to sell it to me for $30." Brown said he saw Henderson later that same day showing off the $15 he got selling the gun to Laymon Almon.

Another neighbor, Thomas Harris, testified he, too, was at Henderson's the night Clark shot Sampson.

"Do you remember when the shooting took place," Lipford asked.

"No, sir. I don't remember the day," he said. "Somewhere about August 13." That was a Friday, not Sunday, as Brown had recalled.

Harris said he saw Henderson "the following Sunday," August 15, along a creek in a pasture. He had a gun on him. Lipford pointed at the murder weapon and asked, "Is that the gun?"

"I couldn't say," Harris said. "It was one just like it."[9]

As with his other witnesses, Lipford was trying to establish that Clarence Henderson had had a nickel-plated revolver in his possession prior to Buddy Stevens's death, using the shooting of Sampson by Clark as a marker. But if Harris's recollection was accurate, it would mean that the gun Henderson had could not have been the murder weapon. The gun sitting on the prosecution table was stolen August 25, nearly two weeks later, when a masked man raped Mrs. Parker at Stripling Chapel United Methodist Church. Cook's testimony that the murder gun was larger than the one he recalled Henderson having cast new doubt on the state's narrative.

Lipford might have had little concern over the details in the testimony of his Black witnesses. All the dates and conflicting recollections meant little to the all-white jury, but doubtless they heard Henderson had a gun—maybe several guns. And Lipford had another key witness: Henderson himself.

After his arrest, Henderson was taken out of Carroll County to a jail in Newnan—about twenty miles southeast of Carrollton, in neighboring Coweta County, for questioning. The jail was under the authority of Sheriff Lamar Potts.

One of the striking aspects of the Henderson trial is that the judge, the prosecutor, and Potts had only recently completed the trial of land baron John Wallace, one that made them instant celebrities and burnished Potts's image as an honest lawman beholden to none. In the Henderson case, he was little more than a jailer, but one who had spoken at length to the defendant prior to trial and oversaw the dictation of two jailhouse statements.

Ever since the Stevens murder, Potts's jail had been where Lipford and the criminal investigators had stashed suspects for interrogation. Tyler North spent months there. Potts said Henderson hadn't been in his jail long when he called for the sheriff.

"He said he wanted to plead guilty," Potts recalled. "I said, 'Plead guilty to what?' He said, 'For killing that man.' I said, 'I don't imagine they would accept a guilty plea.'"

Potts said he told Henderson to write it down—or, because he couldn't write, to tell it to someone who would put it on paper.

"The next day, I carried him up to the courthouse and that is what he said," Potts said, pointing to the statement.

On January 16, Potts said he took Henderson to the chambers of the Coweta County board of commissioners and had him dictate a statement to the commissioners' secretary, who took it down in shorthand and typed it up. Potts wrote "Clarence Henderson" on the page. An "X" supposedly indicated the illiterate Henderson had made his mark, although other documents show Henderson could sign his name in cursive.[10]

Henderson had been in Potts's jail a little more than a month by the time the statement was prepared. What had happened during that time, Wiggins wanted to know.

"If he wanted to plead guilty, why didn't he plead guilty?" Wiggins asked the sheriff.

"I don't know," Potts said, although he had just testified moments ago that he had planted doubts in Henderson's mind that he could plead guilty.

"You did not lay your hands on him in anger?" Wiggins asked. In 1950 in rural Georgia, beating a Black suspect to get a confession was not a novel idea. It was more like routine police work.

"You mean hit him?" Potts asked. "No, sir."

"Did you ever witness anyone striking him?" Wiggins asked.

"No, sir."

"Did you ever see any marks on him where anybody struck him?" the young attorney asked.

"I have seen no marks," Potts said flatly.

"You ever see him with a bloody jacket?" Wiggins said, his voice rising. "Did anybody bring him to jail with a bloody jacket?"

"No, sir."

Then an accusation. "Never take a jacket off and wash the blood off?" Wiggins said.

"Me?" Potts said. "No, sir."

"Were you ever present when this Negro was given a large injection?" Wiggins pressed, pointing back at his client.

To this question, Potts said yes. Henderson had been given injections by a county physician. For syphilis, he said.

"I believe he had several shots," Potts said.

So-called truth serums were among the many dubious and violent interrogation tools used by white law enforcement against Black suspects in the South. Almost two decades earlier, President Herbert Hoover commissioned a report on the state of law enforcement in the nation. The Wickersham Commission, named after the former attorney general who chaired it, found widespread use of torture by police in interrogating prisoners, including the use of truth serums, usually the drug scopolamine, which can cause hallucinations and drowsiness in patients. An example of this, around the time of the Stevens murder, was the arrests of Army staff sergeant Robert Burns and Private Herman Dennis, who were accused of raping a female shopkeeper in Guam. Both men denied the charge and fought it to the Supreme Court. Burns said his interrogators gave him truth serum, rendering him unconscious.[11]

Penicillin, the primary treatment for syphilis, generally does not knock a person out, but Wiggins said that's exactly what happened to Henderson.

"Were you present at the time this Negro was given a shot where he stayed unconscious for a long period of time?" Wiggins said, again motioning to his client. "Were you present when he was given a shot that made him unconscious?"

"No, sir. I didn't see him unconscious."

"You have never seen him given a shot where he became unconscious?"

"I didn't stay around," Potts said.[12]

As soon as Wiggins sat back down, Lipford popped up holding two sheets of paper. They were statements the prosecutor claimed Henderson made during his stay in Potts's jail. One, dated January 16, 1950, was typed on stationery for the Newnan Baseball Association, the partnership behind the Class D Newnan Browns baseball team. Potts, among other things, was the president and general manager of the minor-league club and often let his players bunk down in a portion of the county courthouse, a move clearly illegal by modern standards but considered boosterish in 1950.

"My name is Clarence Henderson and my home is in Carroll County," the statement began, "and at present I am being held in the Coweta County Jail, charged with the murder of a white man."

The statement went on with boilerplate proclamations that this was his first statement—which was, in fact, not the case—and that it was made "freely and voluntarily with no fear of harm" and other declarations that an illiterate tenant farmer likely could not make without a lot of help.

After the preamble, Henderson claimed he got the murder weapon from Bo Dunson in October 1948, shortly before the murder. "Him and Junior Clark were together and split the $10 I gave him for the gun," the statement read.

On Sunday, October 31, Dunson and Clark borrowed the gun from him and returned it the next morning "pretty early."

"All the cartridges had been taken out and when I asked him what he did with the cartridges, he said he shot at a rabbit," the Henderson statement claimed. "If Mr. Stevens was killed with my pistol, then Junior Clark must have killed him because he had my pistol on the night Mr. Stevens was killed."

Then Henderson attempted to bolster his alibi with a strange claim. Clark, he said, had been seen with "a big sum of money."

"I know he wasn't working, but he never did say where he got the money."[13]

Nan Turner said the man who attacked her and Buddy robbed Buddy of $15. If Henderson was, in fact, the murderer and was attempting to cast blame on Junior Clark to escape the electric chair, then this would be a strange part of the deception. Buddy's true murderer would know that the robbery portion of the attack did not result in a "big sum," even by the standards of a Black sharecropper in 1948 Georgia. Instead, it suggests that Henderson did not know the details of the attack and was attempting to throw suspicion toward Clark by guessing that a white boy had a lot of money on him.

Lipford had the statement marked Exhibit A. Exhibit B was also a statement by Henderson made to Potts but taken down five weeks earlier. It told a much different story.

In early December 1948, about three weeks before Christmas, Henderson caught a bus from Carrollton to Villa Rica, about fifteen miles north. He was looking for a game of Georgia Skin, a betting game where single cards are dealt faceup to each player and players bet on whose card will be matched first with a like card from a different suit as cards are drawn from the deck. If your card is matched, you lose. It's pure chance, but generations of gamblers played it until their own bad luck caught up with them.

Henderson didn't know exactly where the game was, but he knew where Black folks lived in Villa Rica and went there. The only Black man in the city Henderson knew was Bo Dunson. When Henderson found the skin game, he found Bo, who was broke but watching the action. Henderson got in the game, gambling awhile and drinking a little whiskey, when Bo approached and showed him a shiny .38 Special revolver. Henderson looked it over—it was unloaded—and offered Dunson $10 for it. Henderson jammed the gun in his pocket and went back to the game.

Pretty soon, Bo came back. He had lost the $10 pretty quick and tried to renegotiate the price of the pistol already in Henderson's pocket. Henderson was up $40 and not looking for trouble, so he packed up, left the game, and thumbed a ride back to Carrollton. When he got home, the gun went in a drawer and was forgotten for a week or so. But Henderson was a gambler and pretty soon he was broke. He remembered the pistol he got from Dunson and sold it to Laymon Almon for $18 and a wristwatch.

He saw Dunson again on Christmas Eve when Bo came calling at his home, asking about the gun. Henderson said he had sold it already. Dunson said nothing.

"I never thought anything about it until I was arrested about it last week," Henderson said. "I still don't know anything about it."

"The reason I didn't tell the officers who arrested me about where I got the gun: I was drunk," he said.[14]

In cross-examination, Wiggins attempted to introduce doubt about the gun. There was no way to know what gun was referenced in either statement, Wiggins suggested. Yes, there was, Potts countered.

"That gun had been found and had been identified by its numbers. That was the gun we were referring to," he said. Then, catching himself, he added, "That is the gun *he* was referring to."[15]

Both jailhouse statements looped Dunson into a shifting alibi. Lipford called him—a Black gambler from Villa Rica in the highest-profile murder trial Carrollton had ever known—to the stand.

Dunson was sworn in and asked to identify himself. He cleared his throat.

"My name is Harvey Moses Stanley Junior Gussie Lee Carley Waters Dunson," he said.

Lipford paused. "They call you 'Bo' most of the time?"

"Yes, sir," Dunson said.

Yes, Dunson said, he knew Clarence Henderson but he never sold him a gun, especially not that gun. What he knew about the gun he learned from

Henderson. Dunson testified he and Henderson shared a cell in December in Coweta County and it was there that Henderson suggested a deal to free them both.

"He told me to tell I let him have the gun and he would get a lawyer to get me out," he said.

Take a murder charge in exchange for a lawyer? Not a convincing offer, but perhaps something a desperate man might suggest.

Police picked up Dunson in late December 1949 in Douglasville, where he worked as a sawmill hand. The record isn't clear why Dunson was arrested or why he was jailed with Henderson. But it is curious: Why would police arrest a man in Douglas County, a contiguous county to the east of Carroll County, and house him in Coweta County to the south? And why put him in a cell with a prisoner so highly valued that he was being secretly held there?

Wiggins didn't dig into the peculiarities of Dunson's arrest. Instead, he tried to get one more bite at Junior Clark. Dunson was of little help in that regard. He had not seen Clark with a gun and never knew Clark to be in trouble with the law. Dunson said he wasn't even at Eli and Flo Cosper's dance.[16]

Following Potts's testimony, Lipford rested the state's case. No motive had been established and Henderson's alibi—that he was home with his wife—had not been challenged. But Lipford had put the gun in his possession for the required time.

In response, the defense's case consisted of a single witness: Clarence Henderson.

In 1950, defendants in Georgia were allowed to make unsworn statements from the witness stand without opening themselves up to cross-examination. Jurors were warned that the statements should be taken with a grain of salt, but for decades defendants were able to make their cases directly to the jury. Given the limitations of his defense team, it was Henderson's best shot.

As a Black sharecropper, Henderson knew how to speak to white men, how to approach them, how to talk to them when he needed something. If he was the confident and powerful Clarence Henderson who Flo Cosper said fired a shot in the air to break up a domestic dispute at Eli Cosper's party, then he was the suppliant Clarence Henderson now. He turned toward the jury, literally holding his hat in his hands. He kept his head tilted down and started speaking.

Henderson said he had "taken the gun in pawn" from Bo Dunson in 1948 and Dunson and Junior Clark had borrowed the gun hours before Buddy Stevens was killed. The gun was loaded when it left, empty when it came back.

"I asked Bo what he done with the cartridges, and he said he shot a rabbit in the bed," he said. "I never thought anything else about it. He said he would buy me some more cartridges."

Henderson said he "never filed a bullet in my life."

"I always knowed what kind of cartridges to go to the store and buy," he said.

Henderson claimed to have loaned Dunson and Clark a .38 Special loaded with the correct ammunition, even though an expert in ballistics had testified that Stevens was killed with a 9mm bullet. It might have been smarter to claim to have filed the ammunition using the file in evidence while still claiming to have lent the pistol out the night of the murder, but Henderson was adamant.

"I never filed any bullets," he said. "The night of this killing, the night it occurred, I was at home in my bed asleep. Next morning, I went to my bossman's and they told me a man got killed. That's all I know about it—that's all in the world I know about it."

Now Henderson looked at the jury. Twelve white men. Carrollton wasn't that big. He knew some of them and called to them by name.[17]

"I am innocent," he said. "This is a frame-up just because I gamble, drink liquor, and sold liquor. They know me all around Carroll County, but I've never taken one dollar. I never bothered that woman and did not kill that man.

"I've got something to live for," he said, sobbing. "I wouldn't mess up my little family. I've got a wife and two children to raise."[18]

Henderson scanned the crowded courtroom. Rows of white faces looked back. White reporters scribbled madly in their notebooks from the front row. In back, he could see a handful of Black faces, his wife, Lizzie, among them. The aisles on either side were flanked with armed state troopers. It had been a long day. Night had fallen, but it was still hot in the courtroom, thanks to a combination of the unseasonable weather and the crowded conditions.

"I have been beat to make me plead guilty," Henderson said, his voice carrying to the back of the courtroom. The Black spectators turned to each other. "Over the head, handcuffed, and beat me up to make me tell who I got the gun from."

Henderson pointed at Wright Lipford. "That man right there," he said. "He was there and saw it. Mr. Gaston drew a pistol on me and stomped me—beat me and stomped me like I was a dog."

Henderson said Sheriff Potts had overseen the injections that knocked him out.

"I went to sleep and waked up about one o'clock," he said. "Mr. Potts says, 'When you were asleep you had lots to say.'" (A common side effect of scopolamine is amnesia.)

Henderson shifted back to the jury, pleading with them.

"I ain't guilty. I may die for it, but if I die for it someday you all will understand this Black nigger didn't have anything to do with that killing," he said, tears now running down his face.[19]

"I worked, I worked for white people," he continued. "I have been raised up with white people."

He scanned around the room, then pointed to a local attorney in a front row. "Mr. Earl Staples, he is a good man, and I was raised up right around him. When we was little kids, I played with him," he said. "I called him to take my case. He said he couldn't take it"—Henderson paused and shrugged—"because he couldn't take it. I don't know why he wouldn't take it. But he is a good man."

Henderson looked around some more, finding a former boss man.

"Another man I stayed with, Mr. Jimmie Lee Thompson," he said, hoping for some recognition. He cropped for the man for three seasons. "Ask him if I ever insulted a white lady. They would tell me what to do and I would do it."

Henderson was spent. He turned back to the jury.

"I guess that is all. I am going to ask for mercy from the court, gentlemen of the jury," he said. "Let me go home and raise my kids."[20]

Wiggins and Driver rested their case. They never called a single witness—not even Henderson's wife to testify that he was home the night of the killing. Perhaps they thought the word of a Black laundress would have little effect on the white, male jurors. Or perhaps the idea of offering an affirmative defense for a Black man accused of killing a well-bred white man didn't occur to them.

Boykin had pushed the pace of the trial all day, but it was late when he gave his instructions to the jury. They were lengthy and extraordinary. His own brother was on the prosecution team, but Boykin filled his remarks with cautions about the evidence supplied by the state.

No one saw Henderson with Buddy Stevens or Nan Turner—he had no prior relationship with them.

Regarding Nan's belief that the voice of the person who attacked her and Buddy belonged to a Black man, Boykin instructed the jury to disregard it. "It is of no evidential value," he said.

While the gun was a striking piece of evidence, nothing else connected Henderson to the murder, or any of the other attacks for that matter. The rest of the evidence was circumstantial. No eyewitness put Henderson at the scene, and he offered an alibi that he was home in bed at the time of the murder. If Henderson's alibi and the state's case were equally possible scenarios, Boykin told the jury it was their duty to set him free.

"I charge you, gentlemen, to warrant a conviction on circumstantial evidence alone, the proved facts must not only be consistent with the hypothesis of guilt but must exclude every other reasonable hypothesis," he said. Every fact in the state's case "which goes to make the chain of circumstances" must be evaluated alone, Boykin said. If one of those facts in the chain is not proven beyond a reasonable doubt, the jury could not convict Henderson of the crime.

Boykin also warned the jury that, while Henderson had a right to make an unsworn statement, it was up to them how much weight to give it. But he said they might consider it persuasive. "You may believe the statement of the defendant in preference to the sworn testimony in the case," he said. If Henderson's alibi was reasonable to the men, they should acquit him, he said.

Lastly, he told the jury that, should they find Henderson guilty, they could recommend mercy. If not, Boykin would have no choice but to sentence him to death in the electric chair.

Boykin's charge to the jury was so filled with caution, it's hard to imagine that he was completely convinced that sixteen months of police work had found the man who killed Buddy Stevens.

The jury left the courtroom at 8:35 P.M. Despite a long day of testimony, the courtroom was still filled to capacity. No one was leaving.

"The courthouse was guarded by state patrolmen and local police, but no incidents were reported and the crowd was quiet and orderly, behaving in a such a manner as to be a credit to Carroll County justice," *Georgian* reporter Hal David wrote in typical *Georgian* style.[21]

The jury returned less than two hours later with a verdict of guilty and no recommendation for mercy. The judge complied, sentencing Henderson to die in Georgia's electric chair in just four weeks. The trial was over by 10:30 P.M. The entire trial, from opening to verdict, had taken less than twelve hours. Wiggins and Driver told reporters Henderson would appeal.[22]

The local press proclaimed victory in the process.

"Attorneys proclaimed it one of the most orderly murder trials of local history," the *Times–Free Press* reported the following day.[23]

The Associated Press lapped up the lurid aspects of the trial for its national audience. Nan Turner was "a pretty young woman" and Buddy Stevens was her "college student escort," but Henderson was a "thug" rightly sentenced to die.[24]

Not everyone was as satisfied. News of the trial and verdict was printed in papers across the nation, including in Northern cities where readers were suspicious of Southern justice when it came to Black defendants.

The *Chicago Tribune* ran a story the next day challenging the verdict in its headline: "Sentence Negro to Die; Identity 'Proved' by Gun." Nan Turner, the crime's only eyewitness, "made no attempt to identify" Henderson as the culprit, the *Tribune* reported.[25]

The *Pittsburgh Courier*, the most widely circulated Black weekly in the nation, cast a similarly jaundiced eye on Henderson's trial.

"Considerable doubt surrounded his 'circumstantial evidence' conviction," the paper reported. "Residents of Carroll County have expressed the opinion that the doomed man has been unjustly convicted and that it bears the mark of a 'white man's crime.'"

The *Courier* report was the only contemporary account to point out that the murder weapon had been owned by a white man, Leonard Pendergrass.[26]

Three months later, the *Times–Free Press* reported Boykin's court had adjourned its regular criminal session "in near record time." At the bottom of the brief, the paper noted a forgery charge against "Eli Cosper, blind Negro" had been held over until the October term. Whether by choice or simply because no one noticed, the *Times–Free Press* made no connection between Cosper's delayed felony trial and the damning role he and his wife played in Henderson's case just a few months earlier.[27]

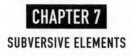

Clarence Henderson would not go to Georgia's death chair as quickly as Boykin's sentence indicated. Even Jim Crow justice wasn't that fast.

By the end of the week, the defense team of Wiggins and Driver had filed a motion for a new trial. Boykin set a hearing for February 18, 1950, a Saturday. But the motion guaranteed Henderson a longer delay. To fully argue their case, Wiggins would need a transcript of the trial, which would have to be prepared by the court reporter. After receiving the transcript, Wiggins said he would file an amended motion.

"When this will be done is, of course, indefinite depending on the time the record is received," the *Georgian* reported.[1]

At the hearing, Henderson's defense team asked Boykin for more time. The judge agreed, scheduling a new hearing date for March 25, also a Saturday, to accommodate delays in preparing the transcript. But that delay was hardly the most interesting tidbit for reporters. Suddenly, Henderson had a new, expanded defense team with the addition of two Black lawyers from Atlanta.

"Two Atlanta Negro lawyers Saturday joined two Carrollton white attorneys to represent Clarence Henderson, a Negro under [a] death sentence for the murder of a Georgia Tech student," reported the *Atlanta Daily World*, the capital city's leading African American newspaper.[2]

The *Daily World* had carried brief accounts of Henderson's trial; Carrollton was a long way away for most of their readers. But interest heightened when S. S. Robinson and E. E. Moore Jr., prominent attorneys with offices in the heart of Atlanta's famed "Sweet Auburn" Black commercial district, announced they had been hired to defend him.

The arrival of Robinson and Moore, alongside Wiggins and Driver, caught everyone off guard. "Four Attorneys in Henderson Case," the *Times– Free Press* announced on its front page. "Those attorneys, both Negroes, . . . announced that they hope to work in cooperation with state-appointed attorneys, William Wiggins of Carrollton and Claude Driver of Buchanan."[3]

More directly, the *Georgian* reported, "Henderson Hires Negro Attorneys," declaring it "a new and unexpected twist" in the saga of the Buddy Stevens murder.

The new lawyers surprised Boykin as well. Robinson and Moore had been silently taking notes as Wiggins and Driver argued for more time to prepare their motion for a new trial. When they introduced themselves, Boykin instructed the four lawyers to work out the details of their new arrangement.

"I just want to make one point clear," he said, "and that is you are sure that this Negro's rights are protected."[4] Of course, this came from a jurist who just oversaw a murder trial where the defense called no witnesses and offered no alternative theory to their client's guilt while allowing the accused to be tried in a garrison atmosphere under armed guard.

Outside Boykin's second-floor courtroom, a young white man, George Wannamaker, nervously stalked the hallways of the county courthouse. Wannamaker was a theology student at Emory University's Methodist seminary and cochairman of a new committee set up to raise money for Henderson's defense. A burly white deputy eyed Wannamaker with distaste.

"If those nigger lawyers talk too loud," he said, nodding to the closed doors, "I'll throw them through that window."[5]

The Henderson Defense Committee met at Big Bethel AME Church in Sweet Auburn to plan and raise money. Big Bethel, founded a century earlier, was the oldest African American church in Atlanta and a central place for meetings, religious and political, in the city's Black community.[6] The church remains a landmark today, proclaiming "Jesus Saves" in illuminated blue letters from its spire to millions of motorists traveling the interstate through the heart of downtown.

The arrival of the two Black attorneys and the organization of a defense committee was just one unsettling development following the Henderson trial for Carrollton's white power structure. Hundreds had attended the day-long trial, and some left feeling unsatisfied. There was even talk that Buddy Stevens's own father did not believe the right man was convicted. (In an editor's note, the *Georgian* attempted to steer the narrative by reporting that Carl Stevens Sr. "believes Henderson guilty and that the verdict was just.")[7]

That a Black-led defense committee in Atlanta now was questioning Carroll County justice was too much to bear for *Georgian* reporter Hal David, who broke into a passionate, if wordy, first-person defense of the court in the middle of a story about the arrival of Henderson's new legal team.

"This Georgian reporter heard every word spoken at the Henderson trial and it was his opinion that Clarence Henderson got a fair trial, was ably represented by counsel, the crowd was quiet and orderly throughout the day and night, and 12 of the most respected men in the county heard the case and deliberated for one hour and 45 minutes before making the verdict they thought proper based on the evidence submitted," David wrote.

Not everyone agreed. "It's a matter of record that many citizens of Carrollton and Carroll County were not satisfied with the Henderson verdict," David allowed. "Court officials have received many letters and newspaper clippings from throughout the nation in which the writers have discussed the verdict, some favoring it and some opposing it."

David reported that his own employer, editor Stanley Parkman, had "heard widespread expressions of dissatisfaction with the verdict" and called for a retrial.[8]

Delays in preparing the transcript pushed Boykin's decision on a new trial into April 1950. By that time Henderson's new attorneys, Robinson and Moore, had taken the leading position in the defense. At the hearing on April 3, Moore made the primary appeal, speaking for more than two and a half hours before the judge and attacking the verdict on multiple grounds, including Boykin's own conduct. The courtroom was packed with Black and white spectators, many drawn simply to see the unique appearance of an African American lawyer in Boykin's court. It had never happened before.

The *Atlanta Daily World* reported that Moore's speech "was at the same time eloquent and factual."[9]

Moore claimed Boykin had erred by not telling the jury specifically that Henderson should be acquitted if the state had not proven its case beyond a reasonable doubt. He also said the judge's charge to the jury referred to "acts" or "crimes" without the caveat that these were only allegations. Moore questioned the casual chain of custody of the supposed murder bullet, a chain that rested on the testimony of police rather than a written record. He challenged the assertions that a 9mm bullet could reliably fire through the barrel of a .38 revolver and the introduction of the file as evidence without proof that the residue on it belonged conclusively to a brass bullet jacket.

Finally, he charged that the trial had been unconstitutionally "secret." Boykin's decision to clear the courtroom for Nan Turner's testimony robbed Henderson of his right to a trial in open court, Moore said.

"The defendant in a murder trial is entitled to a public trial and not a secret trial," he said.

If Boykin was not inclined to grant a new trial, Moore asked the judge to set aside the verdict of death and sentence Henderson to life in prison.

Predictably, Lipford disputed Moore's critique of the trial and especially the sentence.

"The evidence amply authorizes the verdict," he said.[10]

Boykin took the case under advisement and adjourned the hearing. He had a busy day ahead. A new grand jury session was starting, and he had to make his charge to them. This grand jury was notable in that it included a single Black juror, likely by his instruction.

In his charge, Boykin made a grim pronouncement that "subversive elements" were at work in America.

"The future of our democratic form of government is hanging by a small thread," he warned. His concerns were deeply rooted in the Henderson appeal.[11]

Six weeks after Henderson's guilty verdict, white Carrollton received a shock as elemental to their fears as the racial unease caused by Buddy Stevens's murder: Communists had come to Henderson's defense.

"Commies in drive to save C. Henderson," the *Georgian* warned. The brief, ripped from the prior day's *Constitution*, said Communists in Atlanta had "launched a movement aimed at winning a new trial for Henderson" and were circulating fliers in the state capital drumming up sympathy—as well as appeals for money—for the convicted murderer.[12]

In an editorial, the *Times–Free Press* regretted the Communists stirring "the racial question" in defense of Henderson. This was an attempt to divide the South, something that played into Communist hands, the editor warned.

"The Stevens murder underwent a thorough and paintaking [*sic*] investigation," the paper explained. "Evidence under which the Negro was condemned to die in the electric chair was circumstantial, but strong, and was presented in a fair and peaceful manner and the verdict rendered by 12 reliable and fair-minded citizens."

The *Georgian* echoed with a similar editorial, adding that Blacks in Carrollton "distrust and dislike Henderson and believe him guilty of the crime." (There was no evidence of Black residents being polled on this question.) If state troopers had not been present, the Communists likely would have complained about the dangerous atmosphere and state neglect, the paper argued.

Despite the fact that Henderson faced certain death in the electric chair, the *Georgian* reported the Communists were doing Henderson "a disservice" by involving themselves. The *Times–Free Press* concluded they were just "making trouble."[13]

That the Communists were involved in the Henderson Defense Committee was a not a secret. Weeks earlier the *Daily Worker*, the official newspaper of the Communist Party of the United States, had run a story advertising the fact that Henderson was being defended by the Civil Rights Congress, an organization directly affiliated with the Communist Party. The *Daily Worker* reported that attorneys Robinson and Moore were being paid by the Civil Rights Congress and that Henderson "was greatly encouraged to learn of outside interest in his case." The *Daily Worker* article encouraged readers to wire Judge Boykin and demand a new trial. It also advised where to send donations.[14] And donations arrived, including $50 from an all-Black mill workers union in Macon whose members made less than $35 a week.[15]

For nearly two decades, American Communists had developed a strategy of involving themselves in the defense of Black men accused of attacking white people in the South. Communists correctly saw African Americans as an oppressed working class victimized by an unjust, white-ruled system that conspired to keep them oppressed, often as forced labor in the notorious chain gangs of the South. Throughout the South, African Americans were subject to arrest on minor charges such as vagrancy so they could be placed on work crews and leased to private industry. The practice mirrored slavery and lasted into the 1940s before media scrutiny forced the state to outlaw the practice under reformist governor Ellis Arnall.

The test case for the Communist Party's involvement in the defense of Black men actually came in Scottsboro, Alabama, some 120 miles northwest of Carrollton, in March 1931, when nine Black teenagers were arrested on a freight train outside of town and accused of raping two white women who had been on the boxcar with them. The case drew the attention of the

International Labor Defense (ILD), an arm of the Communist Party of the United States of America organized to defend leftist radicals charged with crimes and the predecessor of the Civil Rights Congress. The ILD's strategy was to hire lawyers to defend the accused while simultaneously demonstrating and pressuring for their release.

The Scottsboro Boys, as they came to be known, were an opportunity for the Communists to make inroads among African Americans in the South. When the boys were arraigned on March 31, 1931, two Communist Party members from Chattanooga, Tennessee, were in the audience and reported what they saw to the ILD in New York. Two days later a story appeared in the *Daily Worker* describing the boys as Black "workers" under threat of lynching by the "bosses" in Alabama, casting the conflict in terms of class even more than race. A series of trials followed from April 6 to 9, with the juries finding all but one of the boys guilty and sentencing them to die by electrocution. Within days the ILD organized demonstrations around the nation, beginning in Cleveland, where 1,300 workers protested the verdicts, followed by 20,000 in New York. Other labor protests were held around the Northeast and Midwest, with Communist leaders vying for African American loyalty while criticizing Black-led groups like the NAACP and the National Urban League for their silence. The critique found its mark, with the NAACP actively encouraging its membership to contribute to the ILD-led defense fund even as the defendants publicly stated (though their white attorney) they wanted no help from the Communists. The parents of some of the boys would later solicit the help of the ILD, and in short order all of the Scottsboro Boys were appealing to the Communists for help.[16]

Predictably, the Alabama press recoiled at the influence of the Communists. The *Birmingham Age-Herald* wrote that Alabamians resented the interference.

"They believe that the efforts of certain radical organizations to make the condemned Negroes appear as martyrs in a class struggle are vicious and assuredly misplaced," the *Age-Herald* opined. But the Communist Party of the United States of America's interest in Southern Blacks didn't begin with Scottsboro, nor would it end there. In 1930 the party developed a policy statement that "a serious change in its attitude and practices in regard to the work among the Negro masses" was needed. "The party must openly and unreservedly fight for the right of Negroes for self-determination in the South, where Negros comprise a majority of the population . . ."[17]

The exposure placed the ILD and the NAACP as rival suitors in a suddenly high-profile judicial drama. The Communists were at a disadvantage, since the NAACP had, for much of the century, strategized its fight for civil rights as one that revolved around the federal courts. The organization was the standard-bearer for African American rights, and the Communists were eyed with grave suspicion. But the NAACP had allowed the Communist Party a window of opportunity by initially hesitating to rush to the aid of the Scottsboro Boys. The ILD filled the void quickly, leaving the NAACP scrambling. African American ministers in Chattanooga came to the organization's defense, criticizing the Communists for attempting to wrest the case from the NAACP and warning the Black faithful that the ILD was attempting to weaken the NAACP and co-opt them into the Red fold.[18]

All of this worked to the Communists' advantage, positioning the party's revolutionary activism against the methodical approach of the NAACP.[19] The ILD strategy was twofold, with equal importance placed on legal defense and demonstrations at home and abroad. The ILD retained an influence in the boys' defense, eventually working their way up to the U.S. Supreme Court on claims that the defendants were denied effective legal counsel. A majority of the justices agreed, providing the Communists with a major legal victory in a case with an international profile.[20]

The Henderson defense was out of the same Communist playbook. The flyers claimed the trial was a frame-up. Henderson had been tried at gunpoint, with state troopers flanking the courtroom. How could this be a fair trial? To a great extent, the questions were being pushed by a white man who had quietly attended every hearing of the Henderson case: Homer Bates Chase.[21]

CHAPTER 8
THE COMMIES COME TO TOWN

The Communist Party of the United States saw opportunities for recruiting and expanding their support in the South among African Americans struggling under Jim Crow. Toward that end, Homer Bates Chase came to Atlanta in 1947 to register them to vote and convert them to "the cause." Chase was tall and gaunt, with dark eyebrows. His Roman nose accentuated his receding hairline, giving him an angular appearance. He was just thirty, but he looked a decade older. He had lived a lot already.

Chase had been chosen for the job because he had fought alongside Black soldiers in the Spanish Civil War as part of the Abraham Lincoln Brigade, an international fighting force that included thousands of leftist Americans eager to challenge the rise of fascism in Europe. He was captured and spent time in a fascist prison camp in Spain before being released in a prisoner exchange in the fall of 1938. The *Daily Worker* ran a photo of an unsmiling Chase lifting his hat with a dozen fellow former prisoners. In the accompanying article, Chase told the newspaper General Francisco Franco's fascist troops were demoralized and his Italian guards were anxious to return home.[1]

When America entered World War II, Chase volunteered for duty as a paratrooper, but when it came time for deployment, his well-known political leanings became a problem.

Chase came by his activism honestly. He was the son of prominent Communist parents in New Hampshire. His father, Fred Bates Chase, considered by some to be among the founding members of the Communist Party of the United States, ran for governor of New Hampshire in 1930 as the Communist candidate; two years later he ran for Senate. His mother, Elba Korb Chase, ran for governor in 1940 on the Communist ticket.

This political pedigree did not impress the U.S. Army, but as people who knew him later could attest, Chase was a bulldog who ran over critics. In short, he could be an obnoxious bully. The family story goes like this:

Chase had finished his paratrooper training in the 17th Airborne Division, 513th Parachute Infantry Regiment, and was prepared to go overseas, when an Army intelligence officer told him he couldn't go to Europe because of his Communist ties. Chase allegedly told him there was only one man who didn't want him in the fight: Adolf Hitler.

Apparently, that bravado was convincing: Staff Sergeant Homer Chase did go overseas, where he and the rest of the 513th were flown into France to fight alongside General George Patton in the Battle of the Bulge, pushing through German ranks in brutal bayonet assaults against fixed enemy positions.[2]

It's a wonder that Chase made it to Georgia at all. On March 24, 1945, he and the rest of the 513th took part in Operation Varsity, the final airborne deployment of the war and one that gave Allied forces a foothold across the Rhine River. While the 513th had seen heavy fighting, its soldiers had not been asked to parachute into combat. For the jump, Chase and his comrades were loaded aboard the new C-46 Commando troop transport airplane. The plane's fatal flaw became apparent when they started taking German antiair-craft fire. The C-46s lacked self-sealing fuel tanks, so when hit by enemy flak they began streaming highly flammable aviation fuel across their fuselages. Fourteen C-46s burst into flames in midair; Chase was on one of them but was among the eleven paratroopers who bailed out before his plane went down, earning him the honor of drawing German fire away from Allied forces crossing the river.[3]

"They say never volunteer," Chase later recalled, "but if I hadn't volunteered for the machine gun, I wouldn't have been placed near the door."[4]

In Georgia, where he was state chairman of the Community Party, Bates was under constant federal surveillance. Declassified reports from the FBI show that agents kept close tabs on Chase's actions in 1947, including his attendance at NAACP meetings in Atlanta and his association with rebel Southern poet Don West and other important figures, such as Ellwood Bod-die, a Black dentist and officer in the Communist Party who was watched by the FBI and Army intelligence.[5]

In February 1947, FBI Special Agent in Charge Edwin J. Foltz wrote to J. Edgar Hoover seeking permission to install listening devices in West's office at Oglethorpe University to capture conversations between Chase and West. Foltz noted that Chase appeared to be in Atlanta "for an undetermined length of time and is in constant contact with West."[6] While FBI informants painted West as a "friend and constant associate" of Chase,[7] West recalled the relationship differently.

"If I ever knew anybody that was a Stalin or a dictator, it was Homer Chase," West recalled in an interview three decades later.[8]

West was state chairman of former vice president Henry Wallace's presidential bid in 1948 under the banner of the newly formed Progressive Party. West said Chase attempted to dictate who would run on the Progressive ticket under Wallace in Georgia. When West pushed back, Chase launched "vicious attacks" against him, he said.

"He even spread the word that he had expelled me from the Communist Party. I wasn't a member of the Communist Party. But he spread it around that he had expelled me from the Communist Party. It was in order to discredit me," West said.[9]

The FBI wasn't alone in keeping a close eye on Chase. Ralph McGill, editor of the *Atlanta Constitution*, was another. McGill was a larger-than-life figure in Atlanta and a radical moderate on the pressing issues of the 1940s.[10] He had come to the *Constitution* as a sports editor, but his curious mind and confident writing style lifted him off of the sports pages and into political coverage. In 1936, McGill followed a young senator, Richard Russell, as he fought off a primary challenge from Governor Eugene Talmadge, earning the respect of the former and the undying enmity of the latter. Two years later, McGill was promoted to executive editor of the paper, a job that included a daily column on the editorial page that he used to fly his flag as a progressive Southern Democrat. A Roosevelt New Dealer, McGill banged the drum for Southern progress, fought for the farmer, and railed against the Ku Klux Klan and the Jim Crowism of Eugene Talmadge and his son, Herman. But he was just as ardent a foe of communism, and for several years beating up Homer Chase became something of a hobby for him.[11]

"What we need to do with the Communists is keep the spotlight on them," McGill wrote in April 1947 in a column headlined, "The Commies Have Come to Town."[12]

The column was entirely about Chase's arrival in town and McGill was sounding the alarms while simultaneously telling people there was nothing to fear.

"We have plenty on the newest comrade, all of which will be presented later on," McGill said. "He currently is seeking a place to live and when he gets that it will be made known." In a subsequent column, McGill not only reported where Chase lived but printed his telephone number and some aspects of his daily routine.

Chase had come to the South to sow discord and prey on "suckers," McGill wrote. Labor unions and Blacks were his particular targets, but white Southerners played into their hands, he said.

"They will attempt to make suckers of the police by forcing them into some act of violence or brutality against a Negro," McGill observed. "The fact that some police in every city seem to like to do such a thing has made the Communist job easier."

McGill suggested that Chase might go by other names and was an "experienced Communist from the East, skilled in various forms of sabotage. He is being checked for a criminal record."

Walking a fine line for 1947—and perhaps protecting his own anti-Red bona fides—McGill warned his readers not to "play the Communist game by calling every person a Communist who thinks Negroes have rights and that poverty is wrong."[13]

Ultimately, McGill was right when he told readers that Chase was nothing to worry about. The Communists had been working in the South for years with little to show for it. "Georgia, incidentally, has about 20 persons regarded as Communists and fellow travelers," he wrote. "The FBI knows them."

McGill was anxious about balancing his progressive notions on civil rights with his position as an anti-Communist Southern Democrat. The two halves of him had to coexist and Chase didn't make that easy. Chase had no such conflict. He had come to Atlanta because of his deep conviction that Blacks in the South were oppressed and that the road to socialist revolution would be paved over the dead body of Jim Crow.

But Chase was swimming upstream in his own party, which was fighting its own internal war over white leftist dominance. In a deeply biting essay published a decade later in the *Daily Worker*, Chase railed against "poor national leadership on the Negro question" and claimed attempts to root out white supremacy inside the party were a ruse used to purge dissenting members from leadership.[14]

McGill and Chase, both brawlers, were a match made in heaven. Both were driven by passion and an unwillingness to brook disagreement. McGill's biographer, journalist Harold Martin, recounted a story of his old friend's trip to the 1936 Democratic Convention in Chicago. McGill, a legendary drinker, had drunk lustily at a bar set up in the train's baggage car while enduring teasing from anti-Roosevelt delegates about his love for the president and the New Deal. At one point the ribbing crossed a line.

"Piss on the lot of you," he said, and unfastened his trousers to do exactly that, leaving delegates scrambling over suitcases to get away.[15]

Chase was more bellicose than McGill. On a visit to Georgia, the head of the North Carolina Communist Party described Chase as a man "unfortunately endowed with a strong tendency toward aimless contentiousness in nearly all of his interactions." While noting that Chase blamed his personality on "a faultlessly consistent class consciousness," his comrade from North Carolina said under his leadership "Georgia was the location of a number of stillborn Party plans, a great deal of inner-Party chaos, and an enraged hue and cry" from Communist critics (no doubt a nod to McGill).[16]

McGill must have been thrilled when Chase responded to his initial salvo with a letter blasting the editor for his "many crude lies and outright distortions." McGill "cheerfully" reprinted it in its entirety.[17]

In his response, Chase said the only sabotage training he had had came courtesy of the American government during his paratrooper training more than one hundred miles south of Atlanta, at Fort Benning, near Columbus, Georgia.

"I, together with thousands of other paratroopers, used this information on March 24, 1945, in a parachute jump by the 17th Airborne, five miles behind the German lines near Wesel, Germany," Chase wrote.

Regarding his criminal history, Chase replied, "Why didn't you check before you wrote that column? I have no criminal record."

Turning the tables, Chase mounted a fierce defense of the Communist Party's record of "Americanism," including "the fight for the Scottsboro boys," which he described as "a great victory for the Negro people and all freedom-loving people throughout the world."

By contrast, McGill was an unoriginal Red-baiter, a "weak-kneed liberal" who must be dragged along by more progressive actors. Chase said the

Communist Party was needed in Georgia to "fight against Talmadge's fascist white supremacy attacks on democratic government."

"Red-baiting confuses the main issues," he wrote. "The enemy of the people of Georgia is Wall Street and its political henchman, Herman Talmadge."

Both sides were bloodied and had a taste for it. For Chase, it was publicity; for McGill, who had a daily column to feed, it was gold.

McGill responded the following day with a column equating the Communists with the racist ideology of Gerald L. K. Smith, a far-right populist and Holocaust denier who had mounted an abysmal campaign for president as the America First Party candidate. People like Chase and Smith were attracted to the South because the region had failed "to adjust some of its social wrongs, namely, those affecting the poor white and Negro people who have just grievances."[18]

McGill described Chase's response to his original column as "so typically Communist" but useful in understanding his aims, including the desire to associate communism with "worthy causes," including the defense of the Scottsboro Boys.

"The truth—Communist interference greatly delayed the freeing of the men," McGill wrote. "The Communists actually sought to delay their freedom so as to make capital of the case."

People like Chase had no desire to right the wrongs done to African Americans in the South, the editor wrote. In fact, they attached themselves to civil rights organizations to sabotage them.

"These injustices give the Communists their only hope of getting members," he wrote. "They seek to make it possible for the reactionary forces to charge Communism against every person who may oppose lynchings, injustices, and unfair legislation."

Again McGill told readers not to worry. Chase "is getting nowhere, not even among Negroes, where he has a fellow-traveler assistant."

McGill had readers' attention. Shortly after the back-and-forth with Chase, the *Constitution* printed a letter asking whether Communists identified themselves as such when joining organizations. In an editor's note, the paper answered, "Only when they join the Young Communists' League."[19]

Early in 1948, Chase again was featured in the Atlanta press, this time as the target of an investigation by the American Legion after he attempted to enroll in the organization late the prior year. Beginning in the 1930s, the American Legion had developed a strong anti-Communist stance and would emerge as a backer of Senator Joseph McCarthy during the Red Scare in years to come. In February 1948, the *Constitution* reported in an unbylined article that Chase was under investigation by the Legion's Committee on Anti-Subversive Activities.

"Although Chase reputedly has an excellent war record as a combat soldier, Legion sources implied he was inadvertently taken into the organization which is famed for its principles of Americanism and its militant opposition to foreign 'isms,'" the *Constitution* reported.[20]

The Legion did move to expel Chase while at the same time holding that he had never become a member because he had not taken the Legionnaire Oath, which includes a promise to "foster and perpetuate 100 percent Americanism." It is possible that Chase was not that interested in joining the American Legion in the first place and was signed up as part of a membership drive among local veterans. But he never missed a chance to dig at Georgia's inequities and told the *Constitution* the Legion should investigate "Herman Talmadge's subversive slander against the Negro people in Georgia."[21]

McGill continued to use Chase as a punching bag, with columns in 1948 characterizing him as a charlatan who used misdirection and lies to fool "the poor Negro and the poor white" into buying his Stalinist claptrap. In a column rebutting a radio address by Chase on a local station, McGill hit on the deep fear that African Americans were being pushed toward communism by the stubbornness of Jim Crow. Chase's promises to abolish segregation were wrongheaded, McGill wrote.

"Segregation can be ended in its vicious forms without abandoning the pattern of the South which will not be abandoned and which could not be enforced save by arms," he wrote. "This is typical of the Communist pattern of focusing attention, not on what is best, but on what will best serve the Communists."[22]

McGill's personal campaign against Chase was symptomatic of the age. Fear of Soviet-inspired communism was on the rise nationally. In 1947, President Truman issued an executive order requiring loyalty investigations for federal employees. And in January 1949 the longest federal trial in American history began in New York with the prosecution of a dozen leaders of the

American Communist Party on charges of advocating the violent overthrow of the government.

The trial began January 17 and would last nine months, with the defendants appearing in court under the guard of four hundred New York City policemen. The spectacle of the "commie chieftains" trial appeared on the front pages of newspapers around the nation, including the *Atlanta Constitution*. Included among the defendants was Benjamin Jefferson Davis Jr., a lawyer and New York City councilman from Harlem. Davis, who it was noted was "Negro," was a native of Atlanta before leaving to graduate from Amherst College and Harvard Law.[23]

In the South, the fear of the Communist menace was inextricably linked to progressive Southerners' own conflicted feelings about race and class. Communists' appeal to Blacks in the South threatened a fragile racial ecosystem. It was one of the reasons the death of Buddy Stevens hit Carrollton so hard. A white boy from the city's professional class killed by a masked Black man bent on rape—the entire scenario threatened the system that kept Blacks as a subjugated class. McGill reflected the Southern uncertainty in his columns. But when it came to an easy target like Homer Chase, he hit hard.

Chase had bigger problems than McGill. In May 1949 he was arrested for "harassing" Evans Wilder, a twenty-year-old from Cartersville, a small town about forty-five miles northwest of Atlanta. Wilder, a grocery store clerk, had attended party meetings for several months in 1948 and 1949, but got in trouble with police in Bartow County when he came back from Atlanta and tried to recruit locals to communism. Now Wilder said his association with Communists had cost him his job and subjected him to "public ridicule." Indeed, once the initial story broke, McGill had painted Wilder as "infantile" and a "dim bulb" for swallowing Chase's ideology. The editor had gone so far as wonder—without evidence—if Evans's susceptibility to Communist teachings could be traced back to his poverty and the personal failings of his father.[24]

According to McGill, Wilder had returned from his meetings with the Atlanta Communists "like a quacking gosling . . . babbling Communist threats." Among those threats was a supposed plot to blow up the dam at the Lake Allatoona reservoir, northwest of Atlanta. Once he fell under police scrutiny, Wilder told everything he knew to the FBI about suspected

Community Party members and filed charges against Chase, testifying the state's chief Commie had threatened him if he talked.[25]

In truth, Wilder was a sensitive kid and a likely recruit for the Communist Party. The child of impoverished white mill workers, Wilder had grown up seeing the heavy hand of the bosses used against the working poor. During the Depression, police were brought in to break a textile strike in Wilder's hometown. He was just a boy, but tear gas thrown by the police so damaged his eyesight that Wilder had to wear thick glasses to see.

"I was just six when the strike came," he later recalled. "I remember the bitterness and the hunger and the trouble of that period. . . . My father, and others, were unfairly blacklisted. I saw kids in winter without shoes."

In the local white schools, poor mill kids were segregated from the other students. There were no free textbooks in Georgia schools at the time, and many of the children of mill workers couldn't afford them. By his junior year of high school, Wilder had to drop out to help support the family.

"That nearly killed me," he said. "Maybe you can imagine how it makes you feel not to be able to go when the others can. You feel like life is pretty hard and unfair."

He was a dropout, but Wilder tried to self-educate. He read. "I wanted to learn," he said. "I bought magazines and books. I got books at the library." And he got political. One day while reading the *Nation*, he saw an advertisement offering information about the Communist Party and answered it.

Rather than literature, Wilder received a personal visit from Chase, who introduced himself as "Nelson" and provided the young man with Communist pamphlets and treatises and a warning not to discuss their activities over the telephone. Chase introduced Wilder to other members of his group and was encouraged to start recruiting in his hometown.[26]

In his affidavit, Wilder said he was "being shadowed and watched, spied upon and harassed by Homer Bates Chase and his associates, agents, and stooges and fears they will commit physical violence against his person." Of course, Wilder—the terrified "dim bulb" of a rural grocery store clerk—didn't write that. It was written by his attorney, a fiery lawyer named Dan Duke, who had been hired by Wilder's labor union to represent him. A former state prosecutor, Duke made a name for himself by battling the Ku Klux Klan, but, like McGill, he was no defender of communism.

In an affidavit, Wilder said he met with the "leading Georgia Communists" and "visiting Communists from New York City."

"Wilder said 'so far as he knew' he was not a member of the Party himself, but that he once gave Chase a dollar, which he understood was to 'go to the Communist Party and the Young Progressives,'" the *Constitution* reported.

Wilder went to meetings with the Communists and their associates for about a year, but said he became frightened by the secrecy of the outfit and the threats Chase made if he should talk.

"We have ways of looking after people who talk too much," Wilder said Chase had told him. Duke said his client went to the FBI out of fear, and while he had been sympathetic to the Communist cause, "his eyes have since been opened."[27]

Wilder swore out a warrant against Chase and police started looking for him to answer the charge. A week later Chase emerged with his lawyer. In a twist, Chase, who was trying to recruit Georgia Blacks to the Communist cause, hired as his attorney James R. Venable, a leader of the Klan.[28] Venable would use his representation of Chase for the rest of his life as an example of his sterling character as an attorney.[29]

The harassing charge was minor, but, given the national backdrop, the local papers played it like the road company version of the Communist trial in New York.

"Revolution Plot Laid to State Reds," screamed the headlines spanning six columns of the front page of the *Constitution* following the first day of Chase's bond hearing. During the hearing, Wilder testified that Chase and his compatriots "talked about world revolution, the writings of Lenin, Stalin, and other Communists." He was advised to study and commit to memory Communist Party documents, but also the U.S. Constitution and the Bill of Rights.

"Chase told us to study them as they were handy to a Communist in court," Wilder said.

He claimed Chase bragged that foreigners were being smuggled into the United States through Atlanta. Wilder testified for hours and no detail was too trivial. For instance, he said the group's dangerous talk occurred while listening to "records of Paul Robeson, Lena Horne" and "The Internationale."

"Such music has meaning," Wilder said Chase told him.[30]

Wilder said it was local labor organizer William Stafford, not Chase, who wondered aloud about the amount of dynamite Allatoona Dam would require. But he said Chase had been out to the dam site and he "didn't seem to be sightseeing . . .

"I'd like to bet Chase has notes on all dams and power installations," Wilder said.[31]

Wilder named everyone he could think of who had attended meetings. Oglethorpe University senior Jack Lorenz and recent Agnes Scott College graduate Eudice Tontak each were called to the stand and asked whether they were members of the Communist Party. They took the Fifth. All of them had been influential in the failed Wallace campaign of the Georgia Progressive Party, which local politicians and newsmen alike suspected was little more than a Communist front organization.[32]

Chase personally cross-examined Wilder about the nature of the meetings, which Chase described as "social gatherings" with coffee, cake, and jazz music. "I think they were political," Wilder said.

The bond hearing stretched into a second day, with Chase taking advantage of the press's rapt attention to hold forth on Governor Talmadge, "turncoat Wilder," white supremacy, and the aims and gifts of the Communist Party of the United States. He also fired back at the opposing counsel, Duke, as a tool of white supremacy.

"Wall Street is using Daniel Duke and other white chauvinists to divide the people and bring about war and fascism in this country," Chase said.

"Duke poses as a friend of Negroes on Auburn Avenue," Chase continued, referring to the main commercial drag in Black Atlanta, "but practices white chauvinism and spreads it in a snide vicious manner such as being done here—not openly like Talmadge."

Chase warned Duke to remember that German Nazis who persecuted Communists in the 1930s were later put on trial for their actions.

If he said anything to Wilder, Chase said it was to warn him against talking to the FBI, "which is playing a reactionary role in the politics of Georgia and the United States."

William Stafford also took the stand, testifying that he merely had tried to help Wilder, who had claimed he was in trouble with the local Klan. Now it was Stafford who needed help.

"Bricks have been thrown twice into the home where I live with my wife and baby," he said. "These charges are being used to inflame the people. Why, while I was sitting outside the courtroom, I overheard a man say we all ought to be lynched."[33]

While the Henderson capital murder trial was accomplished in a single day, the hearing over what was essentially a restraining order against Chase lasted three days, beginning on a Thursday and stretching across a weekend into the following Monday. The weekend break gave McGill and the *Constitution* a chance to wring further ink from the affair, with two stories for the Sunday paper, including a stand-alone profile on Rachel Chase, Homer's recent bride. Before her marriage, Rachel had served as a WAVE (the U.S. Navy's women's auxiliary) in Washington, DC, during World War II. More recently, she had worked in Atlanta for the National Labor Relations Board. Such a position would have granted her access to labor complaints, the *Constitution* warned.

"Disgruntled labor is the most fertile field for Communist organizers," the paper explained in the unbylined story.[34]

The other story was a recap of the action so far, but it included this chilling bit of analysis: "One fact seemed clear was that Georgia for some time has had an active Communist cell."[35]

The shadow play concluded Monday with closing arguments by the lawyers for both sides—unusual, to say the least, in a peace warrant hearing. In the end, Fulton County judge Ralph McClellan sided with Wilder, commending the grocery clerk for unveiling the Communist menace among them and finding probable cause that the young man faced dangerous reprisals for his newfound patriotism. The judge slapped Chase with a $5,000 peace bond, a legal instrument similar to a restraining order except that the defendant had to agree to the terms of the court or forfeit the bond amount. Peace bonds largely are not in use today, in part because of constitutional questions created when an accused person cannot afford the bond and ends up in jail. The *New York Times* claimed the large bond required for Chase to maintain his freedom was "unprecedented against a political leader."[36]

Either for reasons of principle or pocketbook, Chase chose jail over putting up $5,000 (roughly $51,000 in today's currency). He cast the decision in lofty, even heroic terms.

"Many a good man has gone to jail before me to promote the cause of justice," he told the press.

But before heading to jail, the truculent Communist organizer again used the bully pulpit the trial provided to get in a few good licks against the prevailing injustices in 1940s Georgia. He started at the top with one of the most politically powerful companies in the state and its largest utility.

"This ruling was handed down by the Georgia Power Company—not by that poor old cripple judge who's just trying to keep his job," Chase said.

The courts and their corporate masters were behind this show trial—not surprising when you consider the white supremacist underpinnings of the system, he concluded.

"Just stop and think how many Negroes and working men are judges," Chase said. "This decision points out the need for Negro judges in Georgia."

Duke, however, hailed the bond as "a lick struck for the American way of life," one that sent a message to any Commie bully who sought to threaten a red-blooded American man like his client. In his closing, Duke, who had endured Chase's insults on Friday, called his adversary "an intellectual prostitute who teaches treachery, falsehood and violence."

"Georgia has many sorrows," Duke said. "But they can't be cured by either Communists or the Klan."[37]

The *Constitution* printed the exchange, along with a tall, two-column photo of Chase under police escort with the caption "No. 1 Georgia Communist Goes to Jail." In the photo, the lanky Chase appears to smirk as he moves past a deputy sheriff.

While expensive in time and materials, any political radical would kill for the platform handed to Chase during the three-day hearing. Gavel-to-gavel coverage in the local press, plus national press recognition? In his decision to testify against his former comrades, Wilder had done the Communist Party a tremendous service.

In a verbatim echo of the *New York Times*, the *Daily Worker* called the decision "unprecedented against a political leader" while underscoring the hypocrisy of a state with a history of lynchings now jailing Chase for political "violence."

"A certain youth says he believes that the American Communist Party is a 'menace' to him," *The Worker* wrote on its editorial page. "On the say-so of this crackpot or stoolpigeon, the local police have arrested the leader of the local Communists."[38]

The *Daily Worker* decried Wilder as a "renegade from the Communist Party" and said the $5,000 peace bond was more than ten times the usual amount for such an alleged offense.

"This frame-up comes against a background of a breakdown of democracy in Georgia," the *Worker* reported. "Unemployment is skyrocketing with the closing of many textile mills. Violence and lynching against Negroes are on the increase."[39]

For his part, Duke was cast by the Communist press as "protecting and covering up the violence of [Governor Herman] Talmadge and the Ku Klux Klan," an accusation that would have made Duke—had he seen it—laugh.[40]

While Chase's attorneys immediately moved to have the bond declared unconstitutionally excessive, the Communist Party began distributing handbills and raising money off the arrest, tying Chase's political imprisonment to Talmadge, the Klan, lynchings, and Wall Street's corrupting influence. Duke and McGill were "stooges," the handbill claimed.

"Instead of prosecuting the lynchers, they are attacking the Communist Party which has always fought against white lynching and all forms of white supremacy," it said. The handbill included information on how to join the Communist Party and where to send money.

In the meantime, supporters of Chase put up a property bond to get him released from jail. He spent three days locked up before he was released.[41]

While Chase was free from jail, the situation was terrible for Communist Party bosses in New York. In October, a jury convicted eleven of the party's top officers of attempting to overthrow the government. Prosecutors did not present direct evidence of the supposed plot, relying instead of the writings of Karl Marx and Vladimir Lenin as proof of the conspiracy. The leaders were sentenced to five years in prison. "Democrats and Republicans in Congress applauded the conviction," the Associated Press reported.[42]

"Now, what about the local commies," McGill wondered, following the New York verdicts.

In perhaps his most below-the-belt move, McGill once against went after Chase in a column about his formative years in New England. "He was the son of Fred Chase, a small farmer, who was reportedly a small-time machinist in Boston when he met a Russian girl and followed her into the Communist Party," McGill wrote, as though he could not indicate enough that Chase's late father was "small" and under the sway of a woman and working "at his wife's direction."

Homer Chase, he said, was similarly emasculated and "not a forceful or effective member."

"Chase works in second place to a feminine Communist in the South, as his father was directed by his Russian wife." If the column was not person-ally insulting enough, McGill included a picture of Fred Chase's gravestone, which is adorned with a Communist hammer and sickle.

Like Chase and his father before him, the Communist Party of the United States was similarly weak and flaccid and treated with "contempt" by its bosses in Russia, according to McGill. The Soviets' American subordinates were often not informed of changes in the party line, leaving their American cousins "in a most ridiculous position," he wrote.

Dancing on Chase's dead father's grave was McGill's parting shot at Chase for 1949. Ironically, McGill would return to that column five years later in a personal letter to the editor of *U.S. News & World Report* regarding the dangers he saw in portraying critics of Senator Joseph McCarthy, like himself, as pro-Communist. McGill said he had done "a rather thorough job of keeping check on a fellow named Homer Chase."

"I published pictures of his father's grave under a stone in the New England cemetery with a hammer and sickle on it," he said. "I believe this would entitle me, by McCarthy's qualifications, to an anti-Communist status."[43]

Following the gravestone column, the *Constitution* rested its case on Chase, although in December 1949 the newspaper published a brief item on page 14 acknowledging the end of the Evans Wilder drama: "Homer Chase Bond Lifted." After six months the bond expired and no move was made to reinstate it. It is hard to imagine Chase giving much more thought to Wilder from that point on. Free on bond, Chase had caught wind of another organizing opportunity. A sharecropper in a West Georgia city had been railroaded in a one-day trial and sentenced to the electric chair. This was just the kind of case that appealed to American Communists and their supporters. Chase's next move would be as a member of the Henderson Defense Committee.

CHAPTER 9

"HIS FIGHT IS OUR FIGHT"

Henderson's conviction on pure circumstantial evidence attracted new supporters to his cause. Along with Chase and the Communists, local civil rights leaders began working on his behalf. The Reverend Benjamin Joseph Johnson Sr. of Greater Mt. Calvary Baptist Church, an associate of the Reverend Martin Luther King Sr. and an early leader in Atlanta's civil rights movement, joined Henderson's defense committee. Johnson, who spent fifty years as leader of his church, hosted civil rights meetings there in the 1940s and 1950s, and the church was used to install Atlanta's first Black police officers in 1948.[1] Johnson was joined by George Wanna-maker, the white theology student at Emory University. Both were listed as chairmen of Henderson's defense committee, as was Barney Rutledge, a recent Morehouse College graduate and classmate of Martin Luther King Jr.

Thanks to their efforts, Henderson had the new legal team of E. E. Moore and S. S. Robinson.[2] The committee had raised funds by distributing a flyer claiming Henderson had been framed. The flyer enumerated the reasons why someone should contribute:

> There were no Negro jurors; he was not identified as the murderer; the prosecutor is the judge's brother; there were 30 to 40 state troopers present at the trial; he swore in court that he was beaten while handcuffed.

The flyer painted Henderson as emblematic of Southern Black men. "His fight is our fight," it said. "An innocent man's life is at stake."

While the white press pushed a narrative of Henderson as a dark-skinned criminal, the Black press highlighted his sharecropping family: the Hendersons never had much wealth, but Clarence's arrest and conviction had pushed his wife and children into destitute poverty.

Lizzie Mae Henderson already had two children by her husband: Clarence Jr. and Sarah. In March, she gave birth in an Atlanta hospital to a third, Lutricia. The Henderson family had been taken out of Carrollton for their safety and were staying with a family in the English Avenue neighborhood of Atlanta just northwest of downtown. The *Atlanta Daily World* published a picture of the family, advertising that they had "absolutely no resources" since Clarence's arrest. That story, amplified by the Communists, fueled contributions to the defense fund.[3]

The play made by the Communist Party for Henderson angered the NAACP, which found the presence of the Communists both irritating and unhelpful.

"The Henderson case is considered a 'hot potato' and it is obvious that the doomed man needs help," the *Pittsburgh Courier* reported. "The NAACP has moved out of the case, claiming that it did so because the Civil Rights Congress 'took over.' The NAACP said it has no intention of re-entering the case unless the CRC 'gets out.'"[4]

In classic fashion, the Communists soft-pedaled their role while also claiming property rights to the case. Rachel Chase, Homer's wife, wrote a letter to the *Courier* claiming that the Henderson Defense Committee was "non-partisan," but said that members of the Civil Rights Congress and the NAACP were working together on the case.

"It will require all the efforts of all organizations to right the terrible wrong done the Henderson family," she wrote.[5]

The defense campaign caught the attention of the Atlanta police, who notified officials to the west in Carrollton. In April 1950, Lipford filed a contempt-of-court action against the men based on information provided by Sheriff Gaston. In reporting on the contempt filing, the *Times–Free Press* wrote that Moore and Robinson had been before Boykin the prior week to argue a motion for a new trial for their client and that "the Negro attorneys at no time charged that Henderson was framed as alleged in the circular." In the story, the *Times–Free Press* relied on Lipford's account of the hearing, an indication that no reporter was present. Following Henderson's conviction, the *Times–Free Press* and the *Georgian* had mostly dropped coverage of the Stevens case. That's not surprising. After sixteen months, reporters and readers likely were burned out and ready to move on.

Burned out or not, Lipford mustered outrage in his filing, claiming the circulars were "scandalous in tone and spirit . . . designed to incite prejudice and passion" and created "a false and defamatory reflection on the judicial integrity of the Superior Court of Carroll County."[6]

Judge Boykin called for the parties to appear in his courtroom in a Saturday morning session.

"The Commies are loudest in demanding their rights under the Constitution they seek to destroy," the *Constitution*'s McGill warned, returning to a favorite topic for his daily column. "They wanted the umbrella [of] those rights held over them while they worked at trying to sabotage this country and the Constitution by which it lives."

An object lesson in understanding anti-Communist paranoia and the racial politics of the period is the case of the white radical poet Don West, who had taken a teaching position at Atlanta's Oglethorpe University after the war.

West's verse tapped into a deeply discontented political underground of Blacks, progressive white Southerners, and Communists. West was riding the success of a collection of his poems, *Clods of Southern Earth*, an energetic defense of working-class whites and oppressed Blacks, both of whom he saw as beset by the racist Bourbonism of the South. The book had a preorder of more than 13,000 copies, in part from support generated by labor unions and progressive Southern religious leaders who saw West as one of their own.[7]

West used his platform to publicly criticize Talmadgism, comparing the young Herman Talmadge to Hitler in a widely heard radio address during a political crisis in 1947 when Herman claimed to be the rightful heir to the political legacy of his late father, Eugene.

Hitler and Talmadge both "used prejudice and hatred to split in order to divide and conquer," West said. "I want to warn you, my fellow Georgians, that unless we alert ourselves to the tremendous importance of what goes on, we too, will be the victims of an open fascist dictatorship."[8]

In the address, which was reprinted and distributed by Southern progressive groups, West passionately advocated for restoring Blacks' right to vote in the state's whites-only primary.

"Thousands of Negro soldiers and sailors fought and died bravely and gallantly to defeat Hitlerism and to maintain democracy in this land," he said. "Is their reward now to be a denial of their fundamental rights as American citizens to vote? The conscience of the people of Georgia will not, must not, permit this to happen."[9]

Don West's FBI file during this time is voluminous. His every movement was monitored; his office at Oglethorpe was bugged. Although he distanced himself from actual membership in the Communist Party, the federal government considered him one of Georgia's most powerful Reds.[10]

As he did with Homer Bates Chase, Ralph McGill favored Don West as a repeat topic for his column, calling him "an enemy of the country" for his association with the Southern Conference for Human Welfare and Henry Wallace's presidential campaign under the Progressive Party banner. Records from a House Un-American Activities Committee investigation linked West and Chase together, providing even more fodder for McGill's anti-Communist rants.[11]

Although mainstream liberals like McGill sought to discredit West by tying him closely to Homer Chase, the relationship between West and Chase was strained to breaking over the Wallace campaign. West objected to the use of Progressive Party activists to distribute Communist Party literature, and Chase attempted to block West's appointment to the Progressive Party's national committee. Chase went so far as to send Wallace a telegram at the party's national convention in Philadelphia advising him to resign. West told Chase to "go to hell" and referred to him as a "junior Lenin." To McGill, the pairing of West and Chase was grist for the column mill and he hammered them both.

In the end, the Wallace campaign tallied fewer than 1,700 votes statewide and the Georgia Progressive Party went into a fast death spiral fueled by internal discord.[12] West retreated to Douglasville, a rural village between Atlanta and Carrollton, to a four-hundred-acre farm to resume his writing.

On April 15, 1950, Henderson Defense Committee members Johnson, Wannamaker, and Rutledge presented themselves before Judge Boykin's court alongside lawyers Moore and Robinson to face the contempt charges. Tensions were high as Lipford began his questioning of the men before a packed courtroom, including, as one observer noted, "an unusually large number of Negroes."[13]

Accompanied by lawyers paid for by the Georgia NAACP, the four Black defendants, each in turn, denied responsibility for the flyer. Reverend Johnson said he had allowed his name to be used "for influential purposes," while the lawyers said they had no idea why their names were on it. Then Lipford called Wannamaker, the only white defendant, to the stand.

Wannamaker's father, a school administrator and U.S. Army colonel who served in World Wars I and II, had worked out a deal with Lipford for his son's testimony using a white Atlanta prosecutor as an intermediary. The deal called for the young evangelical to throw himself on the mercy of the court, corroborate the state's account of the distribution of the leaflets, blame the action on Communist influences in the Progressive Party, and apologize. All young George had to do was nod his head and point fingers. But as John Calhoun, executive secretary of the NAACP's Atlanta branch, described him, the younger Wannamaker was "a zealot in the cause" and knocked those plans into a cocked hat.[14]

In the courtroom, Black reporter C. W. "Pete" Greenlea leaned forward to hear the young white preacher hold forth on the injustices heaped upon African Americans in the South. Those in the courtroom "sat amazed as a young white religious student, one of five Atlantans cited in a contempt of court hearing, used the witness stand to preach for justice for Negro People," Greenlea wrote in a dispatch carried by the *Atlanta Daily World*, the *Memphis World*, and other Black papers. Wannamaker had been called by Lipford to implicate his Black codefendants. The move backfired, Greenlea wrote.

"But the young Rev. Wannamaker dropped a proverbial bomb into the courtroom," he reported.[15]

"Where did this this business of defending Clarence Henderson start?" Lipford asked.

"I think it started many years go," the seminarian said, "with Jesus Christ."[16]

A white reporter in the audience heard Wannamaker's testimony with radically different ears. "Wannamaker surprised everyone, and most of all his lawyer, when he made a complete confession on the witness stand," *Georgian* reporter Hal David wrote.

David described the ministerial student's statement as "wild" and "rambling" in which he took complete blame for the pamphlet, absolving his Black codefendants. The flyer had been developed in the Progressive Party headquarters and mailed from there, Wannamaker said. The two Black attorneys had only agreed to accept payment from the committee and allow mail generated by the appeal to come to their office, he said.

"I had a lot to do with writing that pamphlet and am ready to assume whatever guilt there is," Wannamaker said, pushing aside protests from his attorney that he not be allowed to say any more. "I wish to apologize to the Carroll County Superior Court. I do not think Judge Boykin is dishonest and I hold him in high regard."[17]

But he said Boykin and other Southern jurists "have a lot to learn."

"It's wrong to go on treating Negro people like dogs," he said.[18]

In a letter sent to the NAACP's legal headquarters in New York, Calhoun described the scene as "quite interesting."

"To everyone's surprise, when placed upon the witness stand, Mr. Wannamaker repudiated the statement which had been read by his attorney, Mr. Webb, and although a thoroughly confused young man, expounded his views on the race question and absolved each defendant of guilt in preparing and mailing the circulars," he wrote.[19]

The young Wannamaker's decision on the stand was fortuitous. Myer Goldberg, the white attorney representing the Black defendants in the case, including Robinson and Moore, was aware of the agreement for Wannamaker's testimony and was prepared to unveil it in cross-examination. But doing so would have revealed the role of the Atlanta prosecutor who had helped to broker it. That wasn't a fight the Atlanta NAACP was eager to pick if it could be avoided.[20]

Following Wannamaker's testimony, a perturbed Boykin interrupted. He scanned the courtroom attempting to find the people he thought might be pulling the young preacher's strings.

"Other persons should be made parties to this," he observed. "They are whites and colored, and there are some of them in this room." Then, from the bench, he pointed to a man seated in the audience and ordered him to identify himself. The man stood and identified himself as William Stafford, former leader of the Georgia Progressive Party. Boykin pointed to a young woman, who stood and identified herself as Rachel Chase. The final man ordered to rise was, of course, Homer Chase. Boykin said he recognized Homer and Rachel as well as Stafford because they had attended "each hearing in the Henderson case." The judge continued pointing at faces in the crowd, requiring white students from Georgia Tech and Emory to rise and announce themselves, as well as three other men from Atlanta, including Jim Kamm, another executive in the Georgia Progressive Party.

Boykin immediately adjourned the hearing, ordering that the investigation into contempt be broadened to include Chase, Stafford, and the others. Boykin said he wouldn't rule on the contempt motion until he had gotten "to the bottom of the whole thing."[21] Lipford responded to the judge's charge with a promise to bring all of the resources of his office to bear. The stress of the hearing was apparently too much for Wannamaker, who was admitted to a hospital the following day.[22]

In its next edition, the *Times–Free Press* rued that the case against Henderson was now "serving as a smokescreen to bemuddle the public and make it forget the earlier and basic facts upon which the now-jumbled mess started."

Stevens was white and Henderson Black, the newspaper observed. And, yes, Henderson had been convicted on circumstantial evidence. But, the paper editorialized, there was no evidence that the sharecropper was framed.

"The -ism groups saw a chance to develop another Scottsboro Case, to achieve publicity for their nefarious organizations and raise money for their purpose," the paper wrote, adding its endorsement to the Lipford/Boykin probe "to bring out the real facts."[23]

The expansion of the contempt probe infuriated the Communists. A Southern judge had attacked citizens, white and Black, for doing nothing more than attending open court hearings, The *Daily Worker* reported, using readers to send telegrams of protest to Boykin and contributions to the defense committee.[24]

John Pittman, an African American journalist and columnist for the *Daily Worker*, said the actions of Boykin and Lipford illustrated the desperate plight of Southern Blacks when cast into the white man's justice system.

"In other words, if you dare to speak out against a verdict and sentence in Georgia, or even show interest in a case, you can be cited for contempt and sent to prison," he wrote.[25]

The Communists were hardly cowed by Boykin's threats. An article recounting the extraordinary hearing, probably written by Chase himself, said the Henderson Defense Committee had begun work on another leaflet. And the Civil Rights Congress put Clarence Henderson's wife, Lizzie, on the speaking circuit. Before an all-Black crowd at the Church of God in Christ on Jones Avenue in Atlanta, she spoke about her husband's case and "some facts the public hasn't heard." It was one of several appearances Lizzie Henderson made to raise money for her husband's defense.[26]

Ralph McGill, who had no one to please in Carrollton, took a more nuanced approach than his white colleagues in Carrollton. In a few short sentences the editor described the case against Henderson as "strong" but circumstantial, based largely on testimony from people who didn't like him. His wife said he was at home asleep when Stevens was killed, the editor observed.

"The convicted man was a good father, devoted to his children, and had a good reputation with his employer," McGill wrote, and inferred that Henderson's legal team should have called Henderson's boss—or anyone—to testify on his behalf.

Innocent or guilty, Henderson deserved an advocate, McGill said. He said the Communists had come to prey on the marginalized people who were working in good faith to raise money for the defense, a situation "which must be on our conscience."

With more than a little hint of the patrician, McGill explained, "There originally were obscure, inarticulate, uninfluential persons seeking to raise a defense fund and to hire lawyers.

"The stark reality of the situation was that the Communists were the only persons who looked them up," he wrote.

McGill believed the Communists cared little about Henderson's guilt or innocence. They, like the Klan, used the weak in Southern society—white and Black—to further their goals and to bleed them dry of what little money they had. That members of Atlanta's Black community had turned to Homer Chase for help was as much of a stain on the state as the ignorant and desperate white farmer who sent his $10 to join the Klan, he said.

"No American should have to turn to either of these un-American organizations," he said.

McGill wrote that Henderson's planned execution should be delayed or commuted until the slime the Communists had smeared on the case could be cleared away and the truth underneath revealed. "By all means let those convinced of his innocence continue their work," he concluded. "But let them know that the pious, honeyed words of the Communists are lies."[27]

McGill's column did not sit well with Carrollton's white power structure and they let the *Constitution* editor know it. Two days later a chastened McGill returned with a semi-apology where he admitted the Communists had fooled him "in some minor points by their propaganda."

Henderson, most likely, was guilty, he wrote. McGill said the Communists had so deliberately hijacked the defense fund that no reputable personage—least of all him—would be associated with it and sided with Lipford and Boykin in pursuing the contempt charges. The entire affair "indicates how the Communists involve others and exploit the credulous and those neurotics whose load of idealism keep them close to the nervous crack-up stage," he observed. He drew on Wannamaker's dramatic testimony as evidence that association with Communists was dangerous to one's mental health, since the young seminary student "went to pieces on the stand."

Attempting to save a shred of his initial column, McGill said solid whites should still take pity on the families the guilty leave behind—and, by so doing, rob the Communists of their prey.

The man who two days prior had urged a delay in Henderson's execution concluded, "There seems to be no reasonable doubt about the guilt of the defendant." But the court and the public should care for his wife and children. "To fail in this opens the door to the Commies," he wrote.[28]

While McGill wrestled the Communists on the pages of the *Atlanta Constitution*, interest was stirring in Henderson's case elsewhere. In a Manhattan office building on the morning of February 2, 1950, a letter reached the desk of the NAACP's top lawyer. Inside was a newspaper clipping with the confusing if intriguing headline "Gets Chair for Killing Man Who Refused to Rape Girl." The sender had clipped the article from the January 31, 1950, edition of *New York Post* and scribbled the NAACP Legal Defense Fund mailing address in the margin with the underlined instructions "Act Quickly!" The sender had underlined and drawn an arrow pointing to a sentence in the second paragraph: "The companion of the slain student did not attempt to identify the man on trial."[29]

It was just the type of case that appealed to the man holding the clipping: Thurgood Marshall.

CHAPTER 10

THE NAACP TAKES CHARGE

The offices of the NAACP Legal Defense and Educational Fund (LDF) were in the Wendell Willkie Memorial Building, a gabled, nine-story building in the Flemish Revival style, its gingerbread flourishes towering over brownstones on either side. The building sat across from the main branch of the New York Public Library and Bryant Park, named after abolitionist and newspaper publisher William Cullen Bryant.

Inside the building, in a cramped two-room suite, a small team of lawyers, led by future Supreme Court Justice Thurgood Marshall, plotted the downfall of legalized segregation, painstakingly assembling the suite of civil cases needed to disassemble centuries of America's oppression of its Black citizens. At the same time they also coordinated the fight for the lives of Black men accused, often with scant evidence, of raping and murdering whites across the South. The conviction of Clarence Henderson was such a case.[1]

Within a week of receiving word of Henderson's plight, Assistant Special Counsel Jack Greenberg wrote to Onis Bexley, head of an NAACP branch in Carroll County, looking for more information on "suspicion that Mr. Henderson did not have a fair trial."[2]

Bexley's reply said much about the strength of African American organizing in West Georgia. Bexley, a Black farmer in his mid-fifties, lived in Bowdon. To him, Carrollton was a distant spot on a small map.

"I have no information at all. I live twelve miles from Carrollton," Bexley said in a handwritten reply sent a few days later. "I don't stay thire and is not over thire much."[3]

Greenberg wrote back, asking for names of friendly people in Carrollton who might help. "We do not have names or addresses of any persons in Carrollton," he explained.[4]

Bexley sent some names and partial addresses of people he knew in Carrollton, including "Croffert Marlin Baber shop man and undertaker." Greenberg immediately sent out another letter to "Croffert M. Baber, Mortician," a man he assumed ran a mortuary. However, Bexley meant Croffert Marlin, a Black barber in Carrollton who did double duty preparing the bodies of deceased neighbors on the side. The letter to "Mr. Baber" was returned as undeliverable.[5]

If Marshall's office was groping for information about Henderson, they didn't let on. On February 16, not quite three weeks after Henderson's one-day murder trial in Carrollton, LDF lawyer Constance Baker Motley wrote to a concerned woman in West Virginia that Henderson's case "is already being investigated."

"I can assure you that this association will do all within its power to protect Mr. Henderson from any wrongful deprivation of his life," Motley wrote to the woman.[6]

Meanwhile, Greenberg ran into dead ends on the other names offered by Bexley. By April, he gave up trying to find anyone in Carroll County and asked the state chapter to intervene.

"We have been receiving correspondence about the trial of Clarence Henderson in Carrollton, Georgia," Greenberg wrote to Dr. William Madison Boyd, president of the Georgia NAACP. "There has also been considerable newspaper comment about the case. I am writing to inquire whether you believe this man was deprived of constitutional rights during his trial and, if so, to request you send a copy of the record in his case to this office."[7]

The LDF was stretched thin. The Henderson case was on their radar, but progress was slow. More than two months after Constance Motley's calm assurances, Marshall's office was uncertain how directly involved it needed to be in the case. Of real concern was the influence of local Communists and fellow travelers in Henderson's defense. That was a deal breaker for Marshall. The NAACP was in the middle of a campaign of cleansing itself of Communists in the local branches. At the upcoming national convention in Boston in June, delegates would pass a resolution "directing and instructing the board of directors to take the necessary action to eradicate" Communists from their ranks. The organization passed another resolution supporting American efforts to stop Communist expansion on the Korean Peninsula. A staunch and strategic anti-Communist, Marshall even passed along to the FBI information on suspected Communists attempting to influence the NAACP, perhaps as a way to protect the organization during a time of heightened fear.[8]

Atlanta NAACP executive secretary John Calhoun wrote to Marshall in April that the Henderson Defense Committee was in the process of extracting itself from the clutches of local Communists.

"Just how easily they can get Mr. Chase and other Progressive Party leaders to agree to this will not be known until they meet today," Calhoun wrote on April 18, 1950. The local branch's legal committee "insisted that we will not enter the case unless the activities of the Henderson Defense Committee are entirely divorced" from the Civil Rights Congress, he concluded.[9]

As part of the divorce, Reverend Benjamin Johnson and young Morehouse man Barney Rutledge, both active in the NAACP, resigned from the committee. Georgia Progressive Party leader William Stafford promptly replaced them. Robinson and Moore, Henderson's Black attorneys, were working with the doomed man to distance themselves from the Communists and their Progressive Party allies but still retain some way to raise money for the defense. It was tricky and politically sensitive work. At the urging of the NAACP, Robinson and Moore prepared an affidavit for Clarence to sign, repudiating the Civil Rights Congress and allowing the NAACP exclusively to raise money on his behalf. This was no easy decision. In addition to his looming death sentence, Henderson's wife and three children were living in Atlanta and surviving on the good graces of the Defense Committee.[10]

In a letter to Calhoun, Franklin Williams, another of Marshall's subordinate attorneys, indicated that the LDF was leaving the case in the guiding hands the local branch.

"The steps which have been taken by you to date in this matter appear proper and indicate your thorough understanding of NAACP policy and procedures," Williams wrote. "This office has full confidence in Attorney A. T. Walden's decisions in matters of this type."

Translation: You guys take it from here.

Walden was the dean of African American attorneys in Atlanta and served as the LDF's lead attorney for civil rights cases.

Williams mailed the letter in a package that included the Henderson trial transcript and legal filings they had worked for months to get.[11]

On the very day the LDF appeared to be washing its hands of the Henderson case, Clarence and Lizzie Henderson signed a statement revoking the Civil Rights Congress's permission to raise money in Clarence's defense.

The oath, signed in Henderson's scrawled hand (but not the "X" he allegedly used in his jailhouse statements), stated that the NAACP was authorized, "specifically and irrevocably," as his sole legal counsel.[12]

Williams quickly sent a telegram to Atlanta:

RECORD IN CLARENCE HENDERSON MATTER RETURNED YESTERDAY BY ERROR. PLEASE RETURN TO US IMMEDIATELY UPON RECEIPT FOR OUR FILES.[13]

As soon as the records were returned, Marshall dashed off a letter to Calhoun about the case. Calhoun replied, giving a brief update on Robinson and Moore's motion before the Georgia Supreme Court for a new trial.

"The meantime, Judge Samuel Boykin has set June 17 for hearing on the contempt proceedings against Attorney Robinson, Attorney Moore and members of the Henderson Defense Committee," Calhoun reported.

Calhoun shared Marshall's concern over the committee's Communist entanglements and reported that the committee had elected new leaders. In the meantime, Calhoun asked if Marshall might get in contact with Moore to give "your reactions on the case and any suggestions that might help."

In the margin of the letter, Marshall wrote, "Bob will be down on school case." Along with defending Henderson, Robinson and Moore were the lead local attorneys gathering material for a lawsuit against the Atlanta public schools that would strike at the heart of the "separate but equal" doctrine of public school segregation. The suit sought to compare facilities of Black schools with those of white schools. Marshall was keenly interested in the case and had dispatched LDF assistant special counsel Robert L. Carter from New York to meet with them. They could use the time to discuss how to approach the Georgia Supreme Court on Henderson as well, he figured.[14]

"It looks like things are moving along," Marshall wrote regarding the Henderson case in a letter to Calhoun a few days later. Carter would handle strategy in person on his behalf, he said.

After Henderson signed the paper severing his ties with the Civil Rights Congress and Homer Chase, the Atlanta branch of the NAACP wrote a letter to the *Atlanta Daily World* on Lizzie Henderson's behalf to "express her gratitude to the citizens who showered her family with clothing and gifts." The letter stated the NAACP was now in charge of the defense "and trial records have been sent to the NAACP national office in New York." To complete the extraction, the *Daily World* published a piece announcing a meeting of the Women's Auxiliary of the Atlanta NAACP to plan for the care of the Hendersons, "for whom two weeks' rent has already been paid."[15]

Henderson's signed statement accepting the help of the NAACP arrived on Marshall's desk on April 28, 1950, just as Prosecutor Lipford was investigating the Henderson Defense Committee. It also came as lawyers Moore and Robinson were asking the Georgia Supreme Court to overturn Boykin's decision and order a new trial. They submitted their brief to the state's high court in the middle of delivering their client to the NAACP and defending themselves against contempt charges alongside Homer Chase. Moore and Robinson argued their motion on June 13, 1950, a Tuesday. On Saturday, the two men were due back Carrollton to answer contempt charges in Boykin's court.[16]

It was a tense summer in Georgia. Governor Herman Talmadge, having won a special election in 1948, was running for election to a full four-year term. Former governor Melvin E. Thompson was running against him in the primary, and Talmadge, who had basically been running the same campaign nonstop since 1946, promised Georgia would continue as a state where the white man reigned supreme. In a rally in Carrollton, Talmadge promised, "We will never have mixed schools in this state and there will be no mixing of the races in public places."

J. Robert Elliott, a former state representative who would later serve as a federal judge, viciously attacked Thompson as a "friend of [former vice president and Progressive Party candidate] Henry Wallace and Homer Bates Chase."[17]

Lipford took five weeks to complete his expanded, judge-directed contempt probe, doubling the roster of people cited for contempt to ten. Leading the pack were Homer Chase and Jim Kamm, Chase's young associate from the Georgia Progressive Party. The three others were Erwin Daniel, William Porter, and Ruby Edwards, all Black activists from Atlanta, but the effort seemed geared more toward rooting out Chase and the Communists than them. Boykin set a hearing for June 17, 1950, for those newly cited by

Lipford, but the prosecutor told the *Carroll County Georgian* that the charges against Chase were "separate and distinct" from the others.

Chase, Kamm, and the others charged were cited because they had distributed a flyer, "scandalous in tone and spirit," questioning the Henderson verdict and trial. Ironically, the contempt charges only resulted in more attention being called to it. In fact, the *Times–Free Press* reprinted the wordy leaflet in its entirety in its story about Chase. The *Daily Worker* boasted that Boykin was "obviously afraid that acquainting the public with the facts will expose the rottenness of the Henderson trial." Much like the peace bond hearing filed against him in Cartersville, Chase and the Communists were getting more mileage out of their courtroom escapades than anything else.[18]

Townsfolk crowded into the Carroll County Courthouse's massive courtroom for the Saturday morning contempt hearing, eager to hear what the state's top Communist had to say for himself. Chase would not disappoint, but, as in any good drama, his testimony would wait. Instead, Lipford called Kamm, a young man who had only recently been a student at Emory University, to the stand. Kamm's parents, having arrived from Columbus, Georgia, sat in the audience, waiting on their son's testimony.

By the day of the hearing, Lipford had decided against pursuing charges against Ruby Edwards. Daniel and Porter arrived with their defense team, led by A. T. Walden. Also representing the men was Myer Goldberg, the state legislator and attorney from nearby Newnan who had been appointed to represent Tyler North, the first Black man charged with the Stevens murder.

By contrast, Chase and Kamm came to the hearing in rural west Georgia with representation from New York City, assuredly provided by the Communist Party. Their lawyer was Samuel P. Shapiro, a practiced attorney better known for handling civil lawsuits for labor unions in the North than for negotiating the Jim Crow courts of the South. Shapiro immediately objected to the calling of Kamm on grounds that a defendant cannot be called to testify against himself.

Lipford shrugged. The hearing was only "quasi-criminal," he told the judge, and the testimony was not intended to "incriminate the witness." Boykin agreed and Kamm marched to the stand to be sworn in.

Lipford's first question in the quasi-criminal proceeding: "Are you a member of the Henderson Defense Committee?" Kamm said nothing. Shapiro objected, but Boykin commanded him to answer.

When Kamm refused to answer, Boykin acted quickly. He sentenced Kamm to twenty days in jail for contempt and ordered a bailiff to escort him out of the courtroom to jail. Shaken, Kamm's parents left the courtroom, his father in tears. Turning to the other defendants, Boykin said, "I'm going to get to the bottom of all this at all costs, and I want to warn the other defendants of this fact."

The contempt hearing took place amid a national atmosphere of increased government pressure against leftist activists. The House Un-American Activities Committee had become a permanent committee of the U.S. House in 1945 and its hearings were already legendary. In 1947 the committee famously held a group of Hollywood screenwriters in contempt of Congress for refusing to cooperate with HUAC. The so-called Hollywood Ten fought their conviction all the way to the Supreme Court. Just two months prior to the hearing in Carrollton, the justices refused to hear their appeal and the Ten began serving their prison sentences. All of this would have been known to the defendants in the stifling courtroom in Carrollton.

It was hot. Spectators had insisted bailiffs turn off the overhead fans so they could hear the testimony. The temperature that day would rise to the mid-90s.

Following Kamm's abrupt sentencing, Lipford called Porter and Daniel to the stand. Porter said he was on the committee but said he had no knowledge of the leaflet. Daniel, who had been listed as the committee secretary, said he had no idea who had authored the flyer or how they had been distributed. All he knew was the money raised was being used to hire Henderson some lawyers and take care of his family. Had he been he framed? Lipford asked. Daniel said he had no idea.

While Lipford questioned the two Black men, Kamm, likely after conferring with Shapiro, had a change of heart and agreed to testify. Boykin rescinded his sentence. Back in the courtroom, Kamm copped to writing a press release on the Henderson case that had been sent to the *Atlanta Constitution*. By now it was clear the strategy from the earlier contempt hearing was again being used: Black defendants pleaded ignorance; white defendants sermonized.

Kamm said he had not been present at Henderson's one-day trial but maintained any trial in Georgia where a Black man faced an all-white jury was "unjust" by definition. Every American was owed a just trial, he said, and Americans had a right and duty to hold the courts to that standard. As such, the communiqués from the Henderson Defense Committee were performing a service, he said: "The people should know what is going on." Shapiro, perhaps unhelpfully, then read aloud from an *American Bar Association Journal* editorial on free speech, irritating Boykin.

The judge pointed out that "contempt of court, libel and slander constitute abuses of free speech." Furthermore, the courts must have the public's respect and openly claiming a verdict was framed undermines their authority, he said.

"The courts are big enough and strong enough to withstand such charges," Shapiro replied.

"I don't know whether or not the courts and the government are big enough or strong enough to stand such attacks as these," Boykin said.

In his mind, Boykin must have been thinking about more than a few hundred leaflets distributed in Black neighborhoods in Atlanta. There were larger threats afoot—international threats—and a symptom of this existential dilemma was sitting, sweating, in his court that day.

Finally, Homer Bates Chase took the stand, again over the objections of his attorney, who claimed the forced testimony violated his client's constitutional guarantees. Chase was less concerned. He was more than ready to expose the Henderson trial as farce, regardless of how the cards were stacked in that stifling Georgia courtroom. Yes, he said, he wrote one of the bulletins and "distributed several hundred."

Despite Boykin's claim that Chase and Kamm had attended every Henderson hearing, Chase said he, in fact, had not attended the trial. He didn't need to be there to know that the sharecropper hadn't gotten a fair shake.

"There were no Negroes on the jury, the trial was concluded within a day's time and the general situation in Georgia is such that the population is 33½ percent Negro but the conviction rate of Negroes is 58 percent," he said.

With his New England accent filling the Southern courtroom, Chase explained the built-in biases of Georgia courts.

"The lack of Negro judges," he said, glancing at Boykin behind his oaken bench, "and the general situation, including segregation in the courtrooms, does not give justice to Negroes charged with crimes."

Not all of this was the fault of a white judge, Chase allowed. Henderson didn't have adequate defense counsel, he said. "I believe if the defense had put up the kind of case it should have, it would have lasted more than one day," he said.

He continued, now more for the Blacks sitting in the back rows reserved for them. "Murder trials for Negroes are finished quickly," he said, "but those for whites, especially wealthy whites, take more time."

In what the local papers called a "rambling defense" and national wire services called "a court-room eulogy of Communists as champions of the under-privileged," Chase walked through a century of injustices African Americans and other ethnic minorities had endured in white courtrooms, beginning with the Dred Scott decision and continuing through the Scottsboro trials and the use of the Alien and Sedition Act to inter Japanese Americans during World War II.

Boykin was unimpressed. He leveled his eyes at Chase.

"You hide behind the Constitution," he said, "but you are trying to break it down. You plead the Constitution in court but get out and try to break it."

Chase protested. He was among thousands of Communists who fought to preserve the country during World War II, a war America and the Soviet Union had fought as allies.

If he had a real "taste" of Communism in Russia, the judge said, "I'm sure you would be glad to be back in Georgia." Jumping in, Lipford suggested Chase should be grateful he was in a democratic nation. If this hearing had been held in Russia, he would face a firing squad, he said.

"I'm sorry it's not within my power to give you twenty years in prison instead of twenty days," Boykin said. Applause erupted among the locals in the courtroom.

"My advice to you," the judge said, jabbing a finger at Chase, "is to stay out of this section. As long as I am on the bench, I'm going to see that you get punished every time you come around."[19]

As for Kamm, Boykin treated the young man as he would a wayward child.

"Your father and mother were here, broken-hearted," he said. "Your father was dumbfounded and said that he pleaded with you but was unable to do anything for you."

If Kamm would not renounce his beliefs in communism, the judge said it left him little choice.

"They ought to take up a collection and send you to Moscow," Boykin said. "And I would be the first one to contribute $10 to the fund. There is no place in the United States for people of your belief."

With that, the judge passed sentence: twenty days in jail or a fine of $200. The punishment was a parody of the high drama of the daylong hearing. Daniel and Rutledge, no doubt relieved at the prospect of putting Carroll County behind them for the Sweet Auburn district of Atlanta, left with their attorneys after promising to mail their fines to the sheriff.[20]

Boykin had collected the heads he wanted. Consequently, he found Henderson's new defense team of Moore and Robinson not in contempt but advised the Black attorneys to sever their ties with the defense committee. Likewise, he did not find Reverend Johnson in contempt. "Stick to preaching from now on," he told him, "and let the court run such things as the Henderson case." The contempt charges against Porter also were dismissed, but he issued a warning to the Black activists.

"Georgia," Boykin said, "is not ready for this thing of bringing whites and Negroes together."[21]

The case against Wannamaker, the white seminarian whose surprise testimony served as gasoline to Boykin's raging fire, was continued to a later date.

For Chase and Kamm, their opposition to the verdict was a matter of principle. Shapiro declared Boykin's ruling unconstitutional and announced his intention to file an appeal. Boykin obliged and set an appeal bond for the two men at five times the amount of the fine. Both men were led to jail from the courtroom.[22]

"2 Face Jail for Fighting Frameup of Negro," the *Daily Worker* announced. Chase and Kamm had been held for "fighting the legal lynching" of Henderson, the paper decried.[23]

Kamm's father returned to Carrollton after the hearing and attempted to bail his son out of jail, but Sheriff Gaston refused. Boykin had put some unusual bond requirements on the jailed duo. The $1,000 bond had to be made in cash and without the aid of a professional bondsman. A property bond would suffice, but only if the property used was in Carroll County. By Monday, Kamm's bond was arranged but Chase remained in jail, much to the delight of Parkman and the *Georgian*.[24]

"Communist Leader for Georgia Learns How to Live in Carroll County Jail," the *Georgian* wrote in its Thursday edition. Chase had served a quarter of his sentence by then and agreed to sit down with Parkman's reporter Hal David for a jailhouse interview.

David came armed with a series of questions about communism and its designs on the American way of life, but Chase was uncharacteristically uninterested. Chase's face was "an unrevealing mask which hid his inner thoughts and emotions," the *Georgian* reported.

"I have no comment," Chase said. "No hard feelings, of course."

Chase was interested in how the contempt hearing was received locally. "Do they hate us?" he asked.

Chase said he believed he had as much right to question Henderson's verdict as others had to accept it and that he based much of his opinion about its fairness on the *Atlanta Constitution*'s reporting. But the *Georgian* reporter noted Chase took shots at the big city paper's top man.

"He lashed out against Ralph McGill, editor of the *Constitution*, who has been on a crusade against the Communist Party and the Ku Klux Klan," the *Georgian* reported.

"Freedom of the press has reached a low ebb in this country," Chase said.

The experience left David with more questions than answers, including whether locking Chase up was accomplishing anything at all.

"Does this man, Homer B. Chase, represent a menace to our way of life?" David wrote. "Is jailing people for criticizing courts and public officials in leaflets the cure for the Communist ills?"[25]

Back in Atlanta, residents in an apartment building on Capitol Avenue heard the rhythmic clacking of a mimeograph machine through the night as Rachel Chase and her husband's supporters prepared thousands of new leaflets. "Peace Not Jailings," the new bulletin cried.

Two people were jailed and two others were given heavy fines for fighting for a new trial for Clarence Henderson, Negro sharecropper of Carroll County. These people and many others believe that Henderson was not given a fair trial and stated their beliefs in a leaflet.

The new flyer cast Chase's plight large, connecting Boykin's twenty-day sentence to the "cold war policy" of President Harry Truman and former Ohio governor James M. Cox, who owned the *Constitution* and supported "the atom-bomb policies of Truman."

"The court is taking its cue from the Truman Administration and Truman is following Hitler's path," the flyer warned. The government was persecuting Chase, just as it had Eugene Dennis, the general secretary of the Communist Party of the United States of America, and the Hollywood Ten. It was the time to act.

"Unless you are a big landowner or Wall Street banker or one of their Klan stooges, you have a stake in freeing those in Carrollton," the flyer added, concluding with a plea to write to Judge Boykin and contribute money to the Communist Party via a P.O. box.[26]

The flyer had an immediate effect. An Atlanta man and a woman landowner in Carrollton worked together to post Chase's bond nine days into his sentence. Questioned by the press, a local Carrollton attorney who helped arrange the bond quoted the Georgia oath of office required of attorneys: "I will never reject, from any consideration personal to myself, the cause of the defenseless or oppressed."

The noontime release was well attended. Chase emerged from the jail looking gaunt but well in a jacket and tie. Boykin, Lipton, and Sheriff Gaston had done their best, but their prize catch was about to walk free. "I guess that's it," the sheriff said, once Chase had signed the bond. Chase nodded. "OK," he said.[27]

Both Chase and Kamm were free on bond, but technically they still faced charges in Boykin's court. Within a few days, Boykin granted the duo their request to have a new hearing on July 15. Of course, their rehearing would be in front of the same judge, but it was a required step before they could argue their case up to an appellate court.[28]

A day before the hearing, McGill hammered Chase again in his daily column, calling him an ineffectual lapdog for Moscow. It was a clear attempt to rattle him.

"He is an intense, but bumbling fellow, who seemingly enjoys and fancies himself in a sort of cloak-and-dagger existence," McGill said.

Just a month earlier, McGill had moved his column from the editorial page to the front page, giving it even greater exposure. McGill quoted from Chase's New Hampshire birth certificate and once again wrote about his father's death and Communist gravestone. The column even cast Chase's military record in a suspicious light without actually presenting evidence.

"It has been determined there were Communists in the Army with certain orders to follow if the opportunity came and all are believed to have been active or passive agents of the Kremlin," McGill wrote.[29]

The depth of McGill's research suggests someone was feeding him information. McGill's papers are housed in the archives at Emory University in Atlanta and are filled with items from the FBI, including correspondence and background information on Communists labeled as on loan from the Bureau. McGill would occasionally pass along information on suspected Communists to FBI agents in Atlanta.

"I am sending you this to pass on to whoever keeps a list of Commie suspects," McGill wrote to the FBI agent in charge of the Atlanta office. He enclosed a letter from a reader insulting one of his columns. "This guy is a new one to me."[30]

There is no record of a response.

McGill's passion for rooting out Communists in his Southern sphere knew no limits. On the day it ran, he forwarded his column along to Westbrook Pegler, a nationally syndicated conservative columnist. Pegler was a vocal critic of the New Deal, FDR, and Truman, all revered by McGill. But he also ran a successful smear campaign attacking the Wallace presidential bid, an act McGill must have admired.

McGill wrote, "I have uncovered the background of the southern Communists' front man, and I enclose column of this morning for your files if you are keeping any on the southern Communist front persons."[31]

The Atlanta editor doubled down with another column the following day, delivered across the state the same morning that Chase and Kamm presented their appeal in Boykin's court. In this column, McGill warned of the American inclination to "walk on eggs where traitors are concerned."

"We are confronted with the fact that the Communists of this, or any other country, are loyal first of all to Soviet Russia. They would sell out this country without a qualm," he wrote. "They are eager to be traitors in the sense they would destroy this government and assist the Soviet Union in conquering it should the issue arise."

McGill warned that should war break out between America and a Communist country, American Communists could not be allowed to "roam at large, sabotage and treason being their objectives."[32]

Homer Chase's next visit to Judge Boykin's court had a new, international context. On June 25, thousands of Communist soldiers streamed across the border separating North and South Korea. The Korean War had begun. Seoul fell to the North Korean People's Army the day after Chase made bond and President Harry Truman announced the United States would conduct "police action" in support of the United States' allies in South Korea.

The war would bring added pressure on American Communists like Chase.

CHAPTER 11

A NEW TRIAL ORDERED

"New Trial for Henderson," screamed the headline in the *Times–Free Press* the morning of July 13, 1950. The type in the headline was as large as the newspaper's nameplate. "Suffering Renewed in Stevens Case," the *Georgian* responded.

The Georgia Supreme Court's order for a new trial came a month after Henderson's defense team of Robinson and Moore had argued his case. The opinion was written by Associate Justice Bond Almand, a thin, bald, bespectacled jurist and a recent addition to the court, appointed by Governor Herman Talmadge.

Robinson and Moore had challenged the verdict from three directions. First, they complained that Judge Boykin had failed to instruct the jury to consider Henderson's alibi—that he was home asleep at the time of the murder—when determining his guilt. They also claimed Boykin had violated Henderson's Fourteenth Amendment rights to a public trial when he cleared the courtroom for Nan Turner's testimony. The court rejected both of those claims. Henderson's court-appointed white attorneys had signed off on allowing Turner to testify in relative privacy. The justices agreed that Henderson—an illiterate sharecropper—did not object in the moment, so they tossed out that objection. Likewise, since Henderson's defense team did not explicitly offer an alibi defense—or any defense at all—the justices did not fault Boykin for his jury instructions.

However, the justices were more impressed by the claim by Moore and Robinson that the jury's verdict was based entirely on circumstantial evidence without excluding other, reasonable theories.

The only eyewitness to the crime was Nan Turner, Almand wrote, and she "made no attempt" to say Henderson was the man she saw in brief glimpses that dark night fifteen months prior to the trial. "Nor is there any evidence that the defendant was seen in the vicinity of the killing either immediately before or after the killing," the justice wrote. "There was a total lack of evidence as to the whether other men were or were not in the immediate vicinity at the time of the killing." And while ballistics expert George Cornett testified that the murder bullet came from the .38 Special revolver that police had tied to Henderson, Almand said there remained the possibility that Cornett, despite his personal confidence, was wrong.

In a troublesome conclusion for Lipford, Almand wrote that the prosecution had not excluded "every other reasonable hypothesis" for the crime and remanded the case back to Boykin's court for retrial. The verdict from the all-white supreme court was unanimous.[1]

Both the *Times–Free Press* and the *Atlanta Constitution* reported the news, each prominently linking the case with the Communist Party.

"Following Henderson's conviction, pamphlets viciously denouncing the Superior Court procedure and the conviction were circulated in Carrollton as the Communists launched a defense project for Henderson," the *Constitution* reported in an un-bylined story.

Beyond that, the papers reported the opinion in a straightforward manner.[2]

The *Georgian* wrung its hands at the "regrettable" verdict and worried about "old heart wounds" that would be reopened in the white community as they once again confronted "one of our more terrible tragedies." In an editorial, the *Georgian* acknowledged doubt that Henderson was guilty "has been uppermost in the minds of our local people since the trial." But at the same time, the newspaper rued the high court's decision to overturn a solid if circumstantial case.

"We certainly do not put ourselves in the position of questioning the judgment of the court," the *Georgian* opined (although Parkman certainly was), "but we wonder how it will be possible to build a stronger case of circumstantial evidence than the one presented against Henderson."

The *Georgian* concluded with hopes of a speedy retrial, "because our people have been made to suffer too long already with the uncertainty of this brutal crime."[3]

The reversal took on a different hue outside of Georgia. From New York, the *Daily Worker* trumpeted the decision with the headline "Framed Negro Wins New Trial" and tied the decision to "the role of the mass campaign" for Henderson's defense and the contempt charges brought against Homer Chase, Jim Kamm, and others in Judge Boykin's court. Despite having receded from the defense committee, the *Worker* framed the victory as a cooperative effort between the Civil Rights Congress and the NAACP. "Actually a broad defense committee undertook to save Henderson's life," the paper reported. "The committee retained two Negro attorneys of Atlanta, E. E. Moore Jr. and S. S. Robinson. Later the NAACP retained the two lawyers."[4]

The nation's Black press framed the case in ways its audience understood. On its front page, the *Chicago Defender* reported the Georgia high court "reversed a decision of Carroll County Superior Court where Henderson's trial was held in an atmosphere of tension, hostility, and mob terror."[5]

Overturning the verdict of a Black man accused in the death of a white man was a tremendously encouraging victory for the NAACP's Atlanta branch. But it was also an added financial responsibility. The Atlanta branch was busy raising money through a series of carnivals and festivals to fund its upcoming budget, which included hosting the 1951 NAACP national convention. Having ousted the Civil Rights Congress, the branch had assumed the chore of raising money for Henderson's defense. "This favorable decision, we consider, is an outstanding decision for the Atlanta branch and for Georgia," wrote John Calhoun, executive secretary of the Atlanta branch, in a letter to the home office in New York. "We found it urgently necessary to capitalize upon publicity that the announcement of this decision carried."

In his letter, Calhoun asked permission, obviously after the fact, to raise money specifically for the defense of Henderson "and other similar cases." Calhoun's letter and the victory scored by Robinson and Moore impressed New York. The NAACP executive in charge of managing contact with local branches wrote Thurgood Marshall a memo describing the Henderson defense as a "worthwhile case, and for that reason it seems that we should do everything we can to help."[6]

Within days the Atlanta NAACP moved to create a new "Freedom Committee" to raise money for the defense team. Branch president Charles Lincoln Harper said the new committee would coordinate with the legal redress committee, of which Moore and Robinson were members. "Congratulations to the NAACP and to its lawyers in this case are in order," the

Atlanta Daily World wrote in an editorial, "but it is going to take cold, cash money to defend Henderson and place him on the ground again so that he can return to his wife and his large family of dependent children."[7]

Without donations from within Atlanta's Black community, Henderson would be in desperate trouble. Leaders in the Atlanta branch of the NAACP knew they could not look to the national office for much in the way of financial help. Money was so tight in Marshall's small office that he could not afford to replace a lawyer, and two secretarial positions were cut. The NAACP executive committee voted to sell $10,000 in bonds to keep the office afloat. At the same time, the NAACP's legal team was coordinating criminal defenses in Florida, housing discrimination cases in Detroit and New York, and school desegregation actions across nine states, including North Carolina, Louisiana, and Virginia.[8]

On Sunday, July 23, 1950, members of the executive committee of the Atlanta NAACP planned to speak in forty Black churches, hitting morning and evening services with their fundraising appeal. The *Atlanta Daily World* urged pastors to pave the way by making personal donations, which the newspaper said would be published in their pages.[9]

The appeal worked, after a fashion. Ministers personally donated $357 to the cause. Many of the pastors of the forty Black churches asked for more time to prepare their congregations for a money plea from the NAACP, so the organization's leaders hit less than half their target. Much more money was needed. The NAACP had set a $2,500 budget for the retrial.

The largest contribution came from the pastor of Ebenezer Baptist Church, the Reverend Martin Luther King Sr., who donated $60 to the defense fund.

"That's where our ministers belong," the *Daily World* wrote, "right out there in front with their people. That's what makes a minister influential and strong, not only with his own congregation, but with the community of which he is a part. . . . Let the other ministers and churches look at this Henderson case as their major Christian obligation. It is going to require many thousands of dollars and we have no other place to get the money except from the people of Atlanta."[10]

For Henderson's attorneys, the supreme court verdict was a victory, but a temporary one. Their client would be retried in the same courtroom where he had been tried and convicted in a single day and where they had recently faced contempt charges. But they were prepared to do something Henderson's white lawyers never contemplated: They were going to defend him. Moore and Robinson went to work immediately, hitting the case at one of its many weak spots: ballistics.

Moore knew he would need to disrupt the state's contention that the 9mm slug that killed Buddy Stevens had left the .38 Special they said Henderson had once owned. To do that, they would need a rival ballistics expert, but in Atlanta there were exactly none of those. Less than forty-eight hours after the supreme court ordered a new trial, Moore wrote to New York asking Thurgood Marshall for help finding an expert who would come to Georgia to testify.

"We would appreciate an early reply," he concluded, knowing the Boykin and Lipford would push for an early retrial date. In fact, within a few days, Boykin announced that Henderson would be tried again in just three weeks. Robinson and Moore objected and asked Boykin to delay the retrial until the court's regular October term. Boykin denied the request, saying he wouldn't let the Henderson trial "clutter-up" his court calendar.[11]

Marshall tasked another of his lieutenants, Frank D. Reeves, to help find an expert witness. Reeves was a key member of the NAACP legal squad constructing the civil cases challenging segregation, especially the landmark *Brown v. Board of Education* case. Finding a ballistics expert for a criminal trial in Georgia was not at the top of his list. When no word came from New York, Moore asked John Calhoun, head of the Atlanta NAACP chapter, to check on it. Calhoun called and spoke to Jack Greenberg.[12]

"Can we get the FBI to testify?" Calhoun asked. "The trial is in two weeks!"

Marshall was traveling and didn't get Greenberg's memo until the following week. Writing notes in the margin, Marshall was perplexed. He thought Reeves had handled it already. Regardless, the FBI was not going to stick its neck out to defend a Black tenant farmer accused of murdering a white boy in the Deep South, he thought. Time was short. Marshall shot a memo back to Greenberg. "Can you find a ballistics expert for these people?" he asked. Greenberg started calling. With a pencil, he scribbled down names and addresses in the margins of Marshall's note.[13]

While New York scrambled to line up an expert witness, Robinson and Moore worked to assemble a defense strategy. With nine days to go, Robinson drove to Carrollton with R. E. Thomas, another Black lawyer with whom he shared an office, to take a look at the jury pool for Henderson's next trial. No Black man—much less a Black lawyer from Atlanta—could enter the Carroll County Courthouse unnoticed. As Robinson left the superior court clerk's office, he saw Lipford, his face florid, his gait purposeful. Robinson tensed up; Thomas took up a position behind his friend.

"You are a smart son of a bitch," Lipford yelled, his voice echoing loudly through the marbled hall. "You are so goddamn smart! You have been talking to my goddamn nigger witnesses!"

Defense attorneys have a right to depose prosecution witnesses, and doing so makes good sense, especially when the state's case relies so heavily on knitting together multiple sources, each of whom can testify only to a part of the whole. But for Henderson's attorneys there simply had not been time. Robinson told Lipford he had not spoken to any of his witnesses. Lipford balled his fists, shaking them angrily at the two Black lawyers.

"If you speak to any of my witnesses, I will kill you, you son of a bitch. I'll cut your goddamn throat."

"I'm not going to argue with you, Mr. Lipford," Robinson said. He turned and went back inside the clerk's office, where there were more people. The women in the office turned their heads and some rose as the Black men came back inside, Lipford on their heels.

"You listen to me," he said. "I will kill you if you talk to those witnesses. Do you hear me?" Lipford said.

"I hear you," Robinson said, sounding more calm than he felt. He was far from Auburn Avenue and there was a lot of lonely road between Carrollton and his office. Satisfied, Lipford left the clerk's office. Robinson and Thomas looked gravely at each other as the office workers returned to their desks.

Robinson returned to Carrollton two days later to continue his work and brought Calhoun along as a witness. This time Lipford was out of his office and intercepted the men on the steps of courthouse. He was not as angry, but the threats had been made and the clerks had heard him. No one was interested in helping the Negro from Atlanta prepare his defense of the man accused of killing Buddy Stevens.[14]

Robinson and Calhoun returned to Atlanta and met with Moore and NAACP leadership. Not only were they being hampered in their attempt to defend their client, but Lipford had made it clear they were in danger just being there. Calhoun dashed off a telegram to Marshall, who he knew had experience with angry white politicians in the South and dealing with their threats.

KINDLY ADVISE AS TO JURISDICTION OF FBI AS TO PROTECTION FROM VIOLENCE BY A STATE OFFICER STOP IF AT ALL POSSIBLE WE WOULD LIKE THEIR INTERVENTION STOP

Calhoun closed with a reminder that they still were seeking a ballistics expert.[15]

While he waited on advice from Marshall, Calhoun started calling state officials and lodging complaints. He started with the office of Governor Herman Talmadge, a staunch segregationist and race baiter. The governor's officer referred him to the office of Attorney General Eugene Cook, another hardline segregationist, who in turn referred him to Carroll County sheriff Denver Gaston. Calhoun had little confidence in any of these white politicians, but he had put them all on notice.

In a letter to Gaston, Calhoun pointed out the lengths to which the NAACP had gone to purge Henderson's defense of "all of those influences which tended to upset the citizens of Carroll County" and stressed that the organization's only interest was to see that justice was done.

"If he is guilty, we feel that he should be punished, if not, then he should be freed," Calhoun wrote. "We feel certain that you, as an officer of the law, have the same interest."

Lipford might harbor grievances over the circulation of the "framed" flyer, Calhoun continued, "but you will probably agree that a personal difference between a state officer and an attorney should not be allowed to interfere with the administration of justice. Furthermore, that legal authorities should do everything in their power to protect the citizens, as well as the good name of the state of Georgia."[16]

Marshall advised Calhoun and Robinson to take their complaint to federal authorities, doubtless knowing that the Talmadge machine would have little sympathy. Robinson wrote out his account of the encounter, sending a notarized copy to J. Ellis Mundy, the federal prosecutor for the northern district of Georgia. There was at least some reason to hope the Georgia-born Mundy would take the matter seriously. Earlier in the year, Mundy had successfully prosecuted a North Georgia sheriff for his role in the beating of seven Black residents by a mob of Klansmen. That Mundy pursued the case even after an earlier jury had deadlocked, causing a mistrial, was another mark in his favor.[17]

"I make this affidavit so that those interested may know . . . that the incident has created a very grave and serious interference with the progress of my work as a lawyer," Robinson wrote. "Although my associate, Mr. Moore, was not in Carrollton at said times, the effect of the threat caused him to announce his readiness to withdraw from the case, if further participation therein meant his going to Carrollton. Although I continued my work, it was under the constant fear of serious violence to my life."

Robinson asked Mundy to investigate the threats "and, upon proper finding, prosecute the Solicitor General, Wright Lipford, for his offense as related."[18]

How seriously Mundy took the complaint is not known, but he replied almost immediately, saying the charges would "be given attention by the property authorities." Robinson had not gotten much in the way of direction from Thurgood Marshall, so he went over his head with a letter to NAACP executive secretary Walter White, asking that White use "the influence and power of your office" to urge the U.S. attorney general to investigate the threats. Eventually it was Marshall—who had been on vacation—who replied, saying he had made the request to Washington himself. In fact, Marshall had written the head of the Justice Department's criminal division asking for help, enclosing a copy of Robinson's affidavit.

"If lawyers representing Negro clients in the Deep South are to be intimidated by local state officers, we will certainly have serious difficulties," Marshall wrote. "Unless full affirmative action is taken by the Department, there is no doubt in my mind that the Talmadge forces of reaction in Georgia, supported by the Ku Klux Klan, will extend their violent practices into the courtrooms themselves."[19]

The week of the new trial, Lipford announced, without explanation, that it had been postponed. No reason and no new date was given.[20]

* * *

Lipford's racist threats and the NAACP's pleas for justice were playing out amid heightened concerns in Georgia and Washington, DC, over subversive activities. In the Georgia General Assembly, lawmakers were crafting legislation to outlaw the Communist Party in the state.

"We shall, of course, stay within the bounds of the state and federal constitution," said one state representative involved in the effort, "but I feel that a special measure of this kind is needed to smoke out the Red influence we can see around us."

Governor Talmadge threw his weight behind the effort, as did state attorney general Eugene Cook, who argued such a ban would withstand a constitutional challenge. On Capitol Hill, Georgia congressman Edward Eugene Cox filed federal legislation making membership in the Communist Party a crime.

"The Georgia congressman pointed out that, in view of the present world crisis, it was not in the national interest to have sworn enemies of the Constitution at large in the United States where they could do irreparable damage to the defense effort," the *Constitution* reported.[21]

Red fever was not limited to the halls of government. The American Legion was planning seminars at the University of Georgia "to expose Communist conspiracies and methods of actual and psychological sabotage." And that July, Atlanta police received an emergency call from a police callbox in the center of downtown.

"Send the police, quick!" the man on the line shouted.

"Do you need help?" the dispatcher asked.

"Two of them!" the man replied.

A dozen patrol cars responded to find forty-year-old Thomas Brock, exhausted but holding on to the belt of a younger man.

"He's a Communist!" Brock cried. "He told me he was a Communist and I'm locking him up."

Police learned that Brock had seized the man and dragged him three blocks to the nearest callbox. The alleged Communist was freed, but police arrested Brock for being drunk and impersonating a police officer.[22]

Brock should have waited a few weeks. In August, the Atlanta City Council got into the act as well, drafting an ordinance banning Communists from the city. The ordinance was patterned after a similar one recently passed by the council in Birmingham, Alabama, that gave Communists forty-eight hours to leave town or face criminal charges for each day they remained. As the Atlanta council members debated the measure, Homer Chase, still out on bond from the Carrollton jail, sat in the audience.[23]

A week later the situation got materially worse for Chase. The eleven remaining top officials of the Communist Party of the United States of America, all of whom were on bond pending an appeal of their conviction the prior year under the Smith Act, were ordered to appear in a federal courtroom in New York to defend against Justice Department allegations that they represented a danger to national security amid the crisis on the Korean Peninsula. The very next day Wright Lipford aped federal prosecutors by filing a nearly identical petition in Boykin's court asking the same to be done.

"The United States is today engaged in actual warfare against the Communist aggressors," Lipford reasoned. "Chase, individually and as chairman of the Communist Party of Georgia and a Communist, is a menace to society and a danger to the security of the United States."

Boykin quickly ordered Chase and Jim Kamm to return to Carrollton to determine whether to revoke their bonds for reasons of national security. It would be a Saturday matinee on a steamy August morning.[24]

Chase had been heavily surveilled by the FBI over his five years in Atlanta, but the local field office was interested in what more it could learn. In early August 1950, the special agent in charge of the FBI's Atlanta office asked permission to tap the phone line in Chase's home, which also served as the headquarters for the state party.

"It is believed this surveillance will develop considerable information regarding Communist Party members and current policies," the field office wrote in an August 10, 1950, memo. FBI director J. Edgar Hoover signed off on the request and asked Attorney General J. Howard McGrath for permission to proceed. The installation was relatively simple, but the paperwork took weeks to process.[25]

Chase drove to Carrollton a few days before his scheduled hearing in Boykin's court to get some papers regarding his property bond. That morning Americans awoke to read news of a major military offensive underway against Communist forces in Korea. The atmosphere of heightened tensions may explain why a local reservist approached Chase as he attempted to put a nickel in the parking meter in front of the courthouse.

"Hey," the reservist said. "What's your name?"

No sooner had he replied than blows started raining down on the startled Chase. A trained paratrooper and veteran of two wars, Chase could defend himself. Blocking the younger man's punches, Chase swung and landed a cross-hand punch across his attacker's chin, stunning him long enough for Chase to turn and run east along Newnan Street, turning alongside the courthouse on Dixie Street and toward the sheriff's office in back. Chase arrived at the sheriff's office out of breath, his young attacker rubbing his chin on the sidewalk.

Inside, Sheriff Denver Gaston was unimpressed with Chase's requests for protection. How indeed did the young reservist even know Chase was in town? Flustered, Chase emerged from the office and began walking to his car, searching his pockets for his keys. As he turned back on Newnan Street, he found his path blocked by two men his own age, veterans of World War II and members of the local American Legion. Immediately he was set upon. Kicking and punching, Chase held his own, but he was outnumbered. A small crowd gathered and watched from a distance as the two local men punched and scratched at the lanky Chase, who pushed and fought his way toward his car. Bruised and bleeding, Chase reached for the driver's-side door and, finding it unlocked, pulled himself inside. The two veterans pounded on the glass and the roof of the car as Chase again searched for the keys. The car rocked as several other Carrollton men joined in harassing and jeering at the Yankee Red within. "String him up," yelled several in what did not seem an idle threat. Finally, Chase located his keys and the car lurched forward and roared away.[26]

The "Battle of Newnan Street" led the afternoon edition of the *Times–Free Press*. "Communist Chase Beaten Here and Flees Bleeding," the newspaper crowed in a story that decidedly placed the blame on Chase.

"A prominent businessman, [who] witnessed the whole affair, stated that at no time was Chase mobbed and that the Communist had several opportunities to drive off following his return to the car," the *Times–Free Press* explained.[27]

In a back-patting editorial, the *Times–Free Press* hailed the "pushing, shoving, slugging and tongue-lashing" as a fitting demonstration that "Carrollton is not a welcome spot for Communists."

"They want to overthrow the present form of government, but yell loudly about infringement of rights and privileges when a door is slammed on their unwelcome foot," the newspaper opined.[28]

News of the scuffle was carried the following day on the front page of the *Atlanta Constitution* and by wire reports in newspapers around the nation, including in the *New York Times*. NBC radio commentator H. V. Kaltenborn took the row before a national radio audience. Ever conscious of his image, Chase denied being bested by his attackers and blamed local authorities for failing to render aid.

"I deny I cursed anybody or that I was badly beaten," he said. "I received only some scratches."

The attack on Chase only heightened the fear of violence around the Henderson case. Calhoun again wrote to Marshall's office urging them to press the federal government for help.

"What attorneys Robinson and Moore are most interested in at present is that the Department of Justice be alerted to the situation which exists in Carrollton," he wrote.

Calhoun included with the letter newspaper clippings describing Chase's misadventure at the courthouse.

"Whereas we are not concerned about Mr. Chase nor his activities, we do feel that the atmosphere created by his group is not conducive to the best relations in the community," Calhoun concluded.[29]

The attack on Chase occurred less than a week after Georgia congressman Henderson Lovelace Lanham lunged across a congressional committee room in an attempt to beat William L. Patterson, a Black Communist and activist with the Civil Rights Congress, when Patterson challenged him on Georgia's record on lynching. The violence in Washington and Carrollton disturbed McGill, ever worried that progressive forces were being harmed from either side. The fisticuffs "played right into the hands of Communist Chase and his followers," McGill warned from the *Constitution*'s editorial column. "The history of the Communist movement is a long one of similar provocations."[30]

Chase saw things differently. It was he who was being provoked. If he returned to Carrollton, there was no guarantee a mob wouldn't be waiting for him or his associate, Jim Kamm. While Gaston denied setting up the beating, the sheriff told the United Press International reporter looking into the incident that "it's damn little protection he'll get down here."

"We've got about 60 boys leaving here in September for active duty with the National Guard. They don't feel so good about it," he said. "I don't know how you feel about it, but we think about him the same way we do about North Koreans."[31]

In an editorial, *Georgian* editor Stanley Parkman suggested that perhaps constitutional protections did not apply to people like Chase.

"It has seemed a little on the ridiculous side all along for us to continue spending time and money in the courts, extending the long arm of freedom to characters like Chase," Parkman wrote. "Our Constitution never intended that liberty should go so far. . . . Frankly, we believe one of the reasons so many of the world's people hold contempt for the United States is because of our willy-nilly, tolerant ways of dealing with our enemies."[32]

The *Georgian* also printed a letter from a woman in nearby Rome, Georgia, congratulating the men who pummeled Chase on the street and the sheriff who offered him no protection. She had sent two of her sons to fight in World War II and was sending a third to Korea "to fight against those filthy murderous Communists."

"Why don't the mothers and sons join together and demand our government to clean out our country and make it a decent place to live in?" she wrote.[33]

As Homer Chase faced the prospect of a return to Carrollton, he had to admit that things had taken a grim turn. Even if he made it into the courthouse unharmed, Lipford and Boykin waited within to revoke his bond and return him to jail as a threat to national security. Given the atmosphere, he might very well be jailed for the duration of the Korean conflict.

In less than five years Chase had been jailed twice, turned on by a grocery clerk he tried to recruit, threatened and harassed endlessly by newspaper editors, and now beaten in the streets by a mob while police washed their hands of him. Chase made a decision many would make during the Red Scare: he would go underground and wait for things to cool off. In the predawn hours Saturday morning, Chase, Rachel, and his friend Jim Kamm pointed Chase's car north and left town.

A few hours later, Carrolltonians filled every seat in the cavernous courtroom as Judge Boykin called the case.

"Is Homer B. Chase in the courtroom?" the judge asked. He repeated the question for Jim Kamm. Then he asked again. Heads swiveled as people in the crowd whispered among themselves. Some were in uniform. Veterans of the most recently completed world war clasped their American Legion or Veterans of Foreign Wars caps in their fists.

When it was clear neither man was present, Boykin ordered Gaston to hunt them down. But, he said, bring them back to Carrollton unharmed "regardless of your personal feelings."

"It is the court's duty to see that Chase and Kamm are protected until they are brought to trial," Boykin said as the disappointed crowd filed out.

Within minutes, Gaston and Lipford met in the prosecutor's office to fill out the arrest warrants, stopping only briefly to pose for press photos. Lipford applied a transitive principle to justify hunting down Chase and Kamm on a charge that he had earlier described in court as "quasi-criminal."

"Chase and Kamm are members of the Communist Party of Georgia and we are at war with Communists in Korea," he said. "These men should not be allowed to go free."

Gaston personally drove to Atlanta to check out Chase's Atlanta home and the boardinghouse where Kamm lived. At Chase's home, just a few blocks south of the Georgia State Capitol, Gaston found the shades drawn, the doors locked, and the car gone. Accompanied by his chief deputy and an Atlanta police officer keen on hunting Communists, Gaston checked out "known Communist hangouts" in the area but struck out there as well. An informant told the police Chase and Kamm had left the state, headed for New York.

Chase owed eleven days on a twenty-day sentence for a very dubious contempt charge, yet he was now a fugitive in Georgia.[34] He landed in New York City, taking a job driving a fur truck and cleaning railroad cars. Within a year he would be back in New Hampshire, where he returned to Communist Party politics and a position within the Teamsters Union.[35]

CHAPTER 11 — A NEW TRIAL ORDERED

Things cooled down in Carrollton following the alarm raised by the NAACP to Lipford's threats and the departure of Chase and Kamm. The Henderson retrial Boykin had hoped to hold in early August was pushed into the court's regular October term. It had been two transformative years since Buddy Stevens was gunned down.

CHAPTER 12

DAN DUKE

The *Carroll County Georgian* broke the news of Henderson's retrial during the October court term, not that there was any doubt it was coming. In *Georgian* style, the newspaper was carrying water for local officials eager to show they were not cowed by the NAACP, the Communists, or, for that matter, the Georgia Supreme Court.

"This newspaper has been informed by a high official that the court is anxious to dispose of the case at the October term," the *Georgian* reported in a short front-page story that ran without any quotes or named sources.[1]

Despite his fears the Henderson case would clutter his fall term, Boykin had set the trial to begin on Tuesday, October 10, 1950, at 9:00 A.M. That morning Pete Greenlea, the reporter from the *Atlanta World*, slipped into a back bench with his African American brethren and turned his notebook to a fresh page. Closer up, white reporters for the *Georgian,* the *Times–Free Press*, the *Constitution*, and its competition, the *Atlanta Journal*—as well as Associated Press and UPI wire service reporters—took their spots.

Those unlucky enough not to arrive early lined the courthouse hallway, craning their necks to look inside. Despite intense interest, the state toned down its security presence. This trial lacked the ornament of armed state troopers flanking the courtroom walls.[2]

But, if anything, Boykin was even more vigilant. The Homer Chase affair had both rattled and enflamed him. A week before the trial, Boykin had shared his concerns with a newly seated grand jury.

"At this critical period in our history, subversive elements are trying to bring chaos," he said. "We are on the brink of another war to keep from losing everything."

No one in Carroll County needed to hear more, but Boykin carried on, explaining the peril they all shared. Times were changing in Carrollton and beyond, he said, and they were not at all for the better.

"We are moving too fast, our requirements are too great, and our desires are beyond expectations," he said. The judge spoke directly to three local ministers who were among the white men empaneled, congratulating them on their decision to serve even though they could have been excused under state law. Boykin said the county was "spiritually starved" and in need of God's blessing.

The grand jury, which would pass bills of indictments on crimes other than the Stevens murder, named as its foreman Stanley Parkman of the *Georgian*.[3]

While the first trial largely had been a local affair, this retrial had attracted considerable attention, especially within the Black community. And for good reason: A Black man sentenced to death for killing a white man had temporarily escaped both the lynch mob and Georgia's electric chair. No less than the Supreme Court of Georgia had sided with Henderson's Black attorneys over white authority. The NAACP had wrested control from the Communist Party, which had been driven from the case in dramatic fashion. And Clarence and Lizzie Henderson and their three small children, a dirt-poor family from rural western Georgia, had become a cause célèbre of Atlanta's burgeoning civil rights movement.

As the retrial neared, Henderson's defense lawyers, Moore and Robinson, had a lot on their plates. Over the summer, the pair had worked with two of their colleagues to challenge Georgia's Jim Crow system of racially segregated education with an NAACP-led lawsuit attacking the unequal nature of Atlanta's schools facilities. A separate suit was working its way through the federal appellate courts, challenging unequal pay for Black and white teachers in Atlanta.

Cost and manpower were a problem for the NAACP at both the local and national levels as they pursued these cases. In a letter to the Atlanta NAACP president, Thurgood Marshall warned of the significant costs the facilities case would incur.[4]

There were other hurdles facing Henderson's legal team. Just four months earlier, Robinson and Moore had been accused by the prosecutor and trial judge of contempt of court. Although they had escaped punishment, they had been lumped in with Communists and their sympathizers from the moment they came to Boykin's attention. Moreover, Lipford had threatened to kill Robinson if he even tried to interview the state's witnesses.

"All rise!" the bailiff commanded. The capacity crowd of several hundred spectators quieted and shuffled to their feet as Boykin entered from a door to the left and took his seat.

"Are you ready for trial, Mr. Lipford?" the judge asked.

"The state is ready," Lipford responded. Flanking the prosecutor was Shirley Boykin. The judge's brother had returned for the retrial to assist again in the prosecution.

Turning to the defense, Judge Boykin saw a new face at the defense table, a white lawyer well known in the legal community and in state politics: Dan Duke.[5]

Lawrence Daniel Duke was just thirty-seven, but he had already made a name for himself as a brash, swaggering lawyer and a progressive Democrat who fought extremists from the left and right with equal relish. With sharp features, slicked-back hair, and penetrating eyes that peered from behind round spectacles, Duke looked and acted the part of a pugnacious Southern lawyer. But his deep, sonorous voice had the syrupy quality of the planter class and none of the nasal twang his red-clay background might suggest.

Duke was born southwest of Atlanta in Palmetto, Georgia, in 1914, the son of a failing cotton farmer father and a librarian mother who implanted in him a love of books and learning. After high school, Duke worked his way through Oglethorpe University, a private school on Atlanta's north side. After graduation, he taught school for a few years before enrolling in law school at night, taking and passing the bar exam before completing his courses. In short order he was working as an assistant solicitor for Fulton County with an office in the county courthouse in downtown Atlanta. He was the youngest man in the prosecutor's office, but he had a chin-forward way of approaching life.[6]

Early in his career, Duke set himself against the segregationist and white supremacist Talmadge machine. In 1938 he campaigned for Lawrence S. Camp, the U.S. attorney in Atlanta, in his primary run to unseat Senator Walter F. George. Former governor Eugene Talmadge was running as well, and President Franklin Roosevelt, who was searching for a more reliable supporter of the New Deal, had thrown his weight behind Camp over the incumbent.

George held on to the seat, but Duke developed powerful friends—and enemies—among the state's various Democratic factions.

In 1940, Duke took on an investigation that came to define his political and legal life. For some time, poor white men from south of Atlanta had been victimized by beatings at the hands of the Ku Klux Klan. The beatings, delivered with a long, barbed leather strap, were being handed out by a klavern in East Point, a working-class white suburb just south of Atlanta.

Such violence against Blacks was commonplace, but those victims were unlikely to seek help from the Fulton County Solicitor's Office, as the solicitor at the time was rumored to be a Klansman himself. White prosecutors would have had a hard time getting juries to convict a white man for beating a Black man. But white victims were another story, and their complaints provided enough for Duke to build a case.[7]

The klavern in East Point, like many such groups, viewed itself as a kind of vigilante police force, there to keep both racial order and to enforce a moral doctrine. If a white man drank and beat his wife, the Klan might throw him in the trunk of a car, drive him out to a secluded spot, and beat him nearly to death to illuminate a better path. This particular klavern was further emboldened to take the law into its hands because membership included a number of sheriff's deputies. But the Klan's program of moralistic beatings was a smoke screen for the settling of personal grudges.

One such case was that of a steel mill worker named Tony who disagreed with a man named Guffin over whether the church they both attended should move to a new building. Tony said yes; Guffin, a Klansman, said no. To settle his grievance, Guffin told his fellow Klansmen that Tony was a Communist and was trying to organize a union in the mill—both high crimes.

"Tony didn't know anything about a labor union or anything else," Duke recalled years later in a typical blunt assessment.

The deputies in the klavern faked up arrest warrants and showed up in uniform at Tony's house, handcuffed him, and carried him several miles away to a secluded spot.

"They almost killed him," Duke said. "Tony was a good, unoffensive man. He exuded that—a loving type fellow to his family."[8]

Another case involved a Pentecostal preacher severely beaten by the Klan because his church services were too loud and went on too late in the night.

Duke later recalled the irony that the preacher had a lot in common with his attackers because he was a "narrow-minded, very, very prejudiced fellow."[9]

The breaking point, however, was the beating of Ike Gaston, a white barber and coincidentally the uncle of Carroll County sheriff Denver Gaston. Ike didn't have a lot of enemies, but his reputation as a drinker and a poor provider for his family came to the attention of the East Point Klan. On the icy morning of March 8, 1940, Gaston's frozen body was found on some farmland a few miles west of East Point. He had been stripped and severely beaten. He staggered seventy-five yards before collapsing. A leather whip decorated with Klan symbols and sharp metal cleats was found with him. The Klan's flogging crew had killed someone. *Constitution* editor Ralph McGill was incensed and attacked the "big, brave men" who killed the barber.[10]

"How majestic must be their spirits! How meek and satisfied their souls," McGill wrote in a Sunday column. "I find myself wondering how loud their voices will rise in song this morning as they praise the Lord for his many mercies? And I wonder, too, if between them and the hymn book there rises the picture of the beaten, tortured body lying there dead with a light snow covering it?"[11]

Duke's boss gave him an investigator and two county police officers to build a case against the Klan. The young prosecutor began by showing up at the county coroner's inquest. Displaying a skill with the press that would become a hallmark of his career, Duke addressed the local media, asking any victims of Klan beatings to contact him at his office. When he returned, his boss, who was not accustomed to dealing so openly with the newspapers, was waiting for him.

"You put me on the spot," he told Duke. "Now you'd better make this thing stick."

Within a few days a parade of victims—white and Black—came forward. One startling fact quickly emerged: at least some of the Klansmen were wearing the uniforms of the Fulton County Sheriff's Office when they abducted their victims. They presented false warrants and led their victims away in handcuffs. As they knitted the facts together, one of the county policemen assigned to Duke gave him a revolver for protection.

Duke's team got a lucky break when an Atlanta doctor approached them about his brother, who had been involved in driving one of the cars for the flogging crew but hadn't participated in the violence. Duke brought the man in, and he provided details of how the gang drove through Black sections of town in cars with an electrified cross burning on the hood. Their aim was to scare Blacks and to disrupt labor organizers who were trying to get workers with the Ford auto plant to form a union. They also learned the Exalted Cyclops of the East Point Klan was a sheriff's deputy named W. W. Scarborough.

That night Duke's investigators raided Scarborough's home, seizing Klan records showing Ford Motor Company had paid the terror crew to bust the union. "Without a warrant," Duke recalled later. "I didn't ever go to the trouble to get warrants to search. I just sent them out and said, 'Get this,' and, hell, they got it."[12]

Duke got more from the doctor's brother. All of the details about the Klan's operation proved useful when questioning suspects.

"If you give me everything, you will never be named," Duke promised the man. Rather than hold the man as a witness, perhaps risking his life, Duke took the testimony and had it typed up as a confession, packed with names and dates, and forged the signature of a prominent suspect identified by the Pentecostal preacher as a ringleader. He then had his investigators bring him another suspected member of the crew and slid the confession to him.

"Some of these fellows are going to get by," Duke told the Klansman. "And you'll be left holding the sack."[13]

The ploy worked. Within days the flogging crew was exposed and indicted for the series of beatings.

"They take this blood oath," Duke explained. "And hell, I don't know how you break a through a thing like that unless you trick them or something."[14]

The investigation resulted in the conviction of nine Klan members and shattered the klavern. Among Duke's admirers was Atlanta mayor William B. Hartsfield, a moderate Democrat who would eventually become known as the architect of Atlanta's ethos as a "city too busy to hate." Wild gangs of Klansmen, county police among them, beating people in the streets was not Hartsfield's idea of progress.[15]

Not everyone was as pleased. Eugene Talmadge, who had been reelected governor in 1940, held a hearing in November 1941 in the Georgia Senate to openly debate offering the imprisoned Klansmen clemency. Talmadge was the standard-bearer for Georgia's hard-core segregationist voter and he had the backing of the Klan. He viewed the Klan's wrecking crew as little more than good intentions gone wrong.

"I've seen some pretty good people get misdirected and act the fool," he said. "I got mixed up in a thing like that once."

Incensed, Duke strode forward with the very whip used to beat Ike Gaston to death in his hand and thrust it in Talmadge's face, demanding to know whether the governor had whipped men like the Klan crew. Flashbulbs popped from either side, freezing the image of the young prosecutor angrily confronting the segregationist governor with the bloody emblem of Southern oppression.[16]

Talmadge brushed off Duke's questions, but the damage was done. The photos ran around the nation and the world. Talmadge, who already was dealing with the fallout of an attempt to purge the university system of alleged integrationists, withdrew plans to commute the Klansmen's sentences. Duke emerged from the episode with a reputation as a fearless and principled Southern progressive.

While Duke was not afraid of publicity, he had not engineered the drama. His boss had sent him to the hearing and suggested he take the whip along with him as a prop. Only later did he find out that his boss was working behind the scenes with Mayor Hartsfield to thwart Talmadge's plans to commute the sentences and that Hartsfield had tipped the press that the fiery young Duke was bringing the whip to the hearing.[17]

The following year Talmadge, running for a fourth term as governor, lost the Democratic primary in a landslide to Ellis Arnall, the state's young, liberal attorney general. Arnall, like Duke, hailed from one of the chain of cities southwest of Atlanta and was friendly with the young prosecutor. Certainly, Arnall had to have admired the way Duke stood up to "Old Gene." Duke could have named his post in the Arnall administration, but the timing was bad. With World War II raging in Europe and the Pacific, he resigned his position in the Fulton County solicitor's office and enlisted in the Marine Corps.

Duke's career in the military was short-lived. While in officer training school, he was thrown from a horse and damaged his kidney. He spent his seven weeks as a Marine shuttling between training and return trips to the hospital before being medically discharged.[18] When he returned, Arnall hired him as a lawyer in the state revenue department. When his boss was appointed to fill a vacancy in the state attorney general's office in 1945, Duke moved with him as an assistant state prosecutor, a powerful post for a lawyer just thirty-one years old.

Quickly, Duke was tapped to again battle a resurgent Ku Klux Klan, which had only recently been thought dismantled in a heap of criminal convictions and unpaid taxes. But on May 9, 1946, Grand Dragon Samuel Green led a group of new initiates up Stone Mountain and set a three-hundred-foot cross afire. Green, an Atlanta obstetrician and longtime Klan member, sold the exclusive photo rights to the "naturalization" ceremony to *Life* magazine and heralded the reborn Klan as a nativist, anti-Communist organization.[19]

Governor Arnall made a priority out of breaking this new Klan, which had a long and powerful association with state politics. Georgia had granted the Klan a charter to operate as a fraternal society soon after its first rebirth in 1915 in a similar cross-burning ceremony on Stone Mountain. The charter had been a sort of seal of respectability for the Klan, but Arnall saw it as a weakness. The state could publicly cripple the Klan if it could strip it of its charter. Duke enjoined the local press in the campaign by painting the Klan as a for-profit criminal organization duping otherwise honest citizens into joining its ranks.[20]

"A number of good people, who didn't know about the Klan's secret committees which were plotting the violation of civil rights, and the abuse and threats to peaceful citizens, unwittingly allowed themselves to be used by profiteers to give the Klan a cloak of respectability," Duke told the *Constitution* in a front-page profile that described him as both a "hard-hitting young lawyer" and "a good churchman" leading the men's Bible study class in his local Baptist church.[21]

Painting the Klan as a crooked organization making profits on well-meaning whites was a page right out of *Constitution* editor Ralph McGill's book, and the newspaper followed Duke's every move as the local Eliot Ness. The Black press was even more thrilled that Duke was taking on "the hooded order."[22]

Duke's first move in his 1946 campaign showed how the racial landscape had shifted since 1940. Whereas it took the death of a white barber to launch a criminal investigation six years earlier, this time the signature victims were Black.

In a press conference, Duke revealed that investigators had succeeded in infiltrating a local klavern and heard Klan members boasting about the stabbing death of Porter Flournoy Turner, a Black cabdriver whose body was dumped on the lawn of an Atlanta-area doctor the prior August.[23] In addition, Duke charged the Klan with the beating of a Black World War II Navy veteran earlier in the year. Duke fed that story to McGill's paper in vivid detail: The twenty-one-year-old man, a bellboy in a downtown hotel, was on his way home when he was attacked and viciously beaten by a gang of nine Klansmen.

Forced at gunpoint to his hands and knees, the man was flogged fifty-two times with a two-tailed leather whip. Duke said one of the Klansmen told the victim that "he had seen a white man struck by a Negro soldier overseas and he was determined to get his revenge." Duke's investigators believed the beating was a case of mistaken identity and that the Klansmen had been after another Black man who earlier was acquitted of stealing vegetables from a local store. The same night, police received a call from the home of that man saying that several men flashing badges had shown up seeking the man, who was not at home.

The young Navy vet was kidnapped shortly after police received the call, suggesting that the Klan crew had cruised the neighborhood and picked up the first Black man who vaguely matched their target's description. Duke pointed out to the press the similarities to the 1940 rash of beatings, including the implication that police were involved.[24]

Duke emphasized the dangers of Samuel Green's newborn Klan by accusing the Atlanta Police Department of harboring Klan members in their ranks. In a speech before a Kiwanis Club in June, Duke claimed thirty-eight uniformed police officers demonstrated their fealty to Green by laying their pistols at his feet in a secret Klan meeting. Klan officials were said to have boasted that they were immune from prosecution in the city because of their police connections. In truth, the Klan was filled with Atlanta police officers. A mole inserted into Klavern #1 by the Non-Sectarian Anti-Nazi League, a New York–based hate group watchdog, reported that eighty-three of the two hundred members of the klavern were cops.[25]

Duke also said the Klan was preparing for race riots in the wake of the Democratic gubernatorial primary in July in which former governor Eugene Talmadge was seeking a fourth term in office.

An awareness of the politics of 1946 is essential to understanding Duke's campaign against the Klan. Gene Talmadge's run for governor was based almost entirely on preserving white supremacy in Georgia. In four years Arnall had moved the state toward greater political freedoms for its Black residents, abolishing the poll tax and ordering the state to comply with the U.S. Supreme Court by allowing Blacks to vote in the Democratic primary. He also had lowered the voting age to eighteen, making Georgia the first state to do so. But Arnall couldn't run for another term. The state constitution had been changed in 1942 to allow governors to serve four years instead of two-year terms, and it forbade them from succeeding themselves. With Arnall out of the running, Talmadge seized upon white fears in his attempt to regain the executive's chair, promising to undo what his rival had done.

"I shall see that the people of this state have a Democratic white primary, unfettered and unhampered by radical, Communist, and alien influences," he said in his campaign announcement.[26]

Industrialist and former state legislator James V. Carmichael had been tapped to run against Talmadge as the heir to Arnall's progressive record. Talmadge's campaign was endorsed by Samuel Green's Klan, and in a speech before a group of college students in Atlanta, Carmichael promised "to unmask the Klan and publish its membership, so that they can answer for their crimes."[27]

Three weeks prior to the Democratic primary, Dan Duke formally filed suit to revoke the Klan's charter, accusing the organization of murder, numerous assaults, and false arrests. Moreover, Duke claimed the Klan had put in place a plan to take over state government by enrolling police officers, as well as truck and cabdrivers to move members quickly around the state. Duke charged Sam Roper, an Atlanta police officer and former head of the Georgia Bureau of Investigation, with instigating the plot.[28]

Much of Duke's information came from Stetson Kennedy, a crusading journalist who went undercover as a Klansman to learn their secrets. Kennedy, using the Klan ID card of his dead uncle, learned of a secret subgroup within the Atlanta klavern known as the "Ass-Tearers." The group was limited to members with a history of beating and torturing Blacks. On their robes they wore an insignia with the letters A and T on either side of a corkscrew, reportedly the tool they favored when anally torturing Black men.[29]

Talmadge won the Democratic primary—and was therefore the de facto governor-elect. "Old Gene" won despite having 19,000 fewer votes than Carmichael, thanks to the "county unit" system, a method Georgia used to elect its governor similar to the Electoral College system. The county units gave more weight to less populated, rural counties and weakened the votes in urban counties. The system favored Talmadge's gallus-snapping campaign strategy to appeal to white voters outside of Atlanta, Savannah, and the state's other urban hubs. Nearly 100,000 African Americans voted in the Democratic primary, overwhelmingly casting their ballots for Carmichael, but those votes were mostly cast in the state's largest, most densely populated counties and were diluted by the county unit system. If Talmadge had his way, the 1946 Democratic primary would be their last, as he had run on a pledge of returning to an all-white primary system.[30]

Duke's campaign against the Klan, which had paused in the weeks prior to the primary, heated up. In August, Duke told the press that he had information that "one of the candidates for governor in Georgia" had sought money from the Ku Klux Klan in New York. Duke declined to name the candidate, but no one could have been confused. Moreover, Duke said he had evidence linking the Klan with former members of the German-American Bund, an American pro-Nazi organization that reached its zenith prior to World War II. The former Bund officials had asked Georgia Klan officials to help reestablish a klavern in New Jersey, he said.[31]

Even though Duke had his hands full with the Klan, Attorney General Cook asked his young protégé to take on yet another extremist group: the Columbians.

While the Klan had been around in its various forms since Reconstruction, the Columbians coalesced suddenly from the postwar mists of 1946. The group was the brainchild of Homer Loomis, a Princeton dropout and New Yorker, and Emory Burke, a bookish Alabamian with a burning desire to climb the ladder of the white supremacist movement. Loomis and Burke met in early 1946, and by the summer and early fall, they had tapped into a wellspring of white rage in Atlanta's West End, a white working-class neighborhood where returning Black World War II veterans were increasingly attempting to buy houses. Soon the Columbians numbered more than five hundred dues-paying members who lined up behind Burke's white supremacist ideology and the handsome Loomis's inspiring oratory, charisma, and access to money. And by year's end, gangs of white men in brown shirts with lightning bolt insignias cruised the West End, beating Blacks and threatening worse.[32]

In the predawn of October 31, 1946, a group of Columbians set off a dynamite charge on the front porch of a house recently purchased by a Black couple. The couple was unharmed, but the planting of a bomb was a new degree of terror. The Atlanta police chief, the Fulton County prosecutor, and others lined up to condemn the fascist group, each saying such religious and racial intolerance had "no place in Georgia." Within days, Duke had been tasked with breaking the Columbians and stripping them of their state charter as well. The job had come at the specific request of Mayor Hartsfield.[33]

Less than a week later, the Columbians met for a rally and Emory Burke theatrically tore the group's charter to pieces, stomping on them. A subordinate quickly swept the pieces up and dumped them into an envelope addressed to Duke.

"Give the little pieces to the Jews," one follower yelled.

"The Columbians, Inc., is now dead," Burke announced. "But the Columbians as a party are still alive. We are a political party . . . and within two years we will be electing the officials of Atlanta and Fulton County."[34]

Dan Duke's battles against the Klan and the Columbians had a quixotic aspect to them. Gene Talmadge was set to be the new governor, and Duke had no reason to suspect his own service to the state would extend into the new administration. Talmadge had announced he saw no reason to continue with the case against the Klan and did not plan to do so when he was inaugurated in January. So it was with some frustration that Duke attended a hearing in late November over the revocation of the Columbians' charter. (Tearing up the paper was good theater, perhaps, but it did not carry legal weight.) The Columbians had asked for another delay, something a prosecutor with limited time left in state service could ill afford. The meeting was in the massive Fulton County Courthouse, in the chambers of senior judge Edgar E. Pomeroy, an elderly jurist who, after hearing brief arguments, agreed to a five-day delay.

"They have defied the judicial system of this state," Duke complained to the judge, pointing at a sneering Emory Burke a few feet away in the judge's office. "Their charter says the organization is benevolent and charitable and yet there is not a nickel behind it to protect the people of this state."

Frustrated, he concluded, "The filth of the nation is gathering here to make a spectacle of us."[35]

Duke's passion did not sway Pomeroy, who ruled for the Columbians and started to leave the room. That's when Duke put Burke on the floor with a single punch above his eye. The young prosecutor's blood was near the boiling point all the time, so his decision to slug the fascist could have been tipped when Burke reportedly whispered "Nigger lover" into his ear at the conclusion of the hearing. Burke, a birdlike man of about 120 pounds, was a poor match for the stocky Duke, and bled profusely from a cut caused by the roundhouse punch.

"You'll pay for this," Burke said.

Dismissively, Duke offered to pay Burke's medical bills. Instead, Burke used the episode later in the week at a Columbian rally where he challenged Duke to a rematch.[36] In reality, Burke wanted no more of Duke and had instead filed assault charges against him.

The appeal to law and order was a putrid ruse. At the same time Burke was playing the victim, the Columbians were hatching a plan to kidnap and beat Duke, along with U.S. Representative Helen Mankin and *Constitution* editor Ralph McGill for their public barrages against the group.[37]

Despite his fiery temper, Duke was strategic and smart, and he had the Columbians at more of a disadvantage than they knew. When given the task of dismantling the organization, Duke had reached out for the assistance of the Non-Sectarian Anti-Nazi League, a New York–based group that had formed prior to World War II to organize economic boycotts against the Nazi regime in Germany. After the war, the group started investigating homegrown fascist groups and assisted Duke's mission by using undercover agents to infiltrate the group. NSANL agent Renee Fruchtbaum easily insinuated herself among the mostly male Columbians and gained the confidence of two members who were bitter about the lifestyle Burke and Loomis led while dues-paying members scraped along. Fruchtbaum extracted detailed information about the organization from the men and fed the information to Duke. In a final coup, Fruchtbaum took boxes of records and two disgruntled Columbians to the NSANL headquarters in New York, where they spent days giving long depositions, information that led Atlanta police to the group's storehouse of dynamite. As word spread of coming criminal indictments, three more turncoat fascists made their way to Duke's office for grim meetings and to sign statements saying they had been "misled."[38]

The following day, Duke held a press conference where Fruchtbaum and her two prize witnesses told the press about the inner workings and plans of the Columbians, including their secret "lynch list" and how they planned a government takeover by building a private arsenal of weapons and explosives. The next day McGill's *Constitution* pronounced the organization dead.[39]

While Duke was cleverly outwitting the Columbians and chasing the Ku Klux Klan back to oblivion, a political storm on a millennial scale was approaching. Eugene Talmadge had won the Democratic primary and thus the governor's seat. The general election in Georgia was a tedious formality. Democrats won everything, largely on the promise, either stated or implied, that they would maintain the state's culture of segregation. In 1946, no Republican had offered himself up as a sacrificial goat to Old Gene, and amid the light turnout, Talmadge captured nearly all of the popular vote. The *Constitution*'s story reporting the election results barely made the front page. Even so, it struck a casual tone, mentioning that Talmadge gave the election little of his attention, spending it in the hospital where doctors "are prodding at his body to see how tough he is."[40]

Talmadge's health was questionable, but what the *Constitution* didn't know—in fact, what only Talmadge's inner circle knew—was that Gene was dying. Years of drinking had ruined his liver and it looked like he might not live to take the oath of office. But the Talmadge machine had a plan. In the lightly attended November general election, some voters in Talmadge's home county were encouraged to cast write-in ballots for thirty-three-year-old Herman Talmadge, Gene's only son. Sure enough, Eugene Talmadge—populist demagogue and virulent racist—shuffled off this mortal coil on December 21, 1946, creating a political crisis unlike any in Georgia history.[41]

The *Constitution* announced Talmage's death with a restrained remembrance in which he was described as "picturesque" and "colorful."[42] But the real news ran beside the front-page obituary: "3 Leaders Loom for Governorship." Under the terms of the new state constitution, incoming lieutenant governor Melvin E. Thompson claimed the office by right of constitutional succession. Thompson came from the state's anti-Talmadge faction and his right to the office was supported by outgoing governor Ellis Arnall, another Talmadge enemy.

The Talmadge faction, having planned for this, asserted that the state constitution vested the Georgia General Assembly with the duty of tallying the votes from the general election and announcing which person would be the next governor. As a dead man, Eugene Talmadge was no longer a legal "person," they said, so the state legislators should select the "person" to be governor from the remaining candidates with the two highest vote totals, one of whom they assumed would be Herman Talmadge. Upon hearing the Talmadge machine's plans, Arnall made his own gambit and announced he would not relinquish the governor's office "until his successor was chosen and qualified."

"Technically, under the constitution, I could remain in office for four years longer," he said.[43]

The Talmadge plan ran into temporary trouble when the legislature met to count the write-in votes: James V. Carmichael, who had lost to Gene Talmadge in the primary, got 669 votes, and D. Talmadge Bowers, a Republican, garnered 637. Herman Talmadge, who had just 619 votes, came in third. But then 56 uncounted write-in votes were serendipitously discovered in Talmadge's home county, bringing Herman's total to 675.[44]

On January 15, 1947, Talmadge loyalists in the general assembly met in a marathon session to decide which candidate would become chief executive. Debate stretched into the night, and state lawmakers, some far from home and hearth, began nipping from bottles hidden beneath their desks. Talmadge and anti-Talmadge forces tried to woo fence-sitting legislators with strong drink. One senator had to be carted in from the Capitol lawn, where he had passed out.

"As fast as we could sober them up, the other crowd would take them off and get them drunk again," one recalled.[45]

Where drink failed, partisans tried threats and offered cash bribes—thousands of dollars, according to some—to vote for either Talmadge or Thompson.[46]

In the wee hours, the conservatives got the numbers and voted Herman Talmadge as their new governor. Pandemonium broke out among Talmadge loyalists, who flooded the House chamber. A floor below, Arnall sat behind locked doors in the executive suite, vowing to refuse Talmadge access. Assistant Attorney General Dan Duke was across town, attending an event at Emory University, when his hosts told him he had an urgent phone call. When Duke took to the telephone, he heard the anxious voice of Mrs. Fellows, Governor Ellis Arnall's personal secretary.

"We want you to be over here," she said. "The governor is in his office and he is not going to leave and we think there is going to be trouble."

Duke sped across town, walking past the statue of Tom Watson, a racist, populist politician from a prior era, and up the west steps of the Capitol. The statue portrayed Watson with an angry fist thrust into the air, a fitting sentiment for a revolutionary moment in Atlanta. A knot of rough country types loitered by the doors. "That's that Duke," one said, spitting tobacco juice on a step. "Son of a bitch!"

Inside, the scene was all chaos.

Wild hoots and hollers rang through the Capitol as Talmadge's "wool hat boys" smashed whiskey bottles and celebrated their victory. Duke quickly made his way into the governor's office to confer with Arnall. The young lawyer believed this likely was his last day as an assistant attorney general. As Arnall and Duke waited, they could hear the whooping and marching of feet coming near. Talmadge, flanked by supporters, advanced from the third-floor House chamber and down the Capitol's wide marble steps to the executive suite, intent on installing himself as governor that very moment. Some of his supporters had cut down a small tree from the Capitol grounds, intending to use it as a battering ram to break down the door to Arnall's office. Someone—likely someone less drunk—decided it would save taxpayers the cost of replacing a door if they just removed it from its hinges.[47]

Men flooded into the office, barreling past the governor's staff until they reached Arnall, Duke at his side. But there was little for a lawyer to do, even one who had shown he was willing to use his fists, when necessary. This was mob rule. While some in the crowd wished to use bodily force to remove Arnall, Talmadge tried to persuade.

"I presume that you have been informed that I have been elected as governor by the General Assembly," he said.

Arnall was unimpressed. "The General Assembly cannot elect a governor," he said. "I refuse to yield the office to you, whom I consider a pretender."

Flummoxed, Talmadge turned and left. "You were nice to come in," Arnall called.[48]

The outgoing governor's bravado was not enough. A day later, Arnall returned to find he had been locked out of his office, which now was under military guard. He found a similar situation at the executive mansion.[49]

Barred by state troopers from entering his own office, Arnall set up a temporary "office" thirty feet away in the Capitol's wide, circular rotunda. The brief, embarrassing display ended when the Arnall forces were blocked by Talmadge men. Arnall instead set up a government-in-exile in his Atlanta law office.

On January 18, Arnall resigned as governor, handing his claim to the office to Lieutenant Governor Thompson. Thompson adopted the title of acting governor, saying he would serve until the people could hold another election. In the meantime, Thompson made muscular moves to secure his position and "end the confusion and chaos that is existing in our state." He ordered Talmadge to move out of the official office and executive mansion. Reporters pointed out that Talmadge was unlikely to leave voluntarily. What would Thompson do? "Just yet I do not have a strong military force at my back, so I am not in a position to answer," he said. Talmadge said he would wait for the courts to decide.[50]

The decision took two confusing months, during which Talmadge and Thompson held rival swearing-in ceremonies for various executive appointments. The nation was transfixed; Georgians were anxious. Ultimately, the Georgia Supreme Court sided with Thompson but ordered a special election to be held in 1948. Talmadge, whose stature rose immensely in what became known as the "three governors controversy," vowed he would return. The crisis did end Duke's time in the attorney general's office and he returned to private practice.

Duke's stand with Governor Ellis Arnall against the rowdy, racist Talmadge crowd was in keeping with the character of a man out of step with his time—or, at the very least, his place.

Later in life, Duke often spoke of a childhood memory of riding with his father on a short rail line that carried riders from Fairburn, at the outermost edge of metro Atlanta, a few miles south to the "sure 'nuff" country town of Palmetto. On this trip, his father gave up his seat to a tired Black woman, a serious breach of racial etiquette but, as his father explained, morally just. That lesson stayed with Duke as a mob of drunken Talmadge men swarmed the governor's office, displacing the most progressive governor in the state's history to install a "pretender" whose rise rested solely on the fact that he was the son of a white supremacist. In the coming years, Duke accepted the mantle of the conscience of the New South, opposing injustice, fighting intolerance, and exposing charlatans. And often losing.

For liberals in the Northeast, the situation in Georgia was appalling and reinforced deeply held opinions about Georgia and the South. In Dan Duke, however, they found a virtuous Southerner. Amid the chaos of the three governors crisis, Duke was chosen by the Junior Chamber of Commerce as one of ten "outstanding young men" in the nation for his work against the Columbians and the Klan. Duke shared the honor with Harvard historian and Pulitzer Prize–winning author Arthur Schlesinger Jr., world heavyweight boxing champion Joe Louis, and a young Boston congressman named John F. Kennedy.

"I accept the honor humbly," Duke said, "for I am only one among a great majority of Georgians who stand unalterably opposed to the un-Christian and ungodly practice of preaching and using hatred and religious intolerance as a means of exploiting ignorance and prejudice."[51]

If Duke sounded like a politician running for office, he was. As early as April 1947, his name was mentioned as a potential candidate for governor in the 1948 special election. In a speech in Thomaston, Georgia, seventy miles south of Atlanta, Duke blasted both Talmadge and Acting Governor Thompson as "political vultures." But he said he wasn't running to replace them.[52]

Instead, Duke ran for Fulton County solicitor in a bitter race to unseat the man who replaced his old boss. He lost despite carrying Atlanta majority-Black precincts. That same election, Herman Talmadge won the governor's race, completing the takeover he had been denied by the courts.

In private practice, Duke emerged as an even more fiery crusader, always searching for an opening to wound the Talmadge machine. In September 1949, Duke announced his plans to sue several county solicitors and the state revenue commissioner for unfairly enforcing state liquor laws. Duke's client, a wholesale liquor dealer, had his state license pulled after being caught selling liquor in a "dry" county. Duke claimed the license was a casualty of the Talmadge machine, which turned a blind eye to political allies, who were free to sell liquor wherever they pleased.

He continued his battles against political extremism too. It was Duke who had represented Cartersville grocery store clerk Evans Wilder in his claim that he was being harassed by Homer Chase and other Communists. He also tangled with circuit court judges over excluding Blacks from juries. In February 1950 a judge threatened to toss Duke in jail during a hearing for a Black client for "making insinuations" that the all-white grand jury system was unconstitutional.

"I'll have you placed in jail with the Negro," the judge warned.

That judge was Samuel Boykin, whom Duke now rose to address in a packed courtroom in Carrollton.

"May it please the court," he began, "I have been employed in this case to take the lead in this trial."

CHAPTER 13

THE SECOND TRIAL

It was no surprise that the NAACP reached out to Dan Duke. With a Black man's neck on the line, the organization wanted a white face to present to an all-white Southern jury, and Duke was a natural fit. He was a capable lawyer with a crusading streak. He also was a politician, and, in the turbid waters of *State v. Henderson II*, there was some politicking to do. Even so, Duke's first move in Boykin's courtroom was risky. The case had already been delayed and a jury seated, but he asked for a continuance.

Slicking down his dark suit coat as he stood, Duke poured out the grease as only a seasoned Georgia politician could.

"My only reason for making this statement is because of the intrusion of certain people to exploit this case," he explained. "These people have only sought to use the events of the trial, which they know nothing about, for the purpose of propaganda."[1]

Boykin nodded. It had been just a few months since the judge angrily ordered Homer Chase, chairman of the Georgia Communist Party, locked up indefinitely. Chase was a fugitive from Boykin's court, a fact that had the judge fuming.

Duke pivoted from outrage to flattery.

"I wish to state I have every confidence in this court, every confidence in the learning of the judge on the bench, and his desire and his ability to insure a fair and impartial trial," he said, then added as another nod to the Red menace, "in accordance with the American conception of justice."[2]

This flattery was a hard bit to swallow, but it was a necessary show of fealty to the man in the black robe. After all, just four months earlier, Duke's co-counsel, Robinson and Moore, had stood before Boykin on charges of contempt of court for their role in the "framed" flyer that suggested Boykin, among others, had conspired to convict Henderson unjustly. And only a few months before that, Boykin had threatened to put Duke in jail.

But Duke wasn't only aiming at Boykin. His soft words flowed in luscious baritone for the "able and capable prosecutor" Wright Lipford and the fine people of Carroll County and their "love of liberty and justice."

The jury listened appreciatively. In making a routine motion, Duke was managing an extra opening argument.

"I think proper for me to make this statement, not for the purpose of flattery," he said without irony, "but in order to make my position clear that I am here primarily in an attempt to see that the trial is conducted in accordance with the law and that complete justice be done, in so far as our legal system permits it to be done."

Under the circumstances, Duke's motion for a delay in the trial was a dead letter. The trial was going to happen. But that was hardly the point. He was softening hardened ground.

He took a deep breath and launched back in. Henderson was "an ignorant man" facing the prospect of death. This is a serious matter, and the air should be cleared, he said.

"Those who clouded up and raised a stumbling block as to the conduct of the trial in this case have no place in any court of justice," he said, moving his client farther and farther away from Homer Chase, the Communists, and even the Henderson Defense Committee, whose efforts were paying his fee.

"At this particular time, there are those who do not love our system of justice and seek to use the events of this trial for the purpose of propaganda," Duke said. Such people were not part of Clarence Henderson's defense team, he concluded.

His preamble finished, Duke read his motion asking for additional time to conduct forensic tests on the gun and the alleged brass filings. He pointed out that he had only officially been hired five days earlier and the money for the expert tests had become available only in the last twenty-four hours.

"I am making this motion in the interest of justice," he said. "There should not be any cloud hanging over this case, regardless of the outcome."

The trial had yet to begin, but Duke had left little oxygen in the room.

"What do you say to that?" Boykin asked Lipford.

It had been several months since the Supreme Court of Georgia had ordered a new trial, Lipford said. Regardless of when Duke was brought on,

Henderson's defense team had ample time to conduct any tests they wanted, he said.

"I am anxious to try this case," he told the judge. What few knew was that Lipford had reasons to be anxious and to not want further ballistics tests.

Duke jumped in with an outrageous claim for a defense attorney: he didn't want the forensic tests for his client, he said. In fact, they might implicate Henderson in the crime. Regardless of their outcome, justice would be served, he said.

"This motion is addressed to the sound discretion of the court, by the very deep consciousness and very deep desire of a fair and judicious judge to bring every fact which can be bought so that there will never be any shadow hanging over the case," Duke said, emptying the last drop from this deep well of sweet talk. The oratory, which the *Times–Free Press* declared "a sensation," had taken an hour of the court's time.[3]

"I appreciate the position you are in," Boykin said, after taking a short recess to consider Duke's argument. "I overrule the motion."[4]

Duke had lost, but he had sent an important signal. The first trial had been a model of orderly Southern justice. Witnesses came and went quickly and the trial had been concluded in a single day. This time would be different.

Spectators could feel that difference. The opening day of trial began with an arduous jury selection. The defense and prosecution plowed through five panels of prospective jurors, requiring additional groups to be drawn in before a jury—all male, all white—could be seated and the trial begun in earnest.[5]

It was well into the afternoon when Lipford called his first witness, Dr. Elwyn V. Patrick, the physician who had gone with Sheriff Bunt Kilgore to the scene and who later removed the bullet taken from Buddy's knee. Lipford's examination was straightforward: Patrick had gone to the scene, taken Stevens's pulse to assure he was dead, then later conducted an autopsy at the funeral home, during which he discovered the bullet.

"To whom did you deliver that bullet?" Lipford asked.

"I delivered the bullet personally to the then sheriff, Bunt Kilgore," Patrick said.

"At what place did you deliver that bullet to him?" the prosecutor asked.

"I went back to the scene of the crime and I delivered it to him there," Patrick said.[6]

Moore and Robinson looked at each other and started leafing through pages of the transcript of the first trial with Duke looking over their shoulders. The two Black attorneys had months to study the case, but Duke was less familiar.

Duke popped up as soon as Lipford finished.

"You said you delivered the bullet to then Sheriff Kilgore. Where did you deliver the bullet? At the scene of the crime?"

"Yes," Patrick said. "I went back out there and that is where he was. And I gave it to him personally."

"Are you positive now that you delivered the bullet at the scene of the crime?" Duke asked.

Somewhat uneasy, Patrick looked toward Lipford. The prosecutor, studying papers in front of him, offered no help.

"I am positive it was at the scene of the crime," Patrick said.

Duke held up a typewritten page of the transcript from the first trial. "I will ask you if you remember at the last trial, upon direct examination, if Mr. Lipford asked you, 'Did you give the bullet personally?' Your answer was yes."

Duke turned to the jury and continued reading. "The next question: 'Where did you deliver the bullet?' Answer: 'At the funeral home.' Question: 'Delivered it personally?' Answer: 'Yes.'"

Duke turned back to the doctor.

"Did you, or did you not, testify to that at the last trial?" he asked.

Patrick stammered. "I don't think that is what I said," he offered.

Duke hammered on the inconsistency.

"You are now positive you delivered it to Sheriff Kilgore at the scene of the crime and it was wrapped in paper?" he asked, leaning hard into the word "positive."

Patrick was a country doctor, not a forensic pathologist. He'd had few such occasions to sweat on a witness stand.

"If I had to swear to it, I wouldn't," he said. "But my firm conviction is I delivered it to him out there."

Duke ended his questioning, having turned a perfunctory part of the first trial into a doubt-instilling witness in the second. Lipford sprang up for redirect examination of the doctor and what followed was a ping-pong match of redirects and recrosses by Duke and Lipford with Patrick as the ball.

Did you take the bullet extracted from Buddy Stevens to Bunt Kilgore? Lipford asked. Yes. Did you examine it for bone, blood, or fibers? Duke wanted to know. No. "I took the bullet and put in an envelope," Patrick said.

Is this the envelope, Lipford asked, holding up a smallish wrinkled envelope bearing the name of the funeral home. Yes, "or one similar," the doctor said. Are you certain? Duke asked. Don't envelopes look alike? Patrick shrugged. "Yes, sir."

"You have nothing to go by in making the statement except the fact Mr. Lipford presented it to you and you just assumed that is the envelope?" Duke said.

As limp as a washcloth, Patrick replied. "That is right."[7]

The second witness was Dr. Eldred C. Bass, the young physician who had assisted Patrick in the examination of Stevens's body and in the extraction of the bullet. Again Lipford's direct examination was a basic recitation of the events: Bass met Patrick at the funeral home, where they observed the wounds to the body. A bullet was removed from Stevens's right knee.

Bass said Patrick gave the bullet to the sheriff. Jurors might have wondered how Bass could have known that if Patrick had taken the bullet to the scene of the murder, but Lipford made no attempt to sort it out.

In his cross-examination, Duke began to probe. And he made it clear he was probing much more than either doctor did that night.

The only thing that the state had connecting Clarence Henderson with the murder of Buddy Stevens was a single 9mm bullet and a .38 revolver that supposedly fired it. Duke wanted the jury to know all there was to know about that bullet. Or, more to the point, how little was known about it.

Duke started with the extraction itself. What tool was used to cut it from Buddy's leg? Scissors were used to cut the skin, Bass said, then "it fell right out."

How did it look? Duke asked. Was it scarred? Covered in blood? Disfigured by striking bone? Was the knee examined to determine whether any bones were struck?

The doctor's answers showed very little investigation besides observing the chest wound and extracting the bullet from the knee. Bass said he did not even look closely at the knee wound to determine whether bone had been struck.[8]

The afternoon was late by the time Duke had finished his cross-examination. This trial was different in another important way: the first trial was wedged into a single day. This one would at least go two.

Boykin commanded jurors not to discuss the case among themselves or read any of the coverage in the newspapers and dismissed them to a downtown hotel to be sequestered.[9]

Robinson, Moore, and Duke made their way back home to Atlanta. Even if money had been no object (and it very much was), and even if suitable accommodations could be found for two Black Atlanta attorneys (and it is doubtful they could), they would not have been eager to pass a dark night in Carroll County.

That evening Dan Duke's phone rang. The man on the other end wouldn't give him his name. He had seen Duke in Carrollton but drove to Atlanta to call him with some information. After the supreme court reversed Henderson's conviction, the state had done new ballistics tests and found the bullet taken from Buddy Stevens's leg could not have come from the .38 Special revolver, he said.[10]

* * *

The second day of Clarence Henderson's second capital murder trial dawned with the testimony of former sheriff Bunt Kilgore. As he had the previous day, Lipford walked Kilgore through the night of October 31, 1948: the finding of Buddy Stevens's body, taking possession of the bullet, passing the bullet on to Georgia Bureau of Investigation agent Jim Hillin. When he had finished, also like the day before, Dan Duke rose and began to tug and pull at Kilgore's testimony, particularly when it came to the bullet.[11]

"You state positively Dr. Patrick delivered this bullet to you out at the scene of the crime," Duke asked, reminding the jury of yesterday's contradiction.

"Yes, sir," Kilgore said.

"You put it in your pocket?" Duke asked. Yes, the former sheriff said. "Did you make any mark on the base of the projectile of that bullet so you could correctly identify it?" Duke asked. No, Kilgore said.

Duke cast a meaningful look at the jury before peppering Kilgore with follow-up questions in which Kilgore said neither Patrick nor Jim Hillin marked the bullet and admitted he could no longer distinguish it from any other bullet.

"Did you ever attend the crime prevention and detection school that comes around over the state?" Duke asked.

Kilgore's face reddened. The question harkened back to the 1948 Democratic Party primary and the campaign of Denver Gaston. Gaston, a state patrol officer, had run on a platform of making the sheriff's department more professional, even down to such things as providing proper uniforms. Gaston unseated Kilgore in that race. Now this Atlanta lawyer was questioning Kilgore's basic understanding of criminal procedure.[12]

"Is it true that the first thing they tell you to do if you have evidence you wish to be examined is to make a particular mark on the object so you will be able to identify it?" Duke asked.

"That is right," Kilgore said.

Shirley Boykin objected on the technical grounds that what a third-party criminologist might recommend on preserving evidence wasn't relevant to the case at hand. Shirley's younger brother tacitly agreed but did not sustain the objection. Duke carried on.

"You didn't do it in this case?" Duke asked. "Was the envelope sealed?"

Kilgore said he couldn't recall. Duke asked the sheriff if he could swear that the bullet he never examined was, in fact, the bullet the prosecution claimed took the life of Buddy Stevens.

"No, sir," Kilgore said.[13]

A murmuring from the prosecution table caught Duke's attention. As he swung his head around, Shirley Boykin, who had been talking to Lipford, looked up.

Turning back to the judge, Duke announced, "I want to ask for a mistrial."

Duke claimed the judge's brother had said loud enough for the jury to hear that the defense attorney was putting on "a show" in his cross-examination. "It was a prejudicial and improper statement," Duke said. "It would tend to deprive the defendant of a fair and impartial trial."

Shirley Boykin raised his hands up to his brother. "I told Mr. Lipford to show him the bullet," he said. "To take the bullet and *show* it to him."

"All right, all right," the judge said. "Do not make any private remarks where the jury can hear." Then he told the jury to ignore any comments from either counsel.[14]

With his next witness, GBI agent Jim Hillin, Lipford again tried to establish the chain of custody not only for the bullet but also for the murder weapon.

"Did Mr. Pendergrass give you the serial number of the gun?" Lipford asked. He was referring to Leonard Pendergrass, the taxi driver, former cop, and original owner of the weapon before it was allegedly lost in an attack on Lee Hardman and his date in August prior to the Stevens killing.

"Yes, sir. I have it right here," Hillin said, flipping through a notebook. "A Smith & Wesson .38 Special, serial number 527398."

Did Pendergrass give Hillin the serial number before or after Stevens's murder, Lipford wanted to know. "It was before," Hillin said.

At the defense table, Moore and Johnson began thumbing through the transcript of the trial nine months earlier, furiously making notes, with Duke craning to see.

How long before the murder did Pendergrass provide that information? Lipford asked.

"I don't recollect," Hillin said. "But Mr. Hardman furnished me the number, I would say, within the next 24 hours."

"After Mr. Pendergrass gave you the serial number of the pistol he had lost, what did you do with the serial number," Lipford asked.

Hillin paused. "After I got the serial number from Mr. Hardman . . . ," he began. Then he started again. "The first time I got it from Mr. Hardman, I went to the Atlanta Police Department and gave it to them and they placed it on file."

Lipford had asked Hillin about getting the serial number from *Pendergrass*; he answered about getting it from *Hardman*. If Lipford noticed, he didn't ask his witness to clarify.

When it was his turn, Duke again rose, holding several pages of transcript from Henderson's first trial in January. "You stated the serial number of this weapon had been given to you by Mr. Pendergrass?" he began. "You state it was prior to the death of Mr. Stevens?"

Yes, Hillin said. Pendergrass gave him the information "about, approximately, six weeks or two months" before the Stevens murder.

"At the previous trial you testified?" Duke asked.

"Yes, sir," Hillin said.

Duke read from the transcript from the first trial. "Mr. Lipford asked you the question, 'Was it in 1948 or 1949?' Answer: 'It was in 1948. It was several days or a week *after* Mr. Stevens was killed.'"

Hillin shifted in his seat. "I just approximated it," he said. "I don't know the date. . . . It was sometime *before* the death of Mr. Stevens. . . . Hardman reported it and Pendergrass did too."

"Both of them reported the serial numbers of the lost gun prior to the death of Stevens?" Duke asked skeptically. "In the last trial you responded as to Mr. Hardman, 'It was several days or a week after Mr. Stevens was killed,' did you not?"[15]

"I know it was several days after the robbery of Mr. Hardman down there. That is what it should have been," Hillin said. "I had the serial number right after the pistol was taken."

Duke handed Hillin a page from the transcript. "I will ask you to read this testimony right here," he said, fingering a line on the page, "in order to refresh your recollections."

Hillin read from his words from the first trial. So, Duke asked, was all this testimony in January "just error?"

"Yes, sir," Hillin said.[16]

Following Hillin, the state called a series of witnesses—Police Chief Threadgill, funeral home owner Jack Aycock, and Atlanta police detective E. H. Harkins, who had found the .38 Special in an Atlanta pawnshop—all of whom Lipford used to trace the bullet and the gun from the night of the murder until the day they were linked. Duke had little in the way of cross-examination for any of them. Any questions merely underscored the tenuous nature of the circumstantial evidence against his client.

For example, Duke noted that from the date of the murder to the date the gun was found "is nine days and fifteen months."

"Yes, sir," Harkins confirmed.[17]

Duke meant, but did not say, that it was a long time, for what that was worth.

His cross-examination of GBI agent Tom Price was a different matter. For jurors to believe Henderson was guilty, they had to accept a number of strange premises, including that he had filed down a 9mm bullet to fit into a .38 chamber.

In the first trial, testimony on when, where, and how Price discovered the file supposedly used to file the 9mm rounds was as clear as red Georgia clay. This time, under Lipford's questioning, the agent was more direct: he searched Henderson's tenant shack on his employer's farm south of Carrollton, then "later [went] to the home where his wife had moved to at Sand Hill," several miles northeast of the city. It was there that he found the file—in a house where Clarence Henderson had never lived. In fact, Duke objected to Lipford asking if the file was found "at Clarence Henderson's house."

"The evidence shows it was not Clarence Henderson's house," Duke said. Lipford rephrased the question.

Price recalled the file was found tucked in a dresser drawer but, oddly, he had no recall of the dates he conducted the searches, even though he had been asked about it during the first trial.

In cross-examination, Duke began by emphasizing that the search for the file was conducted some sixteen months after the murder.

"I imagine so," Price allowed. "I don't remember what month."

Through a series of questions, Duke clarified that the Sand Hill house was where Henderson's father-in-law lived. Henderson's wife, Lizzie, had moved there after Henderson was arrested. She and the three Henderson children were living there with her parents and sister.

"I don't know who stayed there," Price said.

"Did you go to any other houses looking for a file?" Duke asked.

"No, sir," Price said flatly.

"You were told prior to that time you had to have a file because the bullet had been filed?" Duke asked, although it was a less a statement than an accusation.

Price agreed. "The reason I searched that house for a file was we received information the bullet had been filed," he said.

Do other people live in that house? Duke asked. A brother-in-law, maybe? Price shrugged. He couldn't say.[18]

As Price left the courtroom, Lipford announced his next witness: Leonard Pendergrass. Murmuring from the audience and the sounds of men shifting in their seats accompanied Pendergrass as he strode to the witness chair. Once the witness was sworn, Lipford kept his questioning short, even terse. The prosecutor's dozen or so questions and Pendergrass's clipped answers took less than five minutes. The cabbie testified that he took Lee Hardman and Mrs. Parker to Stripling Chapel United Methodist Church, he lent Hardman a gun, and he never saw it again. Lipford handed Pendergrass the revolver.

"Did you report the loss of this gun to the officers?" he asked. Yes, Pendergrass said. "Did you give them the serial number?" Yes. "Was that immediately after it was lost?" Yes again.

There was little more territory to cover to benefit the state's case against Henderson. Pendergrass had once owned the murder weapon, he lent it out, it was stolen, and he reported it—*before* the murder. That was all. Despite any rumors they may have heard, Lipford was signaling to the jury Pendergrass's relative unimportance.

Duke began his cross-examination in typically dramatic fashion, asking Pendergrass if he was driving a cab in late October 1949—a year after the murder. Pendergrass said he was.

"You remember the time that you and two other men picked up Clarence Henderson out here in a cab?" Duke asked, motioning to his client.

Pendergrass's eyes widened. "I don't remember ever hauling Clarence Henderson," he said.

"You don't remember picking him up, purporting to take him home, and taking him out in the country and shooting at him and running him off?"

"I never done that in my life," Pendergrass stammered. "It wasn't me!"

Duke let it go, shifting quickly to the former police officer's familiarity with the gun, the ammunition it took, how to fire it, and how to clean it afterward. Pendergrass settled down, responding in one- or two-word answers. Duke then asked about his loan of the gun to Hardman.

"It was August 1948 when you let him have it," Duke said. "It was two or three months before Carl Stevens got killed?"

"It was a year or more," Pendergrass said.

It was Duke's turn to be rattled. He cast a glance back at Moore and Robinson. Their expressions were as puzzled as his own.

"That's when you loaned it?" Duke asked.

"In 1948," Pendergrass said. "He was killed in '49."

Duke shook his head. "If he got killed in 1948—the 31st of October—it was about two and a half months—"

"Yes, he was killed in 1948," Pendergrass said.

"—or three that you let him have it," Duke finished.

Duke didn't know what to do with Pendergrass's confusion, so he focused on the relationship with Hardman. Pendergrass testified that he regularly lent the gun to his friend. Duke asked if Hardman had fired the gun and, if so, if Hardman had provided replacement bullets. Yes, Pendergrass said. Why would he borrow it? Duke asked.

"When he would go fishing, he wanted to carry the gun with him," Pendergrass said.

"When he finally told you the gun had been taken from him, he wasn't going fishing," Duke said. "You know what mission he was on that night?"

"I didn't know what he was going to do. He said he wanted to go out," Pendergrass said. "I don't pry into anyone else's business."

"When was it you heard that Hardman had reported the serial number of the pistol?" Duke asked.

"Hardman didn't report it. I gave it to them," he said. "He was with me down at City Hall and I told the police about it that night."

It was another inconsistency. In the first trial, Hillin had testified Hardman gave him the serial number to the stolen gun a week or so before Stevens was killed and Pendergrass provided it a second time a few days after the murder.[19] In his revised testimony, Hillin had just testified that Hardman had given him the serial number of the gun a few days after the robbery from Hardman and from Pendergrass sometime after that, but well before it was used to kill Buddy.

"You gave it to the officer?" Duke asked.

"Gave it to the officers after they questioned me about it," Pendergrass said.

That Pendergrass had been questioned the night of the Stripling Chapel attack was news to Henderson's defense team. They had not been able to interview the state's witnesses after Lipford's threatening comments to Robinson.

Duke asked Pendergrass if he saw Hardman in the days prior to Stevens's death. Pendergrass said he wasn't sure. Hardman was a mechanic at the cab company, so it was possible.

"Where he worked, [they] have a lot of instruments for fixing things?" Duke asked. He didn't say the words "like a file," but that was what he meant.

Pendergrass said he wasn't sure.[20]

Piecing it together, Duke was creating the possibility that Hardman had borrowed Pendergrass's pistol, shot it, and returned it loaded with filed-down bullets of the wrong caliber. If Pendergrass was the culprit, it could explain the curious notion that Stevens was killed with 9mm bullets shot from a .38 revolver.

Duke released the witness. Lipford let Pendergrass leave the courtroom without any further questions. Nothing he could say would help the state's case against Henderson.

Lipford followed Pendergrass by calling Eli and Floy Cosper, the blind truck farmer who testified that he had pawned the pistol in Atlanta and his wife, who testified that she saw Henderson with it at a party on Sunday, August 28, the weekend after the incident at Stripling Chapel. Compared to their white counterparts, the Cospers' testimony was airtight and in line with their testimony in the first trial.

Eli Cosper testified he had bought the gun from Laymon Almon for $20 and pawned it later the same day in Atlanta for $25. In the first trial, Cosper was weak on the date, at first testifying that he had bought the gun in September—before Stevens's murder. Lipford tried to head it off.

"You remember when you bought the gun?" he asked.

"I remember it was one Monday," the farmer said.

"December 1948, just before Christmas?" Lipford asked.

Although he was new to the case, Duke was ready and quickly objected to Lipford's leading question.

"I think the date is material," he told Judge Boykin. "I object to him leading any witness as to the time or date—matters that are directly at issue."

"Don't lead your witness," Boykin said.[21]

Lipford called Floy Cosper, Eli's wife and one of the state's strongest witnesses in the first trial—and as in the first trial, Floy was unshakable, resolute. She testified that she saw Henderson with the nickel-plated .38 Special on the last weekend in August 1948 at a party at her home and that he had pulled it out and fired it in the air to quell a domestic squabble between a couple from LaGrange. The next time she saw the gun was more than a year later when her husband bought it from Laymon Almon.

Duke's cross-examination did little to rattle Floy Cosper, but he homed in on the weakest part of her story from the first trial: that she had recognized the gun by markings on the butt of the gun, which she saw from a distance at party now more than two years ago. Duke came at the issue from the purchase of the gun from Almon in December 1949, more than a year after the party and Stevens's murder. Was that the first time you noticed the marks? he asked.

"That is the first time I ever paid it that much attention," she said.

You didn't see the marks the first time you saw the gun?

"I didn't see the marks there," she said. "I was looking at it in his hand."

If the gun was in Henderson's hand, it would have been impossible to see the marks on the handle.

"Still, you are testifying positively you know this is the same gun Henderson had at that time?" Duke said, grabbing the gun and holding it out.

Floy turned her face away, without regard to Duke's proffer. "I know a gun when I see it," she said.

"Did somebody talk to you before the trial," Duke asked. It was an accusation of planted testimony, but Lipford ignored it. Eli still had a felony charge hanging over him.

"No, sir," Floy said.

"The only way you identify it by the marks was when Laymon Almon turned it over to your husband?" Duke said.

"He sold it to my husband and he pawned it the next day," Floy said. Eli had just testified he pawned it the same day. Another inconsistency, but Duke was concentrating elsewhere and did not catch it.

Floy Cosper was dismissed. She was a key witness for the state, putting the gun in Henderson's hand after the Stripling Chapel attack and before the Stevens murder. But Duke's cross-examination revealed that her only method for identifying that gun—the marks on the handle—were from more than a year after the murder, when Eli bought it from Almon.[22]

The next witness against Henderson was Junior Clark. Clark was the only state witness to testify in the first trial having seen Henderson filing down bullets prior to the Stevens murder. In that trial, Clark was a shaky witness, testifying about an unknown black revolver and claiming Henderson was filing "long" bullets to fit the shiny .38 Special. He was also the man Henderson tried to implicate in one of his jailhouse statements.

Lipford ran through a quick series of questions about the filing of bullets. Duke barely intervened, objecting only to the most leading of Lipford's questions about the method Henderson supposedly used to file them down. On cross-examination, Duke focused instead on Floy and Eli Cosper's house party. Clark was at that party and had been arrested after shooting a man named James Sampson. Following on his questioning of Floy Cosper, Duke wanted to know whether Clark had seen Henderson with a gun at that party.

"Was it this gun or another?" Duke said, holding the .38 Special up for Clark.

"It was another," Clark said. Lipford looked up from his notes.

Speaking slowly, Duke emphasized, "When he shot there that night, it was another gun?"

"Yes, sir. He didn't use that one," Clark said, pointing.

"You do know on that night at Eli Cosper's it wasn't this kind of gun he used," Duke said. He couldn't ask it enough.

"No, sir. It wasn't that gun. It was the black one I saw."

Through Clark, Duke had given the jury an alternate theory. Floy Cosper had seen Henderson with a gun, but not the gun he had supposedly taken in the Stripling Chapel attack.

"Prior to that," Duke said, "sometime before the party at Eli Cosper's house on that Saturday night, you had also seen Clarence and Eli Cosper's wife up at a fellow named Brown's place? That was about two weeks before the party at Eli Cosper's house?"

"Yes, sir," Clark said. "I think it was about two or three weeks."

Lipford and Shirley Boykin leaned toward each other, conferring. Clark was one of the "goddamn nigger witnesses" Lipford had warned Robinson to stay away from prior to the trial.

"Your best recollection was the party at Brown's house was two or three weeks prior to the time they had a party down at Eli Cosper's," Duke repeated. Then he asked Clark if it was at that earlier party that Clarence fired his pistol to break up a fight.

The question prompted low whispers and a rustling from the spectators, especially from the back benches where the Black audience sat.

"Yes, sir," Clark said.

If Clark was testifying truthfully, Henderson's run-in with the couple from LaGrange happened at a different party two or three weeks earlier, well before the Stripling Chapel attack. That meant Floy Cosper was not only mistaken about the gun Henderson had but she was confused about at which party he had fired it to quell an argument.

Duke spun and walked to the prosecution table and retrieved the nickel-plated revolver, holding it up for Clark to see.

"Give your best recollection of the first time you saw Clarence Henderson with this gun," he said.

"The first time I seen him with it, he was at my house," Clark said.

"When was the first time you saw him with it? Before you were down to Eli Cosper's house?" Duke asked.

"It was two or three weeks," he said.

If Clark had seen Henderson with a shiny pistol two or three weeks before the Cosper party, it could not have been Pendergrass's revolver.

"Two or three weeks before you were down to Eli Cosper's house, you had seen him with this pistol?" Duke asked.

"That is the best I can remember."

Henderson's defense team had turned two of Lipford's key Black witnesses against him. Floy Cosper testified she first saw the marks she used to identify the gun a year after the Stevens murder. And now Clark was testifying to seeing the pistol weeks before he should have had it.

Before he let Clark go, Duke had one more question.

"You know a fellow named Cook?" he asked.

Clark answered warily. "Yes, sir. C. H. Cook?"

"You talk to him about this case?"

"No, sir. We didn't talk none about this case," Clark said, then glancing up at Judge Boykin, he added, "while we went to court up here."

"You haven't talked to him at any time after your testimony last time?" Duke said.

"No, sir. Me and him never said nothing at all about it."[23]

Lipford called Cook to the stand. In the first trial, Cook was simply another Black man who testified he had seen Henderson with guns in 1948. In January, Cook testified he bought a blue-steel .38 Special from him and had seen a nickel-plated revolver around the same time, but exactly when that was, he couldn't say. In fact, in that trial, Cook testified that he didn't think it was the same gun as the one in evidence.

On this day, Cook offered little more, repeating his testimony, full as it was with fuzzy dates and remembrances. As Duke rose for cross-examination, Cook looked at the white man and then down to Robinson and Moore, who met his gaze.

"You know Junior Clark," Duke began. Yes, Cook said. "You see and talk to Junior Clark after he testified in the last trial of this case?"

Cook said he had, but characterized it as "just in there talking."

"Did Junior Clark tell you at the time the reason he testified about Henderson filing some bullets?" Duke asked. "Was it because Henderson put the gun in his possession?"

Perhaps because they were apprehensive about the answer, Lipford and Shirley Boykin both failed to object to Duke's leading question. In jailhouse statements and in an unsworn statement from the witness stand in the first trial, Henderson had said Clark and Bo Dunson had borrowed the gun the night of the Stevens murder, returning it the next day.

Cook leaned back and spoke plainly. A neutral party.

"I asked him, 'Did you see Clarence Henderson filing any bullets?' And he says, 'Yes, he filed the bullets.' I says, 'How come you to tell he filed the bullets?' He says, 'Clarence told he bought the gun from me and I told about him filing them.'"[24]

Clark might be sticking to his story about seeing Henderson file bullets, but according to Cook there was revenge, too, in his testimony.

Sticking with his playbook from the first trial, Lipford called J. T. Brown, a Black farmworker, Henderson's neighbor, and the man who threw the house party early in August 1948. In the first trial, Brown testified that he saw Henderson with a shiny revolver and tried to sell it to him. In brief questioning, Brown repeated the memory.

Brown saw Henderson the Monday after Junior Clark shot James Sampson. Henderson had a nickel-plated revolver he planned to sell to Laymon Almon. Hours later, he saw Henderson again, flashing $15 in cash from the sale. Lipford sat down; Duke rose.

"What time of year in 1948 was that?" Duke asked.

"I couldn't tell you," Brown said. Trying to place it, he added, "I was working."

"What type of work were you doing?"

"Farm work."

Duke moved in—but casually, hands in his pockets.

"Was it cotton-picking time?"

"No, sir. Fall is when we usually pick cotton," Brown said. "I was laying by."

"Laying by" is the growing period between planting and harvesting— summer.

"You sure it was laying-by time in 1948?" Duke asked.

"Yes, sir," Brown said. "It was sometime about the latter part of July."

Lipford called Thomas Harris, a Black man and another of Henderson's neighbors, who had testified in the first trial to seeing Henderson with a shiny pistol. After repeating that testimony, Duke asked him what time of year it was when he saw this.

"Along June or July," Harris said. "Along there somewhere."

Duke, cutting to the chase, picked up the murder weapon.

"You wouldn't pretend to say this is the gun you saw him with," he said.

"No, sir," Harris said.

Witness after witness had claimed to see Henderson with a gun weeks before he could possibly have gotten it in the Stripling Chapel attack. And J. T. Brown had Henderson selling the pistol to Laymon Almon months before the murder. Every fantasy in the state's timeline that had gone unchallenged by Henderson's court-appointed attorneys in the first trial was on full display this time around.

Duke released Harris and sat back down, smiling at the prosecutor. Lipford fumed. Shirley Boykin was sanguine.[25]

The prosecution's next witness was Henderson's jailer, Coweta County sheriff Lamar Potts. The lanky sheriff strode to the stand wearing a coat and tie and carrying a white Stetson hat in his hands. Potts testified to holding Henderson following his December 1949 arrest and that he took two statements from him. Potts recounted the first statement Henderson gave about buying the gun from Harvey "Bo" Dunson in a Georgia Skin game in Villa Rica for $10.

"He kept it a week, got broke, and sold it to a darkey named Laymon something," Potts said. "Laymon Almon, I believe."

Potts also testified that had he arrested Dunson, whom the sheriff called by his alias, "Bo Boykin," as a material witness, placing him in the same cell with Henderson. Then, although it wasn't revealed in the first trial, Potts said he had the telephone company place a secret listening device in the cell so he could hear the two men talk.

"You could hear them just as distinctly as you hear me," Potts told Lipford. "Henderson said to the Boykin boy, 'They got me in a spot. They got me charged with killing a man. I want you to help me out.' Boykin replied, 'I don't know nothing about it. I have got nothing to do with it and don't want to have anything to do with it.'"

Potts said Henderson told Dunson/Boykin that he would get an aunt in Chicago to hire a lawyer for him if he would take the murder charge. "Then you can say you got [the gun] from the other Negro," Potts said, quoting Henderson. Dunson refused the offer, the sheriff said.

"I listened continually, off and on, for three days before I separated them," Potts said. "He made that statement more than once, on the proposition that he would take Boykin to his aunt if he would take it on himself."

Duke objected to Potts's suggesting that Henderson was shifting guilt. "He has not testified to a thing here that would show any admission of guilt," he said.

Potts shrugged and Lipford asked about the days prior to Henderson's first trial. Potts said Henderson called him to the cell to talk to him.

"He said, 'They are going to take me over to Carrollton to try me, ain't they?' I said, 'Yes.' He said, 'I'm going to plead guilty.'"

A confession of guilt had the jury's attention.

"I said, 'I don't imagine they will let you plead guilty, Clarence,'" Potts said.

"He make any statement as to why he was pleading guilty?" Lipford asked. "What reason?"

"That was about all he said," Potts said. "He wanted to plead guilty."

Duke's cross-examination of Potts was a study in passive aggression. The sheriff was obliged to answer Duke's questions, but he would do him no favors.

Duke began by asking Potts if he agreed Henderson was held in the Coweta jail "for safe keeping."

"No, sir. I did not say that," the sheriff said.

"You know why it was he was brought over there?" Duke asked.

"I have an idea," the sheriff said, blankly staring the Atlanta lawyer square in the eyes.

Duke tried again. "Was it for safe keeping?"

"I don't know."

Frustrated, Duke asked, "Was it for any *other* reason?"

Potts paused, appearing to think hard on the answer.

"I don't know," he said. "I imagine that was the reason."

Duke and Potts circled each other with a series of questions about Henderson's jailhouse statements and their reference to the .38 Special. How, Duke asked, did Henderson know about the gun? Who told him? From Potts's perspective, Henderson knew about the gun because he held it in his hand when he shot Buddy Stevens. From Duke's, someone had to tell him so he could incorporate it in this fake statement. Henderson was illiterate and the statement was filled with semi-lawyerly police gibberish.

"You don't purport that was in his own language?" Duke said.

"No," Potts said. Potts typed up the first statement himself, more or less as Henderson had related it, he said. "The second statement was made in the county commissioners' office and written by Mrs. Bailey," he said.

"You mean transcribed by Mrs. Bailey," Duke said. It was a roundabout way to make a point that this statement wasn't to be trusted. "Anywhere in this statement he made did he make any admission he did this killing?"

"No, sir," Potts said.

"Never did," Duke said, punctuating his point. "He has never made a specific statement of guilt to you, verbally or otherwise, as to have taken a human life."

"No, sir."

"When he told you he was going to plead guilty, you told him they wouldn't let him because the judge wouldn't consent to a life sentence?" Duke asked.

"I told him I didn't believe they would accept it," Potts said.

"He said he was going to plead guilty to get a life sentence?" Duke pressed.

"I told him I did not believe they would accept a plea of guilty," Potts said.

"You only *thought* that he was willing to do that in order to save his life?"

"I thought it was that way," Potts said flatly.

At this point Duke was less interested in poking holes in Potts's testimony than he was in getting his points made. The sheriff could have excused himself as Duke peppered him with questions about the jailhouse recordings.

"He told the Boykin boy he was on the spot, they had him charged with killing a white man in Carroll County?" Duke said. "He told him he was in a bad fix and he had to do something to get out of it?"

Yes, Potts said.

"He was charged with a crime and he was trying to get out of it, if he could?" Duke said.

"I don't know that," Potts said.

Potts had built a reputation as a solid lawman, a rare honest man among the moonshiners and crooked country cops of rural Georgia. He was a folk hero following the conviction of Meriwether County land baron John Wallace in 1948, so Duke's next question took courage.

"You remember the occasion when Mr. Wiggins, appointed by this court to represent him, came over there to talk to Clarence Henderson at the Newnan jail?" Duke asked. "Would you swear you did not listen to the conversation?"

Potts looked at Duke. "I swear I wouldn't do it," he said. It was an answer to a slightly different question and Duke knew it.

"You won't swear that did not happen," Duke said.

"I'm very careful about what I state," Potts said. "I swear that did not happen."[26]

Irritated, Lipford chose to question Potts again.

"Clarence has been over there in your jail since the trial in January," he began. Potts nodded and said, "Yes, sir."

"Did you ever have any conversations with him in reference to this case since then?"

Potts nodded again. "Yes, sir." For the moment, Potts seemed content to answer Lipford's questions with the same number of syllables as he had offered to Duke.

"What, if anything, did he say to you?" Lipford said.

"He said this: One night he was going down the road, walking down the road going home, and a car drove up behind him with four or five white men," Potts began. "One of them opened the door, two of them got out and jerked him in the car and gave him this pistol."

Duke objected. "Unless he had the pistol there," he said, pointing to the murder weapon, "and he testified he gave him this pistol—"

Boykin raised a hand to stop Duke, then turned to Potts. "Go ahead," the judge said.

"He said they gave him this pistol, made him take it and threw him out of the car and went on," Potts said. "He said they told him if anything came up, he better keep his mouth shut."

"Did he say he knew them?" Lipford asked.

Potts nodded.

"Who was it?"

"Mr. Pendergrass," the sheriff said.[27]

A murmuring erupted from whites and Blacks alike in the courtroom.

On its face, the story seemed unlikely, the concoction of a Black man who had just been convicted of murdering a white boy and sentenced to die in "Old Sparky," as Georgia's electric chair was unoriginally named. Still, no one in the courtroom—white or Black—could have heard the testimony of Hardman and Pendergrass and not wondered.

The gun had belonged to Pendergrass. It was stolen in an attack hours after the cop-turned-cabdriver had taken Hardman and Mrs. Parker to a remote church south of town. Although he denied it later, Hardman himself had told a grand jury he thought Pendergrass had attacked him. How hard would it be to believe that a disreputable crew of rough white men had decided to pin Stevens's murder on a random Black sharecropper? For the African Americans in the back of the courtroom, not hard at all.

Why Lipford chose to dedicate his redirect of the sheriff to such an endeavor isn't clear.

CHAPTER 14

BALLISTICS, NAN, AND A VERDICT

In preparing for trial, E. E. Robinson and S. S. Moore had sought in vain to find a ballistics expert willing to travel to the Deep South for low pay to testify on behalf of a Black man accused of shooting a white man. Even Thurgood Marshall had been unable to secure an expert in time for the trial. Finding an expert was such a priority because of the damning evidence given by George Cornett, deputy director of the Fulton County Crime Laboratory, in the first trial. While a string of witnesses—some more believable than others—placed the shiny .38 Special revolver in the hands of Clarence Henderson, only Cornett could explain why the bullet dug out of the boy's body was a 9mm instead.

As he had nine months earlier, Prosecutor Wright Lipford called on Cornett to provide this key testimony. And in a series of authoritative answers, Cornett explained how the lands and grooves found on the bullet taken from Buddy's body corresponded to the .38 Special retrieved from the Atlanta pawnshop. He also described how the 9mm bullet would not ordinarily fit a .38, but by filing down the midsection of the bullet casing he was able to get it to chamber and fire. The resulting tests, conducted with microscopic observation but displayed on large sheets of paperboard for the jurors, indicated the bullet taken from Stevens had been fired from the gun in evidence, he said.

"Five lands and five grooves, right-hand twist," Cornett explained. It was a magical explanation by a white wizard in horn-rim glasses.

The testimony was largely a repeat of the first trial, although Lipford's questioning delved deeper into Cornett's process, laboring over the photos comparing the Stevens bullet to a test bullet Cornett fired.

"I will ask you, whether or not, in your opinion, the .38 Smith and Wesson, serial number 527398, fired the evidence bullet?" Lipford concluded.

"In my opinion, it did," Cornett said, directing his answer past Lipford to the jury.[1]

The words echoed as Dan Duke rose. Like Cornett, there was something authoritative about the white lawyer with the wire-frame spectacles, the deep voice, and the sorghum-sweet Southern accent. The anonymous phone call the night before had rattled him, but without more information, Duke had to focus on the task at hand.

Henderson's defense team had been unable to secure an expert to challenge Cornett, so Duke—over the course of nearly an hour of cross-examination—presented himself as one. In fact, Duke's intense questioning suggested he was not only Cornett's scientific equal but his superior and that the limits of the former beat cop's knowledge of ballistics were easily reached. The *Georgian* described the cross-examination as "grueling and lengthy . . . and highly technical."[2]

Duke began with a series of detailed questions about the manufacture of firearms and the boring and rifling of barrels. Within a few minutes the examination gave jurors the impression of a conversation between two experts speaking the same mysterious language.

"They use a really hard substance as the boring apparatus," Duke said.

"The reamer," Cornett said.

"And that extends through the barrel, leaving a right-hand twist to the barrel or the other, by turn?"

"You turn it according to the pitch of the rifling you want."

"You mean right or left," Duke said.

"They put a left-hand twist or a right," Cornett said.

"The reamer would turn in a right-hand direction and the rifling is cut into the barrel?"

"Yes, sir."

"And the bullet passing through the barrel would receive the exact impressions of this filing," Duke said, "according to the amount of powder pressure behind the bullet and according to the size of the bullet?"

Cornett paused, cocking his head and looking past Duke to the prosecution table. Lipford stared back.

Finally, Cornett said, "I am not a ballistics expert. I'm am an identifying man. I identify projectiles."[3]

Duke waited an extra second, letting Cornett's new reputation as a mere "identifying man" settle in before moving on. He asked if Cornett agreed that the specific rifling of the barrel of a gun—its unique fingerprint, as it were—was the result of the manufacturing process. Yes, Cornett said.

Duke then asked if the markings left on a bullet passing through such a chamber would be the result of a number of factors, including the caliber of the bullet, but also the pressure behind it and the hardness of the barrel as it spun out. Yes, the witness said.

"And the amount of powder pressure behind the bullet," Duke said. "If there was 10,000 pounds of pressure behind the bullet, there would be a more direct impression?"

Cornett shifted in his seat, his eyes darting up as he considered the question.

"I don't know about that," he said. "I know projectiles generally swell as they pass through the rifling. I know you can take a bullet of small caliber and the impression will not be as deep as one chambered for it."

"You know that from experience?" Duke asked.

"Yes, sir."

"But you have no scientific knowledge and are not an expert—and don't claim to be—in making comparisons of an evidence bullet with a test bullet when the test bullet and evidence bullet were fired out of a cartridge having a certain firing power?"

Duke continued listing the things Cornett was not and the things he did not know.

"You don't have any way of formulating any opinion as to whether they would leave a different marking if there was a different amount of powder behind the bullet?'

Duke was suggesting that, in his experiments, Cornett might have used bullets from different manufacturers, with differing amounts of gunpowder from the bullet that killed Stevens.

"I never did study ballistics," Cornett said. "I would have to study it to know about the powder power."

Duke moved on with questions about identifying and comparing bullets by sight alone and the exactness of that science. If Lipford had hoped to use Cornett's authoritative lecture to convince the jury, then Duke hoped to bury that lecture in a confusing avalanche of words and Cornett's frequent admission that he was not an expert in the field.

Eventually, Duke turned to Cornett's laboratory tests and the ammunition he personally filed down to fit the .38 Special.

"You know the name of the manufacturer of the test bullet you fired?" Duke asked.

Cornett shuffled through his notes. "I think I can give it to you," he said.

Duke looked up at Judge Boykin. "I'd like to get it for the record," he explained.

"Remington ammunition, metal jacket," Cornett said, finding the page in his notes. "The 9mm was a Remington Luger 9mm."

"Made for a foreign-make weapon?"

"Yes, sir. Made for a foreign-made weapon by the Remington Company," Cornett said.

"The evidence bullet," Duke said. "What type of bullet was that?"

Cornett said the bullet taken from Stevens's body was made by the Western Company. Bullets made by Western, the parent company of Winchester rifles, were less common, although the company had made billions of rounds for the Army in World War II.

"You knew at the time you fired the test bullet the make of them?" Duke asked. "You knew that the evidence bullet was not of the same make?"

"Yes, sir," Cornett replied. Then he turned toward the jury box. "May I say that the reason I did not use that type of ammunition was that I did not have it. I went to the hardware store and searched diligently for it, trying to find that type of ammunition and was unable to locate it."

Duke scoffed. "You are aware," he said, "that all of the scientific authorities say that the powder pressure is a necessary element in making the investigation?"

"No," Cornett said flatly.

Duke went on to list various experts by name—Scott, Riff, Darnell—running Cornett through a gauntlet of scientific studies. At one point he handed an academic paper to the man and had him read it before the jury. Duke peppered him with questions on powder loads and firing power, often without waiting for Cornett's reply.

By this point Cornett was spent.

"I know nothing about the component parts of metal and the powder pressure, or anything like that," he said. "I know when there is enough pressure to pass it through the barrel and if I have another that passed through the barrel—the same barrel—I can make an identification of it."

"You know the amount of pressure of the .38 Special bullet made by the Remington Manufacturing Company and the one you fired?" Duke asked. "Do you know whether the pressure was 12,000 [pounds] or 50,000?"

"I have no record," Cornett replied, adding that even if he did, he was not an expert in ballistics.

"Did you have anybody in the Fulton [County] Crime Laboratory who worked in conjunction with you—who *was* a ballistics expert—who could determine the amount of fire pressure upon the bullet?" Duke asked.

"Not now," Cornett said. He acknowledged the county had previously had a ballistics expert and that expert had matched ammunition for test-firing purposes.[4]

At this point Duke asked Cornett if he was the only man capable of conducting firearms tests at the lab. "I was until two or three years ago," Cornett said.

Turning to Judge Boykin, Duke said, "I expect to show there were others who claimed to be firearms experts in the Fulton County Crime Laboratory at the time and there is a difference of opinion—"

"I object to that," Lipford interrupted. "It is irrelevant and he knows it!"

Boykin quickly sustained the objection. The color rose in Duke's face.

"You rule that evidence out as irrelevant?" Duke asked.

"Yes, I rule it out," the judge said.

Duke gathered himself. When he resumed his cross-examination, he attempted to find another way into the topic, asking Cornett about a prior murder in Atlanta. This time Shirley Boykin objected and his younger brother ordered the jury to leave. Once they were gone, Duke approached the judge.

"I want to get this on the record," he pleaded.

"Ask the question," Judge Boykin said.

The courtroom was packed with observers, but the only ones that mattered were out of earshot when Duke asked Cornett about his boss, Dr. Herman Jones.

"Dr. Jones is a firearms expert, and in addition, he is a chemist?" Duke asked. "He made an investigation of the comparison of these bullets—the evidence bullet and the test bullet and the .38 caliber pistol in this very case?"

Judge Boykin listened intently. All of this was new information.

"I will tell you what I know about it," Cornett said, his mouth drawn tight.

When Cornett had completed his examination of the evidence bullet and the test bullet and developed his photographs for use as evidence, he had a meeting with Lipford, Carroll County sheriff Gaston, and Jones. Jones had looked at his work and found it "absolutely correct," he said.

"You know he has now made a test of the bullet?" Duke asked. When Cornett said nothing in response, the judge looked toward the sheriff's deputy, who had led the jury out and ordered them brought back in. When they were seated, Judge Boykin looked at Duke. "You want to ask that question?" he said.

Duke looked at Cornett. "Do you know whether [Dr. Jones] made an independent examination of any of the tests you made?"

Cornett shifted in his seat. "The test is something I do," he said.

Judge Boykin cut in. "That is not responsive to the question," he said. "Answer the question, yes or no."

"He didn't go through the whole examination," Cornett said.

"Did he or did he not?" Duke asked.

"No, sir," Cornett shot back. "Not to my knowledge. He went through the comparison part."

Duke turned to the judge. "I want Dr. Jones as a witness," he said.

Lipford jumped up. "Did he cooperate with Dr. Jones with this test?" he asked. "I would like to ask him what part he went through with him."

Cornett wasn't Lipford's witness at the moment. Judge Boykin didn't care. "All right," he said. Confused, Cornett looked at the judge and then the prosecutor before saying that Jones had made his own microscopic examination of the test bullet and the evidence bullet.

"What did Dr. Jones say?" Lipford asked.

Duke interjected. "I object to that as hearsay testimony!"

Boykin sustained the objection. Lipford sat down and Duke was allowed to continue his cross-examination.

"Are you a microscope expert?" he asked.

"I do use the microscope," Cornett said, not offering anything now.

"Are you a photographic expert?"

"I make photographs."

Duke asked Cornett a few more questions, delving into his process of photographing the lands and grooves of bullets. Cornett, unsure now, admitted under questioning that he took photographs of the bullets from one side only—just enough to match the grooves. After a few minutes, Boykin interrupted. Through the windows, the gloom of dusk cast shadows on the far wall.

"Court will recess until nine o'clock A.M.," the judge said, rapping his gavel. *State v. Clarence Henderson* would stretch into a third day.[5]

Henderson's defense team again left Carrollton for Atlanta, but this time Duke drove to the Chastain Memorial Park neighborhood in north Atlanta and knocked on the door of one of its quaint Colonial-style homes. Dr. Herman Jones answered with a curious look as Dan Duke recounted his mysterious phone call from the night before. "Have you made any tests on the gun in this case?" Duke asked.

"I can't talk about the work of the lab," Jones said. "You can call me as a witness, place me under oath, then I'll answer your questions."

Duke was in a bind. New tests could provide important evidence proving Henderson's innocence, but if Jones testified that he concurred with the opinions of his deputy, George Cornett, it only strengthened the state's case. No defense attorney would call a witness in a death penalty case without knowing how he would testify. Duke pleaded with Jones and mentioned his inability to get Judge Boykin to allow independent tests on the bullet and the gun. Duke kept Jones talking for three hours as the clock crept to midnight, but he would not budge.[6]

The new day dawned with George Cornett back on the stand with a tired Dan Duke standing before him. Given the unexpected length of this testimony and the distance back to Atlanta, it's possible that Cornett spent the night in Carrollton, so he likely would have been dressed in the previous day's clothes. The length of the trial had done nothing to discourage local observers, as a crowd of five hundred onlookers jammed Boykin's courtroom when the trial recommenced.[7]

Duke renewed his cross-examination with a series of questions about the chemical composition of gunpowder, the answers to most of which Cornett admitted he did not have. Duke probed Cornett's procedures for determining the similarities between bullets under the comparison microscope using—as

Cornett admitted—measurements between just one set of grooves. Again and again, Duke suggested that the witness, who was perhaps the state's foremost technician of his kind, was both ignorant and sloppy when it came to the finer points of ballistic science.

Duke hammered Cornett with a series of questions on the latest academic standards of microscopic identification until Lipford had enough.

"He's answered that two or three times!" the prosecutor complained.

"He has never given me a full answer," Duke said.

He walked back to the defense table and picked up a thick book titled *Textbook of Firearms Investigation, Identification and Evidence,* by Major Julian Hatcher, one of the preeminent experts of the time.

"How long have you had this book to study it?" Duke asked.

"The book in our laboratory has been there several months," Cornett said. "I don't know how long."

"This is the latest authority on evidence identification and comparison microscope photographs?"

"I don't know," Cornett said. "I don't know how long it has been out and what it says."

The Hatcher book wasn't popularly read, but it was required reading for ballistics and firearms experts. It was first published in 1935 at the request of J. Edgar Hoover. That Cornett hadn't read it indicated his expertise was vocational rather than academic.

"You ever study physics?" Duke asked. Duke had stayed up until midnight the night before talking with a man who had studied physics and chemistry and who knew the Hatcher book cover to cover.

"No, sir. I have never been to college," Cornett said.

"A self-made man?"

"I've studied things."

"You have had this book in your office two or three months, and you have never studied physics?"

Lipford objected. Judge Boykin had the jury go out and then turned to Duke.

"You have the right to cross examine this witness as to any matters relevant to the case being tried," Boykin said. "I will give you every opportunity in the world, but don't go into irrelevant matters. I want to get through."

Duke assured Boykin he wasn't "trifling" with the court's patience.

"My purpose in asking a question here is for the purpose of showing whether the witness is an expert in firearms identification," he said.

Cornett knew nothing of physics or chemistry, Duke said. He couldn't expertly comment on the effects of a smaller projectile being shot from a larger barrel or what that might do to the markings left on the bullet. Duke said he expected to further impeach Cornett by calling "persons of authority" later in the trial.

"He has said he never studied physics," Boykin said. "I just want to get this straightened out. I want to give you every opportunity in this case."

With the jury still out, Boykin allowed Duke to ask Cornett a series of questions about his lack of understanding of chemistry, the effects of heat on projectiles, and the use of an X-ray spectroscope to peer into the chemical composition of bullets. Cornett admitted he was not knowledgeable in any of these areas.[8]

A bailiff lead the jury back in and Duke concluded his cross-examination with a series of questions about how Cornett had photographed the test and evidence bullets, the lighting and shadows used, and the reasons behind his methods. Pulling out Cornett's oversized photographs the prosecution had used for evidence, Duke finally asked him if they were just props meant to make up the jurors' minds for them "rather than to let them make it?"

After hours of cross-examination, the indisputable science of ballistics lay on the courtroom floor in a heap. As he did so often throughout the trial, Lipford failed to counter Duke's strategy and instead focused his redirect with more questions about the file.[9]

"What, if anything, did you find on your examination of that file?" he asked Cornett.

"I found brass," he said.

Duke objected. Cornett had already testified he was not an expert in chemistry, he complained.

"Before he could testify they were particles of brass, he would have to show he is an expert in metals," he said.

"He can state his own opinion," Boykin said, "what it looked like to him."

Duke disagreed. This is an expert witness, he said.

"He has not qualified as a chemist and he is not capable of giving his opinion as to the bullet or the file," he said. Boykin waved him off and allowed the testimony in.

Finally, Cornett was dismissed, a moment that no doubt came as a relief to jurors and spectators as much as it did to Cornett himself.

Lipford called Nan Hansard.

There was not much about the case Lipford prepared for the first trial that he changed for the second. Hansard was the exception. She had been an early witness in the first trial. This time he saved her emotional weight for the end. A low hum of spectators whispering to each other greeted Hansard as she approached.

In his questioning, Lipford dug for more details, establishing a clearer timeline. Buddy picked Nan up at the Presbyterian church at a quarter to eight, it took them a few minutes to buy cigarettes at the Green Front, and they were at the country club just after 8:00 P.M. They listened to a program on the radio for half an hour, so it was around 8:30 when a man approached with a flashlight. This time Nan was confident he was "a Negro man." She added that he was wearing a mask, a detail that made the newspapers but one she never mentioned in the first trial.

"Of course, I couldn't see him quite as plain," she said. "I moved and I could see the gun and flashlight and I could see his eyes."[10]

"Could you tell approximately the size of the man at that time," Lipford asked.

"Not too well," she said.[11]

This time Nan said the man told Buddy to lie down on his back while they were still on the road, before he had robbed him. She also said the man "kept a good distance" from them initially, as far away as forty-five feet.[12]

Did you see him? Lipford asked. "I don't remember looking at him," Nan said. "He had the light on us all the time. Directed us with the light and I saw his hand and shape."[13]

"I will ask you whether or not you could see him and determine his size and color," Lipford said.

"I could tell by his hands, the light on his hand—one time," she said.

As in the first trial, Nan again described how the man with the flashlight had beat Buddy and how he had them lie down. She again described how she was gagged and nearly raped and how Buddy was shot and how he died saving her.

"I tried to hold him back. He tried to choke me. I screamed and Buddy lunged at him and knocked him away from me," she said. "I got up as soon as I could and I started to the pasture. And during that time he shot three times in all."[14]

The weakness in Nan Hansard's testimony was not that she was unsympathetic. It was that she never saw her attacker and had never consistently described his size, his shape, or the color of his skin. At most, she said the masked man sounded Black. But in the first trial she had testified that she had only heard him speak once and in a terribly stressful situation. Now Lipford offered a new detail: Nan had visited the Coweta County jail and overheard Henderson talking in his cell using the bug planted by Sheriff Potts.

"Did you hear all of the conversation?" Lipford asked. "How long did you hear him talk in Newnan?"

"Yes," Nan said. "Thirty or forty minutes."

"Who was carrying on the conversation?"

"Clarence Henderson and Bo Boykin," she said. Catching herself, she looked up a Judge Boykin. "Bo Dunson," she said.

Having heard him speak and having seen him at the trial, Lipford wanted to know if, in her opinion, Henderson was the man who had attacked her. Duke objected immediately. She either could identify him or not. Her opinion—a guess, really—was inadmissible, he said. The judge overruled Duke's complaint.

"In my opinion, he is the man," she said.[15]

Like Potts's testimony, Nan's revelation of eavesdropping on Henderson's alleged jailhouse conversations with Bo Dunson was never part of the first trial. It is possible that Lipford was unaware of the recordings, but that seems unlikely. Why would Potts make the recordings if not to aid the prosecution? More likely, Lipford felt the fact that they had recorded Henderson without his knowledge was something the prosecutor should not share with a jury already sympathetic to his cause. On the second try, knowing that the Georgia Supreme Court had made note of the fact that no one could identify Henderson as the culprit, Lipford saw it as a chance to bolster that weakness.

Duke rose for his chance to cross-examine Hansard. Duke could not, as he had done with Cornett, spend hours brutally questioning Nan's recollection or her ability to remember a voice she had heard one time two years ago. So he was more careful as he walked her through the hours following the attack and what she told the authorities that night.

"Did you tell them what you thought the size of the man was?" he asked.

"I was so disturbed, I don't know whether I did or not," she said.

"Did you talk to Officer Hillin, who was aiding the sheriff?" Duke asked. "Did you give him the size and height and weight?"

"Yes, sir," Nan said.

"You told these officers that your best recollection was the man would weigh about 160 pounds, around five feet nine inches high? Did you tell Officer Hillin that?" he asked.

"About that size," Nan said. Jurors' heads turned to the defendant, whose squat, short frame came up several inches shy of five nine.

"This is the first time you have ever sworn in your opinion this was the man?"

"I've never been asked," Hansard said plainly.

"You've been questioned many times officially," Duke said. "You were, of course, frightened and came through much excitement on that night and badly worried and you were very much strained afterwards."

"Yes, sir," she said.

"After the last trial, after the Supreme Court rendered its decision, who did you talk to and give it as your opinion he was the man?"

"To lots of them," Nan said.

"To Mr. Lipford?"

"Yes, sir."

"And he went over the various elements many times with you? He talked with you and went over all of the elements?'

"Yes, sir."

"And this very element?" Duke said, referring to the identification of Henderson as the culprit.

"Yes, sir," Nan said.

"He told you the reason the court—"

Before Duke could suggest that Lipford told Nan that her failure to forcefully identify Henderson as the attacker in the first trial had prompted the state's highest court to overturn the conviction, Shirley Boykin objected from the prosecution table.

"It's highly improper and he knows it," the judge's brother said, pointing at Duke.

Judge Boykin sustained the objection. Duke started to complain, but the judge raised his hand and ordered the jury out. Once they were out, Duke lodged a formal complaint against Shirley Boykin for adding the "highly improper" grace note to his objection.

"I would like to state for the record—" Duke began, but Judge Boykin waved him away.

"Let the jury come back," he told the bailiff.

Duke resumed his cross-examination with questions about the attack, what she saw and where she was standing when she caught her brief glimpse of a Black hand in the flash of gunfire.

"I said all the time he was a Negro," Nan said.

"You won't say it may be just an illusion of yours?"

"Mr. Duke, if you had been through what I did that night, it would be no illusion to you," she said. "It is my opinion that is the Negro that killed Buddy Stevens."

Duke, knowing he could do no more, sat down. Lipford, satisfied he had done enough, rested the state's case.[16]

The defense's case was not lengthy, but Duke took the opportunity to reinforce the lack of credibility in the state's timeline. He recalled Leonard Pendergrass to ask again when he lost his pistol: August 25, 1948. He then recalled Floy Cosper.

"You remember stating yesterday it was the last Saturday in August 1948 when you saw Henderson here at your house, that you saw him with a shiny pistol," Duke said. He raised the .38 Special in his hands. "Which you identified as this pistol."

"That wasn't the first time I saw it," Cosper corrected.

"And the first time you saw it?"

"Saw it one Saturday night at J. T. Brown's," she said.

"It wasn't the fourth Saturday night? I want you to be sure," he said.

"No, sir," Floy said.[17]

Then Duke recalled Georgia Bureau of Investigation agent Jim Hillin, who testified he had received from local authorities a report listing the pistol in evidence as stolen August 25. And what, Duke asked, was the date of the fourth Saturday in August? August 28, Hillin said. And the Saturday before that? August 21. Hillin was dismissed.[18]

The trial, now midway through its third day, broke for lunch. Duke made his way out of the courtroom. Waiting outside was Herman Jones. After a late night with the pleading Dan Duke, Jones received an early morning phone call from a deputy sheriff in Carroll County telling him he had been subpoenaed to testify in the Henderson trial and needed to appear in court "immediately." As soon as he saw him, Duke officially served the subpoena and asked him if he had done his own tests on the gun and bullet.

"Put me on the stand," Jones said. "Ask me under oath."

Duke was unsure. If the anonymous caller was right and the test showed the bullet didn't match the gun, it was potentially devastating for the state's case. But Jones could testify that he didn't test the bullets, or that he tested them and they concurred with his underling's findings. It was an intractable problem. Duke told Jones to wait and marched to Judge Boykin's chambers.

Duke froze as he opened the door to find Wright Lipford sitting in a chair across from Boykin, who was eating his lunch. Composing himself, Duke followed his nature and came in hard.

"I'm going to put Dr. Herman Jones on the stand and show that Cornett doesn't know what he is talking about," he said, glancing at Lipford. "Dr. Jones will testify that revolver didn't fire the evidence bullet."

Boykin nodded and looked at Lipford, who was mulling the idea when the three men heard a toilet flush and George Cornett emerged from Boykin's private bathroom buttoning his fly.

"I don't care what you undertake to prove by Dr. Jones," Cornett said, waving a finger at Duke. "I'm sticking to my report and to my testimony."[19]

Duke turned and went back in the courtroom, where he, Robinson, and Moore huddled around Clarence Henderson. Henderson would again take the stand in an unsworn statement. When the crowds returned at 1:00 P.M. Henderson, imprisoned for nearly a year, strode to the witness stand. He had given an impassioned speech in the first trial seeking mercy from the white men on the jury, some of whom he had known all his life. This time his statement began with a strong defense.

"The .38 Special what I sold to Laymon Almon, the barrel was about that much sawed off," he said, holding his thumb and index finger about two inches apart. "The gun they have here now, I don't know. I haven't even had it in my hand."

Henderson asked Judge Boykin if he could examine the pistol, something he said he had never done. A bailiff handed him the weapon. Henderson hefted it, then opened the cylinder showing the six empty chambers. His eyes widened.

"Gentlemen of the jury, this gun don't break like the one I sold to Laymon Almon. That gun broke this way," he said. He pantomimed taking the barrel of the gun and pulling it down from the cylinder.

So-called top-break revolvers were less common than side-loading guns, but they did exist, particularly in snub-nose guns with shorter barrels, like the "sawed-off" version Henderson said he had sold to Almon.

"The one I sold to Laymon is not the same gun," he said, handing the evidence revolver back. "The one I got from Junior Clark, it was nickel plated and not this one here. The one I sold at that time had 'J.E.' on it. I don't know what it stood for. I cannot say. It had 'J.E.' on the pistol."

That smaller, nickel-plated pistol was the one he sold to Almon, he said. He had another gun, too, similar to the Smith & Wesson in evidence, but that was the blue-steel pistol Junior Clark testified in the first trial as having seen him carry. Henderson stuck with his story that he lent his gun to Clark the weekend of the Buddy Stevens murder, although his statement didn't make clear to which gun he was referring.[20]

He did make clear that he knew nothing about the Stevens murder, appealing directly to the jury. The state's evidence didn't make sense, he said.

"Talking about filing a bullet," he scoffed. "I never have filed a bullet and don't know how a man could file a bullet to get in a gun."

Henderson said the discovery of the file was just as ridiculous.

"They said they found an old file in my wife's house," he said. "Anybody will tell you my wife is a clean girl and she would not have put a rusty file in her dresser drawer."

Looking out at a sea of impassive white faces, Henderson began to ramble. Some knew him and he appealed directly to them. They knew he wouldn't lie to white people. He had been raised among white people and worked for them. But now he was being "treated like a dog for nothing," he said. Henderson said he had been beaten by Carrollton police chief Rada Threadgill and Sheriffs Denver Gaston and Lamar Potts, all acting under the orders of Lipford.

"The white people that know me," he said bitterly, "they wouldn't have hit me."

As in the first trial, Henderson looked out and saw Earl Staples, a local attorney he knew when they were both boys and played and worked on the farm together before the barrier of race forced their friendship to end. He looked to the jury.

"I call on you to go down the line for me and in the sight of God to win a victory so I may go home and raise my kids," he said. "I have got thirteen men to talk to. You know who the thirteenth man is? It is God.

"Gentlemen, look to the Lord and He will show you I am innocent," he concluded.[21]

Henderson returned to the defense table, his footsteps sounding through the quiet courtroom. When his client was seated, Duke rose and called a witness: Dr. Herman Jones. Heads craned to see as the thin, professorial Jones was led into the courtroom.

The defense lawyers stole glances at Lipford. If he was nervous about Jones's testimony, he didn't show it. After a few moments Judge Boykin cleared his throat. Duke emerged from the conference and said he would not call Jones after all. The risk was too great to jeopardize the case on appeal.

"I prefer to go the jury," Duke said.[22]

In closing arguments, Lipford presented Henderson as a Negro accused of raping a white woman. He told the jury he had grown up on a farm in nearby Heard County with Negro hands and he "knew their habits." This trial was about protecting white women and girls from lustful, criminal Black men, he said. He cannot do that without a guilty verdict, he said. Appealing directly to generational fears about Black sexuality and social order—fears instilled in these men all their lives—Lipford told the jurors they needed to send a message.

Enraged, Duke objected and demanded a mistrial.

"The solicitor general by his argument is going into crime generally in the county," he said. "There is no evidence here about the habits of Negroes."

Boykin ignored the plea for a mistrial and instead instructed the jury, essentially, to forget who they are and from whence they came.

"Gentlemen of the jury," he said, "you will not be concerned with any other crimes. You will make your verdict solely upon the evidence in this case."[23]

The jury received the case at 4:15 P.M. and began their deliberations in a conference room on a floor below Boykin's court. In the first trial, the jury took less than two hours to convict Henderson and condemn him to the electric chair, but this time discussions dragged on deep into the evening. Finally, at 9:30, the foreman of the jury appeared before the tired judge. As newspaper reporters rushed in, he told Boykin the jury was deadlocked 9 to 3 in favor of conviction. Boykin was sympathetic but instructed the jury to continue their work a little longer.

"Everybody wants a verdict in this case" he said. "But I won't try to keep you here all night."[24]

Just thirty minutes later, with no further progress, Boykin told the men of the jury to return to their homes for the night and come back the next morning, Friday, and resume deliberations.[25]

Sleep clarified the thinking of the Carrollton men. When they returned to the county courthouse, the formerly deadlocked jury reached a decision after ninety minutes: guilty, no mercy. Henderson would again face the death penalty. Boykin ordered the sentence to be carried out in one month.

Henderson pleaded for mercy as his defense team tried to calm him. Even the strongest defense usually failed when the victim was white, the defendant was Black, and the district court was deep in the South. Henderson's hope would again reside in a higher court. Duke rose and made a motion for a new trial on grounds that the state's evidence was too weak and too inconsistent to warrant such a verdict. The procedural move triggered an automatic delay in Henderson's execution, and Boykin set a hearing for December 2 to hear the defense argument.[26]

Two other verdicts reached that day in the Carroll County courthouse show the sliding scale of Jim Crow justice. In a one-day trial, a jury found

Jesse Arrington, a twenty-six-year-old white man, guilty of voluntary manslaughter for gunning down another white man with a shotgun. Arrington claimed self-defense and received a sentence of between four and twenty years. Albert Kight, a Black man accused of killing his brother, also with a shotgun, likewise was found guilty of voluntary manslaughter. His sentence of one to three years suggests which lives white juries found least valuable.[27] Boykin oversaw both trials that same day after handing down the Henderson verdict.

CHAPTER 15

NEW EVIDENCE, NEW TRIAL

While the first verdict screamed across the front page of the *Atlanta Constitution* just nine months earlier, Clarence Henderson's second conviction ran deep inside, under the headline "Henderson Condemned a Second Time," followed by a spare, four-paragraph recap. The article did note that, compared to the first trial, the jury in the second iteration initially had trouble coming to an unanimous decision.[1] The Black-owned *Atlanta Daily World* played the conviction on the front page with the detail that the "doomed man's" first conviction had been voided by the Georgia Supreme Court. Unlike the *Constitution*'s brief account, the *Daily World* included that, along with Dan Duke, Henderson was represented by Robinson and Moore and that the NAACP had organized and funded his defense.[2]

The timing of the verdict, coming as it did on a Friday, was inconvenient for Carrollton's non-daily newspapers. It was the following Tuesday before the *Times–Free Press* could recap the events of five days earlier. The story—"Henderson Gets Chair"—led the newspaper but went just eight paragraphs long before transitioning into a recap of other notable verdicts. The off-lead story, "New Monkey Gets Hot Welcome from Lighted Cigarette," was nearly as long and might have had more breaking-news appeal.[3]

The *Georgian*, which published on Thursday, got the last word with its typical verbose and boosterish completeness. In its analysis, Parkman's newspaper noted the second trial's "lack of excitement and its complete maintenance of order."

"Also noticeable was the fact that Solicitor General Wright Lipford and Special Prosecutor Shirley C. Boykin moved slower and the small amount of new evidence they did inject into the record was damaging to the defendant's case," the *Georgian* reported. The story disposed of the defense's destruction of the gun timeline, central to the state's case, in a single sentence.

But by the fawning and expansive standard in so many *Georgian* stories, even this article lacked the zest of the first trial. Parkman played it on the front page but below the fold.[4]

While it's unsurprising that a second trial might elicit less excitement than the first, common among the coverage—whether from the big-city *Constitution*, the local press, or the *Daily World*—was the feeling that the story wasn't over. Each recap included early mention of Dan Duke's motion for a new trial, set for December 2, and the automatic stay of Henderson's execution.

In some ways Carroll County was moving beyond the Stevens murder, forging ahead in uncertain times. In an editorial congratulating a local woman who had been selected to appear on a national radio show, the *Georgian* suggested she might use her time to "remind the radio audience that Carrollton is a center of education and culture" and of the "many advantages here for those who want to move industry into our midst." It's unclear whether young Edith Foster was given such an expansive opportunity during her appearance on *The Betty Crocker Magazine of the Air*, but the column does show the mind of the city's leaders.[5] Around the same time, Carrollton's volunteer Carroll Service Council was hailed as a model of progressivism in a long article in a national magazine. The article praised the council for working collectively to push the community forward in everything from education to agriculture to health care, making special mention of the volunteer fundraising effort to build a new hospital.

"The Negroes in this southern community contributed almost as much as their wealthier neighbors, and a Negro ward in the hospital is today as well equipped as the others," the magazine crowed.[6]

The city itself was in the process of expanding its limits, raising school taxes, and establishing a civil service board to professionalize the hiring and firing of city workers. Much of the grunt work was being done by the city's new attorney, William Wiggins. Carrollton's political elite had not punished Wiggins, part of Henderson's first defense team, after handing him such a delicate case.[7]

But beneath the veneer of progress, white leaders could see the fabric of racial segregation begin to fray. "That racial question," as the *Times–Free Press* put it in its editorial page, loomed over all.

"The Southern whites know the Southern colored people, and in turn, the Negroes in the South know the whites," one North Georgia editorial writer put it. "If other folks would keep their hands out of our affairs and stop their unwanted meddling, we'd fare much better."[8]

The fear of outside agitation and federal intrusion on matters of race was an obsession of ruling whites across the South. Speaking to an audience in Tampa, James Farley, chairman of global exports for Atlanta-based Coca-Cola, warned President Truman that Southern leaders should be allowed to find their own solutions to the region's pressing civil rights questions. While Farley, a Democratic Party boss from New York and former postmaster general under FDR, found a receptive audience among Southern whites, African Americans denounced him and organized a boycott of the soda.[9]

While maintaining a strictly observed color barrier, whites in Carrollton were eager to show themselves as progressive. But the unsettled business in Judge Boykin's courtroom was a reminder of the tension caused by "that racial question."

It was unlikely Boykin would grant Henderson a new trial, but his defense team was required to walk through the formality while also preparing their brief for the Georgia Supreme Court. In the meantime, Dan Duke, now a full member of the defense and baptized by fire, was anxious to make waves. The defense team had decided not to risk calling Jones as a witness, but even if he had testified that the ballistics of the gun and the bullet didn't match, it would have been his word against Cornett's. Jones was more highly qualified than his underling, but that likely wasn't enough to get a Black man past a skeptical white jury. Henderson needed overwhelming evidence.

On October 27, 1950, Duke went to the Carroll County Courthouse and filed a motion asking again that additional tests be allowed on the .38 Special, the evidence bullet, and the supposed brass particles Henderson was accused of creating when filing bullets to fit the gun.[10]

Duke also paid another call on Herman Jones, bringing with him another subpoena and pushing him again to tell him whether he had performed any additional tests on the revolver and bullet. Whether out of weariness or a desire to come clean, Jones relented—a bit.

"Yes," he said. "I did make comparison tests on the revolver."

Jones said he had made several comparisons with new test bullets that he then compared to Cornett's original test bullets and the bullet in evidence. He said he had done so in July after the supreme court overturned the conviction. To Duke's frustration, Jones still refused to say what he had learned unless he was under oath and compelled to tell what he knew.

More hopefully, Jones said he would give Duke and the defense team a sworn affidavit of his findings, provided that his boss, the Fulton County police chief, would allow it. Duke held out little hope that the chief would give that kind of permission, but the fact that Jones had offered it was a sign that he had something to say. Duke decided to risk it by asking Jones to testify before Boykin in the motion hearing for a new trial.[11]

Two weeks later, following one of Judge Boykin's Saturday morning hearings, Duke, Robinson, and Moore burst through the courtroom doors into the Carroll County Courthouse lobby. The weather that morning was unseasonably frigid, but Duke was hot.

"They are trying to bait a Negro," he told the gathered reporters, apparently referring to Henderson. "But this is one Negro they are not going to bait."

The remark drew a shouted warning from an angry deputy. Duke turned and tossed a hard word at him.

"Watch it," the deputy said. "You better leave."[12]

Herman Jones, usually a prosecution witness, trailed awkwardly behind the trio of defense lawyers. The hearing had not gone well for any of the four men or for Clarence Henderson. Duke had argued his motion for additional tests on the gun and bullet—at the defense's expense—and lost. Jones was allowed to testify and told the judge he had performed his own tests on the .38 Special and decided it could not be the murder weapon. Duke accused Solicitor Lipford of intentionally suppressing this contradictory evidence and said Jones would back that up in sworn testimony. Lipford denied it, pointing out to Boykin that Jones had signed off on Cornett's ballistics report.

"I initialed it," Jones said, adding that it merely signified he had received the report, not that he agreed with the findings.

Jones said he would testify in trial that he had reached a different conclusion, but Henderson's lawyers wanted independent tests. Duke said the defense would fund new tests from labs in Alabama and Texas.

At the start of the second trial, Boykin had denied the defense's motion to perform new tests after Lipford objected that the team had had months to perform them. Time was no obstacle now, but for Boykin it made little difference. Duke was attempting to "play with the court" by offering up Jones as a defense witness and claiming evidence suppression, he said.

"There was evidence that the pistol fired the bullet," the judge said, "and the jury had the right to believe it or not."

As for additional tests, Boykin didn't see the point and denied the request.

"We can't send this pistol and bullet to every state in the union," he said. "We would never get through litigation if the court heeded this motion."

Stymied, Robinson, Moore, and Duke left the courthouse and walked out into the chill morning air. A hearing for a new trial—another required step with little hope to succeed—was set to be heard by Boykin in a few weeks. Despite his frustration, the fiery Duke was already having the kind of impact the NAACP must have hoped for. The Jim Crow system of justice, usually efficient in convicting Black men, was under stress and its progress slowed.

Henderson's defense team was back in Boykin's courtroom on December 16 for another Saturday morning hearing on a motion for a new trial. This meeting had already been delayed by two weeks, and Boykin, an orderly jurist, was surely impatient.[13] Speaking for Henderson's defense team, Duke opened the meeting by asking Judge Boykin to summon a court reporter so that a transcript of the hearing might be prepared. It was a signal that everything—every remark and motion denied—would be fodder for the defense's argument that Henderson was being unfairly treated. Back and forth, Duke, Lipford, Judge Boykin, and his brother, Shirley, argued the need for a court reporter until the judge ordered the parties into conference with instructions for them to return when they had worked out an agreement.

When they returned that afternoon, Duke resumed by asking to file an affidavit by Dr. Jones where he would state the .38 special in evidence was not the gun that fired the bullet retrieved from Buddy Stevens's leg. The affidavit would bolster the argument for a new trial. Lipford objected, but Judge Boykin—perhaps wary of appearing obstinate—agreed to accept the document as "newly discovered evidence." Boykin reset the hearing for after the new year.[14]

The claim of new, contradictory evidence angered some in the community who were anxious to see the Stevens case closed. *Georgian* publisher Stanley Parkman, who once pondered whether the right man had been convicted, now openly agitated for an end to the misery. "Why has Dr. Jones suddenly decided, after two years, that the findings of his assistant are not correct? Why, after two years of placing his approval on the work of Mr. Cornett, has he changed his mind and now directly contradicts his righthand man?" he wrote.

Parkman suspected "politics" were at play—or perhaps something more base and sinister.

"Evidently there is a considerable amount of folding money floating around in the background of this case and we are beginning to wonder if it has anything to do with such sensational reversals of expert testimony," he wrote.[15]

The new revelations in the Henderson case played much differently in the Black-owned press. Across the nation, African American readers—many of whom were born in the Deep South and migrated to Northern cities for work and greater liberty—kept up with the Henderson case as a reminder of why they left.

"The Henderson case has become the Georgia NAACP branches' cause celebre," the *Philadelphia Tribune* reported. "Negro leaders believe that the illiterate farmer was arrested as a scapegoat for the bungling of some Carroll law officials."

Now "a sensational disagreement between ballistics experts" and allegations of suppressed evidence added credence to the theory that Henderson was—as Homer Chase and the Georgia Communists had claimed—being framed.

Boykin knew how the Henderson case was being portrayed outside of Carroll County. Carrollton was being painted with the Talmadge brush, tarnishing its attempts to cultivate an image as a progressive Southern city of industry and education. That might have been why something extraordinary happened as he prepared for the coming grand jury term. For the first time in county's history, several Black citizens opened their mail to find they had been summoned for jury duty.[16]

As the new year, 1951, dawned, the state's case against Clarence Henderson suddenly seemed shaky. Dr. Jones's potential testimony was as damaging to the state's case as anything Henderson's defense team had yet brought forward, and its ripples were felt beyond Carroll County. In January, a Fulton County grand jury issued a report urging the county to look into the crime lab and its staff.

"Since science and crime laboratories now play so important a part in the detection of crime and trial of criminals; it is recommended that immediate attention be given by the county in establishing high qualification requirements for those who are employed in the department," grand jurors wrote. The report was a direct response to Duke's brutal cross-examination of Cornett, effectively demoting the police officer from expert criminologist to "identification man." The Black press took notice that "Cornett admitted that he had not been to college, had never studied chemistry or physics," and was "merely a former policeman promoted to assist in the crime laboratory."[17]

Lipford countered the bad press in a hearing early in the new year, filing sworn statements from witnesses claiming Jones not only hadn't contradicted George Cornett's ballistics tests but had complemented them. The statements came from Cornett, Carrollton police chief Rada Threadgill, Carroll County sheriff Denver Gaston, a court reporter, the Fulton County police chief, and Lipford himself. Those assurances were enough. On January 17, 1950, Boykin denied Henderson a third trial. Henderson's lawyers had fought hard, but getting a reversal at the trial court level had always been a long shot. Now they were free to argue the case again before the Georgia Supreme Court.[18]

Justice William Yates Atkinson Jr. wrote the opinion for the majority of the state high court. The sixty-four-year-old Atkinson was the son of former governor William Yates Atkinson Sr., a moderate governor and vocal opponent of lynching during his political career who had been accused by his enemies of advocating "social equality" for Blacks.[19] Prior to his election to the state's high court, the younger Atkinson had been the personal attorney for the progressive Governor Ellis Arnall and ran on the same Democratic ticket with Arnall in 1942. In that campaign, the *Atlanta Constitution* lionized Atkinson as a "rugged and honest lawyer, who can't be classified as a politician" and "the man Diogenes wore out lanterns on."[20] Before running for higher office, Atkinson had for many years been solicitor general for the Coweta Judicial Circuit, the same position now held by Wright Lipford.

In their brief to the court, Moore, Robinson, and Duke listed fourteen grounds for overturning the verdict against their client. In an amended motion, they also begged the court for a new trial so that Dr. Jones could be allowed to testify. The court essentially ignored all the proposed reasons for a new trial and focused exclusively on an exchange between Duke and George Cornett.

In a masterstroke of concision, Atkinson described Duke's interrogation of Cornett at trial as "lengthy and . . . of a technical nature." Henderson's defense team had focused on Cornett's decision to visually compare the lands and grooves of the evidence bullet with a test bullet fired from the .38 Special using the comparison microscope. During cross-examination, Duke asked Cornett why he had not measured the "distance and depth of the grooves." Cornett replied that he had seen no need, since the "comparison microscope is the highest and best evidence." Duke objected at the time that Cornett was drawing a conclusion, something reserved for jurors. Judge Boykin overruled the objection. If Duke hadn't wanted a response, he shouldn't have asked the question, the judge said.

Atkinson and the majority of the justices disagreed with Boykin.

"We can not construe the answer here given as being in response to the question propounded," he wrote. "A thorough and sifting cross-examination is a fundamental right."

Judgment reversed.[21]

In a 5–2 decision, the Georgia Supreme Court had saved Henderson, a Black man accused of killing a white man and attempting to rape a white woman, from the state's electric chair. For a second time. It was stunning, and for some in Carrollton it was infuriating.

"Are legal technicalities replacing common sense?" *Georgian* publisher Stanley Parkman wondered. "If cases are to be reversed on such small points, well might the public ask if there is any real chance for a case to be concluded and justice reached in sensational trials handled by skilled lawyers who create and look for just such technicalities."[22]

Sixty miles away, Dan Duke pondered the news from his office above a delicatessen in an area of downtown Atlanta known as Five Points. Clarence Henderson was free only in the sense that he would not be executed. Likely there would be another trial, and while it was not clear that Duke would be retained by the NAACP, his legal mind was already at work about the "peculiar circumstances" of the case that whoever defended Henderson should consider. The first was venue.

"Twenty-four Carroll County jurors have already sat in judgement on Henderson's case," he wrote in a letter to the NAACP defense committee. "A much larger number of the jurors in Carroll County have disqualified themselves because of prejudice or other legal reasons."

Seating a third jury in a small community like Carrollton would be difficult. The Stevens murder and Henderson's two prior trials had consumed the county for more than two and a half years. One solution to such a problem would be to move the trial to another courthouse in the Coweta circuit, but, knowing the territory, Duke warned the committee against it.

For all of its shortcomings, Carrollton was one of the most liberal towns inside the circuit, racially speaking. The other counties in the district were far more rural, and, with the exception of Newnan, they had no urban centers where an educated, white jury might be impaneled.

"I would, therefore, be very careful and extremely hesitant to make a motion for a change of venue," Duke concluded.

Secondly, Duke emphasized the importance of getting independent ballistics tests on the .38 revolver. While Dr. Herman Jones could be counted on to testify that the gun could not have fired the bullet extracted from Buddy Stevens's leg, that would not be enough, he wrote.

"Where you have two witnesses whose testimony contradicts each other, the jury can believe whichever one they choose," Duke wrote. "It would be doing Dr. Jones a grave injustice to use him as the sole witness to contradict Cornett. It is very likely also that the jury in Carroll County would believe Cornett in preference to Jones for the simple reason that they would prefer to believe him."

Henderson needed at least two additional ballistics tests to "so over-whelm" Cornett's opinion that, even if a jury remained unconvinced, the defense could argue to the supreme court for reversal, claiming they had ignored the facts. Moreover, he said he would not consider returning to the defense without a commitment to paying for such tests "in order to totally demolish and overwhelm Cornett's testimony."

In truth, Duke didn't want to return to Henderson's defense at all. He described the case as both "nerve-wracking" and "tedious." If he did return, he suggested that a local white attorney be added to the team to conduct a probing cross-examination of Nan Hansard "without the risk of offending local pride and race solidarity." The cost of such a defense Duke estimated at $2,000: $1,000 for the lead counsel, $500 for a local attorney to assist, and $500 for additional firearm tests.

Duke closed his letter with a plea for the defense committee to stand firm and "draw a line in this judicial circuit."

"This is an important case and is one which your national office should take an interest in," he concluded. "Henderson is not guilty. . . . If Henderson were not a Negro man, he would have never been brought to trial."[23]

For the Atlanta chapter of the NAACP, the reversal was another huge victory. Not only had the Henderson defense been fully wrested away from the Communist Party, but two Black attorneys had now twice beaten Jim Crow in the Georgia Supreme Court. However, while the judgment had once again spared Henderson's life, there would be another trial, and expenses were piling up.

Moore quickly figured the costs of mounting a third defense. Legal fees for himself and Robinson would be $400 if they were hired to assist, but twice that if they had to go to Carrollton and act as Henderson's sole counsel. The NAACP had yet to pay nearly $600 in costs for Henderson's second trial.[24]

Faced with a similar problem the prior summer, the NAACP had pressured pastors of Black churches across Atlanta to pass the plate for Clarence Henderson's defense, enlisting the *Daily World* in ringing the alarm bell. Could they do it again? Adding to the chapter's financial woes, Thurgood Marshall and the NAACP's Legal Defense and Educational Fund were fighting on multiple fronts in Georgia, pushing along legal challenges to the state's segregated schools, which required funding of their own, both at the local and national levels. If Henderson was going to mount a third defense, the national office would need to help.

A. T. Walden, the most respected Black attorney in Georgia and chairman of the chapter's legal redress committee, appealed directly to Marshall. In his letter, Walden noted the case's unusual history, including the NAACP's battle with the Communists, the tense contempt trial in Boykin's court, the hiring of Dan Duke, and the eventual second reversal.

"The local branch has spent nearly $3,000.00 on the case and now has no funds for further defense," Walden wrote.

The case was "one of great importance to our group," he said, in part because of the ballistics victory won over Cornett. Walden described Cornett as "an evil genius" used widely across the state to "establish the guilt of poor persons, principally Negroes, in cases involving the testimony of ballistics experts." The Henderson case was the first to undermine Cornett's authority and paint him as a self-taught but poorly educated "identification man." The more that could be done to even the scales with poor defendants, the better, Walden reasoned.[25]

Walden's appeal met a skeptical reception in the LDF's Manhattan office. Money was tight there too. "It seems as if the state conference is going to have a hard time raising money to handle the education case," Assistant Special Counsel Robert L. Carter told Marshall, referring to a case the NAACP was building in Atlanta comparing white school buildings with their unequal counterparts for Black students. In addition, the NAACP was suing the state over the rejection of a highly qualified Black applicant to the University of Georgia's all-white law school.

"We may have to spend more dough on it and that is the reason for my feeling that we not get involved" in the Henderson defense, Carter said while admitting to his "general prejudice" against engaging in one-off criminal defenses as a poor use of the national NAACP's resources.[26]

Marshall had no such prejudice against defending Black men across the Deep South, but he also knew the financial realities. He wrote a reply to Atlanta that offered some hope.

"Col. Walden," he began, with a respectful nod to Walden's service as an assistant judge advocate in the Army during World War I. "We will, I am sure, be able to contribute to the educational cases, meaning the case in Atlanta and the law school case. I doubt seriously that we can contribute to the Henderson case without a meeting of the Executive Committee of the Fund and they will not meet until September. You see the difficulties I am up against."

However, Marshall said, if the Henderson case wasn't up for retrial until the fall, he would make the appeal. If nothing else, perhaps a loan from the national office could be arranged, he said.[27]

Henderson's third trial would not occur until the regular fall court term. But that still left little time to arrange for experts and—if Boykin would allow it—to perform needed tests on the revolver, the bullet, the file, and the supposed brass filings that made up the state's physical evidence in the case. By the end of summer, it was clear that there would be no help coming from the NAACP in New York and meager assistance from the local branch. The defense filed a thick brief with Boykin's court asking for permission to test the exhibits and to have Henderson declared a pauper.

The request for pauper status would allow Henderson's attorneys to be paid out of the local treasury while also paying for expert witnesses to be brought in to further undermine the prosecution's theory on the ballistics evidence. The request was logical. Henderson relied on appointed counsel for his first trial. And if he was poor before he was put in prison for a year and a half, he certainly was a pauper now. Perhaps the only surprising aspect of the request was that it was filed by Dan Duke, who, despite the reluctance he expressed in his letter, had again signed on to represent Henderson in another stressful trial.[28]

Moore and Robinson were gone. There was no money to support the cost of three attorneys. Their work for justice for their race would continue on the civil side as part of the NAACP's brick-building plan to tear down Jim Crow, but it left Clarence Henderson solely in the hands of a lawyer who, although he loved a fight, was reluctant to take on this one again.

Boykin scheduled the hearing for the morning of Saturday, September 1, 1951, the first day of the long Labor Day weekend. But while well-to-do Georgians took a final summer trip to St. Simons Island, Dan Duke was swimming upstream before the somber judge. Boykin heard the reading of the motion and shook his head.

"There is nothing to authorize me to set up a defense fund," he began, even before Duke had made his argument.

"The court has appointed counsel to represent the defendant in this case," the judge said, referring to the local attorneys assigned to Henderson's first, one-day trial. "The defendant discharged those counsel and employed three counsel of his own choosing."[29]

Henderson could not now claim pauper status, he said.

In so saying, Boykin was ignoring the fact that the imprisoned sharecropper relied on charity for his defense. Shut down before he had even begun, Duke shifted to his appeal for funds to pay for experts to conduct tests on the gun, the bullet, and the supposed traces of copper on the rusty file and then come to Carrollton to testify.

"I might help you there," Boykin said. The judge said if Duke would provide a list of his witnesses, the court would issue subpoenas for them to appear.

"If they do not come, then that is a matter between them and the court," he said.[30]

That was hardly what Duke was asking, and Boykin knew it. The conclusions of George Cornett, the state's expert witness, were contradicted by his own boss, Duke said. Under state law and the U.S. Constitution, money should be provided for these tests and to pay the customary fees for expert witnesses, he told the judge.

"There are conflicts in expert testimony coming from the same governmental agency," he said. "The court has equitable authority to order independent tests made in order to ensure justice in the case."

Again Boykin shook his head. "No," he said. The money Duke was talking about was for the solicitor to prosecute offenders, not for their defense, he said.[31]

For all his misfortune, Clarence Henderson had succeeded where so many men of his generation—and generations before—had failed when brought before the bar of white justice: he was still alive despite being accused of murdering a white boy and attempting to rape a white girl. Many Black men of his generation accused of far less never made it as far as a courtroom, yet he had twice reversed guilty verdicts from all-white juries by appealing to an all-white supreme court in a Deep South state.

Even so, Henderson faced the same long odds a third time, and—denied support set aside for the destitute—he would not have the money for a robust defense. From his prison cell, he could only count the days as the heat of a dying summer faded into autumn and another date in Boykin's courtroom.

CHAPTER 16

THE THIRD TRIAL

Clarence Henderson's third murder trial was scheduled for Judge Boykin's regular term in October 1951. It had been just three years since Buddy Stevens had died protecting his girlfriend in a cold, wet field on a moonless Halloween night, but Carrollton was a different place.

That year Carrollton began work on its first subsidized housing project through its newly chartered housing authority. Like the building of a modern hospital, addressing the poor condition of housing in Carroll County had been delayed by World War II. A federal housing census in 1940 found 1,100 "substandard" residences in Carrollton. From the outset, city leaders assured whites that the housing project would not be integrated by race and that a separate Black facility would be erected.[1]

Homeownership and the construction of new homes took on a greater urgency in Carrollton and the broader United States following World War II. In 1940 the U.S. Census Bureau recorded the lowest homeownership rate in sixty years; a decade later, in 1950, the Census recorded the highest rate of homeownership for the same time span. In one decade—truthfully, because of the war, it was half a decade—homeownership shot up 55 percent nation-wide. Supply for homes could not keep up with demand.[2]

The federal government began to address this unprecedented, pent-up demand for millions of new homes by adding billions of dollars to federal mortgage insurance programs and even creating a mortgage office within the Veterans Administration to assist returning soldiers in financing a home. As a result, single-family housing construction jumped from just 114,000 homes in 1944 to 1.7 million in 1950. In the suburb of Levittown, New York, developers in 1948 were building thirty houses a day. Easy credit played a role in the boom. In Atlanta, nearly 40 percent of home buyers bought entirely on credit, with no down payment.[3]

The fast growth in residential subdivisions after the war reinforced racial and economic segregation. New suburbs moved middle-class whites farther from city centers into developing suburbs and farther from Blacks and low-income whites. Zoning codes were used to reinforce this racial and economic wall building.[4]

As a result, actually owning a home was mostly a white dream. In Georgia, African American families were half as likely to own their own home than whites. Among farm families, the disparity was doubled, with 89 percent of Black farmers living on rented land, compared to 57 percent of whites. And housing for African Americans, regardless of whether owners or renters, was overwhelmingly substandard compared to whites. The vast majority of Black families in 1940 lived in a home with no running water and only a third had electricity.[5]

This disparity was not a Southern phenomenon. Across the nation, Black families faced similar inequality in homeownership and in the adequacy of those homes. In the South, those differences merely appeared in stark relief. Yet in Carrollton the state of housing for whites and Blacks alike was shocking by modern standards. Federal enumerators found two of every three dwellings in need of major repairs and more than half had no indoor plumbing.[6]

In the kind of progressive postwar push that defined its growth, Carrollton attacked its housing problem by establishing a housing authority in 1950. By 1960 the picture would be much different, with 83 percent of houses with indoor plumbing and two-thirds of houses considered "sound."[7]

While addressing the city's substandard housing for poor and working-class whites and Blacks, Carrollton's white leadership was busy expanding the city's options for its growing professional class of whites. Along with the establishment of the Sunset Hills Country Club development where Buddy Stevens had taken his last breath, developers set their sights on another gem on the opposite side of the city.

Lake Carroll—a planned artificial lake—had originally been conceived prior to the war as a reservoir that could be used to lure manufacturing industries in search of a stable water supply. Those plans were put aside in the 1940s but were revived by a cabal of politicians and businessmen who financed the project by selling one hundred lakefront lots at $350 apiece. Despite initial fears that selling lots on a lake that didn't yet exist would be difficult, middle-class white Carrolltonians lined up to get their piece of the project.

"I was in line at the city hall at 8 A.M. and someone was already ahead of me," a local optometrist recalled.

All one hundred lots were sold in less than an hour.

"Only reason it took 50 minutes is because we spent time writing receipts and arguing with people who were unhappy because they couldn't buy more than one lot," George Syme said.[8] (Syme was the head of the Carroll Service Council and the man whose house Nan Taylor escaped to after she and Buddy Stevens were attacked.)

Some said the success of Lake Carroll wasn't just in the development of a new subdivision or a recreational center. It was a manifestation of community spirit.

"Industry is looking for good towns," Syme told a magazine writer in 1952. "And the story of Lake Carroll quickly convinces people that Carrollton is a good community."[9]

Much of the city's most impactful new industry was homegrown. Prior to the war, Carrollton had emerged as a hub for textile mills, drawing young boys away from the fields and into factories for the first time. But the spread of rural electrification as a result of President Roosevelt's New Deal brought what would become Carrollton's most important industry: copper wire. In 1950 a young and energetic entrepreneur named Roy Richards founded Southwire to feed the region's appetite for electricity. A year later Southwire announced an expansion to triple its factory floor.[10]

Local boosters beamed with pride at Carrollton's postwar expansion and the recognition the once-disconnected county had received. In 1951 the NBC radio network featured Carrollton in a series of shows highlighting "real-life stories of democracy in action." The show, *Red Clay and Teamwork*, focused on the Carroll Service Council. The council had been the driving force behind building the hospital and developing Lake Carroll, as well as smaller educational and recreational projects around the county. The NBC program told the story of a community that, a generation prior, had been backward and undeveloped but, through cooperative effort, had emerged as a bright spot of the New South. *The Times–Free Press* called the program "Carroll County's biggest half hour."[11]

While Carroll County mirrored the optimistic—and opportunistic—spirit of early 1950s America, there were also dark clouds. Americans were worried that an expanded conflict in Korea could provoke an atomic war between the Soviet Union and the United States. New, more modern equipment allowed Carrollton's newspapers to carry more wire service photos of soldiers in Korea, bringing the war home in new, more vivid ways. And the deeply divisive decision by President Harry Truman to recall General Douglas MacArthur from his command of the United Nations forces in Korea led to a high-profile Senate investigation that transfixed the country.

As the stalemated Korean conflict dragged on, the new alliance between China and the Soviet Union put the Cold War on the front pages and editorial columns of even small-town newspapers.

"We are mobilizing and preparing to flex our muscles boldly in the face of the Russian bear," the *Times–Free Press* declared in an editorial that warned of more Carroll County boys being sent overseas, factories moving to wartime production, and rationing of consumer goods.

"Our whole lives may have a military slant for the next several years," the paper warned.[12]

In the two years since the Soviet Union successfully detonated its first atomic bomb, new weight had been given to the Communist menace. In one 1951 article, the *Times–Free Press* offered "Six Survival Secrets for Atomic Attacks." The report carried the helpful label NO WAR PREDICTED but offered better-safe-than-sorry tips for an atomic strike, like burying your face in your hands to "protect your face from flash burns" and to "wait a few minutes" after an A-bomb attack before venturing outside.[13]

With Carrollton changing so much, it is not a surprise newspaper coverage of Henderson's third trial paled when compared with the breathless blow-by-blow of the earlier efforts. The death of Buddy Stevens seemed to have happened long ago in another Carrollton, one before Communists and the Korean War, Black lawyers and the troublesome supreme court reversals. The trial was the third stanza in an unloved hymn, listlessly sung more out of duty than conviction.

The trial began on October 8, 1951, a sunny morning when an unexpected cold snap had dropped the temperature 20 degrees overnight. Once again, Solicitor General Wright Lipford was assisted by Judge Boykin's older brother, but for the first time Lipford opened the trial not with an expert witness or a law enforcement official. Instead, he called Carl Stevens Sr. to the stand.[14]

"Carl Stevens Jr. was my son," he began. "He was sometimes known as Buddy Stevens, which was his nickname."

The appearance of Carl Stevens, known to most of the courthouse crowd, set a powerful tone for the jurors. He wasn't needed for any other reason. Beyond "State your name," Lipford's only other question was the date of Buddy's death, which any number of witnesses could have provided. Henderson's defense team didn't bite and Buddy's father left without any further questions.[15]

Lipford's next witness was former sheriff Bunt Kilgore, who testified to a greater degree than ever before about finding Stephens's body. In a winding series of answers, Kilgore said Buddy's body was as close as three hundred yards from the nearest house, which if true means Nan ran the wrong way, running three times as far to the northeast to George Syme's home when other homes were much closer. Kilgore also said he found the body at 9:30, much earlier than Nan's recollection of events, which had Buddy picking her up from the Presbyterian church at 8:45, stopping for cigarettes, parking on a dead-end street for thirty minutes to an hour, being abducted and marched across several fields, running for safety, and finally alerting authorities. That says nothing of the mishandled phone call to Carrollton police and the actual search for the body.

In the second trial, Henderson's lawyers, led by Duke, had demolished the chain of custody of the bullet when Dr. Elwyn Patrick testified he took the bullet removed from Buddy's leg to the murder scene and delivered it to Kilgore. In the first trial, witnesses had testified the bullet was given to Kilgore at the funeral home. This time Lipford made sure Kilgore's testimony was clear.

"I went to the funeral home," Kilgore said, adding he got there thirty minutes after the body arrived and observed the examination. Then he returned to the crime scene. "After I came to the funeral home, I went down there off and on all night."[16]

It was on one of these occasions that Patrick came to him with the bullet, already in an envelope, which he then gave to GBI agent Hillin.

In cross-examination, Duke grilled Kilgore at length about the location of Buddy Stevens's car, the location of his body, its relation to various streets, where ditches and fences were located, and how those landmarks had changed over the intervening three years. Finally, Kilgore rose from the stand. "I will come down there and show the jury where the car was located when I first saw it," he said.[17]

Duke also drilled into the timeline. "It was about 9:30 Sunday night when I first received the call," Kilgore said, contradicting his reckoning just minutes earlier, adding that he got to George Syme's home about 9:45. After finding the body, Kilgore said he had search dogs on the scene by 10:30.[18]

Lipford called Patrick as his next witness. The young doctor recited his testimony about extracting the bullet and delivering it to Kilgore at "the scene of the crime." But Patrick was less sure about timeline. "It was about an hour, or maybe longer, from the time I left George Syme's house to look for the body until we found the body," he said. "We rambled around a good while."[19]

Factually, the timeline was irrelevant to whether Clarence Henderson was the killer. No direct evidence put Henderson at the scene of the crime whether it was at 9:30 or midnight. He wasn't even arrested until more than a year after that night. But the cursory attention paid to matching up details of that night with earlier testimony suggests a sort of laziness the Jim Crow system of justice paid to the evidence when a Black man's life was at stake.

In cross-examination, Duke questioned Patrick in depth about his examination of Stevens's body, the locations of the bullet wounds, and the method he used to extract the bullet from Buddy's leg. Patrick had used steel forceps. Was the doctor certain he had not made additional marks on the soft lead? No, Patrick said, he didn't think so. Duke allowed Patrick to examine the bullet.

"Are you certain this is the bullet you extracted from the leg?" Duke asked.

Patrick looked at it and shrugged. "It looks like the one. I have no positive knowledge that it is the bullet."

Patrick admitted he had not searched for the bullet in Buddy's chest that claimed his life. In all likelihood that slug still resided with Stevens in the Carrollton City Cemetery. Because he had not conducted a thorough examination, Patrick said he could not say whether or not there was a third bullet. Stevens had a wound on his arm, but Patrick did not know whether it was created by a third bullet or a bullet that passed through his arm and into his chest. Again, this line of questioning did little to establish Henderson's guilt or innocence, but it did show the cursory nature of the initial investigation.[20]

Proving that kind of incompetence was more difficult with Lipford's next witness, GBI agent Jim Hillin. Hillin testified that he took the envelope containing the bullet from Kilgore "at the scene" and that he had marked the bullet with an "E," presumably to indicate that it was evidence but also to establish a chain of custody. Unlike Patrick, Hillin could positively identify the bullet as the one he had been given the night of the murder because he had marked it. Hillin also had taken the step of writing on the back of the envelope "Dr. E. V. Patrick, Adamson Avenue, Carrollton. The bullet taken from Carl Stevens," although he said he got the envelope from Kilgore and did not see Patrick hand it over. Lipford walked Hillin through the steps of taking the bullet from Carrollton to the Fulton County Crime Laboratory, where he handed it over to George Cornett for testing.

Changing topics, Lipford asked if he knew Leonard Pendergrass. It was early to bring the cop-turned-cabbie into the story.

"I did not know Leonard Pendergrass at that time," Hillin said. "But since that time I have been acquainted with him. Mr. Pendergrass gave me the serial number of that pistol that he lost."

In the first trial, Hillin had testified that Pendergrass had reported the serial number of the .38 Smith & Wesson after Stevens was shot to death. In the second trial, Hillin said it was weeks before the murder—shortly after it was stolen from Lee Hardman in the rape of Mrs. Parker. In that trial, Duke's cross-examination of Hillin on that point was a major disruption in the prosecution's theory of the timeline of the gun. Now Hillin again appeared to be saying he did not become acquainted with Pendergrass until after the Stevens murder.

Lipford heard it, too, and circled around. He asked Hillin when he had gotten the serial number of the gun.

"The serial number was given to me before Buddy Stevens was killed," Hillin said, getting back on track. "I knew Lee Hardman. He gave me the serial number of the gun."[21]

That did not exactly track along with his testimony in the second trial, but it was closer. Lipford tried again, and this time Hillin understood the question. "Leonard Pendergrass gave me the number of the gun," he said. "I don't know exactly when but it was before Buddy Stevens was killed."[22]

Duke pounced on cross-examination, reciting Hillin's testimony from the first trial. But despite his muddled testimony on direct examination, Hillin was prepared for this. He simply denied the contradiction. Hillin said he got the serial number a few days after the attack on Mrs. Parker at the church down U.S. 27 south of Carrollton. "I don't know the date, but it was right after this crime was committed," he said.

Duke read aloud from the testimony of the first trial, but Hillin stood fast.

"If this record states I testified that I got the serial number from Mr. Pendergrass several days after Mr. Stevens was killed, that is not correct," he said.

"I ask you to read from the transcript," Duke said, handing the pages to Hillin.

"In the first trial I was asked the question, 'How long after the death of Stevens?' My answer was, 'Several days,'" Hillin read, then handed the pages back. "That was several days after the commission of the crime on Highway 27. That's what it was in reference to."[23]

It was absurd, but Hillin wouldn't be shaken. Duke switched gears, walking Hillin through the initial hours of the investigation in a ticktock fashion beginning from the moment he received the call from his home in Austell, a western suburb of Atlanta. Duke paused when he came to the point when Hillin interviewed Nan Turner.

"Who was present with you when you interviewed her," Duke asked.

"I'm not positive," Hillin began, then he named a fellow GBI agent and another police officer. "I talked to her once in the hospital," he said. "It was the morning following when I saw her the next time. I don't recall the names of the people present when I interviewed her on the morning at the hospital."

"Was Dick Flinn present?" Duke asked.

The cavernous courtroom rustled as white Carrolltonians looked at each other; some in disbelief, others with knowing nods.

"I recall that Reverend Flinn was in the hospital when I got there," Hillin said.

"Did he offer to remove himself?" Duke asked.

Shirley Boykin shot up from the prosecution table. "I object to that as irrelevant!"[24]

Until now, the Reverend Dick Flinn's name had never been publicly connected to the Buddy Stevens murder, although it had been considerably trafficked across kitchen tables and along the corridors of City Hall and the county courthouse. Flinn was the pastor of Carrollton Presbyterian Church, the same church where Buddy Stevens had picked Nan up after Sunday evening services on Halloween night, 1948.

For many years Flinn was one of the best-known ministers in Georgia, in part because of his friendship with *Constitution* editor Ralph McGill, McGill's successor Eugene Patterson, and the legendary columnist Celestine Sibley, all of whom sang his praises as a prime example of a good, progressive Southerner. Flinn was the son of the Reverend Dr. Richard Orme Flinn Sr., the founding pastor of Atlanta's influential North Avenue Presbyterian Church, and had served as a chaplain in the U.S. Army's storied 82nd Airborne Division. After the war and a brief stint as headmaster of a Presbyterian girls' school in Atlanta, he was installed as pastor at Carrollton Presbyterian, becoming one of the city's most influential men.[25]

At the time of the third trial, Flinn was a trim, handsome, forty-four-year-old bachelor with stylish tastes and boundless energy—a combination that endeared him to locals and outsiders alike. For years, Flinn shared the church manse with a series of children—mostly boys—he rescued from some kind of crisis, often sent there by the authorities who did not know what else to do with them. Eugene Patterson, who succeeded McGill when he rose to publisher of the paper, wrote that Flinn's "frame house was a way station to those in distress."

A Carrollton resident, who was a boy when Flinn was pastor, said his father called the minister "the most Christlike person he had ever known."

He said his father once saw Flinn buying new tires for his white Pontiac Bonneville, then two months later, having worn them out, saw him buying another new set.

"He was not sitting in his office at church in the afternoon," the man said. "He was out doing good for the community."[26]

But Flinn had also been the subject of rumors since the morning after Buddy Stevens's death. Nan Turner had been a member of his church, and she had run to Flinn when her home life became troubled. Lifelong Carrollton resident Allen Murrah was a teenager at the time of the Stevens murder and kept up with the trials and heard the gossip about the Reverend Flinn.

"Dick Flinn was mentioned so much," he said. "It was ridiculous."

Decades after the trials, Murrah allowed that Flinn's housing of young people in his home was curious in hindsight. But he said no one raised an eyebrow—at least, not until Stevens died while on a date with Nan Turner.[27]

Shirley Boykin wanted to keep the jury from being distracted by Flinn's interactions with Nan the night of the murder, but his younger brother—who doubtless would have heard the same rumors—overruled the objection. Judge Boykin was protective of the city's reputation, but perhaps he had wondered about the preacher too. Or, maybe more likely, there was no legal reason to keep Hillin from answering after the prosecution had questioned him at length about the details of the early stages of the investigation.

Duke moved ahead, asking the GBI agent about the minister's presence during his interview with Nan.

"He did not offer to remove himself," Hillin said. "He remained there at all times."

"When did you next talk to her?" Duke asked.

Hillin shifted in his seat and looked at his notes from the investigation. "I next interviewed her at Rev. Flinn's residence on Highway 27, or the Villa Rica–Carrollton highway," he said. "That was three doors down on the left, below the red light." Hillin said the interview was conducted a week after the murder on Sunday, November 7, 1948.

Duke asked Hillin for the names of everyone at the interview session, aside from Nan and Flinn. "Some of the officers," Hillin said. "I don't know who." Apart from Flinn, Nan Turner, and her father, Hillin said he could not recall any other names. He said he spoke to Nan for about forty-five minutes.

"Did he remove himself at any time," Duke said, meaning Flinn. Shirley Boykin rose again.

"I object to that," he said. Then he added, "And I object to what house he was at."

Sam Boykin again overruled his brother's objection. Hillin continued.

"He removed himself on one occasion while I was conducting the interview with Miss Nan Turner," he said. "I think he came back in the room with a pistol."

It was an extraordinary detail, one made more so since it had been hidden until Clarence Henderson's third trial. It is unclear why Flinn displayed the gun. Duke was more interested in what kind of pistol it was than why it suddenly appeared. A German Luger? he asked. An Italian Beretta? Both used 9mm rounds like the one that killed Buddy. Flinn, a veteran of the European theater in World War II, might well have brought either home as a souvenir.

"I don't know if it was a foreign gun," Hillin said. "I'm not sure."

"Was it an automatic or a revolver?" Duke asked.

"I remember it was one or the other," Hillin said, smiling.

Duke moved on. Was Flinn's gun taken as evidence? Was it tested in the Fulton County Crime Laboratory? After all, the murder was a week old, the police had no suspects, and here a man with a direct connection to the only eyewitness in the case had appeared with a gun in his hand. Certainly, a trained investigator would be interested.

Just moments before, Hillin had recalled from three years earlier how many doors down from a traffic light the pastor lived. Now he shrugged. "I don't remember whether it was taken or not," he said.

Duke asked if Hillin was in the habit of keeping notes of such things. Yes, he said. "I make a full written detail of everything I did," he said.

"Will you let me see them?" Duke asked. Hillin looked to Lipford.[28]

In a capital murder retrial today, a defense attorney might expect to be provided with the reports of the chief investigator from the earlier trial or trials. But in 1951 such transparency wasn't required. In fact, depending on the court, the defense might have no right to even request that such documents be produced. It would be another twelve years before the United States Supreme Court, in *Brady v. Maryland*, decided that prosecutors must turn exculpatory material over to the defense.[29] Duke had no idea what was in

Hillin's notes, and when he asked the question, he had no idea whether he would be allowed to see them. Lipford said he had no objection, putting the ball in Boykin's court.

The judge looked to Duke, confused. "What was the question?"

"I want him to state, using his notes to refresh his recollection, whether the Luger"—Duke stopped himself—"or the nine millimeter pistol of foreign make, was the automatic pistol that Rev. Flinn showed him or whether his notes show he afterwards delivered the automatic nine millimeter to the Fulton County Crime Laboratory for tests."

Boykin shook his head. "I don't think he testified Mr. Flinn delivered it to him."

Everyone was confused. Duke, who repeatedly referred to the pistol as a 9mm automatic, appeared to know more about this than Hillin. Hillin said he couldn't recall even the most generic aspects of the gun. Duke had decided in favor of the risky strategy of offering Flinn as an alternate suspect. Regardless of local gossip, the jury might recoil at the defense pointing a public finger at the preacher. But the fact that the minister had produced a pistol, perhaps of the same type used in the murder, during a police interview with Nan Turner at his home was startling. Duke backed up.

"I want him to examine his notes and see whether or not he did get automatic pistols, to determine what caliber, and what make automatic pistols he got, and whether or not his notes show he took those pistols of different caliber or make to the Fulton County Crime Laboratory for tests.

"I want him," Duke said, pointing at Lipford, "to deliver the notes to the witness."

Lipford again rose. "I have no objection to that," he said, and, picking up a sheaf of notes, walked to Hillin and handed them over. Hillin flipped through them, scanning the pages until he found the second Nan Turner interview. After a few moments he said, "I don't see it."

"And you made notes on this particular occasion, on this particular interview, at the time you interviewed her at the house of Rev. Flinn and Rev. Flinn brought the automatic pistol in?" Duke asked, once more pushing the idea that Flinn's pistol was an automatic rather than a revolver.

This time Shirley Boykin caught it and objected.

"He didn't say Mr. Flinn brought in an automatic," he complained.

But Hillin shook his head. "Whatever kind of pistol it was, whether it was a German make or a .45, it was an automatic," he said. He turned to Duke.

"I don't think I made any note about the pistol Mr. Flinn brought in to show us," he said. "I don't know whether I delivered the pistol to the crime laboratory or not."[30]

Lipford's next witness was Police Chief Threadgill. The chief was there to testify about the discovery of Stevens's body and the geography of the country club, but on cross-examination Duke continued prodding for details about the Reverend Flinn. Threadgill said he interviewed Nan Turner at the preacher's home a day or so after the murder and prior to Hillin's interview, suggesting that Nan may have been among the group of troubled teens living at Flinn's manse. Threadgill said his interview lasted just a few minutes.

"I didn't talk to her but very little in there because Nan was all torn up and nervous," Threadgill recalled.

Duke asked if he saw Flinn with a pistol. The chief shook his head. But Flinn did mention one, he said.

"It seems like he told me he did have an Army .45 automatic, but it was at his mother's," he said.

Threadgill said he didn't keep notes of his interview and he was not there on November 7 when Hillin met with Nan.[31]

Duke questioned both Hillin and Threadgill on their knowledge of firearms, and specifically on whether a semiautomatic pistol existed that did not eject its empty cartridge after firing. Both men testified they had searched the area around the murder scene for spent shells, the absence of which fueled the theory that Stevens's killer used a revolver with altered 9mm rounds. So-called automatic revolvers did exist, but as curiosities among firearm collectors, and both witnesses testified that they were unfamiliar with them. Perhaps the questioning was merely Duke's attempt to open another crack in the state's case into which doubt could creep.

When Duke finished with the police chief, Boykin adjourned the court for the day. Compared to the prior two trials, the first day of the third version of *State of Georgia v. Clarence Henderson* had begun like a heavyweight match in which the boxers spent the first round circling each other, looking for weaknesses. The third time around, the *Atlanta Constitution* report of the opening of the trial merited a short story, filled mostly with background on the case. The story ran on page 7. Black Atlanta had not tired of the drama, however, so the *Atlanta Daily World* ran its story on the front.[32]

Lipford opened the second day of the trial with testimony by Jack Aycock, the owner of the funeral home where Stevens's body was taken for examination. Aycock testified that he provided the billing envelope Dr. Patrick used to place the bullet taken from Buddy's leg. "The last person I saw with the bullet was Dr. Patrick when he was there at the funeral home," he said.

Did Patrick make any identifying marks on the bullet? Duke asked. No, Aycock said. "There were no marks put on the bullet in my presence," he said.

Next was E. H. Harkins, the Atlanta police detective who discovered the .38 Special revolver in a downtown pawnshop. Harkins testified that they had been looking for it for more than a year when it turned up in early December 1949. Lipford asked how he got the serial number of the stolen gun.

"We were notified by the GBI on October 5, 1948," Harkins said.[33]

This was the most specific testimony in all three trials about when Harkins received the serial number for the .38 Special, and it is significant, even if it wasn't recognized as such at the time. In the second trial, Hillin testified that he received the serial number from Lee Hardman within days after the attack at Stripling Chapel in August 1948 and then again from Lee Pendergrass shortly after the murder of Buddy Stevens. If that were true, Hillin had the serial number of a stolen gun he knew had been taken by a serial rapist but never reported it to the Atlanta police pawn detail. Instead, he waited to report it until after Stevens was killed, even though no available evidence suggested at the time that they were looking for a .38. A much more logical assumption is that the first time Hillin knew the serial number was when he squeezed it out of Pendergrass in early October 1948.

Next was Leon Beeber, the immigrant pawnbroker drawn to Carrollton for a third time to testify about his dastardly luck in taking the nickel-plated revolver in pawn. In rote fashion, Beeber recounted paying blind vegetable farmer Luther Cosper $25 for the gun and then turning it over when Detective Harkins came to call.

"I know Detective Harkins very well," Beeber said. "Detective Harkins came to my place with reference to this pistol with Jim Hillin."[34]

Perhaps Beeber had been too well coached, but this testimony contradicted Harkins's earlier account that he had picked up the pistol and taken it to Hillin's office. Hillin couldn't have been with him at the pawnshop.

Lieutenant Tom Price followed Leon Beeber. As in the prior trials, Price's main role was to introduce the metal file into evidence by testifying about its discovery in a bedroom dresser drawer a few days after Henderson's arrest.

"I went to the home of Clarence Henderson after the death of Carl Stevens Jr. in the latter part of 1949," Price said. "We made a search there of his house and found a file. The file was in the upper-hand drawer of the dresser in the bedroom."

"Whose home did you go to?" Duke asked.

"I went to Clarence Henderson's home," he said. "We searched the house, which was about a quarter of a mile this side of the store at Sand Hill."

"Who lived in the home?" Duke asked.

"It was a house where his wife lived," Price said.

Pointing back at his client, Duke asked if Henderson lived there. Not at the time, Price said, adding that he also searched the sharecropper's dwelling where Henderson lived near Roopville while working for a woman named Traylor.

This was the same tactic Lipford had used in the second trial. In that trial, Duke had pointed out to the jury that the file was found in his father-in-law's home, where Clarence's wife and children had moved following his arrest. Clarence had never lived there and there was nothing to directly connect the file to him. Duke challenged Price on those grounds in that trial and did so again.

"I didn't mean to imply that Clarence Henderson lived in that house or ever lived in that house," Price said. In the next breath he implied it again.

"It was probably ten or twelve miles from where he lived at Sand Hill down to this place where Mrs. Traylor's place is," he said, even though Henderson had never lived at the Sand Hill house. Facts aside, the state's message was clear: Henderson's house; Henderson's file.[35]

Rather than belabor it, Duke turned his attention to a more important part of his strategy for trial three. The attorney asked Price if he was present during ballistics testing in the summer of 1950 after the Georgia Supreme Court overturned Henderson's first guilty verdict.

"I was present in Dr. Jones's office perhaps on more than one occasion when the test made in the Buddy Stevens case was discussed," Price said. "I could not say it was in the months of July or August of 1950, but I was there in the summer of 1950."

"Was George Cornett present? Was Dr. Herman Jones present?" Duke asked. Price nodded and answered yes to both questions. "Was Chief G. Neal Ellis present?"

Ellis was the chief of the Fulton County Police and Dr. Jones's boss. No, Price said, Ellis wasn't there. Duke then went broader with his questions, asking if he had spoken with anyone in his office "for the purpose of being communicated to the Fulton County Crime Laboratory" about ballistics tests on the bullet and the gun. Shirley Boykin rose.

"We object to any communication he said to anybody else or anybody else said to him," he said.

The objection was as broad as Duke's question. While Price's testimony about what others said would be inadmissible as hearsay, logically Price should be able to testify about whether he had spoken to someone. But Sam Boykin nodded to his brother. "Yes, I sustain that objection."

Duke was flustered. "I am not asking him to give me—" he said, stopping. "I am asking what *he* did."

"Read the question back," Shirley Boykin said. "It calls for what somebody else said and what he said to somebody else."

The judge waved the court reporter away. "The question was asked that way. I sustain the objection to it."

"I didn't," Duke began. He took a breath. "I am asking him that question like I am all the others: Did he communicate with anyone in his office?"

Shirley again tried to object. This time younger brother Sam motioned for him to sit. "He can ask that question—if he communicated," the judge said. "So long as he doesn't go into the conversation." There was satisfaction among the prosecutors as to the narrow opening through which Duke now had to crawl.

"I communicated with our office," Price said.

"With Delmar Jones," Duke asked. Jones was head of the GBI.

Price nodded. "About the first of October," he said.

"About the first of October 1950?"

"Yes," Price said.

"Are you sure you didn't communicate with Mr. Delmar Jones in August of 1950, Lieutenant Price?"

Price paused, unsure about where to go.

"I was called from south Georgia back to Atlanta sometime during the summer of 1950," he said. "Possibly thirty to forty-five days before the communication with Capt. Jones in October and was advised that the pistol—"

"Wait a minute!" Shirley Boykin said. Beside him, Lipford was fuming.

Duke looked plaintively to the judge. "I have not asked for that," he said.

"Don't go into any conversations, Mr. Price," Judge Boykin said.

In his affidavit, filed back in December when Henderson's defense team was pursuing a motion for a new trial, Dr. Herman Jones had testified that he performed a series of tests in late July and early August 1950, months before the second trial. Such testimony could show Lipford had conspired to suppress those test results, but Duke was stymied by not being allowed to ask Price about the substance of the conversation.

Again Duke shifted gears and asked Price about his interactions with Nan Turner. Price said he had interviewed her at length at the police station in Carrollton.

"Who was with her?" Duke asked.

"She was accompanied by Preacher Flinn," Price said. But he said he interviewed Nan alone.

"At that time did she give you—I am not asking you to tell what was said, but was there communicated to you any description of any kind?"

"That would be hearsay!" Shirley Boykin erupted. "It necessarily calls for him to state what she said."

The judge sustained the objection, but it wasn't enough for his older brother, who pointed a finger at Duke.

"He is trying to try this case with innuendos and we are trying to get away from that," he said.

Duke turned to face his accuser. "Wait a minute!" he said.

Judge Boykin tried to restore order. "I've ruled on it," he said. "Please go to something else."

But Duke was hot. "I have a motion to make at this time," he said.

Judge Boykin raised a hand and ordered the jury to be led out. Once they were gone, Duke moved for a mistrial based on the prosecution's statements "within the hearing of the jury." The judge dismissed the motion immediately and leaned toward Duke. Whether it was challenging the judge's strict ruling on hearsay evidence or his repeated attempts to bring Dick Flinn into the controversy, Dan Duke was throwing the kitchen sink at the state and Judge Boykin had had enough.

"Mr. Duke, we are going to try this case on evidence," he said. "I agree with counsel that you are trying to try it by innuendos and the court is not going to permit it. Now if you have any evidence to offer, offer it, and when I make a ruling on it I want that ruling understood that it is final.

"You understand now, if we are going to have any trouble in this case at all, we are not going to have it on that!" Boykin concluded. He waved to the sheriff's deputy to bring the jurors back.[36]

Lipford called Eli Cosper, the blind produce farmer, as his next witnesses. Cosper, as he had done in two prior trials, told his story of buying the pistol from Layman Almon for $20, then quickly pawning it in Carrollton for $25 at Beeber's pawnshop, although the years of practice had not improved his memory. He testified that he got the gun from Almon "in 1948 or 1949." He was no more specific.[37]

Duke had no questions for Eli Cosper, so Lipford moved on to his wife, Floy. In the first trial, Floy Cosper had been a valuable witness for the prosecution, having placed the gun in Clarence Henderson's hand at a house party in August 1948. She was less so in the second, when her identification of the gun was linked to a much later sighting when Almon sold it to her husband more than a year later.

In a series of short questions and answers, Floy Cosper identified the gun as the one she and her husband bought from Almon and pawned to Beeber. She said she had seen it before in Clarence Henderson's hand.

"The first time I saw him with it, he had it up to Mr. J. T. Brown's on Saturday night in August," she said.

"Do you remember when Buddy Stevens was killed?" Lipford asked.

Yes, she said. "But I don't know what month it was."

Floy Cosper was more clear about the date she saw Henderson with a gun at J. T. Brown's house party: August 14, 1948, the second Saturday of the month. "The second time I saw it, he had it down at my house on the fourth Saturday night in August 1948," she said. That date was August 28.

Lipford held up the pistol. Yes, Floy said, that was the gun. "My husband bought the gun, I took it and looked at it, and it had some scratches on the handle," she said.

Once again, Floy Cosper recounted how Henderson fired his pistol to break up the domestic dispute between the boy and girl from LaGrange—although, for some reason, this time the story included more boys and more girls, but all from LaGrange.

In cross-examination, Duke asked Floy Cosper whether Junior Clark had been at her party in late August. Although Clark had been arrested at the party for shooting James Sampson, Flo couldn't recall his presence. If he was there, he didn't get into any trouble, she said. She remembered more clearly seeing Clark with Henderson at Brown's house party two weeks earlier.

"This is the gun I saw Clarence Henderson with on the second Saturday night in August 1948 down at Mr. J. T. Brown's house," she said.

"Are you sure of the date?" Duke asked.

Yes, she said. She recalled it was two weeks before her own house party. Satisfied, Duke excused the witness.[38]

Lipford next called Almon, who testified to buying the gun from Henderson in December 1948, keeping it about a year, and selling it to Cosper. Henderson had twice testified to selling a gun to Almon, just not that gun. Duke asked Almon if he had ever purchased another gun from Henderson. No, Almon said, just that one.[39]

Next, Lipford called Junior Clark, who testified that he saw Henderson with a "shiny" pistol several times in the summer of 1948 and again testified that he saw Henderson with bullets, both brass and steel jacketed.

"Did you ever see him do anything with those bullets," Lipford asked.

"He is leading the witness," Duke complained.

"How is that leading?" the judge replied. "I overrule the objection. Go ahead."

Clark said he saw Henderson filing bullets. Lipford held up a copper-jacketed bullet and asked Clark where Henderson was using the file.

"He was filing them around on the hull like," he said. "He would file around right up there at the top."

On cross, Duke went right back to that description. "You saw Clarence Henderson filing the tops of bullets?" he asked. There was no need to file the lead bullet in a 9mm round. It was the jacket that prevented it from chambering in a .38.

Clark shifted in his seat. "He didn't file the bullet right at the top," he said. "It looked to me like he was filing back there." Clark indicated the back or bottom of the example round. Lipford had been holding the round upside down, by the lead bullet, Clark said, looking over to the prosecution table. "Clarence was filing it toward the bottom here," he said.

Duke shifted to Clark's arrest for shooting James Sampson, but Clark said he did not remember what month it was when he shot him, only that he was arrested on a Sunday and that he had not been to a party the night before. He did testify that he had seen Henderson at Brown's house party with the gun in evidence and he had seen him with it before Brown's. It was inconsistent with his testimony at prior trials, but Clark was an inconsistent witness at best.

"Why is it every time I ask you a question, before you answer it you look over there at the prosecuting attorney?" Duke asked.

Lipford objected. "This is improper," Judge Boykin said, but Duke was done with the witness.[40]

Duke was less probing of Lipford's Black witnesses than during the last trial, when he took great pains to set timelines in an attempt to establish that any gun Henderson was seen with could not have been the murder weapon because he would have obtained it prior to the attack at Stripling Chapel. All of that work questioning Black farmhands hadn't impressed the all-white jury last time. This time Duke was less concerned with whether the state could show Henderson had a pistol—even that pistol. Instead, his strategy centered almost entirely on the idea that the gun in evidence was not the one that killed Stevens.

Junior Clark was a bit of an exception. His testimony that he saw Henderson filing down bullets was damaging. When Sheriff Denver Gaston took the stand to testify that Clark was locked up Sunday, August 29, 1948, for shooting James Sampson, Duke was energetic on cross-examination.

"Whatever happened to the charges against Junior Clark?" Duke asked the sheriff.

Gaston looked down at the register of arrests and warrants issued against county inmates. He shrugged.

"This book here does not indicate whatever happened to this case, or how long he was under the charge, or anything like that," he said. If the charge went to trial, it would be recorded in the clerk's office, he said.

Duke looked at the register and asked the meaning of a column of red numbers. Gaston said they indicated the cost to his office for holding prisoners for trial. Another column showed his reimbursement from the court for those costs.

"Can you read those figures in the Junior Clark case?" Duke asked.

Gaston looked down at the register.

"There are no such markings on the Junior Clark case," he said. "There was never but one entry made in there, just the warrant. It does not show any other bench warrant or bond or subpoenas or anything."

"Nothing but the warrant for his arrest?" Duke asked.

Gaston shook his head. "There is no other entry made on it," he said.

"What is a bench warrant?" Duke asked.

"A bench warrant is the second warrant issued after a man is indicted," Gaston said.

Duke repeated the answer for emphasis. Clark was never indicted for shooting Sampson. Lipford got to his feet.

"I object to that as being irrelevant," he said.

Judge Boykin nodded. "I sustain the objection," he said.

Duke nodded and looked to the judge. "I would like to state for the record then why I asked the question, and why I contend it is relevant," he said. "I want to state that I was cross examining the state's witness, who is the custodian of the records, of the warrants made and served."

"The record shows what you are questioning him about, Mr. Duke," the judge said. "Now state what you expect to show."

Duke said he wanted to show that a bench warrant was never issued in Clark's case.

"You already asked him and he said no," Judge Boykin said. "Don't ask him anymore."

Duke countered that he wanted the records of Junior Clark's arrest entered into the court record. "Are you offering it as evidence?" the judge wanted to know.

"I am tendering it at this time," Duke said, "so later I can introduce it."[41]

Lipford might well complain that Duke was again trying by innuendo by suggesting that Clark's assault charge in the Sampson shooting had been put aside in exchange for his testimony, much like Eli Cosper's forgery charge. But the prosecutor said nothing.

George Cornett was the next witness for the state. Much of what had occurred to this point was prologue. Lipford knew Duke, who planned to call Herman Jones as a defense witness, would go hard after Cornett's credentials as a firearm expert, as he had in the last trial. A year earlier, Duke had diminished Cornett's standing by writing him off as a high school–educated, self-taught "identification man" rather than a true expert in forensic ballistics. Heading this off, Lipford asked Cornett to separate the terminology. Cornett said firearm identification was the matching of firearms and the shells from which they were fired.

"Ballistics is the study and science of the motion of projectiles, the charges and projectiles and all those sorts of things," he said.

It's a distinction not often made, since forensic ballistics is more often used as a catch-all term for both the identification of a bullet and the path it traveled, but Cornett's description isolated ballistics as a theoretical adventure of little use in the current controversy.[42]

For the better part of an hour, Cornett walked the jury through his years of study in the art of identification, the books he had consulted, and how he used the accumulated knowledge to match the 9mm slug retrieved from Stevens's leg to test the bullets he filed down and fired. Using oversized photos of the bullets, Cornett painstakingly walked jurors through the lands and grooves of the evidence bullet and the test bullets. Finally, Lipford asked the only question that mattered.

"Mr. Cornett, based upon your study of the pistol, your study of the evidence bullet, and the test bullet, in your opinion—"

"If it pleases the court," Duke interrupted, "I have an objection to make."

"Let him ask the question," Judge Boykin said.

"Before he answers it, I want to get my objection in," Duke stressed.

Lipford continued. "Whether or not, in your opinion, that .38 revolver there," he said, pointing, "fired the evidence bullet."

Duke jumped in. "I object to the witness being permitted to answer that question, because this witness has not been qualified as an expert of firearms identification," he said. "I want to also object to the question in that it calls for an opinion from the witness, not shown to be familiar enough with firearms identification, microscopy, and photography."

For Duke, it was like the past hour of Lipford's questioning of Cornett had never happened. Judge Boykin overruled the objection.

"In my opinion," Cornett said, "this revolver fired the evidence bullet."[43]

Lipford relinquished the witness, and Duke began his campaign in earnest.

CHAPTER 17

CORNETT V. JONES

Dan Duke's cross-examination of George Cornett was a walk through the infancy of criminology in Atlanta and much of the nation. Cornett had been a newspaper photographer prior to joining the Fulton County Police in 1939, but he was never a beat cop or a detective. He was hired to work in the identification bureau taking photographs of traffic accidents and crime scenes. Such photography was a modernizing step in police work.

Cornett came to the county police force around the same time as the identification bureau began upgrading its equipment and methodology. At the time an *Atlanta Constitution* article trumpeted the county's "latest step in the march toward scientific crime detection" with the purchase of a photostatic machine that could make copies of fingerprints to send the FBI in Washington. With this, the paper reported, the bureau had "outdistanced any other identification bureau in the South."[1]

During his time at the bureau, Cornett said he developed an interest in firearm identification, an interest he said was nurtured by Francis Hoyt, the county's resident expert. Cornett said Hoyt showed him how to photograph bullets under the comparison microscope.

"I would study under him and make his photographs for him under his supervision," he said.

Later, Cornett worked under a man named Doris Austin, who did his own examinations of firearms and bullets and supervised Cornett's work. When it came to testifying in court, it was Austin who went.

"Were you ever officially designated or instructed to do this work by your superior officers?" Duke asked.

"I don't know that I was ever called or told to do it, if that is what you are speaking of," Cornett said. "They never stopped me from doing it."

"You just began doing it? Calling yourself an expert, is that right?" Duke said.

Cornett bristled. "No, I didn't begin calling myself an expert, Mr. Duke," he said. "I had not been going into court, but I had been working all that time on firearms identification."

"So, when Mr. Austin went to court, he was rendering his own opinions, based on examinations he made," Duke said. "And any examination you made was to satisfy your curiosity?"

"No, sir," Cornett said. "I was learning firearms identification."

When Austin left the identification bureau for the Navy during the war, Cornett began testifying in court based on his own examinations. "Who passed on your qualifications and designated you to do that?" Duke asked.

"I don't think you have any individual person come and tell another one working in a place whether he is qualified or not," Cornett said.

Well, Duke asked, why hadn't Cornett been giving his opinions in court all along?

"I wanted to get as much experience on the examination of firearms as I could before I attempted to go into court," Cornett explained.

"You say it was 1939 when you went with the county?" Duke asked.

"January 1, 1939," Cornett said.

"Don't you know, as a matter of fact, it was in early 1940 that Mr. Hoyt died?"

Cornett's journey from accident scene photographer to firearms expert under the tutelage of the late Francis Hoyt suddenly seemed quick indeed.

"Mr. Duke, I don't remember when it was," Cornett said. "I am telling you the truth about that."[2]

With Cornett off balance, Duke began a long, exhausting series of questions about ammunition: its weight, the types of bases of bullets (flat and concave), how bullets expand in the barrel of a gun when fired, and how that varies by type of bullet. The questioning went on for an hour or more. If jurors were paying attention, all of Duke's questions were meant to inject doubt into the choices Cornett made when selecting 9mm bullets as test rounds. In an affidavit filed after the second trial, Herman Jones suggested Cornett erred by not accounting for the different weights of the rounds and by choosing flat-based bullets instead of concave ones, like the round extracted from Stevens's body. Duke's questioning was exhaustive. No detail about Cornett's process went unexamined. In one exchange, Duke drilled deep into the care Cornett took in selecting test bullets and how closely he reported his findings to the prosecution.

"You say this is a flat-base bullet?" Duke said, pointing at an oversized photo of a test bullet.

"No, sir," Cornett began. Then, examining the photo, he said, "Well, speaking—it would be a flat base, yes, sir."

"Would you say this is a concave bullet?" Duke said, referring to the evidence bullet.

"That is right," Cornett said. "That is concave."

"Did you take an instrument and measure the diameter of this bullet?" Duke said, gesturing to the test round.

Cornett barely looked up. "I compared it with a known nine millimeter ammunition."

"This bullet here?" Duke tapped the exhibit with a forefinger.

"Yes," Cornett said. "The evidence bullet."

"I'm talking about the test bullet that you fired," Duke said, tapping again.

Cornett paused. "No, sir. I didn't measure that."

"You didn't measure the diameter of any of your test bullets, did you?" Duke said.

"No, sir," Cornett said. "I just compared those with the evidence bullet."

"And in your report, you only gave the factory specification of the different types of ammunition that you used," Duke said.

"Yes, sir," Cornett said. "That is before it was fired."

"And you never attempted to give any specifications of the test bullet—any of them—after they were fired, did you?"

"No, sir," he said. "I didn't measure it. I compared them."

"And if they looked alike under magnification of the comparison microscope, you let them go at that, did you?" Duke said. "Were your test bullets the same type and quality and lot number, made by the same manufacturer as the evidence bullet?"

No, Cornett said.

"Were any of them made by the same manufacturer as the evidence bullet?"

Again no.[3]

Duke walked to the defense table and began leafing through a hefty book, looking through its dog-eared pages for something.

After a few moments Judge Boykin learned forward. "Are you through with this witness?" he asked.

"No, sir," Duke said. "I have certain authorities here," he said, holding up the book. "I will request time, not to be hastened, to develop it."

"Go ahead with the examination of the witness," Boykin said, leaning back. "I will give you all the time you need."

A few moments later, Duke strode back to Cornett with the book open and handed it to him. The book was Julian Hatcher's text of firearms identification, which Duke had used in the prior trial to portray Cornett as a poorly read, self-taught "identification man."

"I will ask you to read page 288, beginning with the second paragraph," Duke said.

Cornett took the book and read silently a passage about the handling of evidence bullets and chain of custody and protecting the bullet during transport. Actually, the passage was more about what *not* to do, and it read as if it had been written specifically for this case. "Unfortunately, lead bullets can be rattled around enough in boxes and even envelopes . . . to quite seriously lessen the chances of a positive identification with test bullets later on; the worst possible place to carry them is in one's pocket," Hatcher wrote. "Proper packaging of weapons and ammunition components is merely common sense, but a lot of people seem to be a bit short of this commodity."[4]

"Any objection?" Judge Boykin asked as Cornett perused the book.

The judge's brother rose and looked to Duke. "Are you offering that?" he asked, pointing at the book.

Duke looked to the judge. "I tender it for identification at this time," he said. "At the proper time I will offer it in evidence."[5]

With that, Duke dove into a series of deep questions about the alloys used in ammunition, the chemical composition of various gunpowders, and how each might reflect on the scoring of bullets as they passed through the barrel of a .38 revolver. Cornett answered each, but often the answer was that he wasn't a ballistics expert, physicist, or chemist. If Duke's questioning of Cornett had been technical and pedantic in the second trial, he was determined to be even more so in the third.

Duke's efforts seemed geared toward blunting the impact of Cornett's testimony in a tidal wave of jargon and minutiae while portraying Cornett not only as uninformed but casual—even sloppy—in his approach. For instance, Duke asked Cornett a series of questions about his testing of the evidence bullet, including how he recorded the findings.

"Did you measure the width of the lands and the grooves on the evidence bullet with an instrument?" Duke asked.

Yes, Cornett said.

"Did you record that anywhere?"

"I recorded it on a piece of paper while measuring it," Cornett said.

"Did you record it in your report?" Duke asked.

"No, sir."

Duke turned to the jury. "You never did record any measurements, or any distances of width of the lands and the grooves on any of your test bullets either, did you?"

"No, sir," Cornett said. "I didn't even examine them. I didn't measure those at all."[6]

Duke's persistent questioning about the finer points of Cornett's job began to wear on Judge Boykin. When Duke questioned Cornett about the prisms used to reflect light back into the comparison microscope, and specifically a type of lens known as a Bertrand lens, the judge finally butted in.

"Mr. Duke, he stated that is the only one we have on that," Boykin said. "Don't ask him anymore. Go on to something else."

"I am afraid that he does not understand what I mean," Duke protested.

"He answered the question," the judge said. "I don't know whether he understood. He said there is only one prism besides the mirror."

Still, Cornett attempted to answer the question. "I don't know the names of the different prisms," he said. "I do know their purposes."

"Do you know whether you have such a thing in the Fulton County Crime Laboratory?" Duke asked.

Before Cornett could answer, the judge, clearly frustrated, jumped in.

"He says he doesn't know what it is," Boykin said. "How does he know whether he has it if he does not know what it is?"

Duke looked to the judge. "I think I ought to be able to get a specific answer on it."

"He doesn't know what it is! Isn't that a specific answer?" the judge complained. "Don't ask it anymore."[7]

Duke complied but he continued with questions about the methodology Cornett had used to compare his test bullets with the evidence bullets, sometimes to the irritation of the judge and prosecutors. When Duke asked Cornett to point out to the jury the markings on the bullets to which he was referring, Judge Boykin appeared close to mandating an end to the marathon cross-examination.

"He has gone over that," Boykin said.

Duke protested that Cornett had pointed out just one marking on one exhibit. He wanted Cornett to identify all the reference points he used to match the bullets. Flustered, the judge agreed.

"All right," he said. He looked to Cornett and said, "Point them out." Then, to Duke, he said, "Don't interrupt him until he has finished pointing them out."

Cornett held the exhibit and started to point, but at an oblique angle to the jury box. Duke moved toward him.

"I would like for him to point them out for the jury," he said, reaching for the photo.

"Will you sit down over there?" Boykin said, pointing to the defense table.

"You mean I can't observe it when he points them out?" Duke said.

The judge inhaled and held it for a second. "You can stand there when he points them out," he said, pointing to a spot in front of the jury box. Then, to Cornett: "Go ahead."

Cornett pointed out the areas of similarity he used to match the bullets, taking about a minute to do so, then Boykin turned to Duke, who had wandered back to the defense table and was scribbling on a legal pad.

"Now, what further questions?" Boykin asked.

Duke raised a finger. "I have one," he said, continuing to write. "If you will let me make a note here at this time for my record."

"Examine him," the judge said. "Make your notes later."

Duke switched tactics and began asking Cornett about when and how he had received the .38 Special, what he did with the gun and the evidence bullet, and when they were in and out of his possession in the eighteen months since the first trial.

When Duke asked about how he had received them prior to second trial, Cornett searched his recollections. He recalled the gun, evidence bullet, and test rounds were sent back to him in August 1950, but he didn't remember the courier.

Duke leaned in and asked Cornett if he recalled a meeting around that time between him, Herman Jones, GBI director Delmar Jones, and Fulton County police chief Neal Ellis in Ellis's office.

"Now, don't state what was stated," Duke said, holding a hand up to Cornett. He was trying to avoid another objection, but Lipford was already on his feet.

"It has nothing to do with the case whatsoever," the prosecutor complained.

Judge Boykin nodded. "Yes," he said. "I sustain the objection."

Duke turned to the judge. "I am seeking to lay the foundation to impeach this witness," he said.

"Impeach him on matters that are not material," Lipford added.[8]

Leaving the meeting aside for the moment, Duke asked Cornett if he was aware of tests Dr. Jones performed on the revolver in August 1950. Yes, Cornett said.

"Were you ever present when he made any comparison tests?" Duke asked.

"I know he was running some comparison tests," Cornett said. "He was in there working on it and filing down ammunition and firing the pistol in there after it was brought back."

"Do you know Mr. Clarence Nelms?" Duke asked. Nelms was a Fulton County police officer who had been detached to the department's new "science squad."[9] "Did you see him anywhere around there on the particular day that you said Dr. Jones was working on the pistol and the bullets?"

Cornett shrugged.

"He was our outside man, went out on calls," he said. "He was in and out of there, off and on, all the time."

"You don't have any recollection now or any memory of his having been there in the laboratory at a specific time when you and Dr. Jones were comparing the test and evidence bullets?" Duke asked.

"Not to the best of my memory," he said.

Duke went back to the defense table and brought out a sheaf of papers—transcripts from the second trial—and started to read Cornett's testimony where he swore Jones had not prepared his own tests but had merely reviewed Cornett's work.

"At the time you answered that, you knew that in August, just two months prior to the time you gave that testimony, that Dr. Jones did make independent tests, didn't you?" he said.

"I knew he was working on filing down ammunition and in there firing the bullets," Cornett said, clearly contradicting his testimony from a year earlier.

Didn't he remember sitting beside his boss, prior to the second trial, and discussing their comparisons, with Jones pointing out his observations and Cornett answering with his own?

"I don't remember anything like that," Cornett said.[10]

The picture Duke was painting for the jury was of a lab divided, a boss and his underling caught in disagreement, and a cover-up by prosecutors heading to trial. As he continued, Lipford and Shirley Boykin, either sensing the strategy or feeling a growing irritation with Dan Duke's endless questioning, grew impatient. When Duke asked Cornett to identify Herman Jones's position as director of the crime lab, attorney Boykin threw up both hands.

"I don't think anybody disputes that," he said. "That is the sixth time that was put in the record."

Sam Boykin ignored his older brother and motioned wearily to Duke. "Go ahead," he said. But for Duke, wearing everyone out was a main point of the exercise.

"I would like to challenge the record that this is the first time I asked that question," Duke said.

Judge Boykin would have none of it. "Go ahead," he said to Cornett, "you can answer it," then, turning to Duke, he added, "faster than you can challenge the record."

Cornett testified that Jones is the director of the lab and a firearms expert. "He is also a chemist," he said.[11]

Not much of a flourish, but with that, Duke ended his questioning. Lipford rose for redirect examination and asked Cornett a couple of questions reestablishing his credentials as a firearm expert and the author of the original report matching the bullet to the gun. As Lipford sat down, Duke launched into a series of questions about guns: the difference between revolvers and automatics, how revolvers work, and whether he had any experience with an "automatic revolver." Cornett said he hadn't seen such a gun, but he did suggest that a double-action revolver—one that fired without pulling back the hammer—had a similar character to an automatic but it did not eject the spent shell.

Regardless, Cornett said, he was unaware of any automatic revolver that would leave the same markings as found on the bullet retrieved from the body of Buddy Stevens.[12]

Duke also asked about the internal processes in the crime lab, specifically about what the initials of Dr. Jones on the bottom his report on the Stevens case meant. Cornett vacillated between describing the initials as a sign that Jones "approved" the report and that he had merely "OK'd" it. Duke pinned him down with a direct question.

"When he OKs a report, it does not necessarily indicate he personally made the test and is approving the contents of the test," Cornett said. But, he added, the initials on the Stevens report carried more weight.

"He had OK'd my report because he examined it with me," he said.[13]

Cornett was at last dismissed from the witness stand, likely to the relief of all save Duke, who had more questions to ask if he could have gotten them past Lipford and the Boykin brothers. As Cornett departed, Lipford engaged in some prosecutorial housekeeping, formally entering the gun, the bullet that killed Buddy, Henderson's jailhouse statements, and enlarged photographs of Cornett's test bullets into evidence. Duke objected to much of it but was overruled by Judge Boykin. Duke most strenuously objected to the photographs, which he said were made by a person who "has displayed an utter lack of knowledge for the mechanics of a comparison microscope." His objection was overruled, but Duke was talking to the jury. In the first trial, the comparison microscope and the accompanying scientific evidence were presented to the jury as proof of the magic of modern criminology. By the third trial, Duke had pulled the robes off the magicians, portraying them as poorly self-educated rubes playing with a science they barely understood.[14]

Next, Lipford called Nan Hansard to the stand. Now a married woman in her early twenties, Nan again cast herself back to that Halloween night in 1948. Her well-worn tale varied little from her prior testimony, although some additional details made their way in. When she talked about being marched across the cotton fields, Nan recalled a new detail about the man she never saw well. It happened when Buddy lifted her across a wire fence and she turned to watch their captor cross.

"He was kind of humming or singing something," she said, "you know, like Negroes do."[15]

With that, the white jury had in their minds the image of a deadly singing Negro.

When recounting the final struggle with the masked man, Nan said Buddy lunged at her attacker and pushed him off. "As I got up, he shot three times," she said. She also said she "could tell he was not very big," a new and important bit of testimony if the jury was to pin the crime on the short and stocky Henderson.[16]

Once Lipford finished, Duke launched into as tough a cross-examination as Nan had yet experienced and managed to extract some new details, including that a car had approached while she and Buddy were parking at the end of the dead-end street in the country club. Nan said she did not know who was in the car, although "it seems I recognized one boy."

"Did you look out and see who it was or did you hear somebody make a statement of some kind?" Duke asked.

"I didn't hear anybody say anything," she said. "But I saw the boy's face."

Duke asked if Nan recalled speaking to Lieutenant Price. Yes, she said.

"At any time have you told Lieutenant Price, at any time he was interviewing you about this specific case and what happened out there," Duke said, reading from his notes, "that a car drove up behind you? That a boy who evidently knew Buddy Stevens said, 'Buddy, you have got my place?'"

It was a cryptic comment. Regardless, Nan said she never told Price that.[17]

Duke asked Nan a series of questions about various statements she made to investigators in interviews following the attack, attempting to point out how unsure she had been three years ago about the man who attacked her.

"Have you ever told any of the officers that interviewed you concerning this that you never did get a view of the man's face, and that when the shots were fired that you had already run approximately fifty feet before you heard the first shots fired?" Duke asked.

Coolly, Nan replied. "You asked two questions," she said. "Ask one."

Unperturbed, Duke started with the distance question. "No," she answered. "That isn't true."

In the first trial, Nan had testified that Buddy had knocked the masked man off of her, she got up and ran, and then she heard three shots, then later appeared to contradict that testimony. In the second trial she was running when the shots were fired. This time she was unequivocal: the man shot Buddy three times and then she ran.

Nan also said she never told any investigator that she didn't get a look at the man. Duke recited her prior statements estimating her attacker's height and weight to various detectives and investigators. Nan denied them all, finally saying, "So many questioned me, I can't remember what I told."

Duke also questioned Nan about the gun she had seen in her attacker's right hand. The gun "looked dark to me," she said. And again she described it as a "dark-colored gun" rather than the shiny nickel-plated gun the state said fired the fatal round.[18]

After Nan Hansard, Lipford recalled Carl Stevens Sr. to testify about the night of the murder and his walk to the scene of the crime. Why Lipford chose to make the elder Stevens his final witness is unclear, as there was little to be gained, with the possible exception of presenting a well-known man and grieving father to the jury for a final few questions. Duke had little for Stevens in cross-examination except to clarify that he was six feet tall, a somewhat pertinent point when he talked about clambering over wire fences in the dark to reach his fallen son. Henderson was significantly shorter and presumably would not have had as much ease with the task.[19]

In the two prior trials, Clarence Henderson's attorneys had tried different strategies. In the first, they offered no defense, which predictably put their client on the road to execution. In the second, a team of Black and white attorneys from Atlanta vigorously defended their client by attacking and unraveling the torturous logic used by Lipford to put the gun in the hands of Henderson for the narrow window needed to kill Buddy Stevens. At the end, the state's case—by modern standards—was in ruins, but Henderson was no better off when the case went to the jury.

For the third trial, Duke went after the science behind the state's accusations. Ultimately, Duke would attack George Cornett with his own boss and the state's—perhaps the South's—leading expert in criminology. But he began with a colleague, Paul Shoffeitt.

Shoffeitt was a criminologist at the Fulton County Crime Lab, but he wasn't a self-taught "identification man," like Cornett. Shoffeitt was on an educational leave from the state of Alabama, where he had been the state toxicologist. He was in Atlanta working on his PhD in chemistry at Emory University and working at the lab at the same time. He had his master's degree in chemistry from Auburn University and a law degree as well. Several years later he would return to Alabama, where he was so highly regarded the state crime lab there carries his name.[20]

Duke's goal was to underscore his earlier cross-examination of Cornett, where he painted him as sloppy and uninformed, by leading the sure-footed Shoffeitt into the weeds where Cornett had stumbled. Duke began by having Shoffeitt describe the methods he used to compare and identify bullets in murder investigations. Along the way, Shoffeitt described his familiarity with various bullets, gunpowders, and the working parts of comparison microscopes—all things Duke had grilled Cornett on in his arduous cross-examination.

Shouldn't an expert know these things? Duke asked.

"I would think that you would have to be familiar with the equipment and apparatus pertaining to examination of bullets and shells, guns, and fire powders, in order to be a firearms identification expert," Shoffeitt said.

Duke's strategy was no secret, and Lipford wasn't ceding the ground.

"I object to what he *thinks*," the prosecutor said.

Judge Boykin nodded. "Yes," he said. "I sustain the objection to what he thinks."

Nonetheless, Shoffeitt carried on. "You would have to be familiar with those elements in order to be a firearms identification expert," he said.[21]

Shoffeitt laid out the meticulous process he used in the microscopic comparison of bullets, including measuring the weight and diameter of the bullets, matching the ammunition types, and comparing the widths of the lands and grooves of the test bullets and the evidence bullet—all steps Cornett had apparently not taken in matching the Stevens bullet to his own filed-down slugs.

All of that was theory or best practices. Duke had yet to get to the evidence in the case at hand when he handed Shoffeitt a magnifying glass.

While saying he would be more comfortable in a lab setting, Shoffeitt used the glass to compare the evidence bullet with Cornett's test bullets. The markings on the bullet retrieved from Stevens's leg appeared to be less scored than those Cornett used for comparison, he said. If anything, the scoring of a bullet fired more than a year earlier should be deeper, since the rifling of a gun barrel wears down over time, rather than becoming more pronounced.[22]

Lipford and Shirley Boykin frequently interrupted with objections throughout Duke's sometimes highly technical questioning of Shoffeitt. Duke was being pedantic, they complained, asking questions about gunpowder mixes and the hardness of various metals. Some of these objections were performative, aimed at jury members who might be suspicious of the Atlanta lawyer and his chemist talking over their heads. In the fading daylight, Lipford kept his cross-examination brief, asking Shoffeitt, who had come to the crime lab just seven months earlier, his history with the case.

"I have never examined this pistol, nor have I made an examination of the bullet," he said. "That is the first time I've seen it, tonight."[23]

Having set the stage with Shoffeitt, Duke raised the curtain on the main act: Dr. Herman Jones. Jones settled into the witness chair and recited the long list of academic credentials and degrees that took him from Auburn University to Columbia to Vanderbilt University and back to Auburn before he came to Georgia. Known affectionately as the "Crime Doctor," Jones was as well-known to Georgians as any lawman. In features and trial stories, Jones had appeared nearly four hundred times in pages of the *Atlanta Constitution* by the time he testified in the third Henderson trial.[24]

With Jones's qualifications established, Duke began to question him about various types of firearms in an attempt to poke holes in the state's case that the .38 Special pistol in evidence was the only weapon that could have fired the 9mm bullets that took Buddy Stevens's life.

The Smith & Wesson .38 isn't the only firearm with five lands and five grooves, Jones said. Earlier in the trial, Duke had questioned Carrollton police chief Rada Threadgill and GBI agent Jim Hillin about the existence of an "automatic revolver," with both men saying they had never heard of one. It was a pet theory of Duke's that such a gun could have been used in the crime, and Jones agreed, to a point. Gunmaker Iver Johnson had produced a "safety automatic" revolver that fired standard .38 rounds, and that gun's barrel had five lands and five grooves. The gun was a "double-action" revolver that retained the cartridge case, but it was a substantially rarer firearm than the Smith & Wesson .38 in evidence. Likewise, Harrington & Richardson made a similar .38 revolver with five lands and five grooves, Jones said.[25]

When Jones concluded his quiet testimony on various peculiar revolvers, Duke, who had been casting daggers at the prosecution table, again asked Judge Boykin to declare a mistrial.

"Mr. Shirley Boykin, at counsel table, is talking audibly to his associate," Duke said, barely containing his fury.

"What did he say?" the judge asked, looking at his brother.

Duke said he would be glad to repeat it, but he didn't want to do so with the jury in the courtroom.

"I merely stated to my associate counsel," Shirley Boykin began, but paused at a warning look from the judge. Frustrated, he began again. "A matter of a question of importance came up," he said. "I know nobody in the world would have heard it unless he was eavesdropping at counsel's table." He glared back at Duke.[26]

Judge Boykin rejected Duke's motion and instructed Jones to continue his testimony. With Duke leading, Jones covered some of the same technical ground trod by his associate Shoffeitt before moving to the case. Yes, Jones said, he recalled when Jim Hillin delivered the evidence bullet to the lab. Consulting his notes, Jones said he and Cornett received the bullet on November 30, 1948, a full month after the shooting. The pistol came a year and eight days later, also delivered by Hillin, he said.

From that time until summer 1950, Jones said he never made any comparison tests with the pistol, not even to check the work of his underling. Duke specifically asked if Jones checked Cornett's work prior to the first trial. No, Jones said.

"I went through the comparison microscope with George Cornett after the first trial and before the second trial," he said, looking at his notes, "on July 31 after the bullet and the gun were returned to the laboratory."

Curiously, Jones said he got the gun, the evidence bullet, and the test bullets by going to Cornett's home the day before, July 30. Jones said he began his examination of the bullets immediately the next day, and he soon found problems with Cornett's conclusions.

The evidence bullet was "lightly scored," Jones said, meaning the markings were faint. Some of the grooves were so shallow, they didn't even begin at the base of the bullet. Duke retrieved the prosecution's enlarged photographs of the evidence bullet and Cornett's test rounds and asked Jones to point out what he saw.

"In test bullet number one," Jones said, tracing his index finger on the exhibit, "you will observe the heavy lines to the left, and how that line spreads, continuing on the left, and the other one going straight through."[27]

The poster-sized exhibit showed regular, well-defined grooves on the test bullets so deep that the ridge created by one groove reflected as a bright white line in the flash from the camera. By comparison, the grooves in the bullet taken from Buddy's leg appeared shallow and irregular, fading away well before the test bullets' grooves.[28] Jones, with practiced patience, walked the jury through the differing characteristics between the evidence bullet and Cornett's test bullets.

"I was very much concerned over it," Jones said as he described his examination. "Being concerned, I proceeded with the work by the use of the microscope."

Jones spent hours trying to match the evidence bullet with Cornett's test bullets. Duke asked why he was so concerned. Jones said the bullet and gun had come back from Carrollton after the first trial for more tests, and the need for additional tests was discussed in a meeting with GBI director Delmar Jones and Fulton police chief Neal Ellis. It was this meeting that formed the basis of what Duke believed to be a conspiracy to withhold exculpatory evidence before Henderson's second trial. Predictably, Shirley Boykin objected. His brother was well ahead of him.

"I don't see where it is relevant if they had a conference," Judge Boykin said. "I rule it out."

Duke asked the judge if the meeting "should become relevant," would he rule it back in? Yes, Boykin said.[29]

Jones continued. After viewing Cornett's test bullets and the evidence bullet through the microscope, he was convinced they could not have been fired from the same gun. To be sure, he fired five additional bullets through the .38 Special.

"This evidence bullet did not match with any of the test bullets that I fired," Jones said.[30]

It was a long windup, but Duke had what he wanted: a well-qualified expert contradicting the state's theory on the gun. The early October sun had long set on this day of Clarence Henderson's third trial. Judge Boykin called for a recess until Wednesday morning. For thrift or safety or both, Duke stayed on a cot in the jail with his client. He had more to ask of Jones.

The third day of the trial opened with Dr. Jones back on the stand professorially lecturing the jury on the details of test-firing the .38 Special. Unlike his underling, Jones said he matched the manufacturer of the test bullets (Western) with that of the evidence bullet in order to have the closest comparison. This interested Duke very much. Cornett had said no such comparison ammunition had been available at the time he performed his original tests. Jones said he knew that was not the case because they had used Western 9mm ammunition to fire test bullets in another case around the same time.

Was Cornett aware his boss was checking his work in the Stevens murder? Duke tried to find out but was stopped by Lipford's objection to "anything he said to Cornett or Cornett said to him."

Ultimately, Duke wanted to show that the state had conspired to keep this new evidence under wraps. To do that, he needed to show they were aware that Jones had redone the tests.

"Do you know of your own knowledge," Duke began, "that Cornett knew—"

"I object to that," Shirley Boykin said. Frustrated, Duke dropped his head, shaking it back and forth.

"Don't shake your head," Lipford warned.

"I saw you," Judge Boykin agreed. "Don't do that anymore."

Duke gathered himself. "I asked him if he knew of his own knowledge," he said. "I did not ask that he repeat anything Mr. Cornett said."

Pausing, the judge overruled his brother. Yes, Jones said, Cornett knew about the tests. And did you file a written report of these new tests? Duke asked. Shirley Boykin, anxious to derail this insinuation, objected. Jones had already said he didn't think the evidence bullet could have come from the revolver. Who cared where he filed a report? From the bench, Boykin's brother agreed. Duke complained that the state had gone into detail about how Cornett had filed his report with Jones and that Jones had initialed it. That report was in evidence. Duke said he wanted to show Jones had made a similar report but that it had been buried by the prosecution. Judge Boykin was unmoved, but he said Duke could check the transcript and restate his objection the following day if necessary.

There was another reason why the report was important to Duke's theory. Jones didn't have the test bullets he had fired. He had turned them over to the GBI shortly before the second trial, along with the gun, the evidence bullet and Cornett's original test bullets.

Duke gestured to the state's display of ballistics evidence. "Do you see the test bullet you fired out of this gun anywhere in the courtroom," he asked.

No, Jones said: "I have never seen or heard from these bullets after I turned them over." Jones said he turned over the new evidence less than two weeks before the second trial, at the request of Solicitor Wright Lipford.

"I object to that," Lipford said. "That has nothing to do with it—who told him to turn it over."

"I think that has got a lot to do with where the five bullets are," Duke countered. "The solicitor now has the pistol, the Cornett test bullets, and the evidence bullet here."

The only things missing were Jones's test bullets, which presumably would cast doubt on the murder weapon. Lipford turned to the judge. He knew nothing about Jones's test bullets, he said. Judge Boykin nodded and turned back to Duke.

"Mr. Duke, the solicitor is generally not the keeper of any evidence," he said. "The clerk is the keeper of the evidence."

Unsaid was where the superior court clerk of Carroll County would get such evidence to keep. It would come from the prosecution.

"Go ahead," the judge said, motioning to Duke and Dr. Jones.

Duke nodded back and turned to Jones. "Did, or did not, Mr. Lipford ever come to Atlanta and hold a conference with you with reference to your findings?"

Lipford shot up again. "What statement I made to him would be pure hearsay," he complained.

"I didn't ask for the conversation," Duke said. "I asked him if it happened."

Yes, Jones said, he did talk with Lipford about his findings. "I have some notes here that I made," he said. He didn't have the bullets, but Jones's notes were precise, showing the measurements, weights, and diameters of his test bullets and comparisons with the evidence bullet, as well as the dimensions of the lands and grooves of each.[31] Again, over the objections of Lipford, Jones said his calculations showed that the evidence bullet could not have been fired by the .38 revolver. And Jones testified—also over Lipford's objections—that he made these precise micro-measurements using an instrument he invented that had since been adopted by the federal government. Lipford and Shirley Boykin complained that Duke was "encumbering the record"—dragging things out with irrelevant details—but Duke fought for every syllable.

"Wait a minute. He asked that same question last night!" Lipford said as Duke pressed Jones again on his conclusions about the ballistics in the case.

"I want to insist that I never asked him that question," Duke said, his regal Southern drawl echoing in the cavernous courtroom. Then he added, "in that form."[32]

Having had Jones testify in several different forms that the evidence bullet did not match the evidence gun, Duke finally relented and allowed Lipford the chance to cross-examine a man whom he had likely counted as an ally in numerous previous cases. Lipford came at Jones like a boxer aware of his opponent's soft spot, jabbing the area most likely to cause injury.

"Dr. Jones, do you recall the case of John Garris?" Lipford asked.

Of course Jones recalled the case, as would most Atlantans. The 1949 murder of Garris, an esteemed tenor with the New York Metropolitan Opera, in a dark alley near the train station in Atlanta was a stain on the city and a lurid story many had followed with great interest. Garris was killed by a single gunshot wound to the chest. Jones had examined the bullet and determined that it had been fired by a .38 caliber weapon. Within a few days police had a suspect, a paroled murderer who had been arrested in South Carolina after he had stolen a car in Atlanta. Jones worked tirelessly firing test bullets from the suspect's Belgian-made .38 and comparing them to the slug extracted from Garris's heart, finally reporting that the bullets matched. But the FBI, brought in at the request of the Atlanta police chief, disagreed and Jones was not permitted to bring his evidence to the case. The case was never solved.[33]

The Garris case was a high-profile failure for the Crime Doctor and an apparent case where Jones's wizardry with ballistics fell short. As Lipford began asking Jones about the case, it was Duke's turn to intervene. If Lipford wanted to know what the FBI said about Jones's work, he should introduce the FBI report, he said. "The actual record would be the highest and best evidence," Duke said, without saying that it would also mean the jury wouldn't have to hear it from Jones's own mouth.

Lipford pointed at Jones, the scientist central in so many convictions. "He comes here as a witness testifying against his own assistant," he said. "I expect to prove by this line of questioning the Federal Bureau of Investigation didn't agree with his findings."

Jones was dismissive of the FBI report. The report was inconclusive, he said. "They left it hanging fire," he said. But Lipford's point was made: Dr. Jones wasn't the last word in forensic science and the jury shouldn't think otherwise.[34]

Next, Lipford walked Jones through the early days of the Buddy Stevens investigation, turning up some new details that hadn't made their way into testimony in trials one and two. For instance, Jones said in the year between receiving the bullet extracted from Stevens's knee and the .38 revolver, the GBI had brought in "numerous" weapons as possible matches.

"They were all automatics," Jones said. That made sense, given the 9mm round already in the lab. But that changed when Jim Hillin of the GBI brought in the .38 Special. In fact, Jones said he heard about it before he saw it. Hillin had called him with a question.

"He asked me if it was possible for a .38 Smith & Wesson to have fired the fatal bullet in the Stevens case," Jones said. "Ordinarily, a .38 Smith & Wesson will not chamber automatic ammunition, and I would say at that time in talking to him that it would not be much possibility of it."

But Jones said he agreed to the tests and several days later Hillin brought the gun. This was a slightly different timeline than was understood in earlier trials, which had intrepid police rushing across the city to the downtown pawnshop and then to the crime lab.

Initially, Cornett was dismissive of the .38, Jones said. He tried to load the automatic round into the .38, but it wouldn't fit. But Jones reminded Cornett of a case in northwestern Georgia in which a World War II veteran had filed a .32-caliber bullet down to fit a single-shot pistol he had brought back from France. Cornett took the pistol and the evidence bullet and, "except for two or three seconds a day or two after," Jones said he did not see either again until shortly before the second trial.

In his testimony, Jones took credit for the ingenious idea of filing the bullets to fit the suspect gun, washed his hands of the results, and then discredited them with his own later tests.[35] Jones's calm, professorial demeanor, which had served prosecutors in Georgia so well in the past, was infuriating now. Lipford questioned Jones about a meeting at the crime lab shortly after Cornett had performed his original test firings of the revolver. Jones remembered the meeting well, including his limited participation in it. Jones testified that Lipford, Hillin, and Sheriff Gaston met privately with Cornett and the Fulton County police chief in a conference room.

"When you all came out, I said that if Mr. Cornett had done that work that apparently he had done a good job," Jones recalled. But he said that was not because he had checked Cornett's work.

"I never told you, or anyone else in there, those bullets matched," Jones said. Then he added, "And I have told you that all the way through."[36]

Lipford produced a typewritten page. "I will ask you to look at this report," he said.

Jones eyed the page with concern. He reached into his file and produced a carbon copy of the same page. "That copy you have there is my office file copy," he said, pointing to the letter in Lipford's hand. "It is not supposed to come out of that office."

The letter addressed to the head of the GBI totaled costs for lab tests on the revolver and court testimony at $650. The original report, held by Lipford, featured Jones's initials at the bottom of the page following a paragraph that read, "It is therefore our opinion that the .38 Smith & Wesson did fire the evidence projectile said to have been removed from the body of Carl Stevens."

"Those are my initials," Jones said. "And that copy is supposed to stay in my office."

"Dr. Jones," Lipford said, "you read this report, didn't you?"

"I don't know. I presume that I probably did."

"And you initialed it?"

"I did. Yes, sir, because it came to my desk," Jones said. But, he said, his initials were not an approval of Cornett's work.

"Do you mean to tell this jury, Doctor, that you would initial a report, which in all probability could take a man's life, with such indifference?"

Jones looked up at Judge Boykin. "If I answer that question, I will have to explain it," he said.

"Answer the question," Boykin commanded.

Duke stood up. "I think he has a right to explain his answer," he said.

"Mr. Duke," Boykin said, "I have told him to answer the question."

"It was not with indifference," Jones said. "I initialed that report to show it came to my desk and was ready for the file."[37]

Lipford then asked Jones about his own tests in late July and early August 1950. If the prosecutor had wanted to assure jurors that he had not suppressed evidence in the last trial, he went about it in a strange fashion. Jones said he had shared his doubts with Coweta County sheriff Lamar Potts during an August car ride to perform an autopsy and again in mid-September in a meeting with Lipford. Finally, a few days before the second trial commenced, Jones came to Lipford's office in Newnan to once again share his findings.

"I told you that the bullet—in my opinion, the gun didn't fire it," Jones said.[38]

More than just ignoring Jones's report, Duke believed Lipford had buried it and actively suppressed efforts to validate it. On redirect, Duke asked Jones if he had "tried to persuade Mr. Lipford to let independent tests be made on this weapon by other crime laboratories."

Lipford protested. By the time of his meeting with Jones, the gun and bullets were already in Carroll County for the start of the trial. Judge Boykin, who at the start of the second trial had denied Duke's motion for additional time to conduct his own tests, nodded his head.

"Yes," the judge said. "Mr. Lipford had nothing to do with it at all."

Duke turned to Jones. "Did you or did you not attempt on that night, two days before the second trial, to get them not to try this man again," he said, pointing at the prosecution table.

"I object to that," Lipford yelled.

Again Boykin sustained the objection. Jones didn't answer that question, but he did say he was instructed "just to keep it quiet."[39]

Lipford had one more shot at Jones, but in trying to emphasize weaknesses in Jones's contradictory ballistics testimony, he only managed to show evidence of a darker conspiracy. The prosecutor pointed out that Jones had no physical proof of this theory.

"Now where is the test bullet that you fired?" he asked.

Jones said he turned them over to a GBI agent, "as per your order."

"As per *my* order?" Lipford said.

"Your order," Jones said.

Lipford suggested Jones was confused. Certainly it was on the order of the head of the GBI, Delmar Jones? No, Jones said.

"You wrote me a letter requesting it," Jones said.[40]

Duke immediately picked at the thread, asking Jones if he ever saw the bullets again. No, Jones said. Not since he turned them over a few days before the second trial. Duke waved a copy of Jones's report and asked him why he had not submitted it prior to the second trial. It was Lipford's case, Jones said. "I felt obligated [to] keep whatever was between us on that case between the state and the county," he said. "It would be between me and Mr. Lipford."[41]

After hours of grueling testimony stretching over two days, Duke released Jones and called W. H. Stephens, a former GBI agent who had been called to these scene the night of the murder alongside Agent Hillin. Stephens had left the GBI to take a job as a district manager for a Pepsi distribution plant deep in Coca-Cola country, but he retained his "just the facts" law enforcement manner on the stand when he testified about his initial interview with Nan Turner. Turner had said her attacker was a "large man," as opposed to the squat Henderson. As far as a physical description, that was it, he said.

"She told me she could not identify him as white or Negro," he said.[42]

Duke called Hillin back to the stand, but the seasoned GBI agent was not shaken. Turner (now Hansard) had described the man as five feet, nine inches tall and weighing around 160 pounds. "She stated from the first it was a Negro," he said.[43]

Duke followed with a series of local witnesses. Two residents who lived near where Stevens was gunned down testified they saw a taxicab turning around in a driveway shortly after the murder. Then he called a young Black man named Carl Harris, who nervously took his place in the witness box.

Harris was Clarence Henderson's nephew and he had been living with his grandfather—Henderson's father-in-law—in the Sand Hill community in the home where police had seized the file allegedly used to file down the 9mm bullets. The state's theory was that he had used the file at his home in Carrollton and, after his arrest, it moved with his wife and family across the county and ended up in a bedroom dresser drawer. But after the conclusion of the second day of the third trial, Harris told Duke he recognized the file. It belonged to his grandfather, he said.

Harris said he had gotten the file from his grandfather to sharpen an axe. He laid it against a tree trunk while he cut up stovewood.

"That was about a week or two before the police came up there to that house," he said. Harris identified the file by a broken corner. "I broke it off with the axe," he said.

The file had always been one of Lipford's most convenient pieces of evidence, but it also was important. On cross-examination, Lipford asked Harris if he had ever mentioned this important fact to the sheriff or police chief or state investigators. No, Harris said.

"The first fellow I told was that man right there," he said, pointing at Duke. "I told him yesterday."

Lipford asked why he was only now coming forward. Harris said he had never been asked about a file and he didn't attend the first two trials.

"Did you know we had a file?" Lipford asked. "Did you know we had introduced it as evidence against Clarence?"

Harris said he didn't know it was *that* file. When he saw it introduced in evidence, he approached Duke.

The afternoon shadows were growing long across the courtroom as Duke's defense of Henderson was winding down. This trial, now into its third day, was markedly different from the previous two, with contradictory evidence on the murder weapon and the strong evidence that the state suppressed Jones's new ballistics tests. The new testimony on the last piece of physical evidence—the file—cast more doubt on the prosecution's case, although Duke likely knew Harris's testimony would have limited impact on the white men in the jury.

From the defense table, Duke rose to call his final witness: Solicitor Wright Lipford. Calling a prosecutor as a witness for the defense is a rare, often desperate gamble, but in this case, a very credible witness had testified about disappearing evidence and instructions to "keep it quiet."

Once Lipford was sworn and seated in the witness chair, Duke handed him Jones's typewritten report of the new comparison tests, which had been given to the defense two months after the second trial. Lipford said he recognized it and had "read it hurriedly."

"He told me that a request had been made of him for his findings," he said. "I told him at that time that as far as I was concerned it did not make any difference to me if he gave it to you or to the paper or anybody else in the country."

Duke asked Lipford a series of questions about the whereabouts of the missing test bullets. Apart from asking the GBI to bring all evidence to Carroll County, Lipford said he had nothing to do with them.

"I did not see the envelope or the contents of the envelope until the second trial," he said. In fact, he said he never even had the envelope in his possession except for a brief time carrying it to and from the sheriff's office. Lipford said he did not recall any additional bullets.

Holding up the gun, Duke asked, "Mr. Lipford, you requested that Dr. Jones make the comparison tests on this the second time, did you not?"

Lipford leaned back. "Now, Mr. Duke, I will have to explain that," he said. Lipford said he had talked about more tests with Lieutenant Price of the GBI. "Whether or not I requested it or the GBI requested it, I do not know."

Regardless, Lipford said he was concerned that the Georgia Supreme Court had reversed the first guilty verdict on a lack of evidence. "I had every confidence in George Cornett. I thought he was a good man and that his findings were correct," he said. But he said Dr. Jones had suggested he might make additional tests in case his own testimony would be needed.

"After he made it, you were aware of it before the second trial?" Duke asked.

"Yes, sir," Lipford answered, ending Duke's questioning.

If anything underscored the unique nature of Clarence Henderson's third trial, it was the cross-examination of the prosecutor by the judge's brother. Shirley Boykin rose and questioned his colleague about his visit to the Fulton County Crime Lab following Cornett's original ballistics tests.

"George Cornett told me that there was no question in his mind but that the gun had fired the bullet that was taken from Buddy Stevens Jr.," Lipford said.

Moreover, Lipford said, Jones had told him that Cornett "was to be commended for the splendid work that he had done." Lipford said Jones told him he had doubts about the gun prior to the second trial. "But he never gave me an official report" until two months after the trial, he said.[44]

* * *

Clarence Henderson's third trial ended as the prior two had: with him on the stand, pleading for his life. Henderson's rambling statement hit the same notes as his earlier two, although he was more forthcoming about the beatings he took while being held in Sheriff Lamar Potts's jail. Through it all, he maintained his innocence, he said. To the all-white jury, Henderson stressed he was a "good Negro."

"God knows I ain't killed nobody. God knows I ain't guilty," he said.

Henderson said he wouldn't "rape no white woman," and spoke personally to the jurors.

"Some of you may know me and know that I worked around some of your people," he said. "I have never bothered no white people in my life."

He praised God for the fact that he was still alive after two guilty verdicts.

"I look up to Jesus and ask him to save my body. I don't believe he will let me down, because he knows I am not guilty," he said.

Henderson closed by talking about his wife and children and his desire to return to them. He was ready to return to his home, to farm and to work. "Gentlemen of the jury, give me my freedom, please. That is all."

Henderson looked up at his lawyer. Duke shot him an urgent look.

"And I weigh 135 pounds," Henderson said, remembering. "I am five feet, six inches."

Then looking at his stocky frame, he added. "I weigh 140 now, I imagine. I have been in a little cell in the jail."[45]

CHAPTER 18

GOD AND THE NAACP

Bob Johnson checked his watch and settled into a back bench, notepad on his knee, as Dan Duke began a twenty-three-minute presentation of the Clarence Henderson case before the Georgia Supreme Court. Johnson was the city editor of the *Atlanta Daily World*, and the Henderson case was important news for his readers.

Six months had passed since Henderson received his third guilty verdict. The deliberations and verdict were again splashed across the front pages of the *Times–Free Press* and the *Georgian*, but without the breathlessness of prior trials. (The *Constitution* ran a small notice on page 2.) But the endless struggle of a Georgia sharecropper against the state's formidable white justice system remained an important story for the Black press.

In Carrollton, newspaper coverage was guarded. Stanley Parkman's *Georgian* acknowledged that Duke's defense "offered the strongest evidence yet" of Henderson's innocence.

"Not only did he put up more witnesses, but he was able to contradict the expert testimony of George Cornett," the *Georgian* wrote, adding that Lipford "followed the pattern of the first two Henderson trials."

The jury got the case a little after 5:00 P.M. on Wednesday, October 10, 1951, following Henderson's statement from the stand and closing arguments by both sides. The jurors deliberated for two hours and retired for the night. By lunch the following day, the foreman announced a verdict: guilty, with no recommendation of mercy. Like the prior two Carrollton juries, this one agreed to send Clarence Henderson to the state's electric chair.[1]

Although the jury's deliberations stretched across two days, it came to a verdict in just over seven hours total—roughly the same length of time as the jury in the second trial. Duke's new evidence, Jones's testimony, and Henderson's pleadings had made no difference.

Judge Boykin ordered Henderson to be executed thirty-six days later, on November 16, but that date was set aside as Duke again filed a motion for another new trial.

Henderson's third guilty verdict occurred on the same day a jury in Detroit convicted Haywood Patterson of manslaughter. Patterson was the most famous—perhaps infamous—of the Scottsboro Boys, whose treatment at the hands of white justice was the spiritual ancestor of Henderson's own case. Convicted of rape in the show trials of the 1930s, Patterson spent years in Alabama prisons before he managed to escape from a prison farm in 1948 and run to his sister in Detroit. The law eventually caught up with him, but the governor of Michigan refused to send him back to Alabama.

In 1950, Patterson published a memoir, *Scottsboro Boy*, describing brutal treatment and his own brutal behavior inside Alabama's notorious prisons. That same year he was arrested and charged with stabbing to death another Black man in a bar fight. Like Henderson, Patterson was tried three times on the charge. The first trial ended in a hung jury. The second was a mistrial. Upon his conviction in the third trial, the Michigan judge sentenced Patterson to serve between six and fifteen years in prison.

"I have read your book, *Scottsboro Boy*, so I know you have been wronged in the past," the judge said. But he said the prosecutor and two jurors were Black, as were many witnesses. "You cannot claim racial prejudice here."[2]

Patterson would not serve long. He died of cancer in prison a year later.

As he had two previous times, Judge Boykin again denied Duke's motion for a new trial, sending Clarence Henderson back to the state supreme court to beg for his life. How that news was received depended on the audience. To readers of the white press, Henderson was the "convicted Negro slayer." To readers of the *Atlanta Daily World*, he was the "thrice-doomed Georgia farm hand."[3]

While Johnson and the *World* covered Henderson's supreme court hearing in great detail, the white papers in Carrollton virtually ignored it. The *Times–Free Press* ran a thirty-nine-word brief on the hearing—about the same space the paper devoted to an item headlined "Car Kills Cow."[4]

Prior to the hearing, Johnson told his readers what many already believed: The white justice system was rigged against them. Henderson's multiple convictions and miraculous escapes illuminated the farce of Jim Crow justice and made him a folk hero among African Americans. Duke's argument before the state's highest court, Johnson wrote, "may begin uncoiling the controversial trial proceedings of Carroll County Superior Court which now lay firm claim on Henderson's life."

In his brief to the court, Duke listed eighteen grounds for a new trial, including a general lack of evidence to sustain an conviction and Boykin's decision at the end of the trial not to allow the jury to examine Herman Jones's written report on his independent ballistics test. Johnson found Duke's oral argument "simple but emphatic" and noted that the young attorney spoke "without benefit of a copy of his printed brief." Duke focused on the contradictory laboratory tests with the passion he was known for.

"It was this singular contradiction that moved the Atlanta lawyer to burst forth with a brief but eloquent plea," Johnson wrote, adding that the seven justices were "religiously grave" in their response.

Dramatic as always, Duke urged the justices to use the Henderson case as a model to protect defendants across Georgia from the unquestioned tyranny of the state's ballistics evidence. The state had allowed an erstwhile photographer and self-taught firearms expert to travel the state, sending defendants to prison with microscopic certainty, he said.

"This case offers an opportunity to create an exacting test to protect the poor and bedraggled persons picked up and sent away to dungeons on what is called scientific evidence," Duke said. "There's opportunity to erect a monument to courts for guiding scientific evidence."[5]

Associate Justice Lee Wyatt wrote the opinion for the majority of the court. Wyatt had been appointed to the high court in 1943 by Governor Ellis Arnall, but he took a leave of absence in 1947 to serve as a judge in the trials of Nazis in Nuremberg, where he oversaw the conviction of SS officers for the destruction of the Bohemian village of Lidice and the massacre of most of its inhabitants. Coincidentally, Wyatt's appointment to the supreme court by Arnall had created a vacancy in the Coweta Circuit that the governor filled by appointing Sam Boykin.[6]

In his ruling, Wyatt recalled the first trial, which he wrote was "substantially the same" as the current case, and ruled that Nan Hansard's ex post facto recognition of Henderson's voice was not enough to warrant sending him to the electric chair.

"The witness was not familiar with the voice of the accused," Wyatt wrote. "So much so that she made no effort to identify him on the first trial, and in the instant case simply gave it as her opinion, having heard him talk since that time, that it was the same voice."

Wyatt was joined by three other justices in the 4–2 decision, with one of the seven justices abstaining. He ignored the rest of Duke's argument, passing on the opportunity to author a precedent-setting manual on scientific evidence. The court had no appetite for that level of reform. However, Clarence Henderson had slipped the noose again.

* * *

The phone started ringing in Lipford's Newnan office early Monday, June 9, 1952. More than 1,300 days had passed since Buddy Stevens's lifeless body was found on the edge of a plowed-up cotton field. Having been through this twice before, Lipford couldn't have been surprised by the results when newspaper reporters began calling. Still, he dodged the obvious question: Would he try Henderson a fourth time?

"I have not seen the opinion of the Supreme Court," he told the *Constitution*. He would need to study it before deciding on whether to bring the case again, he said. The *Constitution* buried the story on page 15 the following day. In Carrollton, the *Times–Free Press* gave the story just two paragraphs, citing the *Constitution* as its source, an indication that the local paper didn't even see the opinion and wrote the brief for its late edition. Two days later, when the *Georgian* published its story, Lipford said he still had not seen the court's decision.

"As soon as I make a thorough study of the decision of the Supreme Court, I will announce, as soon as possible, if prosecution of Henderson will be continued," he told the *Georgian*.[7]

Lipford's tone and willful ignorance were a far cry from how he greeted the first supreme court reversal two years earlier. Back then, the prosecutor confidently told reporters Henderson would be back in Boykin's court without delay—a prediction Judge Boykin made come true.[8] Despite his reluctance to announce it in the press, Lipford filed a motion by the end of the week asking the judge to call Henderson—the farmer, the Negro slayer—back for a fourth trial.[9]

Weeks passed and Henderson remained in jail—not doomed, but not free, either. He was in limbo while Lipford and others weighed the legal and political avenues left to them after the court had turned back the latest verdict with the same reasoning it had used in the first reversal. Getting a conviction from an angry white jury in Carrollton three times was one thing, but Lipford had made no progress with the justices in Atlanta.

Two months had passed when Daniel Duke received a call from Bob Johnson at the *Atlanta Daily World*. Judge Boykin had ruled in favor on Lipford's motion to retry Henderson—for *robbery*. According to Nan Hansard, the man who shot Buddy Stevens had first taken $15 from his wallet. From his office in Newnan, Lipford had told Johnson he had "no plans" to bring Henderson back on the murder charge, but he also said he had no plans to drop it. Unable to get his three convictions to stand up, Lipford wanted to keep Henderson in prison by whatever means available.

Even if he wanted to retry Henderson for Stevens's murder, Lipford had little choice in the matter. He had no new evidence linking him to the crime, and even his circumstantial evidence was crumbling. The split between George Cornett and his boss, Dr. Herman Jones, was deep and personal. Cornett was humiliated by the treatment he had received. He would leave the crime lab and never forgive his boss. Jones, of course, would stay as head of the lab, which would soon be taken over by the state. Today, it is part of the Herman Jones Memorial Forensic Science Complex at the GBI headquarters in southern Atlanta.

A new trial date for Henderson was set for mid-October, near the fourth anniversary of Stevens's death. Duke told Johnson he would be prepared to defend his client once again. He didn't say who would pay for it or what resources he would have for another trip through the Carroll County justice system.[10]

It was a major victory of sorts. Lipford's capitulation on the murder charge meant Henderson no longer faced death. But he also wasn't free.

Boykin called the criminal session to order on Monday, October 13, 1952. In anticipation of a trial, the clerk had called twenty more potential jurors than usual. Finding jurors without deep, personal convictions on the case would be difficult indeed, although the white press in Atlanta and Carrollton took little notice of Clarence Henderson's return to court.[11]

Carroll County residents were more invested in a referendum that would split the county school board into seven regional districts. It was a progressive idea aimed at more equal representation across the county, but that was what worried white voters in Carrollton, particularly middle-class voters. Across the nation, at-large elections for such boards—that is, boards in which each member represented the entire jurisdiction—were an effective barrier to the unwanted (poorer white areas gaining a stronger voice) or the unthinkable (Black voters pooling their power to elect one of their own). At-large seats watered down the poor and minority votes.[12]

Those concerned with broader issues were more interested in the U.S. Supreme Court, to which Ethel and Julius Rosenberg, convicted of passing atomic secrets to the Russians, had turned in hopes of reversing their own death sentences. As Henderson and Duke stood before Boykin, news broke that the Court had refused to hear the Rosenberg case, all but sealing their fates. In addition, Henderson's fourth trial came just weeks ahead of the presidential election between Dwight Eisenhower and Adlai Stevenson. Senator Richard Nixon, Eisenhower's pick for vice president, attacked the Democrat Stevenson for appearing as a character witness in the perjury trial of accused Russian spy Alger Hiss, saying his poor judgment disqualified him for the nation's highest office. Stevenson could not be trusted to confront the Communist threat, Nixon said.[13]

The threat posed by international communism was not merely political. That fall, American and United Nations forces battled the Chinese army for control of several strategic hills in the so-called Iron Triangle of central Korea. One hill changed hands so many times in desperate fighting that by mid-October it was stripped of vegetation, earning the name "White Horse" for its spare appearance.[14]

While beating a crooked system of white justice for a third time was a feather in the cap of the Atlanta branch of the NAACP, Thurgood Marshall and the national office were deep into a massive legal push to topple legal segregation. By the fall of 1952, the case *Brown v. Board of Education* had made its way before a divided United States Supreme Court, which had bundled the Kansas case with four other school segregation cases. Chief

Justice Fred M. Vinson was a Kentuckian and had served in Congress and in the Roosevelt and Truman administrations before President Truman tapped him to lead the court through one of its most difficult periods. A backroom dealer, Vinson had trouble keeping a majority together on the difficult social and racial issues before the Court. By the end of the year, the justices were not in accord. The cases would be reargued the following summer.[15]

If the world's interest in Henderson's plight had waned, it did not lessen his jeopardy. He and his attorney were alone and lacked even the meager resources of their prior appearances. A conviction would mean years of hard Georgia prison time.

Lipford stood and addressed the judge.

"I will ask the court for a ruling whether the law, as laid down by the Supreme Court with reference to identity, applies for the robbery charge," he said. "If the court rules it does, I will not press the charge."[16]

Duke looked up; Henderson looked to his attorney. Lipford, unwilling to have another conviction overturned, had placed the burden on Boykin to decide. If the supreme court hadn't accepted Nan Hansard's identification of Henderson as the murderer, would they accept him as a robber? If Boykin believed they would not, Henderson would be free. The judge agreed to take the matter under advisement.

Two days later, Henderson and Duke were both summoned back to the Carroll County Courthouse to wait while Judge Boykin oversaw the routine pleadings and jury trials that made up the October session. Duke sat in the back of court or roamed the halls, while his client waited in a holding cell until late in the afternoon. Several witnesses whom Duke had subpoenaed were also there, in case Lipford moved ahead with the robbery charge.

Boykin called the case at 4:00 P.M.

"May it please the court," Solicitor Wright Lipford began. "On October 31, 1948, there happened in this county, to my way of thinking, one of the most brutal murders that has ever been committed in this section of Georgia."

Lipford recounted the facts of the case and its many "unfortunate" reversals. Three times, he said, Carroll County juries had declared Henderson guilty of murder, only to have those verdicts turned aside by the justices in Atlanta.

"It is not my purpose nor the purpose of any officer of this court to let this case drop where it is," he said. "An investigation is still being made and an investigation will continue until additional facts are secured."

But until such time as that new evidence appeared, Lipford asked that the charges against Clarence Henderson be placed on the "dead docket." The dead docket was courtroom lingo for a case that was not dropped entirely but was removed from the active criminal docket and was not actively prosecuted.

"Any objection to that?" Boykin said to Duke. In Georgia, defendants had the right to object to a case being dead docketed and the judge had to grant their wish. Duke wasn't about to make such an objection.

"No, sir," he said. "I do have one thing that I think that I ought to call to the court's attention."

Duke asked that Henderson be taken by the sheriff to Atlanta. For Henderson, this incredible turn of good fortune did not come without peril. A Black man accused—indeed, convicted three times—of killing a white man and attempting to rape a white woman was about to slip through the arms of white justice. Certainly, some whites in Carrollton would take offense, and sunset was just a few hours away.

Duke said he was not suggesting "any good citizen of Carroll County" would do anything to Henderson. But, he said, "I am sure this court would be most anxious to avoid any untoward incident that might occur."

"Well," Boykin said, "the court will take that under advisement and consideration."[17]

Boykin said he would write an order placing State v. Henderson on the dead docket. He turned to Duke.

"I'm not going to release him without a bond," he said. "You may make application for a bond if you desire."

Duke was confused. Dead docketing a case typically meant no bond was required. This was a maneuver by Boykin and Lipford to avoid the political damage of releasing Henderson, who had now been in jail nearly three years and was the only suspect in the case. Because he had been in jail and not working, Henderson's family lived in abject poverty. They had no way to bond him out.

There was no case against him that could withstand the scrutiny of even Georgia's skewed justice system, yet the judge and prosecutor intended to keep him in a cell. With a rap of his gavel, Boykin adjourned the court. Duke's face flushed hot and his famous temper boiled. He appealed to the judge to sign for his client's release.

"Court is adjourned," Boykin said. "I will reconvene at 9:15 Thursday morning."

Reporters for the *Georgian* and the *Times–Free Press* rushed up to Duke, who promised to "take such action as will be necessary . . . to get justice."

"But," he said, furiously, "I am not coming back down *here*."[18]

Duke didn't return to Carrollton the following day, but he did receive Boykin's written order indicating the case had been "continued" and restating that Henderson could apply for bond. Continued? That wasn't Lipford's motion. He had asked the court to move the case to the dead docket. A continuance indicated the prosecutor wanted the case to remain on the active criminal docket and new trial date set. Duke was livid. Lipford had concealed evidence and built a case on a gun that, under careful review, didn't even appear to have ever been in Henderson's possession. Now he and Judge Boykin were manufacturing a reason to keep him in jail indefinitely, or at the very least, hold him for ransom.

Duke received a call from the *Atlanta Daily World*, which was anxious to catch up on the Henderson case. The reporter was a young Morehouse College graduate and classmate of Martin Luther King Jr. named Lerone Bennett Jr. Within a few months, both Bennett and his boss, Bob Johnson, would be in Chicago as city editor and executive editor, respectively, of *Jet* magazine. Bennett later moved to *Ebony* magazine, rising to the top editorial position, where he developed a reputation as one the most esteemed historians and social critics of his generation.

Duke said Boykin's written order and Lipford's request to dead docket the case were "not the same thing."

Bennett reached out to Judge Boykin. The judge refused to be quoted, but "an authoritative courthouse source" told the reporter that "dead docket" was "slang," and the judge's written order was all that mattered. Lipford followed by telling the *Daily World* that a "dead-docketed" case was merely one where a hearing date had yet to be set. None of this was true.[19]

In Georgia, continuances in criminal cases were granted from "term to term," meaning they were not indefinite, whereas a case moved to the dead docket stayed there until a judge requested its removal.[20] State law, at the time, was less clear on the topic of bail for defendants in dead-docketed cases, although it was later encoded in state law that bail was not a requirement in such cases.[21]

The wrangling over the freedom of Clarence Henderson continued for more than two months. Finally, on December 12, 1952, three years after Henderson was arrested by the GBI, the sheriff, and the Carrollton police chief, Duke filed a thick habeas corpus motion demanding his release and asserting that "his further restraint is illegal" and constituted "involuntary servitude." Duke argued that Lipford had specifically asked the case be sent to the dead docket and not continued and that motion had been granted. If the plan had been to continue the case, Duke could have objected and insisted that the case be tried immediately. That Boykin's written order decided the case was merely continued to a future date was "vexatious, oppressive, and arbitrary," Duke wrote. He added that the state had no additional evidence against Henderson and the evidence they did have had twice been shown by the state supreme court to be insufficient to warrant conviction.

"Your petitioner avers that to restrain him of his liberty further is tantamount to inflicting upon him cruel and unusual punishment which disgraced civilization in former ages and which makes the modern age shudder with horror," Duke concluded.[22]

Boykin called a hearing on a chilly Saturday morning, January 17, 1953. For a final time, the wide and ornate courtroom was packed, mostly with white Carrolltonians interested to see if Henderson, so reviled as the monstrous Negro who had stalked young white couples and killed Buddy Stevens, would walk free. Lerone Bennett from the *Daily World* slipped into a back pew among the handful of Black residents who had come to see if justice would be done.

Dan Duke, dressed in a dark suit, entered the courtroom from the back and walked to the defense table. "Is that the mayor?" one onlooker whispered. Duke had become such a recognizable figure in town, the confusion was understandable.[23]

Presently, Henderson, dressed in jail overalls, was led in and seated next to Duke, who rose and recited his reasoning for his motion: the supreme court had three times reversed his client's conviction, there was no new evidence linking Henderson to the crime, and his continued imprisonment was against Georgia law and the constitutions of the state and nation. When he had finished, Lipford calmly dismissed Duke's argument. State law required defendants charged with capital crimes to be held without bond, and Henderson was so charged. Technically, Henderson was in jail on two bench warrants, one for murder and one for robbery. Retaining him in jail was "pure and regular on its face," Lipford said.

Boykin turned his stern face to Duke, who had risen to his feet, and asked him to respond, but he warned him not to stray from the peculiarities of the law in the Deep South.

"If you don't have any Georgia authorities," he said, "I'm not going to grant it."[24]

In fact, Duke did have Georgia case law, including the 1805 case of *State v. Marco De Las Maurignos and Jose Sierra*, in which two men accused of highway robbery had been held over two terms of court without their case being called. In that case, the attorney for the two men argued that the prosecutor had no evidence linking them to the crime and was merely holding them indefinitely. The court agreed and released them.[25]

"I agree with you on the principle of the thing," Boykin said. "But there is a bench warrant pending. I have some obligation here."

Tossing the hot potato back to Lipford, Boykin said the situation would be different if Lipford dropped the charges. Lipford shifted uncomfortably in his seat.

"I can't make him *nolle pros* it," Duke said, using the Latin-derived legal phrase for no longer pursuing a charge.

"I can't either," Boykin said.

Duke paused. Boykin was reluctant to release Henderson because of the warrants that the judge himself had issued. Refocusing, Duke pointed out that the state's evidence against Henderson, which had been the pretext for the warrant, had been ruled by the supreme court to be insufficient. Absent new evidence, how could the warrant be valid?

Boykin turned back to Lipford. "Is anything being done?" he asked. Lipford insisted that the case continue to be under active investigation, but Duke was disbelieving.

"The work being done doesn't point to Henderson," Duke insisted.

Boykin was quiet and the crowd was still. Finally, he turned to the clerk.

"I think you had better let him make his own bond," Boykin said. The clerk took the instruction to mean Henderson could make an "appearance bond," a written promise to return to court should new evidence come up. After three years and three death sentences, Clarence Henderson would walk out of the Carroll County Courthouse a free man.

Before the largely white crowd, a deputy led Henderson away out of the courtroom to prepare him for his release. As Boykin adjourned the court, Lipford turned to Duke and warned him that he should get his client out of Carrollton as soon as he was released.

"I don't want anything to happen to him," he said. The whole affair was an embarrassment to him; the last thing Lipford needed was for a mob to try to finish the job he couldn't complete. Whether Henderson took Lipford's words as a warning or a threat, deputies hustled him from the courtroom so he could quickly complete his business in Carrollton.[26]

"You can never tell what will happen," an unnamed court employee told Bennett as the hearing adjourned. "We want to protect him from screwballs."

"Phooey!" interjected a white man nearby. "Why didn't they just turn him loose here? Nothing is going to happen to him. He's no more guilty than you or me."

Lizzie Henderson gathered the children up and began down the marble stairs from the courtroom to the ground floor of the courthouse, when she felt a hand grab her arm. Turning, she saw the smiling face of a stout white woman.

"I'm so happy," the woman said. "I've been praying for you all the time."

The months-long delay between the dead docketing of Henderson's case and his release was legally indefensible, but it is possible it gave white Carrolltonians time to process the news. Whether it was because the evidence was weak or because they preferred another suspect, a segment of the white community had always doubted Henderson was the guilty party. Three times through the Jim Crow justice system might have moved public opinion even further among the more progressive whites. Certainly, his jailers had treated Henderson as a free man in waiting, giving him trustee status and permission to leave the jail to see his family or get a haircut. But the waiting was excruciating.

"I didn't do anything," Henderson said. "Anything but pray—prayed and kept the jail clean."[27]

When Henderson emerged onto the sidewalk, photographers snapped photos of him in an open-collared flowered shirt, jacket and hat. He carried Lutricia, his two-year-old daughter, who had never known her father outside of jail. Lizzie and the couple's other two children, Clarence Jr. and Sarah, walked with him. The photo carried in the *Atlanta Daily World* was a Clarence Henderson readers had not seen before. He was smiling.

"I never gave up hope," he told reporters. "I never did."

Henderson and the Stevens murder were once again national news. Wire services carried his story around the nation and beyond. "Freed After 3 Death Sentences," the *New York Times* reported. "Doomed Thrice in Killing, Georgian Is Freed by Writ," the *New York Herald Tribune* echoed. "Negro Convicted in Shooting Freed" was how the Associated Press story appeared to readers across the heartland.[28]

The *Atlanta Daily World* carried the news in long articles and feature stories bursting with Black civic pride at the improbably victory.

"Clarence Henderson is alive and a free man today, as if saved by some miracle of fate," the *Daily World* wrote. "That miracle, according to Henderson's own words, is the NAACP! Henderson freed Saturday after being allowed to sign his own bond, whisked out of Carroll County immediately, breathed his first sigh of relief and gave thanks to God and the NAACP."[29]

Along with Dan Duke, Henderson praised S. S. Robinson and E. E. Moore, his Black co-counsel in the second trial, and Charles Harper, president of the Atlanta branch of the NAACP, who had made public and private appeals to raise the needed money needed for his defense.[30]

The *Daily World* lavished praise on the NAACP for spending $5,000 on Henderson's defense, much of it collected in coins and small bills wrung from the pulpits of Black churches. Raising money had been a constant struggle and a limitation, but it was an impressive figure to readers, as it was nearly five times the annual wages of a Black worker at the time.[31]

Speaking of which, Henderson was free but now faced the daunting task of finding work to rebuild his life. Poor as he was, Henderson had eked a living in Carroll County as a sharecropper. Removed to Atlanta, he would have to find some new means of support.

"I've got to find a job now and do something for my family," he said.

Henderson knew there was no going back to Carrollton. Even if many white Carrolltonians thought he had been railroaded, certainly some believed he was a serial rapist of white women who had gotten away with murder. If he stayed in the city of his birth, he likely would end up dead.

"I won't go back to the farm. Never expect to do that again," he said. "My idea is to stay here with the people who helped me."

For a while at least, Clarence Henderson was a celebrity and a reminder that it was possible for African Americans to overcome the odds and powerful whites in their quest for equality and justice. Fresh from jail, Henderson was brought to the headquarters of the Atlanta NAACP to receive congratulations from his former attorney, S. S. Robinson. From there, he was escorted to a two-room apartment chosen for him and his family in a Black neighborhood in Atlanta's west side. It was not much removed from the sharecropper shack they had been in before this started, just without fields to work.

"We've got to start from the bottom again," he said. "It's a long climb, but we're willing."[32]

Henderson's victory was a good story, but it didn't change the reality Black people faced in America. *Daily World* editor C. A. Scott described the Henderson case as "not only a vindication of the man but . . . a victory for the courts," but African Americans were horrified by the death sentence handed down to Ruby McCollum around the same time. McCollum, a wealthy Black woman in Florida, gunned down a local doctor who had physically and sexually abused her and fathered her illegitimate children. The lurid and terrifying details of the trial had been carried in the African American *Pittsburgh Courier* in stories written by novelist Zora Neale Hurston. The McCollum verdict was a stark reminder that for every Clarence Henderson there were dozens of Ruby McCollums for whom there was no such good fortune.[33]

Even so, Henderson's hard-fought and improbable victory was a sign of the powerful forces changing Carrollton, Georgia, and America in the early 1950s. In the fall of 1952, as Clarence Henderson bided his time sweeping the floors of the Carrollton jail, the city held a parade through town to honor a local Black woman. Catherine Hardy, who grew up in the county, won a gold medal in 4 × 100-meter relay in the 1952 Summer Olympics in Helsinki, Finland, and was the guest of honor in a ceremony attended by the city's white and Black elite, who spoke glowingly about Hardy but also of the racial situation in the county.

"Most of the speakers brought out the contrast between the afternoon's gathering and the racial situation as it has been pictured by Russia," the *Georgian* reported.[34] Unreported was that Hardy, lauded in the *Georgian*'s editorial page as a "non-racial heroine," was returning to Carrollton from Fort Valley State College, a Black school, because West Georgia College was segregated and did not admit Black students—and would not for another decade.[35] Also downplayed in the coverage was that whites attending the ceremony at a local ball field after the parade had a reserved section in which to sit.[36]

A more significant sign of change was the defeat of a proposed amendment to the state constitution backed by segregationist governor Herman Talmadge. Talmadge sought to have the "county unit" system that diluted the voting strength of densely populated urban counties in the party primaries written into the state constitution and applied to all elections. Talmadge, who greatly benefited from the state's white primary, spun the effort—without apparent irony—as fighting the "political machines" in Atlanta.

"It will keep political power in the hands of the majority of the people throughout the state," he said, "instead of turning it over to a highly organized group of bloc voters, led by the Negro lawyer A. T. Walden within the city of Atlanta."[37]

The effort had to be approved in a statewide vote. Talmadge warned of "mixed schools" should it fail, but fail it did. A coalition of Black voters and progressive whites in Atlanta turned the tide. In Carrollton, *Georgian* editor Stanley Parkman urged his readers to let the effort stay buried. Those who worried about racial equality could depend on the white primary, he wrote.

"Governor Talmadge knows better than we do that the races will never be mixed in the schools of Georgia," Parkman wrote in an editorial shortly after the November ballot issue went down to defeat. "He knows better than we do that Negroes and whites never have and never will dance together in the municipal auditorium of Atlanta or anywhere else in Georgia."[38]

After the Henderson trial, Dan Duke continued to be a thorn in the side of Southern justice. A little more than a year after freeing Clarence Henderson, Duke was held in contempt of court in a much less momentous case involving a woman accused of participating in an underground lottery. An

Atlanta municipal court judge ordered Duke to pay $25 or face twenty days in jail for accusing a police officer on the stand of mistaking himself "for Jesus Christ." When the judge warned him against such outbursts, Duke told him he would rather be jailed than pay a fine for his words. He also refused to be fingerprinted.[39]

In 1955, Duke was in southwestern Georgia, where he fought the removal of 483 Black voters from the rolls in Randolph County. In another impressive victory, Duke convinced a jury in federal court to side with him, awarding damages of $40 each to twenty-two Black would-be voters. In court, Duke said he had been approached by Black voters in several other counties who had been deprived of their right to register to vote and warned local officials against "illegally and wrongfully" removing them from the rolls.[40]

In 1958, segregationist governor Marvin Griffin appointed Duke, a political enemy, to investigate corruption in the application of the state liquor tax. In another of his crusades, Duke had taken to representing liquor dealers in filing lawsuits against the state revenue commissioner. alleging that the state was abusing its constitutional authority to extort money from his clients.[41]

The times finally caught up with the man in 1964 when Duke won a race for judge in Fulton County on the strength of the Black vote, beating the handpicked candidate of the Atlanta Bar Association in an upset.

"I will exercise this awesome power with the consciousness always that the power to imprison should humble any man," Duke said in his victory speech. "I hope that any errors that I may commit will be on the side of mercy."[42]

Duke made the most of his modest perch as a county judge and quickly reignited his campaign against the Ku Klux Klan, urging the state to break up the fractured Klan sects by revoking their state-issued charters "as we did back in the '40s."

"I cannot understand the surprising indifference and inactivity of our leaders in not pursuing with unyielding vigor those who violate the law under the umbrella of a Georgia-granted charter," he said. Duke found his campaign stymied again by segregationist politicians unwilling to take action against the Klan.[43]

Despite his temporary fame and his stated intentions, Clarence Henderson's life after the Buddy Stevens affair was not a happy one. If he was a hard man before his arrest and three years in prison, Henderson was no less angry and dangerous having to begin again in a new place. Fulton County records show he received a twelve-month sentence in jail for assault and battery in 1957. Three years later he got another year in a stabbing and yet another year in jail in 1964 for assault. Family members recalled his bad temper and deep suspicion of white people. For the generation that followed, the story of his arrest, trials, and eventual flight from Carroll County was told only in the sketchiest of ways, his remarkable history lost to his own family.[44]

Indeed, life for the Henderson family was far from peaceful. Nearly thirty years after Clarence Henderson's first murder conviction, his son, Clarence Henderson Jr., was charged with the shooting death of his wife in the midst of a rage about his daughters keeping company with two teenage boys. According to the transcript of the pleading, the thirty-four-year-old Henderson was holding a pistol—a .38 revolver—behind his shoulder when it fired, hitting his wife in the head. One of Henderson's attorneys in the case was James Venable, the Klan leader who had represented Homer Chase three decades earlier in the Communist leader's "peace bond" hearing. Venable took many such public defender cases, often with Black clients who were either unaware of his Klan ties or in no position to object. Venable and Henderson's other attorney successfully argued that the shooting had been accidental and implored the judge not to remove both parents from the home. Henderson received five years' probation and a stern lecture from the judge.[45]

Buddy Stevens's murder was never solved, and despite the decades that have passed, the case remains officially open. After Henderson, the state never pursued another suspect. Leonard Pendergrass, the former cop and cabdriver, had always been considered a likely suspect by some in Carrollton. He had lent the .38 special revolver to Lee Hardman just hours before the attack at Stripling Chapel Church, and the state had linked that gun to the Stevens slaying. Early in the investigation, Judge Boykin had blamed the taxicab industry in Carrollton for playing a role in the attacks, letting slip that police believed the culprit had been taken to the scene of the prior lovers' lane attacks in a taxi.

But fate saw to it that Pendergrass would never emerge as an official post-Henderson suspect. He died in November 1951, a little more than a month after Henderson's third conviction and half a year before that conviction would be overturned.

Just four years passed from Stevens's death to Henderson's release from jail, but Carrollton had changed mightily in ways that mirrored the United States as a whole. With a country club development on one side and a lakefront residential area on the other, Carrollton embraced the postwar suburban dream that would move its white residents out of the central city and farther from their Black neighbors.

West Georgia College saw its inflated enrollment numbers from returning GI fall back to prewar levels, but the institution was forever changed. New dormitories were built and old ones fireproofed for the first time. The college broke ground on a new science building in 1953 as President Ingram opined in his annual report about building the new generation of industrial and agricultural leaders.

The county's new hospital, now named Tanner Memorial Hospital after the wholesale grocer who contributed $75,000 in seed money to its construction, was the pride of the city. In its first year Tanner had 434 new births, virtually all of which would have been in-home births less than a generation before. The hospital also recorded 477 emergency operations, marking another important improvement to the county's quality of life. Perhaps less appreciated at the time were the 130 "charity cases" handed by the hospital's 15-member staff, which the *Georgian* estimated cost the public trust $10,000.

Stanley Parkman eventually bought out the *Times–Free Press*, merging it with his *Georgian* to create the *Times-Georgian*, which still publishes today. In the coming decades he would see much of his "Georgian Plan" for Carrollton come to pass as the once-rural outpost became a white-collar college and factory town.

Over the decades, the murder of Buddy Stevens, the sensational trials, the arrival and departure of Communist leader Homer Chase, and the fiery Dan Duke all became part of the lore locals told each other with varying degrees of fidelity to the facts. Transcripts of the first trial were kept in a large wooden box under the front counter in the clerk's office because so many people came looking for them. The revolver, bullets, and other court records were locked in an evidence vault for more than fifty years until a new courthouse was built. Then all of the transcripts and evidence were moved to the new evidence room and forgotten. Memories of the trials faded for all but local history buffs and senior citizens who had been curious youth at the time.

A block off the downtown square, Carrollton Presbyterian Church looks much as it did in 1948 when two young lovers met on Halloween night. A short walk west from the church is the old city cemetery where the builders of Carroll County—industrialists, politicians, and judges—were laid to rest beneath watchful angels or ensconced in altar tombs with long inscriptions of their achievements. The newer, larger part of the Carrollton cemetery is separated by a narrow street. There headstones are more modest for the graves of the public servants, college professors, and factory managers—the new middle class that shaped the city after the war.

Near the center is the military marker for Staff Sergeant Carl B. Stevens Jr., who died bravely just a few weeks short of his twenty-second birthday and lay in the ground for decades until his parents could join their only child.

ACKNOWLEDGMENTS

I want to offer my thanks to the many people who supported and encouraged me in the long, multi-decade journey I took researching and writing this book.

Foremost, I wish to thank my wife, Kathleen, and my children, Josie and Andrew, who listened to me talk about the project and endured my bleary-eyed countenance at the breakfast table after another late night of writing.

I'd like to also thank my sister and brothers and those friends who are "the family we choose" for their encouragement. I offer my appreciation to my colleagues at the *Atlanta Journal-Constitution,* especially Bill Rankin, who gave helpful (often brutally frank) advice that made the book better. Special thanks to Dorie Turner Nolt for her help in DC and to Matthew S. L. Cate for answering my questions about the world of lawyers.

Thanks to my agent, Matt Carlini of Javelin, who believed in the book and acted as my part-time therapist, and the folks at Abrams Press who guided the project to its completion in the middle of a worldwide pandemic.

In addition, thanks go to the good people at the Carroll County Courthouse, the staff in special collections at the Ingram Library at the University of West Georgia, and the archivists at the Library of Congress Manuscript Reading Room, all of whom assisted in tracking down materials that made the book both broader and deeper than it would have been otherwise.

My great appreciation goes to the descendants of many of the people in the book, including the surviving relatives of Clarence Henderson and Dan Duke. I sincerely hope I told their story well.

Finally, I thank my father, Van B. Joyner Jr., who was proud of his son's work but did not live to see it completed.

NOTES

CHAPTER 1: MURDER AND CHAOS

1. U.S. Census Bureau, 1940 U.S. Census, Carroll County, Carrollton; List of Carrollton Kiwanis Club presidents, accessed September 6, 2018, www.carrolltonkiwanisclub.org/sitepage/presidents-of-the-kiwanis-club-of-carrollton-ga.
2. "Long Investigation Nears End, Stevens Case Trial Set Monday," *Carroll County Georgian*, January 26, 1950, 1.
3. Syme was executive director of the Carroll Service Council, an umbrella social welfare organization established by the county's political, educational, and social elites to push the county into the modern world; Ralph McGill, "Carroll County Does a Real Job," *Atlanta Constitution*, April 24, 1946, 6; Allen Carpenter, "They Built Themselves a Lake," *Rotarian*, 81, no. 6 (December 1952): 56.
4. *State of Georgia v. Clarence Henderson*, No. 63, Carroll County Superior Court, October 1950, 6.
5. *State v. Henderson* (October 1950), 6–7.
6. 1940 U.S. census, Carroll County, Georgia, Carrollton, population schedule, enumeration district 22–13, sheet 12B, digital image, Ancestry .com, accessed September 4, 2018; Eldred C. Bass Obituary, *Atlanta Journal-Constitution*, June 19, 2014.
7. *State of Georgia v. Clarence Henderson*, Carroll County Superior Court, Brief of Evidence, January 30, 1950, 35–37.
8. *State v. Henderson* brief, 36.
9. "Tech Student Slain by Gunman," *Atlanta Constitution*, November 1, 1948. 1.
10. "Posse, Hounds Comb Carroll Swamp for New Suspect in Student Slaying," *Atlanta Constitution*, November 2, 1948, 1; "One Suspect Held,

No New Clue as Stevens Murderer Is Sought," *Carroll County Georgian*, November 4, 1948, 1.

11. "One Suspect Held, No New Clue as Stevens Murderer Is Sought," *Carroll County Georgian*, November 4, 1948, 1.

12. David Teal (son of Junior Teal), telephone interview with Chris Joyner, June 6, 2016. Decades later his son, David Teal, would remember spending weekends with his father. "His reputation wasn't too good as it was," David Teal, born long after the murder, said. "I can remember the police taking me home on a couple of different occasions." The elder Teal would stay in trouble his whole life. He was arrested for bootlegging as late as 1980 and died in a single-car accident. His son suspected he had been drinking, despite recent heart surgery.

13. David Teal interview, June 6, 2016. "My mom didn't even know where he was for two or three days," David Teal said.

14. "Teal Gets Lie-Detector Test in Carroll Slaying Case," *Atlanta Constitution*, November 3, 1948, 8.

15. "Posse, Hounds Comb Carroll Swamp for New Suspect in Student Slaying," *Atlanta Constitution*, November 2, 1948, 1.

16. Keeler McCartney, "Fulton Sets Up Complete Crime Laboratory," *Atlanta Constitution*, August 24, 1947, 3B.

17. *State v. Henderson* brief, 37–38.

18. Ibid., 35–37; Robert M. Thompson, "Firearm Identification in the Forensic Science Laboratory," National District Attorneys Association, 2010, 15.

19. Stanley Parkman, *Stanley Parkman: In His Own Words* (Bloomington, IN: Author House, 2006), 3–20, 33–42.

20. For an example of the Georgian Program, see "The Georgian Program," *Carroll County Georgian*, November 4, 1948, 2nd Section, 2.

21. Stanley Parkman, "Error Made in Judgment," *Carroll County Georgian*, November 4, 1948, 2nd Section, 2. Police would later say that Buddy's death was the sixth attack, the most recent having come about a month earlier.

22. Ibid.

23. Ibid.

24. Ibid., 74–75; Stanley Parkman, interview with Chris Joyner, 1998, Carrollton, GA.

25. "Murder Shocks County," *Carrollton Times–Free Press*, November 4, 1948, 1.

26. Alice Sinyard, telephone interview with Chris Joyner, September 5, 2018.

27. "Time for Emotional Control," *Carroll County Georgian*, November 11, 1949, 1.

28. Ibid.

29. "Stevens Case Still Mystery as Investigation Staff Grows," *Carroll County Georgian*, November 11, 1948, 1. McLemore's tenure as the GBI's top man was brief. He was appointed by Governor Melvin Thompson in 1947 and replaced by Governor Herman Talmadge shortly after the November 1948 election.

30. "Aroused Carroll Citizens Offer $500 for Capture of Tech Student's Slayer," *Atlanta Constitution*, November 8, 1948, 1.

31. "Carroll Holds Five in Probe of 6 Assaults," *Atlanta Constitution*, November 7, 1948, 1; "Stevens Case Still Mystery As Investigation Staff Grows," *Carroll County Georgian*.

32. "Carroll Farmer Accused by Girl, 13," *Atlanta Constitution*, November 6, 1948, 1.

33. "Aged Farmer Arrested in Carroll Assault," *Atlanta Daily World*, November 7, 1948, 1; "Carroll Holds Five in Probe of 6 Assaults," *Atlanta Constitution*, November 7, 1948, 1.

34. "2 Arrested in Tech Student's Slaying," *Atlanta Constitution*, November 5, 1948, 1.

35. "Negro Arrested in Taxicab Altercation," *Carrollton Times–Free Press*, November 16, 1948, 1.

36. "Cuban Is Questioned in Tech Student's Death," *Atlanta Constitution*, November 11, 1948, 6.

37. "Murder Shocks County," *Carrollton Times–Free Press*, November 4, 1948, 1; "Stevens Case Still Mystery As Investigation Staff Grows," *Carroll County Georgian*, November 11, 1948, 1.

38. "County Seeks Ace Investigator to Aid Stevens Murder Hunt," *Carrollton Times–Free Press*, November 9, 1948, 1.

CHAPTER 2: CARROLLTON

1. Rita Gentry, Carl and Charlcie Stevens interview, October 20, 1980, Box 9, Tape OH-139, Myron House Oral History Collection, Ingram Library Special Collections, the University of West Georgia; U.S. Census Bureau historical population tables, accessed November 2, 2018, https://www2 .census.gov/library/publications/decennial/1940/population-volume -1/33973538v1ch04.pdf; James C. Bonner, *Georgia's Last Frontier: The Development of Carroll County* (Athens: University of Georgia Press, 1971), 1.

2. John Sedgwick, *Blood Moon: An American Epic of War and Splendor in the Cherokee Nation* (New York: Simon & Schuster, 2018), 71, 147–48.

3. David Williams, *The Georgia Gold Rush: Twenty-Niners, Cherokees, and Gold Fever* (Columbia: University of South Carolina Press, 1993), 12–13; Sedgwick, *Blood Moon*, 148.

4. Sedgwick, *Blood Moon*, 149–150.

5. Ibid.; Bonner, *Georgia's Last Frontier*, 14–15; Williams, *Gold Rush*, 13–14.

6. Sedgwick, *Blood Moon*, 163.

7. Various, *The Heritage of Carroll County Georgia 1826–2001*, Carroll County Heritage Book Committee (Walsworth, 2002), 4.

8. Bonner, *Georgia's Last Frontier*, 21.

9. Ibid., 30–31.

10. Ibid., 21–22.

11. Ibid., 23.

12. Bonner, *Georgia's Last Frontier*, 33–34; *The Heritage of Carroll County Georgia*, 9; Joe Cobb, *Carroll County and Her People* (Salem, MA: Higginson, 1997), 129–31.

13. Bonner, *Georgia's Last Frontier*, 26.

14. Ibid., 34.

15. Ibid., 50; Williams, *Gold Rush*, 64.

16. Bonner, *Georgia's Last Frontier*, 51.

17. Ibid., 22.

18. Ibid., 22, 76–77.

19. Cobb, *Carroll County and Her People*, 27.

20. Bonner, *Georgia's Last Frontier*, 90, 99.

21. Ibid., 92.

22. Gail Williams O'Brien, *The Color of Law: Race, Violence, and Justice in the Post–World War II South* (Chapel Hill: University of North Carolina Press, 1999), 60, 141–43.

23. *Public Opinion: A Comprehensive Summary of the Press Throughout the World on All Important Topics*, vol. 30 (New York: The Public Opinion Company, January–June 1901), 777.

24. O'Brien, *Color of Law.*

25. Bonner, *Georgia's Last Frontier*, 182.

26. Ibid.

27. Ibid., 181–82.

28. Ibid., 154–55.

29. Cobb, *Carroll County and Her People*, 134–35.

30. Bonner, *Georgia's Last Frontier*, 35, 53–54.

31. Ibid., 34; transcript of interview with Dr. James C. Bonner, February 16, 1982, Myron House Oral History Collection, Box 14, Folder 1. Special Collections, University of West Georgia.

32. President's Annual Report, June 30, 1948; President's annual report, Irvin Sullivan Ingram Papers, Box 1, Folder 15, Special Collections, University of West Georgia.

33. Irvin Sullivan Ingram Papers.

34. "University of West Georgia," *New Georgia Encyclopedia*, accessed November 23, 2018, https://www.georgiaencyclopedia.org/articles/education/university-west-georgia.

35. Bonner, *Georgia's Last Frontier*, 10

36. "Construction Ready to Go on City-County Hospital," *Carroll County Georgian*, October 21, 1948, 1; Bonner, *Georgia's Last Frontier*, 33.

CHAPTER 3: A DESPERATE MANHUNT

1. "Construction of Homes Continues in Sunset," *Carrollton Times–Free Press*, January 6, 1949, 1.

2. Stanley Parkman, "Investigators Brand Rumors in Stevens Case Unfounded," *Carroll County Georgian*, November 25, 1948, 1.

3. "GBI Assigns Two Ace Investigators to Local Murder Probe," *Carrollton Times–Free Press*, November 23, 1948, 1.

4. "Lest We Forget," *Carroll County Georgian*, December 9, 1948, 1.

5. "An Appeal to Local Negroes," *Carrollton Times–Free Press*, December 9, 1948, 2.

6. "KKK Organizers Disappointed Here," *Carroll County Georgian*, December 12, 1948, 1.

7. Numan V. Bartley, *The Creation of Modern Georgia* (Athens: University of Georgia Press, 1990), 208–209.

8. Eugene Cook to J. Lindsay Almon Jr., July 22, 1953, State File for Georgia, NAACP Legal Defense and Educational Fund records, Manuscript/Mixed Material, Library of Congress, Washington, DC.

9. Bartley, *Creation of Modern Georgia*, 210.

10. Ibid.; Edwin L. Jackson, "State Flags of Georgia," *New Georgia Encyclopedia*, July 14, 2020, accessed November 29, 2020, https://www.georgia encyclopedia.org/articles/government-politics/state-flags-georgia.

11. Bartley, *Creation of Modern Georgia*, 212.

12. "Lt. Gov. Griffin Hits Socialism," *Carroll County Georgian*, December 9, 1948, 1; Scott E. Buchanan, "Marvin Griffin (1907–1982)," *New Georgia Encyclopedia*, July 13, 2018, accessed November 29, 2020, http://www.georgiaencyclopedia.org/articles/government-politics /marvin-griffin-1907–1982.

13. Bartley, *Creation of Modern Georgia*, 213–15.

14. "Carroll Slaying Suspect Bound Over," *Atlanta Constitution*, January 13, 1949, 1; "Charge Negro with Murder; Continue Probe," *Carrollton Times–Free Press*, January 13, 1949, 1; "Grand Jury Will Hear Tyler North Evidence," *Carroll County Georgian*, January 13, 1949, 1.

15. "Carroll Slaying Suspect Bound Over," *Atlanta Constitution*.

16. Stanley Parkman, "Break Comes in Stevens Case," *Carroll County Georgian*, January 20, 1949, 2.

17. "Grand Jury List Is Announced," *Carrollton Times–Free Press*, March 22, 1949, 1; "Superior Court Will Convene April 4; Grand Jury Listed," *Carroll County Georgian*, March 24, 1949, 1; "Boykin Blasts Dope Ring and Taxi Situation in Charge to Grand Jury," *Carrollton Times–Free Press*, April 5, 1949, 1.

18. "County Courtroom Again Shines with Beauty and Color," *Carrollton Times–Free Press*, January 13, 1949, 1.

19. "Carrollton Fetes Arnall and Atkinson," *Atlanta Constitution*, October 14, 1942, 20.

20. "Georgian Spotlight," *Carroll County Georgian*, February 23, 1950, 2; "Long-Term Court Reporter Gives Memories of Superior Court Judges," *Carroll County Georgian*, September 13, 1951, 10.

21. "Georgian Spotlight," *Carroll County Georgian*.

22. "Boykin Blasts Dope Ring and Taxi Situation in Charge to Grand Jury," *Carrollton Times–Free Press*, April 5, 1949, 1.

23. "Judge Says Dope Ring Operating in County," *Carroll County Georgian*, April 7, 1949, 1.

24. "Boykin Blasts Dope Ring," *Carrollton Times–Free Press*.

25. "Judge Says Dope Ring," *Carroll County Georgian*.

26. "City Council Pledge Attention to Taxis," *Carroll County Georgian*, April 7, 1949, 1.

27. "Judge Says Dope Ring," *Carroll County Georgian*.

28. "Grand Jury Indicts Negro for Stevens Murder," *Carroll County Georgian*, April 7, 1949, 1.

29. Ibid.

30. "Boykin Blasts Dope Ring," *Carrollton Times–Free Press*; "North Heads List of 15 Indicted; Rape Charge Placed Against Two," *Carrollton Times–Free Press*, April 7, 1949, 1; "Grand Jury Indicts Negro," *Carroll County Georgian*.

31. "Two Given Life Sentences for Murder; Court Nears Recess," *Carrollton Times–Free Press*, April 12, 1949, 1; "Trial of Stevens Case Holds Until Special Term June 20," *Carroll County Georgian*, April 14, 1949, 1.

CHAPTER 4: "A VERY DARK NEGRO"

1. "Trial of Stevens Case Postponed; Return of GBI Agents Requested," *Carroll County Georgian*, June 6, 1949, 1; "Stevens Case Action Begged," *Carrollton Times–Free Press*, June 14, 1949, 2; "Kiwanis Resolution Brings GBI to Town," *Carroll County Georgian*, June 16, 1949, 1; "Lions Adopt Resolution for Bringing Back GBI," *Carroll County Georgian*, June 16, 1949, 5.

2. "Stevens Case Action Begged," *Carrollton Times–Free Press*.

3. "Juror Lists Announced for Grand Jury and Opening Week of Superior Court," *Carrollton Times–Free Press*, September 13, 1949, 1; "90-Man List of Jurors For Criminal Session of Superior Court Published," *Carroll County Georgian*, September 20, 1949, 1.

4. "North Denies Assault on White Girl in His Statement to the Jury," *Carrollton Times–Free Press*, October 11, 1949, 1.

5. Ibid.

6. Ibid.

7. "Court Called for North Trial to Open Nov. 28 at Courthouse," *Carrollton Times–Free Press*, November 8, 1949, 1.

8. "Trial Is Set Here Nov. 28 in Stevens Case," *Carroll County Georgian*, November 10, 1949, 1.

9. "Trial of North Off as Illness Halts Lawyer," *Carrollton Times–Free Press*, November 22, 1949, 1; "Attorney Is Ill, Stevens Case Off," *Carroll County Georgian*, November 24, 1949, 1.

10. "Tyler North Is Released Under Bond," *Carrollton Times–Free Press*, February 7, 1950, 1.

11. U.S. Census Bureau, 1940 U.S. Census, Fulton County, Georgia.

12. *State of Georgia v. Clarence Henderson*, No. 63, Carroll County Superior Court, January 31, 1950, 9–10.

13. "Murder Weapon Tips New Lead in Stevens Case," *Carroll County Georgian*, December 22, 1949, 1.

14. Keeler McCartney, "Carroll Murder Trial to Bare Bullet Test," *Atlanta Constitution*, January 28, 1950, 1A.

15. "Murder Weapon Tips New Lead in Stevens Case," *Carroll County Georgian*.

16. C. W. Greenlea, "Henderson, Free, Thanks 'God and NAACP' for Help," *Atlanta Daily World*, January 18, 1953.

17. "Death Gun Traced; Nab Negro in Stevens Case," *Carrollton Times–Free Press*, December 15, 1949, 1.

18. "Tyler North Convicted in Assault Case," *Carroll County Georgian*, October 13, 1949, 1. Henderson's indictment is included in the final paragraphs of this story as a roundup of other court news. There is nothing suggesting that the charge is related to the Stevens case.

19. At this time Georgia's Black population was about 35 percent of the 3.1 million people in the state, while Carroll County's Black population was about 21 percent of 34,000 people, or roughly 7,250 people.

20. "Grand Jury Gets New Evidence Thursday on Stevens Murder," *Carrollton Times–Free Press*, January 10, 1950, 1; "Farm Youth Held As New Killer Suspect," *Atlanta Daily World*, December 17, 1949, 1.

21. "Death Gun Traced; Nab Negro in Stevens Case," *Carrollton Times–Free Press*, December 15, 1949, 1.

22. "Solicitor Hinds January Trial of Stevens Case," *Carroll County Georgian*, December 29, 1949, 1; "Another Murder Suspect Denies Owning Weapon," *Carrollton Times–Free Press*, December 29, 1949, 1.

23. "Funeral Notices: Mr. Walter Bernard Threadgill," *Atlanta Constitution*, March 8, 1970, 19B.

24. "Grand Jury Gets New Evidence Thursday on Stevens Murder," *Carrollton Times–Free Press,* January 10, 1950, 1; "Grand Jury Will Get Henderson Evidence Today in Stevens Case," *Carroll County Georgian*, January 12, 1950, 1; "Carrollton Man Indicted in Tech Student's Death," *Atlanta Daily World*, January 13, 1950, 6.

25. "Grand Jury Will Get Henderson Evidence Today in Stevens Case," *Carroll County Georgian*, January 12, 1950, 1.

26. U.S. Census Bureau, 1940 U.S. Census, Carroll County, Carrollton.

27. "Henderson Is Indicted for Stevens Murder; Trial Started for Jan. 23," *Carrollton Times–Free Press*, January 12, 1950, 1.

28. Harold Murphy interviewed by Bob Short, December 15, 2008, Reflections on Georgia Politics (video transcript), Richard B. Russell Library for Political Research and Studies, University of Georgia and Young Harris College, accessed July 18, 2019, http://russelllibrarydocs.libs.uga.edu /ROGP-060_Murphy.pdf.

29. Jim Camp, attorney at Wiggins & Camp, telephone interview with Chris Joyner, June 8, 2017.

30. "Trial Postponed, Jurors Selected in Stevens Case," *Carroll County Georgian*, January 19, 1950, 1.

CHAPTER 5: THE FIRST TRIAL

1. "Long Investigation Nears End, Stevens Case Trial Set Monday," *Carroll County Georgian*, January 26, 1950, 1.

2. Keeler McCartney, "Student's Slayer Sentenced to Die," *Atlanta Constitution*, January 31, 1950, 1; John T. Smyly, "State's Chief Communist Is Given Carroll Jail Term," *Carrollton Times–Free Press*, June 20, 1950, 1.

3. *State of Georgia v. Clarence Henderson*, No. 63, January 31, 1950, Carroll County Superior Court (hereafter *State v. Henderson* [I]), 6.

4. Ibid., 8–9.

5. Ibid., 12.

6. "Plea for Life Term Made by Henderson Attorneys," *Times–Free Press*, April 4, 1950, 1; "Henderson Files New Trial Plea," *Carroll County Georgian*, April 6, 1950, 1.

7. "Miss Nan Turner Is Wed to Talker B. Hansard, Jr.," *Carroll County Georgian*, August 4, 1949, 4.

8. Amended motion seeking a new trial, undated draft, Clarence Henderson, 1950–53, NAACP Legal Defense and Educational Fund records, Manuscript/Mixed Material, The Library of Congress, Washington, DC.

9. *State v. Henderson* (I), 12–15, 18.

10. "North Heads List of 15 Indicted; Rape Charge Placed Against Two," *Carroll County Georgian,* April 7, 1949, 1.

11. Keeler McCartney, "Student's Slayer Sentenced to Die," *Atlanta Constitution*, January 31, 1950, 1.

12. *State of Georgia v. Clarence Henderson*, Carroll County Superior Court, Brief of Evidence, January 30, 1950, 48.

13. Major Calvin H. Goddard, "Who Did the Shooting?," *Popular Science* 111, no. 5 (November 1927): 21–22, 171; Robert Grant and Joseph Katz, *The Great Trials of The Twenties: The Watershed Decade in America's Courtrooms* (Boston: Da Capo Press, 1998), 43.

14. *State v. Henderson* brief, 50.

15. Ibid., 51.

16. *State v. Henderson* (I), 32–34.

17. *State v. Henderson* brief, 52.

18. Ibid., 53.

19. Celestine Sibley, "99 Pct. Cop, Reporter Gets Fond So-Long," *Atlanta Constitution*, July 26, 1979, 1B.

20. Keeler McCartney, "Carroll Murder Trial to Bare Bullet Test," *Atlanta Constitution*, January 29, 1950, 1A.

21. Hal David, "Henderson Gets Death for Stevens Murder," *Carroll County Georgian*, February 2, 1950, 1.

22. *State v. Henderson* (I), 38–40.

23. *State of Georgia v. Clarence Henderson*, No. 63, Carroll County Superior Court, October 10–12, 1950, 44.

24. *State v. Henderson* (I), 41–43.

25. Ibid., 43–45.

CHAPTER 6: "LET ME GO HOME"

1. *State of Georgia v. Clarence Henderson*, No. 63, Carroll County Superior Court, January 31, 1950 (hereafter *State v. Henderson* [I]), 11.

2. Ibid., 45–47.

3. Ibid., 48–50.

4. Gilbert King, *Devil in the Grove: Thurgood Marshall, the Groveland Boys, and the Dawn of a New America* (New York: HarperCollins, 2012).

5. *State v. Henderson* (I), 55–56.

6. Ibid., 55.

7. Ibid., 58.

8. Ibid., 58–59.

9. Ibid., 60–63.

10. Authorization signed by Clarence Henderson, April 26, 1950, Clarence Henderson, 1950–53, NAACP Legal Defense and Educational Fund records, Manuscript/Mixed Material, Library of Congress, Washington, DC.

11. Darius Rejali, *Torture and Democracy* (Princeton: Princeton University Press, 2007), 70–73; Herbert Shapiro, *White Violence and Black Response: From Reconstruction to Montgomery* (Amherst: University of Massachusetts Press, 1988), 401–403.

12. *State v. Henderson* (I), 63–66.

13. January 16, 1950, statement by Clarence Henderson marked "Prosecution Exhibit A," *State v. Henderson* (I).

14. December 20, 1949, statement by Clarence Henderson marked "Prosecution Exhibit B," *State v. Henderson* (I).

15. *State v. Henderson* (I), 67.

16. Ibid., 71–72.

17. Keeler McCartney, "Student's Slayer Sentenced to Die," *Atlanta Constitution*, January 31, 1950, 1.

18. Hal David, "Henderson Gets Death for Stevens Murder," *Carroll County Georgian*, February 2, 1950, 1.

19. McCartney, "Student's Slayer Sentenced to Die"; David, "Henderson Gets Death for Stevens Murder." Sources differ: David's transcription of the statement in the *Georgian* uses ". . . this black nigger . . . ," while the official transcript and McCartney heard ". . . this old Negro . . ."

20. *State v. Henderson* (I), 67–70.

21. David, "Henderson Gets Death for Stevens Murder."

22. "Jury Finds Henderson Guilty, Electrocution Set for Feb. 24," *Carrollton Times–Free Press,* January 31, 1950, 1; "Henderson Meted Chair in Slaying; Attorneys Appeal," *Atlanta Daily World*, February 1, 1950, 6.

23. "Jury Finds Henderson Guilty," *Carrollton Times–Free Press.*

24. "Says Thug Slew Escort Refusing to Attack Her," Associated Press, published in the *New York Herald Tribune*, January 31, 1950, 2.

25. "Sentence Negro to Die; Identity 'Proved' by Gun," *Chicago Tribune*, January 31, 1950, 8.

26. "New Defense Planned for Doomed Georgian," *Pittsburgh Courier*, March 4, 1950, 6.

27. "Superior Court Adjourns Monday in Record Time," *Carrollton Times–Free Press*, April 11, 1950, 1.

CHAPTER 7: SUBVERSIVE ELEMENTS

1. "Hearing February 18 for Henderson," *Carroll County Georgian*, February 9, 1950, 1.

2. "Atlanta Lawyers Take Defense in Henderson's Suit," *Atlanta Daily World*, February 21, 1950, 1.

3. "Four Attorneys in Henderson Case; Hearing March 25," *Times-Free Press*, February 21, 1950, 1.

4. "Atlanta Lawyers Take Defense in Henderson's Suit," *Atlanta Daily World*; Hal David, "Henderson Hires Negro Attorneys," *Carroll County Georgian*, February 23, 1950, 1.

5. "CRC Plea Wins Stay for Georgia Negro," *Daily Worker*, March 8, 1950, 8.

6. "Henderson Rally Set at Big Bethel Tomorrow Night," *Atlanta Daily World*, February 19, 1950, 8; Big Bethel AME church website, accessed February 17, 2018, http://www.bigbethelame.org/home/index.php ?option=com_content&view=article&id=1&Itemid=2.

7. David, "Henderson Hires Negro Attorneys."

8. Ibid.

9. "Henderson's Plea Studied by Judge," *Atlanta Daily World*, April 5, 1950, 1.

10. "Plea for Life Term Made by Henderson Attorneys," *Times–Free Press*, April 4, 1950, 1; "Henderson Files New Trial Plea," *Carroll County Georgian*, April 6, 1950, 1.

11. "Judge Urges [headline cut off]," *Carrollton Times–Free Press*, April 4, 1950, 8.

12. "Commies in Drive to Save C. Henderson," *Carroll County Georgian*, March 9, 1950, 1.

13. "Communists and Their Lies," *Carroll County Georgian*, March 16, 1950, 2; "The Stevens Case," *Carrollton Times–Free Press*, March 14, 1950, 2.

14. "Ga. CRC to Defend Negro, Sentenced to Die February 24," *Daily Worker*, February 20, 1950, 4.

15. "CRC Plea Wins Stay for Georgia Negro," *Daily Worker*, March 8, 1950, 8.

16. Hugh T. Murray, "The NAACP Versus the Communist Party: The Scottsboro Rape Cases, 1931–1932," *Phylon* 28, no. 3 (1967): 277–28; James R. Acker, *Scottsboro and Its Legacy* (Westport, CT: Praeger, 2008), 1–6, 36.

17. Acker, *Scottsboro and Its Legacy*, 38–39.

18. Murray, *NAACP Versus the Communist Party*, 279; Acker, *Scottsboro and Its Legacy*, 39; Karen Ferguson, *Black Politics in New Deal Atlanta* (Chapel Hill: University of North Carolina Press, 2003), 56–57.

19. Acker, *Scottsboro and Its Legacy*, 40.

20. Murray, *NAACP Versus the Communist Party*, 286.

21. "Commies in Drive to Save C. Henderson," *Carroll County Georgian*, March 9, 1950, 1; "Judge Boykin Orders Probe of Visitors at 'Framed' Hearing," *Carrollton Times–Free Press*, April 18, 1950, 1.

CHAPTER 8: THE COMMIES COME TO TOWN

1. "It's Real Homecoming When 14 Boys Arrive from Fascist Jails," *Daily Worker*, October 19, 1938.
2. The 513th Parachute Infantry Regimental History, accessed November 30, 2020, http://www.ww2-airborne.us/units/513/513.html.
3. Matthew J. Seelinger, "Operation VARSITY: The Last Airborne Deployment of World War II," Army Historical Foundation, accessed November 30, 2020, https://armyhistory.org/operation-varsity-the-last-airborne-deployment-of-world-war-ii/; "Thunder Mail Call," 17th Airborne Division Newsletter No. 6, September 2008, accessed November 30, 2020, http://www.ww2-airborne.us/18corps/17abn/documents/tfh_newsletter_6_levert_smith.pdf.
4. Donald H. Forbes, *Two Communist Brothers from Washington, New Hampshire and Their Fight Against Fascism* (Morrisville, NC: Lulu Press, 2013), 61.
5. The Black Vault, Don West FBI File, File No. 9, 255, accessed November 30, 2020, https://documents.theblackvault.com/documents/fbifiles/West_Donald_L.-HQ-9_text.pdf; Stephen G. Tompkins, "Army Feared King, Secretly Watched Him," *Memphis Commercial Appeal*, March 21, 1993, 1A.
6. Edwin Foltz memo to J. Edgar Hoover, February 15, 1947, Don West FBI File. https://archive.org/stream/DonaldWest/.
7. The Black Vault, 285.
8. Don West, Southern Oral History Program, University of North Carolina at Chapel Hill, January 22, 1975, 34.
9. Ibid., 34–35.
10. John Egerton, *Speak Now Against the Day: The Generation Before the Civil Rights Movement* (Chapel Hill: University of North Carolina Press, 1995), 257–58.

11. Harold H. Martin, *Ralph McGill, Reporter* (Boston: Little, Brown, 1973), 30–38, 69.

12. Ralph McGill, "The Commies Have Come to Town," *Atlanta Constitution*, April 4, 1947, 10.

13. Ibid.; Ralph McGill, "Homer Uses Tom's Telephone," *Atlanta Constitution*, August 9, 1948, 6.

14. Homer Chase, "The American Road to Socialism: Is It 'Cult of Personality' or Bureaucracy?," *Daily Worker*, August 12, 1956.

15. Martin, *Ralph McGill, Reporter*, 40–41.

16. Junius Irvin Scales and Richard Dickson, *Cause at Heart: A Former Communist Remembers* (Athens: University of Georgia Press, 1987), 293.

17. Ralph McGill and Homer Chase, "A Commie Writes in Protest," *Atlanta Constitution*, April 10, 1947, 10.

18. Ralph McGill, "The Communists and Their Methods," *Atlanta Constitution*, April 11, 1947, 12.

19. "The Pulse of the Public," *Atlanta Constitution*, April 21, 1947, 6.

20. "Red-Organizer Probe Said Under Way Here," *Atlanta Constitution*, February 3, 1948, 2.

21. "Chase Expulsion Trial up for Legion Action," *Atlanta Constitution*, April 11, 1948, 10A.

22. Ralph McGill, "Homer Has Been Talking Again," *Atlanta Constitution*, September 7, 1948, 6.

23. "US Trial of Commie Chieftains Opens Today," *Atlanta Constitution*, January 17, 1949, 1.

24. Ralph McGill, "Commie Appeal to Infantile Minds," *Atlanta Constitution*, April 25, 1949, 8.

25. "Commies Said Eying Allatoona as Target for Dynamite Blast," Associated Press, published in the *Atlanta Constitution*, April 22, 1949, 1; "Red Harassing Charged," *New York Times*, May 27, 1949, 9; The Black Vault, 281.

26. "Communist Net Closed Fast After Georgia Boy Wrote H.Q.," *Atlanta Constitution*, June 28, 1948, 1.

27. Marjory Smith, "Georgian, Citing Red Threats, Asks Protection," *Atlanta Constitution*, May 26, 1949, 1.

28. "Homer Chase Returns for Intimidation Trial," *Atlanta Constitution*, June 1, 1949, 1.

29. James Venable, oral history interview by James Mackay, DeKalb County History Center, May 28, 1982, accessed November 30, 2020, https://www.dekalbhistory.org/documents/2012.3.3JVenable5231982.pdf.

30. DuPont Wright, "Revolution Plot Laid to State Reds," *Atlanta Constitution*, June 3, 1949, 1; "Communist Net Closed Fast After Ga. Boy Wrote H.Q.," *Atlanta Constitution*, June 28, 1949, 1.

31. "Silken-Tongued Reds Entwine Victims—Wilder," *Atlanta Constitution*, June 29, 1949, 11.

32. "Chase Case May Close Tomorrow," *Atlanta Constitution*, June 5, 1949, 2A; James J. Lorence, *A Hard Journey: The Life of Don West* (Champaign: University of Illinois Press, 2007), 141.

33. DuPont Wright, "Chase Flays Talmadge in Red Hearing," *Atlanta Constitution*, June 4, 1949, 1.

34. "Chase's Bride Employed by Labor Board," *Atlanta Constitution*, June 5, 1949, 2A.

35. "Chase Case May Close Tomorrow," *Atlanta Constitution*.

36. "Georgia Red Jailed for $5,000 Peace Bond," *New York Times*, June 7, 1949, 23.

37. Katherine Barnwell, "Case Takes Jail over $5,000 Bond," *Atlanta Constitution*, June 7, 1949, 1.

38. "Jail Home Chase, Georgia Leader of the Communist Party," *Daily Worker*, June 8, 1949, 8; "Homer Chase's Arrest," *Daily Worker*, June 9, 1949.

39. "Hear Writ Today to Free Chase, Georgia CP Leader," *Daily Worker*, June 10, 1949, 2.

40. "Jail Home Chase," *Daily Worker*.

41. "Communist Chase Free on $5,000 Realty Bond," *Atlanta Constitution*, June 11, 1949, 1.

42. "U.S. Jury Convicts 11 Top Reds," *Atlanta Constitution*, October 15, 1949, 1.

43. Martin, *Ralph McGill, Reporter*, 148–49.

CHAPTER 9: "HIS FIGHT IS OUR FIGHT"

1. C. J. Freightman, "Rev. B. J. Johnson Jr., 83, Never Missed a Chance to Help Others," *Atlanta Journal-Constitution*, April 17, 2015.

2. Moore and Robinson would later become involved in an important public access case challenging Atlanta's Jim Crow rules barring Blacks from playing on the city's public golf courses. The case eventually made its way to the U.S. Supreme Court, which in November 1955 ruled the courses must allow Black golfers admission. See "*Holmes v. Atlanta*: Changing the Game," https://pwp.gatech.edu/holmesvatlanta/.

3. "Henderson Attorneys, Commies Under Contempt Charge Here," *Carroll County Georgian*, April 13, 1950, 1; "Henderson Trial Motion at Carrollton Tomorrow Afternoon," *Atlanta Daily World*, April 2, 1950, 1; "Henderson's Plea Studied by Judge," *Atlanta Daily World*, April 5, 1950, 1.

4. "New Defense Planned for Doomed Georgian," *Pittsburgh Courier*, March 4, 1950, 6.

5. "Atlanta, Ga. NAACP Is Not in Henderson Defense," *Pittsburgh Courier*, April 8, 1950, 26.

6. "5 named for Contempt in Calling Henderson 'Framed,'" *Carrollton Times–Free Press*, April 11, 1950, 1; "Citizens Appear in Contempt Hearing Today," *Atlanta Daily World,* April 15, 1950, 1.

7. James J. Lorence, *A Hard Journey: The Life of Don West* (Champaign: University of Illinois Press, 2007), 119–33.

8. Don West, Jeff Biggers, and George Brosi, *No Lonesome Road: Selected Prose and Poems* (Champaign: University of Illinois Press, 2010), 44–45.

9. West, Biggers, and Brosi, *No Lonesome Road*, 45.

10. Lorence, *A Hard Journey*, 119–120.

11. Ibid., 135–36.

12. Ibid., 139–41.

13. Hal David, "Judge Throws Spotlight on Communists of State," *Carroll County Georgian*, April 20, 1950, 1.

14. J. H. Calhoun to Thurgood Marshall, April 17, 1950, Clarence Henderson, 1950–53, NAACP Legal Defense and Educational Fund records, Manuscript/Mixed Material, Library of Congress, Washington, DC.

15. C. W. Greenlea, "Judge Delays Decision in Carrollton Contempt Case," *Atlanta Daily World*, April 16, 1950, 1.

16. Ibid.
17. David, "Judge Throws Spotlight."
18. Greenlea, "Judge Delays Decision."
19. J. H. Calhoun to Thurgood Marshall, April 17, 1950, Clarence Henderson, 1950–53, NAACP Legal Defense and Educational Fund records, Manuscript/Mixed Material, Library of Congress, Washington, DC.
20. J. H. Calhoun to Thurgood Marshall, April 22, 1950, Clarence Henderson, 1950–53, NAACP Legal Defense and Educational Fund records, Manuscript/Mixed Material, Library of Congress, Washington, DC.
21. "Homer Chase Queried from Carroll Bench," *Atlanta Constitution*, April 16, 1950, 1A; "Judge Boykin Orders Probe of Visitors at 'Framed' Hearing," *Carrollton Times–Free Press*, April 18, 1950, 1; David, "Judge Throws Spotlight."
22. David, "Judge Throws Spotlight."
23. "Courtroom Smokescreen," *Carrollton Times–Free Press*, April 18, 1950, 2.
24. "Rules 10 in 'Contempt' For Being in Court," *Daily Worker*, April 19, 1950, 2.
25. John Pittman, "Mundt Bill and Peaceful Change," *Daily Worker*, April 25, 1950.
26. "Judge Threatens Contempt Action Against Friends of Framed Negro," *Daily Worker*, April 30, 1950, 15; "Among the Churches," *Atlanta Daily World*, April 15, 1950, 2.
27. Ralph McGill, "The Commies Are False Advocates," *Atlanta Constitution*, April 20, 1950, 18.
28. Ralph McGill, "How the Commies Confuse," *Atlanta Constitution*, April 22, 1950, 8.
29. Clipping of Associated Press article, "Gets Chair for Killing Man Who Refused to Rape Girl," *New York Post*, January 31, 1950; Clarence Henderson, 1950–53, NAACP Legal Defense and Educational Fund records, Manuscript/Mixed Material, Library of Congress, Washington, DC.

CHAPTER 10: THE NAACP TAKES CHARGE

1. Patricia Sullivan, *Lift Every Voice: The NAACP and the Making of the Civil Rights Movement* (New York: New Press, 2009), 298–99.

2. Jack Greenberg to O. S. Bexley, February 9, 1950, Clarence Henderson, 1950–53, NAACP Legal Defense and Educational Fund records, Manuscript/Mixed Material, Library of Congress, Washington, DC.

3. O. S. Bexley to Jack Greenberg, February 15, 1950, Clarence Henderson, 1950–53, NAACP Legal Defense and Educational Fund records.

4. Jack Greenberg to Bexley, March 1, 1950, Clarence Henderson, 1950–53, NAACP Legal Defense and Educational Fund records.

5. O. S. Bexley to Jack Greenberg, March 1950, Clarence Henderson, 1950–53, NAACP Legal Defense and Educational Fund records; Returned letter, Jack Greenberg to Croffert M. Baber, March 16, 1950, Clarence Henderson, 1950–53, NAACP Legal Defense and Educational Fund records, Manuscript/Mixed Material, Library of Congress, Washington, DC.

6. Constance Baker Motley to Mrs. John H. Waugh, February 16, 1950, Clarence Henderson, 1950–53, NAACP Legal Defense and Educational Fund records, Manuscript/Mixed Material, Library of Congress, Washington, DC.

7. Jack Greenberg to Dr. William M. Boyd, April 3, 1950, Clarence Henderson, 1950–53, NAACP Legal Defense and Educational Fund records, Manuscript/Mixed Material, Library of Congress, Washington, DC.

8. Simon Hall, *Peace and Freedom: The Civil Rights and Antiwar Movements in the 1960s* (Philadelphia: University of Pennsylvania Press, 2011), 94; Denton L. Watson, "Thurgood Marshall's Red Menace," *New York Times*, December 10, 1996, 27A; Neil A. Lewis, "Files say Justice Marshall Aided FBI in 50's," *New York Times*, December 4, 1996, 11B.

9. J. H. Calhoun to Thurgood Marshall, April 17, 1950, Clarence Henderson, 1950–53, NAACP Legal Defense and Educational Fund records, Manuscript/Mixed Material, Library of Congress, Washington, DC.

10. J. H. Calhoun to Thurgood Marshall, April 22, 1950, Clarence Henderson, 1950–53, NAACP Legal Defense and Educational Fund records, Manuscript/Mixed Material, Library of Congress, Washington, DC.

11. Franklin H. Williams to J. H. Calhoun, April 26, 1950, Clarence Henderson, 1950–53, NAACP Legal Defense and Educational Fund records, Manuscript/Mixed Material, Library of Congress, Washington, DC.

12. Authorization, April 26, 1950, Clarence Henderson, 1950–53, NAACP

Legal Defense and Educational Fund records, Manuscript/Mixed Material, Library of Congress, Washington, D.C.

13. Telegram from Franklin Williams to J. H. Calhoun, April 27, 1950, Clarence Henderson, 1950–53, NAACP Legal Defense and Educational Fund records, Manuscript/Mixed Material, Library of Congress, Washington, DC.

14. J. H. Calhoun to Thurgood Marshall, May 29, 1950, and Marshall to Calhoun, June 2, 1950, Clarence Henderson, 1950–53, NAACP Legal Defense and Educational Fund records, Manuscript/Mixed Material, Library of Congress, Washington, DC.

15. "Clarence Henderson Wife Thanks Friends for Their Gifts," *Atlanta Daily World*, April 29, 1950, 3; "Women's Auxiliary of Atlanta NAACP Will Meet Today," *Atlanta Daily World*, May 3, 1950, 3.

16. "Henderson Case Before State Supreme Court Tuesday," *Atlanta Daily World*, June 11, 1950, 1; "Justices Ponder Henderson Case," *Atlanta Daily World*, June 16, 1950, 1.

17. "Elliott Blisters Thompson; Talmadge Cites Record in Local Addresses," *Carroll County Georgian*, June 22, 1950, 5.

18. "Judge Cites Chase As in Contempt," *Atlanta Constitution*, May 28, 1950, 1; "Jail for Contempt Perils Ten Who Defended Negro," *Daily Worker*, June 11, 1950, 7; "State's No. 1 Communist Cited Here for Contempt," *Carrollton Times–Free Press*, April 30, 1950, 1; Hal David, "Contempt Charge Lists H. Chase," *Carroll County Georgian*, June 1, 1950, 1.

19. "Georgia Red Leader Gets 20-Day Jail Term and $200 Fine," Associated Press, published in the *Boston Globe*, June 18, 1950, C6.

20. John T. Smyly, "State's Chief Communist Is Given Carroll Jail Term," *Carrollton Times–Free Press*, June 20, 1950, 1; "Georgia Red Put in Jail," *New York Times*, June 18, 1950, 38; Hal David, "Communist Leader for Georgia Learns How to Live in Carroll County Jail," *Carroll County Georgian*, June 6, 1950, 1.

21. C. W. Greenlea, "NAACP Forms Henderson Freedom Committee," *Atlanta Daily World*, July 16, 1950, 1.

22. Smyly, "State's Chief Communist Is Given Carroll Jail Term."

23. "2 Face Jail for Fighting Frameup of Negro," *Daily Worker*, July 6, 1950, 3.

24. "Bond Frees Student but Chase Stays," *Atlanta Constitution*, June 21, 1950, 7.

25. "Home Chase Declines to Peddle His Communism While Staying in Jail," *Carroll County Georgian*, June 29, 1950, 13.

26. Keeler McCartney, "Red Leaflet Urges Chase Jail Release," *Atlanta Constitution*, June 23, 1950, 1.

27. "Communist Freed on Bond Tuesday," *Carrollton Times–Free Press*, June 27, 1950, 1; "Chase Free on Bond After Serving 9 Days," *Atlanta Constitution*, June 28, 1950, 11.

28. "Chase and Kamm to Get New Trial Hearing July 15," *Carrollton Times–Free Press*, June 29, 1950, 1.

29. Ralph McGill, "Commie Front in the South," *Atlanta Constitution*, July 14, 1950, 1.

30. McGill letter to Paul Slayton, FBI, Atlanta, Ralph McGill Papers, Series V, Box 51, Folder 5, "Communist Suspects," Stuart A. Rose Manuscript, Archives and Rare Book Library, Emory University.

31. McGill letter to Westbrook Pegler, July 14, 1950, Ralph McGill Papers, Series II, Personal Correspondence, Stuart A. Rose Manuscript, Archives, and Rare Book Library, Emory University.

32. Ralph McGill, "The Traitors in Our Midst," *Atlanta Constitution*, July 15, 1950, 1.

CHAPTER 11: A NEW TRIAL ORDERED

1. *Henderson v. State of Georgia*, 207 Ga. 206 (1950), 60 S.E.2d 345.

2. "New Trial for Henderson Is Seen Soon by Lipford," *Carrollton Times–Free Press*, July 13, 1950, 1; "Supreme Court Orders New Henderson Trial," *Atlanta Constitution*, July 13, 1950, 17.

3. "Suffering Renewed in Stevens Case," *Carroll County Georgian*, July 20, 1950, 10.

4. "Framed Negro Wins New Trial," *Daily Worker*, July 17, 1950, 2.

5. "Order Retrial for Man Held in Ala. Slaying," *Chicago Defender*, July 22, 1950, 1.

6. J. H. Calhoun to Gloster Current, NAACP director of branches, July 26, 1950, Clarence Henderson, 1950–53, NAACP Legal Defense

and Educational Fund records, Manuscript/Mixed Material, Library of Congress, Washington, DC; Memo from Gloster Current to Thurgood Marshall, August 25, 1950.

7. C. W. Greenlea, "NAACP Forms Henderson Freedom Committee," *Atlanta Daily World*, July 16, 1950, 1; "A Message to Ministers," *Atlanta Daily World*, July 22, 1950, 6.

8. Minutes of the NAACP Executive Committee, September 11, 1950, NAACP Legal Defense and Educational Fund records, Manuscript/Mixed Material, Library of Congress, Washington, DC.

9. "Churches Asked to Back Henderson Case Sunday," *Atlanta Daily World*, July 22, 1950, 1; "A Message to Ministers," *Atlanta Daily World*, July 22, 1950, 6.

10. "Church Reports Pour in For Henderson's Defense," *Atlanta Daily World*, July 25, 1950, 1; "Good Work, Ministers," *Atlanta Daily World*, July 26, 1950, 6; "Henderson Trial Postponed, Fund Drive Continues," *Atlanta Daily World*, August 2, 1950, 1.

11. E. E. Moore to Thurgood Marshall, July 14, 1950, Clarence Henderson, 1950–53, NAACP Legal Defense and Educational Fund records, Manuscript/Mixed Material, Library of Congress, Washington, DC; "New Henderson Trial Aug. 3," *Carroll County Georgian*, July 23, 1950, 1; "Churches Asked to Back Henderson Case Sunday," *Atlanta Daily World*, July 22, 1950, 1.

12. Thurgood Marshall to Frank D. Reeves, July 18, 1950, Clarence Henderson, 1950–53, NAACP Legal Defense and Educational Fund records, Manuscript/Mixed Material, Library of Congress, Washington, DC.

13. Memorandum from Jack Greenberg to Thurgood Marshall, July 25, 1950, Clarence Henderson, 1950–53, NAACP Legal Defense and Educational Fund records, Manuscript/Mixed Material, Library of Congress, Washington, DC; Memorandum from Thurgood Marshall to Jack Greenberg, August 1, 1950, Clarence Henderson, 1950–53, NAACP Legal Defense and Educational Fund records, Manuscript/Mixed Material, Library of Congress, Washington, DC.

14. Sworn affidavit of S. S. Robinson, August 7, 1950, Clarence Henderson, 1950–53, NAACP Legal Defense and Educational Fund records,

Manuscript/Mixed Material, Library of Congress, Washington, DC; J. H. Calhoun to United States Attorney J. Ellis Mundy, August 5, 1950, Clarence Henderson, 1950–53, NAACP Legal Defense and Educational Fund records, Manuscript/Mixed Material, Library of Congress, Washington, DC.

15. Telegram from J. H. Calhoun to Thurgood Marshall, July 28, 1950, Clarence Henderson, 1950–53, NAACP Legal Defense and Educational Fund records, Manuscript/Mixed Material, Library of Congress, Washington, DC.

16. J. H. Calhoun to Sheriff Denver Gaston, July 29, 1950, Clarence Henderson, 1950–53, NAACP Legal Defense and Educational Fund records, Manuscript/Mixed Material, Library of Congress, Washington, DC.

17. "Convicted Dade Sheriff, Aide File New Trial Motion," *Atlanta Constitution*, March 15, 1950, 4.

18. Sworn affidavit of S. S. Robinson, August 7, 1950, Clarence Henderson, 1950–53, NAACP Legal Defense and Educational Fund records, Manuscript/Mixed Material, Library of Congress, Washington, DC.

19. United States Attorney J. Ellis Mundy to J. H. Calhoun, August 9, 1950, Clarence Henderson, 1950–53, NAACP Legal Defense and Educational Fund records, Manuscript/Mixed Material, Library of Congress, Washington, DC; S. S. Robinson to NAACP Executive Secretary Walter White, August 2, 1950, Clarence Henderson, 1950–53, NAACP Legal Defense and Educational Fund records, Manuscript/Mixed Material, Library of Congress, Washington, DC; Thurgood Marshall to United States Assistant Attorney General James M. McInerney, August 24, 1950, Clarence Henderson, 1950–53, NAACP Legal Defense and Educational Fund records, Manuscript/Mixed Material, Library of Congress, Washington, DC.

20. "Henderson Trial Is Postponed," *Carrollton Times–Free Press*, August 1, 1950, 1. "Henderson Trial Postponed Indefinitely," *Carroll County Georgian*, August 3, 1950, 1.

21. William J. Allen, "Alverson Promises Bill Outlawing Red Activity," *Atlanta Constitution*, August 2, 1950, 4; "Right, Governor!" *Carrollton Times–Free Press*, August 8, 1950, 2; Bill Allen, "Anti-Communist Law Can Stand Up—Cook," *Atlanta Constitution*, August 3, 1950, 2; Gladstone Williams,

"Rep. Cox Offers Bill to Bar Communist Party in Nation," *Atlanta Constitution*, August 3, 1950, 2.

22. "Communist's Arrester Gets Self Cell, Too," *Atlanta Constitution*, July 18, 1950, 2.

23. "Ordinance to Bar Communists is Read to Council Members," *Atlanta Constitution*, August 8, 1950, 5.

24. "Solicitor Seeks to Revoke Bond of Chase, Kamm," *Carroll County Georgian*, August 17, 1950, 1.

25. "Recommendation for Installation of Technical Surveillance," August 10, 1950, Atlanta Field Office of the Federal Bureau of Investigation, file number 100–349078, Federal Bureau of Investigation, United States Department of Justice, Washington, DC; "Memorandum for the Attorney General," August 21, 1950, J. Edgar Hoover, file number 100–349078, Federal Bureau of Investigation, United States Department of Justice, Washington, DC.

26. "Communist Chase Beaten Here and Flees Bleeding," *Carrollton Times–Free Press*, August 17, 1950, 1; "Homer Chase Admits Tussle, Denies Beating," Atlanta Constitution. August 18, 1950, 1; "Red Beaten in Georgia," *New York Times*, August 18, 1950, 6.

27. "Communist Chase Beaten Here and Flees Bleeding," *Carrollton Times–Free Press*.

28. "Battle of Newnan Street," *Carrollton Times–Free Press*, August 22, 1950.

29. J. H. Calhoun to Jack Greenberg, August 19, 1950, Clarence Henderson, 1950–53, NAACP Legal Defense and Educational Fund records, Manuscript/Mixed Material, Library of Congress, Washington, DC.

30. "Playing into the Hands of the Communists," *Atlanta Constitution*, August 19, 1950, 4; John T. Smyly, "Chase, Kamm May Be in New York," *Carrollton Times–Free Press*, August 22, 1950, 1.

31. "Georgia Sheriff Says Communist Leader to Get Little Protection," *Lubbock (TX) Morning Avalanche*, August 18, 1950, 4.

32. "A Communist Is an Enemy—Anywhere," *Carroll County Georgian*, August 24, 1950.

33. Letter to the Editor by Mrs. M. E. Stanford, *Carroll County Georgian*, August 24, 1950, 10.

34. "Chase, Kamm Still Free After Arrest Order," *Atlanta Constitution*, August 20, 1950, 12B; "Red's Arrest Ordered," *New York Times*, August 20, 1950, 41; "Chase Avoids Arrest; Said 'Lying Low,'" *Atlanta Constitution*, August 21, 1950, 4; John T. Smyly, "Chase, Kamm May Be in New York," *Carrollton Times–Free Press*, August 22, 1950, 1; "Chase Goes 'Underground' After Jumping Bond Here," *Carroll County Georgian*, August 24, 1950, 1.

35. Donald H. Forbes, *Two Communist Brothers from Washington, New Hampshire and Their Fight Against Fascism* (Morrisville, NC: Lulu Press, 2013), 67–69.

CHAPTER 12: DAN DUKE

1. "Court Session Begins Monday," *Carroll County Georgian*, September 28, 1950, 1.

2. "Plea for 30-Day Delay Denied: Henderson Retrial Starts Here," *Carrollton Times–Free Press*, October 10, 1950, 1.

3. "3 Ministers Sworn in as Jurors," *Carrollton Times–Free Press*, October 3, 1950, 1; "Able Charge Given by Judge Boykin," *Carroll County Georgian*, October 5, 1950, 1.

4. Thurgood Marshall to C. L. Harper, May 11, 1950, Clarence Henderson, 1950–53, NAACP Legal Defense and Educational Fund records, Manuscript/Mixed Material, Library of Congress, Washington, DC; Thurgood Marshall to C. L. Harper, May 16, 1950, Clarence Henderson, 1950–53, NAACP Legal Defense and Educational Fund records, Manuscript/Mixed Material, Library of Congress, Washington, DC. "We will have to do considerable research as to the particular situation in Atlanta including the taking of pictures of the schools and other details," Marshall wrote. "I think you can safely estimate that the cost for the trial in the lower court will be $5,000."

5. *State of Georgia v. Clarence Henderson*, No. 63, Carroll County Superior Court, October 1950, 1.

6. Interview with Daniel Duke, August 22, 1990, Interview A-0366, Southern Oral History Program Collection (#4007), University of North Carolina Center for the Study of the American South, 1–6.

7. Ibid., 11.

8. Ibid., 9–10.

9. Ibid., 18.

10. Ibid., 11; Ralph McGill, "One More Word," *Atlanta Constitution*, March 10, 1940, 4K; "Flogging Probe Events Traces from Day-to-Day," *Atlanta Constitution*, March 31, 1940, 5B.

11. McGill, "One More Word."

12. Interview with Daniel Duke, August 22, 1990, 14–15; Willard Cope, "Cars Bearing County Emblem Linked in Flog Probe; Jury Gives Open Verdict," *Atlanta Constitution*, March 4, 1940, 1.

13. Interview with Daniel Duke, August 22, 1990, 17–20.

14. Ibid., 20.

15. Ibid., 17.

16. "Sordid Flog Drama Played at Hearing," *Atlanta Constitution*, November 26, 1941, 1; Wolfgang Saxon, "Lawrence D. Duke, Sr., 86; Fought the Klan in Georgia," *New York Times*, April 1, 1999, 11B.

17. Interview with Daniel Duke, August 22, 1990, 35.

18. Ibid., 29; Franklin M. Garrett, *Atlanta and Environs, Vol. 3* (New York: Lewis Historical Publishing, 1954), 289.

19. Chester L. Quarles, *The Ku Klux Klan and Related American Racialist and Antisemitic Organizations* (Jefferson, NC: McFarland, 1999), 82–84.

20. Jack Taver, "Arnall Declares War on Klan," *Atlanta Constitution*, May 30, 1946, 1.

21. Jim Furniss, "Hard-Hitting Dan Duke Again to Lead KKK Fight," *Atlanta Constitution*, June 2, 1946, 1.

22. "Klansmen Threaten Victim of Flogging," *Pittsburgh Courier*, June 29, 1946, 14.

23. "Klan Terrorists Linked to Killing," *New York Times*, June 8, 1946, 28.

24. Jim Furniss, "52-Blow Flogging of Negro Is Laid to Klan by Dan Duke," *Atlanta Constitution*, June 7, 1946, 4.

25. Steven Weisenberger, "The Columbians, Inc.: A Chapter of Racial Hatred from the Post–World War II South," *Journal of Southern History* 69, no. 4 (November 2003): 833.

26. William L. Blevin Jr., "The Georgia Gubernatorial Primary of 1946," *Georgia Historical Quarterly* 50, no. 1 (March 1966): 39.

27. Furniss, "52-Blow Flogging of Negro"; Scott E. Buchanan, "Three Governors Controversy," *New Georgia Encyclopedia*, June 8, 2017, https://www.georgiaencyclopedia.org/articles/government-politics/three-governors-controversy; "Klan Issue Grows in Georgia Poll," *New York Times*, June 1, 1946, 13.

28. Jim Furniss, "Georgia Files Its Suit to Null Klan Charter," *Atlanta Constitution*, June 21, 1946, 1.

29. Weisenberger, "The Columbians, Inc.," 834–35.

30. "Talmadge Cracks Own Vote Record in Clinching 4th Term as Governor," *Atlanta Constitution*, July 19, 1946, 1.

31. "Candidate Asked Klan Aid—Duke," *Atlanta Constitution*, August 14, 1946, 5; "Duke Tells Klan Tie-Up with Bund," *Atlanta Constitution*, August 24, 1946, 2.

32. Weisenberger, "The Columbians, Inc.," 821–22.

33. "Columbian De-Charter Job Duke's," *Atlanta Constitution*, November 5, 1946, 1.

34. "Columbians Tear Up Charter, Mail Bits to Prosecutor Duke," *Atlanta Constitution*, November 8, 1946, 1.

35. Dupont Wright, "Duke Floors Burke in Courthouse Battle," *Atlanta Constitution*, November 24, 1946, 14A; "Cook Pledges Klan Fight to a Finish," *Atlanta Constitution*, November 30, 1946, 8.

36. Wright, "Duke Floors Burke"; Weisenberger, "The Columbians, Inc.," 849.

37. Keeler McCartney, "Columbian Revelations Due Today," *Atlanta Constitution*, December 10, 1946, 1; "Dan Duke Trial Postponed," *Atlanta Constitution*, November 27, 1946, 3.

38. Weisenberger, "The Columbians, Inc.," 849–50; Michael Newton, *White Robes and Burning Crosses: A History of the Ku Klux Klan from 1866* (Jefferson, NC: McFarland, 2014), 91–92; McCartney, "Columbian Revelations"; M. L. St. John, "Confessions Are Called Knell of the Columbians," *Atlanta Constitution*, December 11, 1946, 1.

39. St. John, "Confessions Are Called Knell of the Columbians"; Weisenberger, "The Columbians, Inc.," 850.

40. "Election Day and Governor Again, but Hospital Respite Excites Gene," *Atlanta Constitution*, November 6, 1946, 1.

41. Neil R. McMillen, ed., *Remaking Dixie: The Impact of World War II on the American South* (Oxford: University of Mississippi Press, 1997), 8.

42. "Death Comes Quietly for Governor-Elect," *Atlanta Constitution*, December 22, 1946, 1A.

43. Charles S. Bullock, Scott E. Buchanan, and Ronald K. Gaddie, *The Three Governors Controversy: Skullduggery, Machinations, and the Decline of Georgia's Progressive Politics* (Athens: University of Georgia Press, 2015), 154.

44. Kenneth Coleman, ed., *A History of Georgia, 2nd edition* (Athens: University of Georgia Press, 1991).

45. Bullock, Buchanan, and Gaddie, *The Three Governors Controversy*, 162.

46. Ibid., 162–63.

47. Interview with Daniel Duke, August 22, 1990, 21–22; "Battle of Atlanta," *New York Times*, January 19, 1947, 1.

48. Bullock, Buchanan, and Gaddie, *The Three Governors Controversy*, 172.

49. Interview with Daniel Duke, August 22, 1990, 22; "Armed Moves by Talmadge Block Rival," *New York Times*, January 17, 1947, 1; "Battle of Atlanta," *New York Times*, January 19, 1947, 1.

50. "Arnall Steps Out; Thompson Claims Governorship Post," *New York Times,* January 19, 1947, 1.

51. "Honor Dan Duke for Combating Two Hate Groups," *Atlanta Constitution*, January 19, 1947, 7A; "Men of the Year Range from Boxer to Atomic Physicist," *Delta Times Democrat* (Greenville, MS), January 20, 1947, 2.

52. "Duke Flays 'Factions' as 'Political Vultures,' " *Atlanta Constitution*, April 4, 1947, 23.

CHAPTER 13: THE SECOND TRIAL

1. *State of Georgia v. Clarence Henderson*, No. 63, Carroll County Superior Court, October 10–12, 1950 (hereafter *State v. Henderson* [II]), 1.

2. Ibid.

3. "Plea for 30-Day Delay Denied: Henderson Retrial Starts Here," *Carrollton Times–Free Press*, October 10, 1950, 1.

4. *State v. Henderson* (II), 1–4; "Plea for 30-Day Delay Denied: Henderson Retrial Starts Here," *Carrollton Times–Free Press*, October 10, 1950, 1.

5. "Red Intrusion Rapped by Henderson's Counsel," *Atlanta Constitution*, October 11, 1950, 21; "Henderson Retrial Continues; Proceedings Similar to Old Case," *Carroll County Georgian*, October 12, 1950, 1.

6. *State v. Henderson* (II), 6.

7. Ibid., 9–11

8. Ibid., 11–14

9. Ibid., 14.

10. Affidavit of Herman Jones, December 16, 1950, 34.

11. *State v. Henderson* (II), 14–17.

12. Allen Gaston, interview with Chris Joyner, Carrollton, GA, November 9, 2018.

13. *State v. Henderson* (II), 19–21.

14. Ibid., 21.

15. Note: Duke appears to be confused and reading from the wrong part of the transcript. Hillin testified in the January 30, 1950, trial that he had delivered the serial number of the stolen gun to his office "several days or a week" after Stevens's death. However, in cross-examination, Hillin clearly answers that he got the serial number of the gun "several days" after the murder.

16. *State v. Henderson* (II), 25–27.

17. Ibid., 36.

18. Ibid., 38–41.

19. *State of Georgia v. Clarence Henderson*, No. 63, January 31, 1950, Carroll County Superior Court, 8–9.

20. *State v. Henderson* (II), 42–44.

21. Ibid., 45.

22. Ibid., 45–51.

23. Ibid., 54–62.

24. Ibid., 64–66.

25. Ibid., 66–69.

26. Ibid., 69–76.

27. Ibid., 78–79.

CHAPTER 14: BALLISTICS, NAN, AND A VERDICT

1. *State of Georgia v. Clarence Henderson*, No. 63, Carroll County Superior Court, October 10–12, 1950 (*State v. Henderson* [II]), 81–89.
2. "Henderson Retrial Continues; Proceedings Similar to Old Case," *Carroll County Georgian*, October 12, 1950, 1.
3. *State v. Henderson* (II), 89–90.
4. Ibid., 90–98.
5. Ibid., 98–101.
6. Affidavit of Herman Jones, December 16, 1950, 34–36.
7. John T. Smyly, "Henderson Jury Is Sent to Bed After 5 Hours of Deliberation," *Carrollton Times–Free Press*, October 12, 1950, 1.
8. *State v. Henderson* (II), 106–108.
9. Ibid., 109–110.
10. Ibid., 115–16.
11. Ibid., 116.
12. Ibid., 117.
13. Ibid., 118–19.
14. Ibid., 123.
15. Ibid., 124.
16. Ibid., 126–30.
17. Ibid., 130.
18. Ibid., 131–32.
19. Affidavit of Wright Lipford, December 30, 1950, 114; affidavit of George Cornett, December 20, 1950, 98–99.
20. *State v. Henderson* (II), 132–33.
21. Ibid., 134–35.
22. Ibid., 136.
23. Ibid., 136.
24. In its October 12, 1950, edition, the *Carrollton Times–Free Press* quoted Boykin as saying to the jury, "We'll get [a verdict] if it takes until next week." In its next issue, on October 17, the paper ran a front-page correction saying the judge did not say that at all. The newspaper did not explain how it made such an error.
25. Smyly, "Henderson Jury Is Sent to Bed"; "Henderson Jury Quits for Night, Undecided," *Atlanta Constitution*, October 13, 1950, 4.

26. "Henderson Gets Chair; Appeal Set for Dec. 2," *Carrollton Times–Free Press*, October 17, 1950, 1.

27. Ibid.; Hal David, "Henderson Convicted, Sentenced for Second Time; to Die Nov. 17," *Carroll County Georgian*, October 19, 1950, 1.

CHAPTER 15: NEW EVIDENCE, NEW TRIAL

1. "Henderson Condemned Second Time," *Atlanta Constitution*, October 14, 1950, 16.

2. "Henderson Convicted Again; Lawyers Motion New Appeal," *Atlanta Daily World*, October 14, 1950, 1.

3. "Henderson Gets Chair; Appeal Set for Dec. 2," *Carrollton Times–Free Press*, October 17, 1950, 1; "New Monkey Gets Hot Welcome from Lighted Cigarette," *Carrollton Times–Free Press*, October 17, 1950, 1. (The "new monkey" story referred to a new monkey mascot obtained by the Carrollton Fire Department. The firemen's former mascots, named Amos and Andy, were also monkeys. Andy had recently died and Amos had been returned to its "New York agency" for being unfriendly.)

4. Hal David, "Henderson Convicted, Sentenced for Second Time; to Die Nov. 17," *Carroll County Georgian*, October 19, 1950, 1.

5. "Again the Nation Hears of Carroll," *Carroll County Georgian*, October 28, 1950, 3.

6. "Carroll Service Council," *American City* 65 (October 1950): 112.

7. "Legislation Proposals Are Discussed by Councilmen," *Carroll County Georgian*, November 9, 1950, 1.

8. "That Racial Question," reprint of the *Dalton Citizen* editorial, *Times–Free Press,* November 28, 1950, 3.

9. Stephanie Capparell, *The Real Pepsi Challenge: The Inspirational Story of Breaking the Color Barrier in American Business* (New York: Simon & Schuster, 2008), TK.

10. "Henderson Asks More Tests of Evidence Revolver, Bullet; Cites 'Suppression' of Expert's Testimony," *Carrollton Times–Free Press*, October 31, 1950, 1.

11. Affidavit of Herman Jones, December 16, 1950, 37.

12. "Test in Stevens Case Denied by Court," *Carrollton Times–Free Press*,

November 14, 1950, 1; "Mercury Hits 24 Sunday Morning," *Carrollton Times–Free Press*, November 14, 1950, 1.

13. "Set Henderson's New Trial Motion for December 16," *Carrollton Times–Free Press*, December 5, 1950, 1; "New Motion for Henderson Set at Carrollton," *Atlanta Daily World*, December 16, 1950, 1.

14. "Hear Henderson's Plea for Another Trial January 5," *Carrollton Times–Free Press*, December 19, 1950, 1.

15. Stanley Parkman, "Is There a Payoff in the Henderson Case?" *Carroll County Georgian*, December 21, 1950, 2.

16. "Ballistic Experts Dispute May Save Ga. Lovers-Lane Suspect," *Philadelphia Tribune*, January 6, 1951, 3.

17. "Judge Boykin Denies New Henderson Trial," *Atlanta Daily World*, January 18, 1951, 1; "Gun Expert Aids Farmer," *Afro-American* (Baltimore), January 13, 1951, 15.

18. "New Hearing Delayed on Henderson," *Atlanta Constitution*, January 6, 1951, 16; "Henderson Defense Given Until Tuesday to File," *Atlanta Daily World*, January 7, 1951, 8; "Judge Studies Henderson's Third Trial Motion; Seven State Affidavits Throw New Light on Case," *Carrollton Times–Free Press*, January 9, 1951, 1; "Boykin Considers New Henderson Trial," *Carroll County Georgian*, January 11, 1951, 5; "Henderson Denied Third Murder Trial by Judge Boykin," *Carrollton Times–Free Press*, January 18, 1951, 1; "Retrial Denied for Henderson," *Atlanta Constitution*, January 18, 1950, 3.

19. Edwin T. Arnold, *Carrollton* (Athens: University of Georgia Press, 2012), 99–101.

20. "Popular William Y. Atkinson Nominated to State High Court," *Atlanta Constitution*, October 8, 1942, 12.

21. *Henderson v. State of Georgia*, 208 Ga. 73, 75 (1951), 65 S.E.2d 175.

22. "Are Legal Technicalities Replacing Common Sense and Hindering Justice in Our Courts?" *Carroll County Georgian*, May 24, 1951, 2.

23. Daniel Duke to NAACP Defense Committee, May 25, 1951, NAACP Legal Defense and Educational Fund records, Manuscript/Mixed Material, Library of Congress, Clarence Henderson, 1950–53.

24. E. E. Moore Jr. to Atlanta Branch, NAACP, May 25, 1951, NAACP Legal Defense and Educational Fund records, Manuscript/Mixed Material, Library of Congress, Clarence Henderson, 1950–53.

25. Austin T. Walden to Thurgood Marshall, June 4, 1951, NAACP Legal Defense and Education Fund records, Manuscript/Mixed Material, Library of Congress, Clarence Henderson, 1950–53.

26. Memo from Robert Carter to Thurgood Marshall, June 25, 1951, NAACP Legal Defense and Educational Fund records, Manuscript/Mixed Material, Library of Congress, Clarence Henderson, 1950–53.

27. Thurgood Marshall to Austin T. Walden, July 5, 1951, NAACP Legal Defense and Educational Fund records, Manuscript/Mixed Material, Library of Congress, Clarence Henderson, 1950–53.

28. "Henderson Appeals for Defense Funds; Hearing Saturday," *Carrollton Times–Free Press*, August 28, 1951, 1; "Henderson Defense Asks for Funds," *Carroll County Georgian*, August 30, 1951, 10; "Henderson Case Returns to Superior Court," *Atlanta Daily World*, September 1, 1951, 1.

29. *State of Georgia v. Clarence Henderson*, No. 63, transcript of hearing on a special motion, September 1, 1951, Carroll County Superior Court, Carrollton, GA.

30. Ibid.

31. Ibid.

CHAPTER 16: THE THIRD TRIAL

1. "Contract Let for Survey of Sub-Standard Housing," *Carroll County Georgian*, March 21, 1951, 1.

2. 1950 Census of Housing, Summary of Finding, XXIX, https://www2.census.gov/library/publications/decennial/1950/housing-volume-1/36965082v1p1ch1.pdf.

3. Kenneth T. Jackson, *Crabgrass Frontier: The Suburbanization of the United States* (New York: Oxford University Press, 1987), 232–33; Thomas J. Vicino, *Transforming Race and Class in Suburbia: Decline in Metropolitan Baltimore* (London: Palgrave Macmillan, 2008), 23; "Nothing-Down Big Lure In '49 Home Buying," *Atlanta Constitution*, November 5, 1950, 15B.

4. Jackson, *Crabgrass Frontier*, 241–42.

5. 1940 Census, Occupied Dwelling Units by Tenure and Population per Unit, by Color of Occupants, Georgia, 551–58, https://www2.census.gov/library/publications/decennial/1940/housing-volume-2/housing-v2p2-ch7.pdf.

6. 1940 Census, Data for Small Areas, Characteristics of Housing for Urban Places, and for Wards of Cities of 10,000 Inhabitants or More, 274, https://www2.census.gov/library/publications/decennial/1940/housing -volume-1/housing-v1p1-ch4.pdf.

7. 1960 Census, Data for Small Areas, Characteristics of Housing for Urban Places, and for Wards of Cities of 10,000 Inhabitants or More, Georgia, 12–115, https://www2.census.gov/library/publications/decennial/1960/ housing-volume-1/41962442v1p3ch4.pdf.

8. Allan Carpenter, "They Built Themselves a Lake," *Rotarian* 81, no. 6 (December 1952): 56.

9. Ibid., 58.

10. "New Southwire Expansion Move Helps Triple Original Plant Area," *Carrollton Times–Free Press*, March 22, 1951, 1.

11. "Half-Hour NBC Program Feb. 24 Honors County," *Carrollton Times– Free Press*, February 6, 1951, 1; "NBC To Salute County with Broadcast Sunday," *Carrollton Times–Free Press*, February 20, 1951, 1.

12. "War News Moves Closer," *Carrollton Times–Free Press*, January 1, 1951, 2.

13. "Civil Defense Gives Simple Safety Hints to Remember in Event of Future A-Bomb Attack," *Carrollton Times–Free Press*, February 13, 1951, 1.

14. The transcript of the third trial was recorded differently from the prior two trials. In the third trial, the court reporter, Henry Revill, often transcribed witness testimony in long passages without the questions by either the prosecution or the defense. In some cases the author has imputed the questions based on the answers given.

    The issue of Revill's transcriptions came up in court records, in part because of Revill's advanced age. In 1951, Revill was eighty-one years old. See Leo Aikman, "Meriwether County Took to FDR," *Atlanta Constitution*, September 5, 1951, 4.

15. *State of Georgia v. Clarence Henderson*, No. 63, Carroll County Circuit Court, October 8–10, 1951, trial transcript (hereafter *State v. Henderson* [III]), 1.

16. Ibid., 3.

17. Ibid., 3.

18. Ibid., 4–5.

19. Ibid., 6, 8.

20. Ibid., 7.

21. Ibid., 11.

22. Ibid., 11.

23. Ibid., 12.

24. Ibid., 13.

25. Sam Clarke, "News About Georgia," *Atlanta Constitution*, December 27, 1948, 14; "Honor to Dr. Flinn," *Atlanta Constitution*, July 19, 1947, 6.

26. J. Scott Turner, interview with Chris Joyner, August 1, 2017.

27. J. Scott Turner, interview with Chris Joyner, November 25, 2018.

28. *State v. Henderson* (III), 13–14.

29. Lester B. Orfield, "Discovery During Trial in Federal Criminal Cases: The Jencks Act," 18 Sw L.J. 212 (1964); *Brady v. Maryland*, 373 U.S. 83 (1963).

30. *State v. Henderson* (III), 14–15.

31. Ibid., 19–20.

32. "Both Sides Move Cautiously As Third Trial of Clarence Henderson Opens," *Atlanta Constitution*, October 9, 1951, 7; "Henderson Jury Named As Trial Gets Underway," *Atlanta Daily World*, October 9, 1951, 1.

33. *State v. Henderson* (III), 21.

34. Ibid., 23.

35. Ibid., 23–24.

36. Ibid., 24–32.

37. Ibid., 32.

38. Ibid., 33–34.

39. Ibid., 35.

40. Ibid., 38–39.

41. Ibid., 41–43.

42. Ibid., 52.

43. Ibid., 56

CHAPTER 17: CORNETT V. JONES

1. "Fingerprint Bureau Adds to Equipment," *Atlanta Constitution*, September 2, 1937, 12.

2. *State of Georgia v. Clarence Henderson*, No. 63, Carroll County Circuit Court, October 8–10, 1951, trial transcript (hereafter *State v. Henderson* [III]), 56–59.

3. Ibid., 59–67.

4. Julian Sommerville Hatcher, Frank J. Jury, Jac Weller, and Thomas G. Samworth, *Firearms Investigation, Identification and Evidence* (Harrisburg, PA: Stackpole, 1957), 288–89.

5. *State v. Henderson* (III), 69–70.

6. Ibid., 76.

7. Ibid., 77–78.

8. Ibid., 86–87.

9. Photo "Police Science Squad," *Atlanta Constitution*, May 26, 1946, B10.

10. *State v. Henderson* (III), 88–92.

11. Ibid., 95.

12. Ibid., 96.

13. Ibid., 97–98.

14. Ibid., 100–101.

15. Ibid., 104.

16. Ibid., 105.

17. Ibid., 107.

18. Ibid., 109–111.

19. Ibid., 111–112.

20. Jay Jarvis, *Georgia's Crime Doctor: The Story of Herman Jones and the First 20 Years of the Georgia Crime Laboratory* (Morrisville, NC: Lulu Press, 2009), 63–64; *FBI Law Enforcement Bulletin*, vol. 37, no. 10 (October 1968): 6; Governor Bob Riley of Alabama, Executive Order No. 34, June 27, 2006.

21. *State v. Henderson* (III), 118.

22. Ibid., 118–122, 124.

23. Ibid., 128.

24. Ibid., 128–29; ProQuest search of the *Atlanta Constitution* from 1938–1951 found 384 matches for Dr. Herman Jones.

25. *State v. Henderson* (III), 130. A description of the Iver Johnson .38 can be found at https://www.guns.com/news/2013/04/20/iver-johnson-safety-revolvers-glorious-contradictions.

26. *State v. Henderson* (III), 130–31.

27. Ibid., 132–133.

28. State exhibit 13, *State v. Henderson* (III).

29. *State v. Henderson* (III), 134.

30. Ibid., 135.

31. Ibid., 138–42.

32. Ibid., 144.

33. Jarvis, 57–61; "Atlanta Sleuths Confident Gun Test Will Link Parolee with Slaying of Garris," *Atlanta Constitution*, April 24, 1949, 1A; "Gun Ruled Out as Vital Garris Clue," *Atlanta Constitution*, April 25, 1949, 1A.

34. *State v. Henderson* (III), 145–46.

35. Ibid., 147–48.

36. Ibid., 149.

37. Ibid., 150–51.

38. Ibid. 155.

39. Ibid., 161–62, 164.

40. Ibid., 165.

41. Ibid., 166.

42. Ibid., 167.

43. Ibid., 168.

44. Ibid., 175–79.

45. Ibid., 182–84; "No Verdict, Henderson Jury Recesses," *Atlanta Constitution*, October 11, 1951, 15.

CHAPTER 18: GOD AND THE NAACP

1. "Henderson Given Death Sentence for Third Time," *Carrollton Times–Free Press*, October 11, 1951, 1; "Henderson Case Goes to Jury Wed. After Three-Day Trial," *Carroll County Georgian*, October 11, 1951, 1; "No Verdict, Henderson Jury Recesses," *Atlanta Constitution*, October 11, 1951, 15.

2. "'Scottsboro Boy' Patterson Handed 6–15 Year Term," *Atlanta Constitution*, October 12, 1951.

3. "New Trial Denied," *Carrollton Times–Free Press*, February 5, 1952, 1; Robert E. Johnson, "Henderson Case Heads for Supreme Court for Third

Time," *Atlanta Daily World,* April 9, 1952, 1; "Court Saturday," *Carrollton Times–Free Press,* January 17, 1952, 1; "Henderson Hearing," *Carroll County Georgian,* January 10, 1952, 1.

4. "High Court Gets Henderson Appeal," *Carrollton Times–Free Press,* April 17, 1952, 1; "Car Kills Cow," April 22, 1952, *Carrollton Times–Free Press,* April 22, 1952, 1.

5. Robert E. Johnson, "Dan Duke Asks Supreme Court to Reverse Henderson's Death Decree," *Atlanta Daily World,* April 15, 1952, 1.

6. "Lee Wyatt Dead, Georgia Justice," *New York Times,* February 7, 1960, 84.

7. "Henderson Death Term Is Reversed 3d Time," *Atlanta Constitution,* June 10, 1952, 15; "Court Reverses Henderson Decision," *Carrollton Times–Free Press,* June 10, 1952, 1; "Henderson Death Sentence Reversed for Third Time; Possible New Trial," *Carroll County Georgian,* June 12, 1952, 1.

8. "New Trial for Henderson Is Seen Soon by Lipford," *Carrollton Times–Free Press,* July 13, 1950, 1.

9. "Wright Lipford Files Motion for Rehearing of Henderson Trial," *Carroll County Georgian,* June 6, 1952, 1.

10. "Henderson Must Face 'Rob' Trial, Sharecropper Beats Murder Charge in Case," *Atlanta Daily World,* August 19, 1952, 1.

11. "Henderson to Be Tried on Armed Robbery Charge," *Carrollton Times–Free Press,* October 14, 1952, 1.

12. "School Principals Voice Opposition to Amendment 2," *Carroll County Georgian,* October 16, 1952.

13. "High Court Rejects Atom Spies' Appeal of Death Sentence," *New York Times,* October 14, 1952, 1; Susan Jacoby, "Competing Narratives and Public Amnesia, 1950–1965," in *Alger Hiss and the Battle for History* (New Haven, CT: Yale University Press, 2009), 119–39.

14. Bryan R. Gibby, "The Battle for White Horse Mountain September–October 1952." *Army History,* no. 89 (2013): 26–47.

15. Richard Kluger, *Simple Justice: The History of* Brown v. Board of Education *and Black America's Struggle for Equality* (New York: Alfred A. Knopf, 2004), 587, 596–99.

16. "Henderson's Fight for His Life Continues," *Atlanta Daily World,* October 14, 1952, 1.

17. This exchange contained in the habeas corpus motion by Daniel Duke for a hearing set January 17, 1953, Superior Court, Carroll County, GA.

18. "State Will Not Call for Henderson This Session," *Carroll County Georgian*, October 16, 1952, 1: "Henderson Case Sent to 'Dead' Docket to Await New Evidence," *Carrollton Times–Free Press*, October 16, 1952, 1.

19. Lerone Bennett Jr., "Henderson Case Bogs Down as Court Asks Bond Before Release," *Atlanta Daily World*, October 18, 1952, 1.

20. Georgia Code of Laws 1933, 24–2714(7), 27–2002.

21. Official Code of Georgia Annotated 17–6–31(c).

22. Motion for writ of Habeas Corpus, *Henderson v. Denver Gaston*, December 12, 1952, revised January 17, 1953.

23. "Seein' Things with Windy," *Carrollton Times–Free Press*, January 20, 1953, 1.

24. Lerone Bennett, "Clarence Henderson Freed; Joins Family Here," *Atlanta Daily World*, January 18, 1953, 1.

25. Minutes of Superior Court, *State v. Marco De Las Maurignos and Jose Sierra, al. dict. Joseph Segar*, in *Georgia Reports, Annotated, Book 1* (Charlottesville, VA: The Mitchie Company, 1903), 12; Donald E. Wilkes Jr., "From Oglethorpe to the Overthrow of the Confederacy: Habeas Corpus in Georgia, 1733–1865," *Georgia Law Review* 45 (2011): 1015.

26. Lerone Bennett, "Clarence Henderson Freed; Joins Family Here," *Atlanta Daily World*, January 18, 1953, 1.

27. "Local Citizens Glad at Release of Henderson," *Atlanta Daily World*, January 18, 1953, 1.

28. "Freed After 3 Death Sentences," *New York Times*, January 18, 1953, 67; "Doomed Thrice in Killing, Georgian Is Freed by Writ," *New York Herald Tribune*, January 18, 1953, 34; "Negro Convicted in Shooting Freed," *Palladium-Item* (Richmond, IN), January 18, 1953, 2.

29. C. W. Greenlea, "Henderson, Free, Thanks 'God and NAACP' for Help," *Atlanta Daily World*, January 1, 1953, 1.

30. Greenlea, "Henderson, Free, Thanks 'God and NAACP.'"

31. U.S. Department of Commerce, Census Bureau, "Current Population Reports: Consumer Income," Washington, DC, February 18, 1951, 36, www2.census.gov/library/publications/1951/demographics/p60–07.pdf.

32. Marion E. Jackson, "Henderson, Now Free, to Drop Stakes in Atlanta," *Atlanta Daily World,* January 20, 1953, 1.

33. "A Victory for Justice," *Atlanta Daily World,* January 21, 1953, 6; Tammy D. Evans, *The Silencing of Ruby McCollum: Race, Class, and Gender in the South* (University Press of Florida, 2018).

34. Lucrete Marshall, "Parade Welcomes Catherine Hardy Returning from Olympic Victory," *Carroll County Georgian,* August 28, 1952, 3.

35. "Welcome Home, Cat," *Carroll County Georgian,* August 28, 1952, 2.

36. "Welcoming Monday for Local Olympic Track Star," *Carrollton Times–Free Press,* August 14, 1952, 1.

37. H. H. Martin, "Section II: The Nineteen-Fifties," in *Atlanta and Environs* (Athens: University of Georgia Press, 1987), 185.

38. "Let's Forget Amendment One," *Carroll County Georgian,* November 11, 1952, 2.

39. "Client Freed, Duke Cited in Court Flareup," *Atlanta Constitution,* June 30, 1954, 1.

40. "Restore 483 to Vote List, Duke Warns," *Atlanta Constitution,* September 22, 1955, 12.

41. William M. Bates, "Griffin May Appoint Dan Duke as Prober," *Atlanta Constitution,* July 1, 1958, 1; "Extortion Liquor Tax Suit Killed," *Atlanta Constitution,* September 27, 1958, 1.

42. Jack Strong, "Negro Vote Fails to Turn Tide," *Atlanta Constitution,* September 24, 1964, 1.

43. Bill Westbrook, "State Faces Trouble on Klan, Duke Says," *Atlanta Constitution,* November 23, 1965, 11; "Bolton, Duke Split on Klan," *Atlanta Constitution,* February 26, 1966, 3.

44. Fulton County Misdemeanor Sentence Register, Georgia State Board of Corrections; author's interviews with Ernest Henderson and Lutricia Gray Henderson.

45. *State of Georgia v. Clarence Henderson Jr.,* Superior Court of Fulton County, Case No. A-43377, plea transcript, March 12, 1979.

INDEX

Watson, Tom, 155
Wells, Ida B., 36–37
West, Don, 87–88
  FBI monitoring, 105
  McGill on, 105
  on Talmadge, E., 104
West Georgia College, 2, 20,
  279
white supremacy, 89
  Communists fighting, 98–99
  segregation and, 27–28
  of Talmadge, E., 91, 149
Wickersham Commission, 70
Wiggins, William, 42, 79–80, 200
  in first trial, 45–46, 50–51,
    54–59, 63–64, 69, 73, 75–76
  motion for re-trial, 79
Wilder, Evans, 58, 93–96, 98–99,
  100
Williams, Franklin, 113
women, white, 47
World War II, Carrolton after, 2–3,
  213–15
Wyatt, Lee, 264–65

zoning codes, 213